RESTORING THE
GODDESS

RESTORING THE
GODDESS

EQUAL
RITES FOR
MODERN
WOMEN

BARBARA G. WALKER

Prometheus Books
59 John Glenn Drive
Amherst, New York 14228-2197

Published 2000 by Prometheus Books

Inquiries should be addressed to
Prometheus Books, 59 John Glenn Drive, Amherst, New York 14228–2197.
VOICE: 716–691–0133, ext. 207.
FAX: 716–564–2711.
WWW.PROMETHEUSBOOKS.COM

04 03 02 01 00   5 4 3 2

Library of Congress Cataloging-in-Publication Data

Walker, Barbara G.
    Restoring the goddess : equal rites for modern women / Barbara G. Walker.
        p.   cm.
    Includes bibliographical references and index.
    ISBN 1–57392–786–4 (cloth : alk. paper)
    1. Goddess religion. 2. Women and religion. 3. Feminism—Religious aspects. I. Title.

BL473.5 .W355 2000
291.2'082—dc21   99–059070
                                           CIP

Printed in the United States of America on acid-free paper

CONTENTS

ACKNOWLEDGMENTS

M Y HEARTFELT GRATITUDE GOES TO all the women who contributed their thoughts, feelings, histories, and spiritual
insights to this book: Karen Arnold, Michele Augustyniak, Peggy
Beck, Joleen Benedict, Julia Burgmann, Tracy Colatarci, Elizabeth
Craft, Peg Dickson, Linda Downing, Olympia Dukakis, Lisa Eden-
field, Karen Fraley, Bianca Franchi, Eugenia George, Sedgwick Hes-
kett, Stacy Hoffer, Roberta Kaplan, Kim LeMoon, Judith Livant,
Becky Martin, Leana McCutcheon, Debra McIntyre, Inga Muscio,
Francine Nardone, Joanna Peak, Sandy Powers, Amy Sass-Eilert,
Chris Schorr, Jo Searles, Nora Serotkin, Debra Shaw, Elaine Silver,
Rocky Smith, Mavra Stark, Pat Talbott, Donna Templeton, Lee
Walling, Beverly Weidner, Joan Wynne, Janette Yanas, and the
others who wished to remain anonymous—you know who you are,
and thanks.

B.G.W.

INTRODUCTION

WHEN I WAS A CHILD, a minister told me that all the information in the Bible was completely true, because it came from the very mouth of God, and God could never lie about anything. For a while, I believed this. The assurance had come from an authority figure, one considered respectable and trustworthy, a person who, like God, could not lie. Later, when I began to read the Bible for myself, I was astonished to discover how numerous were the falsehoods, and how shameless the self-contradictions, of both God and his ministers.

I saw problems appearing in the very first chapter of Genesis. God claimed to have created light four days before he created the sun and all other stars. I knew that the only light sources in the universe are the stars, including our local star, the sun. What I didn't know was that primitive peoples often believed that sunlight and daylight were different, because they still saw daylight when the sun was hidden by clouds; this naive belief is preserved in Genesis.

Then I read that God made grass and trees and all other plants before creating the sun. I knew that couldn't be true, because green plants can't live without sunlight. Furthermore, God put grass and trees on land before there was life in the oceans. Another falsehood. I knew the sea had supported life forms many millions of years before the land had any vegetation at all.

Then there was the crazy geography of the four rivers (Gen. 2:10–14) that put Eden at the headwaters of the Euphrates and three other streams, one of which "encompassed" all of Ethiopia. I could see no possible way to envision this on any map in the atlas. Then, craziest of all, there was the story of a unique male childbirth (Gen. 2:21–22) that made Eve the daughter of Adam, and their union, therefore, an incestuous one. I found out only years later that the Adam's rib story was concocted especially to give man primacy over woman, but the biblical version wasn't original. It was copied from a much older Babylonian myth of the Goddess Nin-Ti, "Lady of the Rib," who invented childbirth by allowing women to form their babies' bones in utero out of their own maternal ribs.

Patriarchal Adam himself was a transformation of an earlier female principle of birth giving, *Adamah*, meaning "bloody clay," which male scholars more delicately translated "red earth" to disguise its original implications. The custom behind this name dates back to the time when fatherhood was unknown, the basic social unit was the maternal clan, and the conception of children was attributed to a variety of causes having nothing to do with sex. (That is why the Bible wording always so specifically insists that "he went in unto her, and she conceived, and bare a child," because in biblical times not all peoples understood this sequence of events.)

In the ancient Middle East, women wishing to become pregnant often performed a charm of sympathetic magic by forming clay figurines and anointing them with menstrual blood, the original mystic "blood of life" that was thought to be women's special gift from Mother Moon. For thousands of years, men tried in vain to appropriate women's conception magic, establishing customs of ceremonial castration and/or sacrifice of members of their own sex, in crude imitations of menstruation, culminating in numerous cults of dying savior-gods whose blood could be considered life giving. Jesus was only the most recent of a large number of similar savior-gods whose mythological traditions reach all the way back to Paleolithic cultures. According to Babylonian scriptures, however, the first people were created by the Goddess Ninhursag, who made them as clay figures, and anointed them with her precious magic blood to bring them to life.

When it came to the matter of blood sacrifice, the biblical God apparently wanted it so much that he even labeled Cain a sinner for offering only the first fruits of his fields, which were all he had. God insisted on being fed the blood of goats, sheep, and cattle at regular intervals, for "in the blood is the life," and it was traditionally reserved for the food of deities. Yahweh was as bloodthirsty as any other ancient god, and more cruel than many, as "his" Bible clearly shows.

Since he was omniscient and had perfect foreknowledge of everything, God would have known that Adam and Eve would eat the fruit of the tree of knowledge (which the Bible does *not* say was an apple). God did nothing to prevent their "fall," but used it as an excuse to condemn all future humans to an eternal hell sadistic beyond belief. If a human parent had done such a thing to a child, knowing the child would be led into temptation with no delivery from evil, it would be the parent's crime. Such tales express what seems to be a universal characteristic of patriarchal societies: namely, the idea that guilt is readily transferred to the innocent. Patriarchal gods and their minions seem to have a habit of taking revenge on the wrong parties, those not responsible for the offense. Through the ages, men (and their gods) have made war on, persecuted, sacrificed, or otherwise harmed people and other creatures who had nothing to do with their original grievances. The Bible shows great numbers of innocent civilians, women and babies, slain for the lapses of a few male citizens, or because their kings happened to bow down to idols, or because their land was grabbed by covetous neighbors whose god had "promised" it to them. And of course, the whole Christian religion is based on the premise that God condemned every human being, forever, to an eternity of torture because Eve disobediently sought the knowledge of good and evil— at least, up to the time when a nonsinning Jesus accepted punishment for that primal sin. It seemed somebody had to die to appease God's wrath, even though it was not the original perpetrator.

This Christian version of the custom of human sacrifice was

only a late manifestation of the basic guilt-transference idea that used to be widespread in the ancient Middle East, as the Bible demonstrates. The biblical God demanded sacrifice of every first-born, whether it be human or animal (Exod. 13:2). When the people began to resent child sacrifice enough to overcome their fear of the angry god and protest, eventually an animal was offered as a substitute. The story of Abraham's substitute of a sheep, instead of killing his son Isaac on God's altar as he had been supposed to, represents the transitional period when "scriptures" were written to assure people that the animal replacement was acceptable (Gen. 22:9–13). Still, Abraham was praised for having been perfectly willing to cut his son's throat for God. For those whose gospel tradition promised an eternity to be spent "in the bosom of Abraham," one wonders why a kinder-hearted bosom was not selected. Almost any mother would have been more defensive of her child's life than Abraham was.

The metaphor of the bosom apparently was copied from the Egyptians, who claimed that those who ate the sacramental bread/flesh of the savior Osiris would become immortal, like their god, and spend eternity in the bosom of the Goddess. Several of her incarnations were said to keep the blessed one close to their ever-flowing breasts, and give him the milk of paradise. "They draw their breasts to his mouth, never more do they wean him."[1] This state of paradisiacal pseudoinfancy obviously arose from collective memories of the most comfortable period in a human life, when Mother anticipates all our wants and there are no guilts or punishments. Such postmortem bliss was promised by Egyptian funerary priest-esses, who bared their breasts while carrying a corpse to the tomb, and by the bare-breasted Goddess painted inside the lid of the sar-cophagus, ostensibly leaning down from heaven to clasp the deceased to her bosom. The biblical God became a rather freakish copy of this loving Goddess when he described himself as a "nursing father" carrying the "sucking child" in his bosom (Num. 11:12).

Unlike the biblical God, the Goddess was depicted as a nurturer and preserver of the animal world as well as the human one. Some of her statues, like the famous Diana of Ephesus, showed her entire torso covered with many breasts, to feed all living things. "Many-Breasted Artemis" was known to the Greeks as the mother of animals, and Ishtar was known to the Babylonians as the angry mother who punished the god who caused the flood, because he had wilfully and irresponsibly killed so many of her creatures. She sent a rainbow to bar him from reaching the sacrifices offered on earth; this rainbow still remained in the Noah version but was given quite a different meaning.

Gods had a habit of demanding blood sacrifices, since it was widely believed that blood was what they lacked and needed to live on. Women and Goddesses, on the other hand, had so much life-giving blood that they could even afford to shed some of it every month. When men began to insist that firstborn sons were the sacrifices most pleasing to the gods, it was probably the mothers who raised objections and brought about the substitution of animals.

Substitution of a lamb for the firstborn son naturally led to the description of Jesus as the sacrificial "Lamb of God," whose death was supposed to atone for humanity's original sin and save everyone from an eternity of torture in hell. But in later practice, it was decided that God must not release the whole human race from his curse, because that would leave the church without any salvation to sell, when much of its lavish income depended on scaring people into compliance with hell's ominous threat. So the church fathers declared that the blood sacrifice of Jesus didn't redeem humanity after all; it only induced the vengeful God to relent just enough to allow the possibility of redemption. As Robert Ingersoll put it, "God so loved the world that he made up his mind to damn a large majority of the human race."[2] Then the church had to invent a limbo for the many good souls who had lived and died in previous ages, before Jesus was supposed to have soothed God's ire with his own blood, and who didn't deserve to go to hell but, being pagans, were denied heaven.

Terrible events are still called "acts of God," and the biblical God actually declared himself the creator of evil (Isa. 45:7). It was generally agreed that God created not only disasters on earth, but also hell and all the devils who inhabited it. Church fathers declared that devils either were once worshiped in the form of pagan gods, or were once heavenly angels who became dissatisfied with God's government and staged a rebellion against him: a concept borrowed from Zoroastrian Persia. The rebellion failed, and the rebels were sent down to hell and given the crucial job of tormenting sinners for all eternity. But if the devils were truly rebels against God, why would they obediently carry out God's orders? Real rebels probably would have let the sinners go without any punishment at all.

However, the church claimed that the devils obeyed God's directive to torment humans, just as assiduously as did the Dominican and Franciscan inquisitors whose racks, thumbscrews, and other instruments of torture were inscribed "Glory be only to God."[3] An astonishing depth of sadism is revealed by the writings of churchmen who describe the torments of hell in sickening detail, as also in those who wrote the mythical biographies of hundreds of purely mythical martyrs, piling mortal wounds upon more mortal wounds until the reader's mind boggles at these iron-fleshed saints.[4] It is one of the dirty secrets of the Christian religion, rarely admitted but always evident: "Any body of men who believe in hell will persecute whenever they have the power."[5]

Blatant pleasure in sadism was even attributed by Christian authorities to the "good" people who managed to get into heaven. St. Thomas Aquinas stated that "In order that the happiness of the saints may be more delightful to them and that they may render more copious thanks to God for it, they are allowed to see perfectly the sufferings of the damned . . . the blessed in glory will have no pity for the damned."[6] According to St. Fulgentius, even infants who died in the womb, or perished shortly after birth without the benefit of baptism, "must be punished by the eternal torture of undying fire."[7] Surely women, as mothers or potential mothers, would never have developed any such doctrines. Margaret Knight remarked that in the name of the religion of love, vast numbers of people were "not merely killed but atrociously tortured in ways that make the gas chambers of Belsen seem humane." And Susan Wixon condemned God in one sentence: "Anyone who would make a lake of fire and brimstone in which to incinerate his children ought to be the first one burned in it."[8]

Martin Luther had to admit that his God, as depicted in the Bible, was viciously cruel, unjust, and capricious. He was somewhat troubled by this but twisted his mind around to a belief in the unmerciful God's mercy as a test of faith: "This is the acme of faith, to believe that He is merciful . . . that He is just who at His own pleasure has made us necessarily doomed to damnation; so that, as Erasmus says, He seems to delight in the tortures of the wretched, and to be more deserving of hatred than of love. If by any effort of reason I could conceive how God could be merciful and just who shows so much anger and iniquity, there would be no need for faith."[9] Thus Luther defines faith as belief not only without evidence, but even against evidence.

The Bible is a primary source of evidence for God's mercilessly vindictive character. After issuing his edict that "thou shalt not kill," God went on to order tremendous massacres, to be carried out either by himself or by his chosen people. Among those who fell victims to God's homicidal tendencies were the following:

- All of Egypt's firstborn, after God deliberately hardened the heart of Pharaoh to make the killing possible; 3,000 Israelites, slain by their own relatives at God's insistence (Exod. 12:29, 32:27).
- Fourteen thousand, seven hundred Jews, destroyed by God's plague; all the Canaanites at Hormah; "much" people among the Israelites; 24,000 Israelites on another occasion; and all males among the Midianites, and all females except young virgins, who were to be raped and made into slaves (Num. 16:49, 21:3, 21:5, 25:9, 31:7,17).
- "Men, women, and little ones" of the Amorites; "utter destruction" without mercy for all the Hitties, Girgashites, Amorites, Canaanites, Perizzites, Hivites, and Jebusites; anyone, even a close relative or friend, must be killed for not following God's orders, "neither shall thine eye pity him, neither shalt thou spare, neither shalt thou conceal him; but thou shalt surely kill him" (Deut. 2:34, 7:1,2, 13:8,9).
- All of Jericho, "man and woman, young and old," together with all their domestic animals; 12,000 men, women, and

children of Ai; all the people of Makkedah, Libnah, Lachich, Gezer, Eglon, Hebron, Debir, and Goshen (Josh. 6:21, 8:25, 10:28–41).

- Ten thousand Perizzites and Canaanites; all the inhabitants of Zephath; 10,000 Moabites; 120,000 Midianities; 25,100 Benjamites (Judg. 1:4, 1:17, 3:29, 8:10, 20:35).
- Fifty thousand and seventy men of Bethshemesh, killed because somebody peeked into the ark of the covenant; "man and woman, infant and suckling" of the Amalekites; both sexes of all the Geshurites, Gezrites, and Amalekites (1 Sam. 6:19, 15:3, 27:8,9).
- All the Ammonites, slain by torture; 70,000 people slain by God's pestilence (2 Sam. 12:31, 24:15).
- Forty-two children killed by bears at Elisha's request, because the children angered God by saying to Elisha, "Go up, thou bald head"; 185,000 Assyrians slain in one night (2 Kings 2:24, 19:35).
- Five-hundred thousand Israelites; 120,000 Judeans (2 Chron. 13:17, 28:6).
- Seventy-five thousand Elamites (Esther 9:16).
- All of Job's innocent children, servants, and domestic animals were killed because God made a frivolous bet concerning Job's faith (Job 1:15–19). Job didn't "curse God, and die" after all, so he was more loyal to a tyrannical deity than the deity was to him. But I wondered, on first reading this story, why everyone made so much of Job, the only one left alive? What about all those others who were unfairly murdered for no good reason?

As an animal lover I was most severely disturbed by God's arbitrary destruction of a whole world of living things, countless billions of innocent animals, because a few humans had displeased him with an unnamed "wickedness" in the story of Noah's flood. Two of each species were saved in the ark, but what of all the others, subject to this incredible mass extinction?

After giving it further thought, I realized that the story of Noah's flood was not only cruel, it was also impossible. How could Noah have gathered the pairs of polar bears, Arctic foxes, walruses, wolves, reindeer, ermines, Siberian ponies, Antarctic penguins, and land animals from the Americas, Africa, Australia, and Oceania, which would have had to swim the seas or travel for months through completely incompatible environments to arrive at the ark? Then, to accommodate pairs of every mammal, insect, arachnid, reptile, crustacean, bird, or worm on earth, plus all their food for five months—including extra animals to serve as food for the meat eaters—would require an ark approximately the size of the state of California. Surely there was not enough "gopher wood" (Gen. 6:14) or any other kind of wood in the world to build such a thing, nor could it have been done in one generation by one family, nor even by the entire population of the Middle East in five or six generations. Bible fundamentalists still want us to believe this ridiculous story, which not only places God in a very bad light as a capricious killer but also makes him a liar too careless even to try to make sense.

Scholars are not as naive as Bible fundamentalists. They know that the biblical flood story was not even original; it was copied from much older scriptures belonging to various "heathen" peoples. The Babylonian flood hero was Uta-Napishtim. His Greek counterpart was Deucalion. His Akkadian counterpart was Atrakhasis. His Sumerian prototype was Ziusudra (Armenian Xisuthras), whose ark "came to rest on Mount Ararat." The flood myth was known also in India, where it represented the chaotic passage between the Great Mother's destruction of one world-cycle and her creation of the next one.

Noah was saved, according to the Bible, because he was the only righteous person in an entire world population. But we are never told what actually constituted this unique virtue. Yahweh's Old Testament favorites seldom showed any genuine goodness of character. In general, biblical patriarchs were a disreputable lot. Abraham not only set out to murder his son, he also acted as a pimp for his wife (Gen. 12:11–20). Jacob conned his brother out of his birthright (Gen. 25:31–34). Lot, the only Yahweh-fearing "righteous" man to be saved from the destruction of Sodom, offered his

two virgin daughters to a mob to be gang-raped, and later impregnated both of them while in a drunken stupor (Gen. 19:8, 33–36).

However mean or self-contradictory were the edicts of the biblical God, one is given the impression that no dissent or protesta-
tion is allowed. The victims must never cry, "Unfair!" When God's
people understandably complained of their deathly hunger and
thirst in the desert, their pitiless deity sent fiery serpents who "bit
the people, and much people of Israel died" (Num. 21:6). Moses,
however, was allowed to bring the slaughter to an end by setting up
a brass healing idol of the serpent god Nehushtan (resembling the
universal healing charm caduceus), which seems to have cured the
surviving victims (Num. 21:9). But jealous Old Testament Yahweh
brooked no competition from the snake god, however benevolent.
In the reign of Hezekiah, after nearly a century of reverence, the
worship of this deity was finally forbidden. God ordered complete
destruction of "the brazen serpent that Moses had made: for unto
those days the children of Israel did burn incense to it: and he
called it Nehushtan" (2 Kings 18:4).

Despite this destruction plainly recorded in their infallible Holy
Writ, the Catholic church in Milan for many years displayed as a
sacred relic the very same identical brazen serpent made by Moses,
or so they claimed. In fact, church practices and traditions contradicted the Bible in so many instances that it's hardly any wonder
that lay persons were forbidden to read "God's word" for many centuries, on pain of excommunication or even burning at the stake.
As it turned out, the church need not have worried too much. Even
in later ages of general literacy, when most people did come to own
a family Bible, few seem to have read it with any understanding. Its
inconsistencies were (and are) generally overlooked, and its myths
were (and are) generally dismissed as incomprehensible allegories,
despite the fact that their original writers obviously meant them to
be taken as literal history.

The Bible was written by technologically ignorant people a long
time ago. Its mythology is derivative, its history false, its science
nonexistent. To expect modern educated people to swallow its
absurdities whole is to demand a blind credulity that actually

places God in the worst possible light: He seems to punish humanity's only real species asset, its intelligence. The ultimate act of God's tyranny seems to be his insistence on literal belief, as the price of salvation, in all the biblical absurdities. If our intelligence is a gift of God, then he certainly shows a gratuitous meanness in forbidding its use. But if our intelligence is mythologically attributed to the boldness of Mother Eve, who seized the knowledge of good and evil for all her descendants, then once again it is the ancient Goddess, not the god, who deserves our attention—especially since the old matrifocal pagan world seems to have been happier.

God is inconsistent because he was made in the image of men—many men, with differing ideas and priorities, over many centuries. Almost the only thing those men agreed on was that the old creator deity made in the image of women must be utterly destroyed and forgotten. The effort plunged all of Western civilization into a bitter war against itself, and almost succeeded; but today the Goddess has been rediscovered and is being recreated. Women are making not theology but thealogy.

1

IN THE BEGINNING
The First of All Myths

*I*N THE BEGINNING, IN THE time that was no time, nothing existed but
the Womb. And the Womb was a limitless dark cauldron of all
things in potential: a chaotic blood-soup of matter and energy, fluid
as water yet mud-solid with salts of the earth; red-hot as fire yet
restlessly churning and bubbling with all the winds. And the Womb
was the Mother, before She took form and gave form to Existence.
She was the Deep (biblical *tehom*, Babylonian *Tiamat*, Egyptian
Temu, Greek *Themis*).

In the time that was no time, She divided the elements in the
Womb cauldron into the two spheres of infinity. By the use of Her
magic Om, Her grunt of cosmic birth giving, She caused the fiery
lights and airs to collect in the heaven sphere, and the dark waters,
salts, and solids to collect in the sphere of earth. She shaped the
heavenly lights into sun, moon, planets, and stars. She shaped the
earthly materials into continents, rivers, mountains, and seas. By
the light of the sun She made Day, and by the shadow of the earth
She made Night.

At the point of contact between the two spheres of infinity, Her
blood of the Womb generated living things. To each living thing the
Mother gave a temporary form that would eventually dissolve, back

21

once more into the infinite churning cauldron of potential, where matters and energies are constantly exchanged and recombined. She made the world an image of that uterine cauldron, so that every life form sustains itself by absorbing, decomposing, and assimilating other forms. And She gave autonomy to each form by pronouncing its name in Her primordial language, expressing the verbal magic of creation.

She made human beings able to imitate Her in the use of language. She formed them of reddened earth (*adamah*), moistened in the Womb by Her own holy blood. She gave them consciousness capable of remembering their own passage through dark birthways into the light of seeing and knowing; capable, too, of envisioning their own return to darkness and dissolution. She made woman in Her own image, with the female-mammalian power to create new life out of her interior blood. She made man to be woman's consort and helper, to assist in the long, arduous nurture of the world's most helpless offspring. She taught Her people to sow and reap, preserve food, weave cloth, build shelters, carry fire, make tools and vessels, keep records of the seasons, and a thousand other practical arts and crafts for their survival in the world. She taught Her people not to take more than they needed from the earth, the plants, the animals, the waters, and the woods; for if any creature took too much, others would suffer.

The world and its creatures dwelt in peace until the Mother began to give birth to jealous gods. Each god claimed to be Her first-born and Her chosen lover, privy to Her secrets, sharer of Her creativity. Each god insisted that he alone was both Her son and Her bridegroom, as well as Her helper in the world's creation. Some even went so far as to claim sole responsibility for creating the earth or its living things.

It is written that the Goddess's true firstborn took the form of the divine serpent, to slide into Her terrestrial body, to be anointed by Her wise blood, to know Her inner wisdom, and to learn how to become immortal by periodically shedding his old skin and being reborn in a new, fresh one. The phallic serpent represented sexual "knowing" as man's way to contact the blissful life-giving magic inside woman; and so when men made images of the Mother, they often showed her accompanied by Her snake, or even gave Her a snake form.

Later gods, jealous of the wise serpent, sought ways to discredit him. They pretended that the serpent's connection with the maternal netherworld was an evil rather than a special privilege. They began to claim credit for dividing the Womb into earth and heaven, for the pronouncing of sacred names, and for the molding of clay figures to be brought to life. Some even claimed to be birth givers themselves, despite their male incapacity for that. One even went so far as to declare that he could make man into a birth giver—at least one man, the first, who could then usurp maternal authority over the woman who was his child.

The jealous gods appealed to men, promising them longer lives, earthly riches, or godlike immortality if they would become dutiful worshippers. They taught men to perform blood sacrifices, to imitate the mysterious blood-magic of the Mother, to claim a connection with the giving of new life. Alas, the men never learned to let blood without pain or harm, as women did. Nonetheless, they mutilated their own bodies to imitate women's lunar bloodletting. They even killed some of their own number and claimed that the victims were transformed into life givers by their outpouring of blood. The men promised to feed their ancestral gods on sacrificial blood, to preserve their immortality, hoping for similar immortality in return. Their gods found blood sacrifices acceptable, but rejected the offerings of grain and fruit that had been customary in the elder times of peaceful agriculture (see Gen. 4: 3–5).

The new, jealous gods were not kind to the people they claimed as their children. They tyrannized the people and oppressed them mightily for the most trivial offenses. They threatened the people with plagues, wars, fevers, madness, blindness, slavery, famine, and rains of fire (see Deut. 28) for the least infraction of their rules.

One of the new gods even dared to send a world flood, to drown nearly every creature on earth—even nonhuman ones—because a few of the people had displeased him. The Mother caught him at it and became very angry. She punished him by setting a rainbow in the sky to bar him from feasting on men's altar offerings. She said he should starve, "since rashly he caused the flood storm, and handed over my children to destruction."

Nevertheless, the jealous gods continued to attract men by a combination of promises, threats, and violence. The gods restricted men's expressions of love for women, even for mothers. They allowed men to seize their neighbors' lands and possessions, to enrich themselves, to make slaves of other people. They allowed men to declare themselves kings, and to choose surrogate victims to be sacrificed in their stead. Men knew that many of the things they did were wrong, and their gods' threats made them guilty and fearful. They submerged their fear in acts of cruelty performed in groups, so that other men could justify their behavior. They appointed male priests to condone everything and write that it was all the gods' will.

Male priests wrested power from the tribal mothers and priestesses by organizing men into marauding armies, blessing their violence, and rewriting myths to exclude the Goddess or declare Her an abomination. The jealous gods became even more jealous, and fought among themselves, and each pronounced himself the One God. Their warfare was unremitting, until one devoured nearly all the others, diabolized his few remaining rivals, and proclaimed himself superior even to the Goddess who had produced him and taught him all his ideas.

And so the world was set upon a trail of tears, oppression, and intellectual error that prevails even to this day.

2

WHAT IS THEALOGY?

*F*OR NEARLY TWENTY CENTURIES, WESTERN civilization has been con-
structing a pseudoscience called *theology*. The word means literally "knowledge of God," even though many theologians declare
that God is unknowable. This pseudoscience has been taken seriously
enough by enough people to evolve a mainstream morality; to shape
the spiritual lives of billions of human beings; to foment innumerable
wars, persecutions, and crusades; to support the civilized world's
richest and most powerful institutions; and not incidentally, to create
a patriarchal society that is fundamentally misogynous and sexist.

During the patriarchal centuries, a majority of Western women
certainly accepted the belief systems of theology, because there
were no alternatives available to them. Indeed, in some periods of
history, not to accept the patriarchal god was a capital crime, to be
punished even more severely than murder. Within the system,
many women even managed to think themselves emancipated.
Nevertheless, any system that views a female as something less
than a male; that denigrates her as a source of temptation, sin, or
guilt; that denies her full participation in religious leadership; and
that postulates a god without a Goddess is not only sexist to the
core, it is the core of sexism.

25

Religion creates misogyny. Religion was and is the primary medium of women's spiritual, political, and social enslavement. There is no other aspect of human nature or culture that could have evolved such a phenomenon.

At present a new study is emerging from the neglected prepatriarchal past, and taking a modern form as *thealogy*, "knowledge of Goddess." Judeo-Christian theologians and ecclesiastics have tried many ways to suppress thealogy. They have loftily ignored it as a minor "cult." They have fiercely condemned it as paganism, deviltry, or witchcraft. They have dismissed it as a silly New Age fad. They have preached against it as a radical-feminist error. They have called it immoral, and its adherents confused. They have denounced its history as false—even though their own history stands on a decidedly shaky ground of crude folklore, forgery, and dissimulation. The real problem for theologians is a fear that thealogy may eventually lure women away from the churches that their unsung womanly efforts have so long supported, and so bring about the collapse of the whole construction.

Actually, thealogy is neither new nor faddish, but a philosophy far older and more venerable than the earliest traditions of patriarchal theology. It can be traced back to the very beginnings of the human species, during that long, long cultural infancy when everything seemed to have been created by the Mother of all mothers, when only the birth-giving sex was perceived as having transcendent powers, and when fatherhood of any kind was unrecognized and unknown.

Only with the comparatively recent development of Neolithic and Bronze Age cultures did people begin to understand, in a few parts of the world, that males as well as females possessed some reproductive power, although at first they weren't sure how it worked. Knowledge of fatherhood, and concomitant "knowledge" of a father god, have existed for only a few thousand years at most. The theologians' god is a Johnny-come-lately indeed, compared to the once and future Goddess of thealogy.

This realization has affected increasing numbers of women who are intrigued and empowered by it. Some get together with other women to talk about it, to consolidate their spiritual ideas and feelings, to read and discuss, to create rituals. Such feminine activities go on mostly underground, unnoticed by popular media. They comprise a grassroots movement, gathering momentum, perhaps to burst forth as a full-scale mainstream religion at some not-yet-fulfilled time.

Just as social matriarchy was never patriarchy spelled with an *m*, thealogy is not theology spelled with an *a*. The modern concept of the Goddess is very different from a merely feminized god or an androgynous Father-Mother deity. Goddess is not simply the female face of God. Goddess is a different entity altogether, arising from different psychological and cultural roots, recognizing different truths of human nature, embodying a different philosophy of life and death.

Most sociologists and psychologists regard religious belief as a significantly stabilizing and unifying force in human society. This claim is part of the conventional wisdom, even though it has never been shown that unbelief is particularly disruptive. On the contrary, atheists seem to be generally more law-abiding, socially responsible folk than their believing neighbors. But for many thinking people who would like to be believers in something, the trouble with Judeo-Christian religion is that it lacks believability.

The religious heritage of Western civilization has left us with a hodgepodge of wild improbabilities: virgin births, miraculous idols, talking bushes, curative relics that don't cure, primitive wizardry with rods and serpents, reanimated corpses, magic blood, angels and devils, a bizarre creation myth, an impossible hell, an unplaceable, indescribable heaven, and a spectacularly self-important God whose self-esteem seems to depend on ceaseless flattery. It has been demonstrated over and over that every theological concept has its roots in primitive superstition or in ancient paganism plagiarized without credit, and the theologians' primary job is to obscure these unworthy roots with a gloss of polysyllabic rhetoric.

If religious authorities want the public to believe, they should try to come up with something believable. Faith that must always guard itself against the encroachment of common sense or rationality is not worth keeping. The world needs a new belief system that doesn't demand that its adherents remain ignorant of the discoveries of earth sciences, biology, history, astronomy, physics, paleontology, or archaeology. The world needs a religion that can be believed without insult to human intelligence.

It's possible that thealogy will provide such a religion. Thealogians recognize the symbolic nature of religious concepts and do not require literal credulity Thealogians understand the psychobiological foundations of religion in a way that father-god followers can never comprehend. Thealogians know the Goddess to be humanity's most spontaneous spiritual construct, whereas father gods tended to be artificially imitative. Like a gathering storm, thealogy is building to a point where it may sweep away the patriarchy that has enslaved the world's energies to unworthy exploitations and persecutions for nearly two thousand years.

Thealogy as "knowledge of Goddess" means a woman's knowledge of self, knowledge of nature, knowledge of the life force in all things as revealed by ongoing scientific discoveries, and as much knowledge as possible of the history and evolution of the Great Mother image in human societies, past and present. No transcendent, outside-of-the-universe deity is involved in thealogy. The Goddess is always immanent, a personification of the real universe in which we find ourselves, and especially of the sacred Earth, the only source of life that we know. The Goddess represents ourselves and the environment that supports us, united by the female power that continually creates and nurtures living creatures.

Unlike the biblical God who was said to have manufactured the world, molding clay figures and breathing charms onto them, the archaic Great Mother gave birth to the world. She produced all things from Her own body, and they remained forever a part of Her. That's why many ancient peoples regarded themselves as true brothers and sisters to the animals, plants, and each other. The Mother concept is more unifying than that of the Father. The latter always seemed to evolve vicious we-they dichotomies that set group against group, and one self-important "truth" against all the rest of the world's "error." Beginning with the vast slaughters described in the Old Testament, the Judeo-Christian God has been egregiously intolerant of all but a very narrow segment of humanity, and has respected other life forms not at all. He said, in fact, that man was to subdue and "have dominion over" every other living thing (Gen. 1:28).

The dominion of man (or God) seems to have involved violence, oppression, and fear much more often than any expressions of love or nurturance. All the way up to the middle of the twentieth century, wife abuse was recommended from the pulpit and upheld by secular courts.[1] Sexual guilts were instilled in every child from babyhood on, leading to widespread poisoning of adult sexual relationships. Throughout the Christian era, fear ruled a European society nurtured on horrific visions of hell decreed by a stern, punitive God who apparently hated to see human beings enjoying themselves. Endless violence, crusades, wars, and pogroms were preached and carried out "for the glory of God," including five centuries of the most extreme terrorism directed against women by the Holy Inquisition and other witch-hunters.

Even in today's supposedly more enlightened world, we see ample evidence of religion-based oppression of women. Islam stands as a prime example, with its female genital mutilations, forced seclusions, and harsh theology. Wives are domestic slaves and economic nonentities, forbidden to handle money, drive cars, or even show their faces in public, all by order of Allah. Similarly, Judeo-Christian fundamentalism still goes as far as it can toward enslavement of women by forbidding them control of their own bodies and reproductive functions, suppressing sexual information, demanding wives' obedience even to abusive husbands, and wielding threats of eternal suffering in hell for any infractions of God's arbitrary rules. By the time a woman grows up enough to perceive hell as an imaginative construct of the purest sadism, it's little wonder that she may begin to perceive the fundamentalist God as a sexist tyrant representing the worst aspects of male callousness and ruthlessness. Certainly today's women can find nothing but horror in the pronouncements of St. Thomas Aquinas and other church fathers, to the effect that one of the blissful enjoyments of heaven will be a clear view of all the agony of the damned writhing eternally in hell.[2]

As a general rule, it is the dominant element of cruelty in patriarchal fundamentalism that alienates women and sends them in search of a more humane creed. Women seek here and there for years, often trying many spiritual paths before finding one that frankly affirms and honors femaleness per se. Many are convinced that there will never be true equality between the sexes until the Goddess is as widely accepted, cited, invoked, and revered as the god. Both, after all, are concepts created by human beings, in the image of human beings, and human beings come in two basic sexes. One can't exist without the other. This fact led the ancients to resist establishment of exclusively god-oriented sects for a surprisingly long time, and even maintained traces of Goddess worship in patriarchal Europe, doggedly persisting despite the most severe persecutions, all the way up to the present day.

Humans are imitative creatures. They learn from others how to live and think, work and play, love and hate, not only in childhood but through adult life, too. Culture is the sum total of many thousands of imitations. Moral codes and patterns of behavior grow out of the culture, nearly always supported by the myths that are created by the few and believed by the many.

Myth is a curious creation of the human mind, which usually takes such pride in its own capacity for rational thinking. Myths are always irrational; yet they are part of the furniture of even the most logical minds. Indeed, the more irrational or improbable the story, the more frequently and firmly it is thought literal fact—as shown by Western civilization's collective determination to believe in virgin birth, Adam and Eve, heaven and hell, angels and demons, prophets and soothsayers, miracles, magic, and mysterious "redemption" brought about by drinking someone's blood. People tend to accept the improbable more readily than the provable, even long after it has been exposed as fraudulent. Church father Tertullian wrote *Certum est, quia impossibile est*—"It is certain, because it is impossible"—and considered this a reasonable expression of faith.[3] Even when the literal belief in a myth has had to be abandoned because it simply would not seem sane any more, the story remains popular and is declared "symbolic."

Like folktales, myths change as they are repeated over time; yet they are always considered immutable. When myths are immobilized by literary sources, like the Bible, new translations and interpretations continually alter the sense of them. We are always struggling to bring our myths into some kind of harmony with perceived reality.

The myths that are finding new acceptance today are myths of the Goddess, once replaced by those of the god, now returning to public consciousness in a kind of karmic recurrence. In past generations, Western civilization buried its indigenous Goddess figures under a mountain of revisionism and forgot that they used to be holy. Today, however, many women are rediscovering the symbolic usefulness of such figures as Demeter, Minerva, Aphrodite, Cerridwen, Kali, Tiamat, Ishtar, Isis, Juno, Brigit, Hathor, Astarte, Cybele, and innumerable others.

The Goddess is an archetype, in the Jungian sense, dwelling in the innermost mind of every creature born of woman and psychically bonded, from that instant on, to its mother. Though that bond may be consciously forgotten in later life, it is unconsciously preserved forever in the primitive brain, deeply influencing the ways in which men relate to women and women envision themselves.

Thealogy, then, is a means to understand that archetype, to search the inner self and the environment simultaneously, to discover the best ways in which they can interact. It is a "new" study because it has not yet been widely pursued in the context of the modern world, despite its multitudes of ancient, prepatriarchal traditions. It is the generation of women who are alive today who will carry it forward into the unforeseeable future, and perhaps in time will establish a new woman-church that will truly honor feminine contributions to human culture in a manner once known to every human society for more than two million years, though it has been unknown for a brief and recent two thousand. Thealogy is both new and old: a new view of Woman, her spirituality, and her achievements, plus a much-needed return to her roots. Underneath the surface of our patriarchal society, there are female voices calling out for this—more and more of them each year.

"The Earth is our Mother," says a modern feminist chant, repeating exactly what Neolithic and Bronze Age peoples thought of the land that gave them birth. Earth and Nature have always been Mother, and it has been said that "we serve both ourselves and our hopes for the planet by insisting on a new female reality on which to base a new metaphor for the earth: the female body with its own organic integrity that must be respected."[4] Although theologians have tried for centuries to attribute everything in the natural world to God's conscious manipulations, there has never been a Father Nature.

The Vatican has perceived what it calls the "cult" of the Earth Mother as a threat ominous enough to be denigrated, but even sincere Christian women are beginning to ignore such official warnings. After all, Christianity itself was once a minor "cult" among many similar ones. Women's spirituality is too important to women to be dismissed by any male authority. Furthermore, women's spirituality just might prove to be the very salvation of our precious natural environment, which does literally support all our lives by means of the blooming, water-blessed outer skin of our mother planet. Thealogy may be said to constitute a new development of the immeasurably old Earth-Mother-Nature idea, whose time has come around again.

Vivekananda predicted such a time: "One vision I see clear as life before me, that the ancient mother has awakened once more, sitting on her throne rejuvenated, more glorious than ever. Proclaim her to all the world with the voice of peace and benediction."[5]

Theology has presumed to call itself "science," on the pretext that there is something objective out there for it to study: an actual, sentient, nonhuman god whose characteristics and idiosyncrasies can be discovered. Thealogy's generally more pragmatic approach recognizes the deity as a psychosocial phenomenon based on human culture rather than on any part of the external universe. According to Catholic theologian Uta Ranke-Heinemann, the church has burdened its adherents with "hair-splitting nonsense, and has tried to train them to be moral acrobats, instead of making them more human and kinder to their fellow men and women." She declares that the last thing one can expect from a pope is progress in theology.[6] But today's women are demanding such progress toward a more humane world, and are imagining it for themselves and for others without waiting any more for theologians to trundle their ponderous constructions down the road of progress.

According to Ambrose Bierce, "religions are conclusions for which the facts of nature supply no major premises."[7] Many people think the existence of a god can be "proved" simply by the fact that there is a universe, which they assume had to have been created with conscious intent by a sentient being. But the conclusion doesn't follow the premise. "If the theist has no difficulty accepting an uncaused god, why does he complain when asked to accept an uncaused universe? There is absolutely no evidence to suggest that the natural universe is in any way dependent upon some supernatural agency." As David Brooks wrote, "To explain the unknown by the known is a logical procedure; to explain the known by the unknown is a form of theological lunacy."[8] Not even the old theological doctrine of the Uncaused Cause, the last resort of the Christian rationalist, really serves to support the rootless assumptions of churches. E. Haldeman-Julius says, "The principal objection which a thinking man has to religion is that religion is not true—and is not even sane."[9]

But suppose there were to come into the world a symbol system based not on literal acceptance of irrational untruths, but rather on general recognition of real anthropological history and the fundamentals of human psychology. The only religious symbol that makes rational sense is the Goddess-as-Mother, since the natural teacher and authority figure for every young mammal— including the human one—is none other than its mother. The relationship of child to mother is the foundation of all love, trust, dependence, and yearning for guidance: the constellation of emotional connections that the Hindus called *karuna*.[10] There may be good reasons why societies that recognized a Mother Goddess seemed more serene, more at ease with themselves, than societies that rejected Her in favor of punitive father gods and their manipulative priesthoods.

Suppose we were free to recognize deity for what it really is, an archetypal symbol in some sense evolved by the mind of every individual born of woman: a human phenomenon only, but an important and powerful one. That would be thealogy, and it would be new. And it would lead us back to the Mother.

3

BREAKING AWAY
FROM THE
PATRIARCHY

*O*N THE THRESHOLD OF THE twenty-first century stands the first generation of Goddess-minded women in Western civilization. This is the breakaway generation, the pioneers of feminist spirituality. They have had little guidance on their spiritual journeys. They have had no mainstream cultural sanctions whatsoever. They are blazing a new trail.

Nearly every American woman now alive was taught in her childhood that God is male. She was indoctrinated into one or another brand of Judeo-Christianity. She was given no opportunity to grow up with a generally accepted idea of feminine divinity. It was only in adulthood that some women have come to recognize the Goddess as a primary and primordial metaphor of the sacred, both within themselves and in the shadowed areas of history and prehistory.

These women have had to learn from each other, rather than from an established tradition. Our mothers and grandmothers might have been strong or spiritual women, powerful in their individual hearts and minds, but they had no image of specifically female power to pass on to us. Now, however, we have one to pass on to our children.

The works of many contemporary feminist scholars have shown that our traditional religious organizations have been dedicated to denial or demonization of the Goddess, all the way from biblical times to the present. Bible writers referred to the great Mother Goddess of the Middle East as an abomination (2 Kings 23:13), and even Pope John Paul II issued warnings against what he called "the cult of the Earth Mother." During all the centuries between the former and the latter, no heresy so aroused patriarchal religious authorities to heights of vituperation and violence as the least hint of feminine divinity. Yet many such hints persisted and survived, under cover, underground. Today they are sprouting, leafing out, and flowering anew.

This flowering will require careful nurturance if the present breakaway generation is to have its fruit to pass on to posterity. The tender plant is growing in hostile soil, and there are many who would like to uproot it. Some are even declaring, against quite persuasive evidence, that it isn't there at all. This is largely wishful thinking on the part of those who are too threatened by ideological changes to believe that any evolution can take place in either culture or nature.

In *The Beauty Myth*, Naomi Wolf has pointed out that there is a pernicious fib crippling young women today: the fib called postfeminism. Some traditionalists are contending, and some women are believing, that all the important battles have been fought and won. It is said that young women don't want to be called feminists anymore because feminism is not considered sexy. Wolf says, "It would be stupid and sad if the women of the near future had to fight the same battles all over again from the beginning just because of young women's isolation from older women. It would be pathetic if young women had to go back to the beginning because we were taken in by an unoriginal 20-year campaign to portray the women's movement as 'not sexy.' "[1]

Throughout the Christian era, men have been defining female weakness and passivity as sexy, and female strength or tough-mindedness as a personal threat to their male egos. For many generations, women wishing to be attractive to men have played weak, played dumb, played bubbleheaded incompetence in order to stimulate men's interest. Unfortunately, more often than not, they also stimulated men's thinly disguised contempt, which was patronizing to their faces and degrading behind their backs. And these attitudes were rooted in one primary cause: Western patriarchal religion.

There is no doubt that historical male saints and fathers of the church were bitterly opposed to women. St. Augustine declared that God made man to rule, and woman to obey him. St. Anthony said, "When you see a woman, consider that you face not a human being, but the devil himself. The woman's voice is the hiss of the snake." Other saints insisted that no savage beast is as harmful as a woman, and that although the dragon is fierce and the asp is cunning, woman is the malice of both.[2] Christian theologians had long blamed women for the natural fact that someday their own precious selves would have to die, because the fathers insisted that Eve was responsible for the very existence of death. She "conceived by the serpent and brought forth death," and in her "the whole female race transgressed."[3] Tertullian said every woman is another Eve, the devil's gateway, endlessly guilty of bringing death even upon the Son of God.[4] Sexism exists in Western civilization as a result of the unremitting efforts of churchmen to vilify women and deprive them of basic human rights.[5]

The first generation of American proto-feminists understood well enough that religion was the leading instrument of their subjection, and they boldly defied it. Matilda Joslyn Gage wrote in *Woman, Church, and State*: "The most stupendous system of organized robbery known, has been that of the church towards woman, a robbery that has not only taken her self-respect but all rights of person; the fruits of her own industry; her opportunities of education; the exercise of her own judgment; her own conscience, her own will." Elizabeth Cady Stanton wrote in 1896: "The Bible and Church have been the greatest stumbling blocks in the way of women's emancipation. . . . The whole tone of Church teaching in regard to women is, to the last degree, contemptuous and degrading. . . . The religious superstitions of women perpetuate their bondage more than all other adverse influences."[6]

Stanton spent many years writing *The Woman's Bible*, a thoughtful assessment that exposed the biblical foundations of our civilization's antiwoman prejudice. In her time, the science of Bible criticism was yet young. If she had known some of the facts that have come to light more recently, her analysis of Judeo-Christian responsibility for sexism in our society would have been devastating indeed.

These early feminists were groping toward a nonpatriarchal spirituality that would support their human rights, but they only got as far as rejection of the patriarchy that they correctly perceived as their ideological burden. They had little to put in its place. It would take a new generation of feminist scholars to demonstrate how the patriarchy long ago attacked, and after many centuries managed to overthrow, ancient established religions of the Goddess, the Mother Creatress, who preceded the male gods in every mythology of the world. Sexism has been identified as the product of that ideological battle, which extended over some three thousand years and caused some of the worst manifestations of man's inhumanity to woman, including the Inquisition's reign of terror that paralyzed most of Europe for centuries.

Nineteenth-century American feminists allied themselves with the wave of rationalism then stemming from the Enlightenment. Consequently, they were closely identified with the freethought movement. Their leaders declared openly that God is a myth, Eve's alleged responsibility for sin and evil is a myth, and men had been putting women down for two millennia on the basis of a primitive, obsolete legend. Stanton sweepingly rejected all churchmen who had been cursing women on Eve's account throughout history. She said, "Take the snake, the fruit-tree, and the woman from the tableau, and we have no fall, no frowning Judge, no Inferno, no everlasting punishment—hence no need of a Savior. Thus the bottom falls out of the whole Christian theology."[7]

As much as a century ago, Stanton put her finger on the very reason why today's fundamentalists are still insisting that their children be taught the literal truth of the Eden myth, against every known principle of geology, paleontology, archeology, zoology, prehistory, and common sense. So-called creation science (an oxymoron if there ever was one) demands that the story of original sin be preserved at all costs, because without it, God's execution of his son becomes just another archetypal symbol of the jealous father's propensity to child abuse, and the believer is left without any really compelling reason to be a Christian at all. As a result of fundamentalism, many children today are straitjacketed into a crudely primitive worldview that forcibly reduces our Mother Earth's 4.5 billion years to a mere five thousand, and obliges the children of the *Jurassic Park* decade to believe that the dinosaurs' 165 million years somehow never happened. This seems a sort of pinnacle of hubris, considering that this opinion comes from creatures whom old Mother Earth brought forth less than a mere three million years ago, and whose patriarchal gods were postulated only in the most recent five thousand.

Modern feminists' new personification and celebration of Mother Earth is compatible with ecological considerations that Western patriarchy unfortunately ignored for much too long a time, having been misled by the biblical God's directive to "subdue" the earth and "have dominion over" every other living thing (Gen. 1:28). In much the same sense, Bible writers directed men to subdue and have dominion over women, equating women with the earth, which has always been female. We can now recognize the Great Mother Goddess as a symbol of our planet, of whose substance we are made, and to whom we owe all we know of life and beauty.

Some people clearly comprehend the Goddess as metaphor for the life force in general, but see little difference from the god concept, other than the change of pronouns. They ask how, if both god and Goddess are constructs of the human imagination, can one be any more or less valid than the other? The crucial point here is that the validity of the image depends on its effect on human behavior and acculturization. There is no doubt that the Goddess image has induced more tolerant, peaceful, kind, and caring societies than the god image, whose societies always tended toward war, violence, puritanism, and hierarchy.

Nowadays it's fashionable for various religionists to claim that their churches promoted reform movements like those of the nine-teenth-century suffragists. Actually, the reverse was true. American churches firmly supported all the political, economic, and social inequalities that plagued women in those times. What people nowadays seldom realize is that there was much more at stake for women than winning the vote. For example, married women were legally barred from signing contracts, making wills, or even keeping property inherited from their own families. Everything belonged to their husbands, including their children, who could be willed away or sold into bondage by their father, whether their mother consented or not. When a wife worked for wages, all her earnings belonged to her husband. When a wife died, her husband automatically took everything; but when a husband died without a will, in many states the widow was allowed to live in her home for only forty days. The home was then sold; the widow received only one-third of its value, and was sent to live with the nearest male rel-ative. If both husband and wife died together, the estate went to the husband's family.

Widows and single women who earned money were forced to pay taxes, even though they couldn't vote. When religious women began speaking out for the abolition of slavery in the 1800s, the most influential churches in New England demanded a ban against the abolitionists, because they "set aside the laws of God by wel-coming women to their platforms and allowing them to speak in public."[8] It should be remembered that Abe Lincoln's vaunted "gov-ernment of the people, by the people, for the people" was actually a government of men, by men, for men. Women had no part in it.

While suffragists were fighting to free themselves from the ideological burdens of patriarchy, most of the men of their time remained serenely convinced of St. Thomas Aquinas's dictum that every woman should have a man as her personal master, because her intellect is no better than that of a child or an imbe-cile; and fathers deserve more love than mothers, because they are "the active principle of generation" and mothers are only passive vessels.[9]

Jean-Jacques Rousseau had insisted in his popular *Emile* (1762) that every woman's primary characteristic must be "sweetness," and that she must learn to submit without complaint to even the most abusive husband, however wrong and unjust his actions might be. Abusive men often cited the Bible as their justification for torturing women. At the Fifth National Women's Rights Convention in 1854, the Reverend Henry Grew had the effrontery to stand up and say that "the Holy Scriptures show that it is clearly the will of God that man should be superior in power and authority to woman. . . . No lesson is more plainly and frequently taught in the Bible than woman's subjection."[10]

A Catholic theologian has written that the church's long-held insistence that Christianity meant liberation for women is a false claim. On the contrary, church fathers consistently maintained that wives should be their husbands' slaves. Even the reform movements within the church were aimed at repressing and silencing women, and depriving them of human rights. "The whole of church history adds up to one long arbitrary, narrow-minded masculine despotism over the female sex. And this despotism continues today, uninterrupted."[11]

In fact it was the rise of rationalism and the increasing rejection of Judeo-Christian mythology that contributed most to the women's cause. Joseph McCabe says, "The world grows more humane as it discards Christianity. That is the subtle grievance of the modern priest."

Proto-feminists like Lucretia Mott, Susan B. Anthony, Ernestine Rose, Abby Kelley Foster, Anne Royall, and Voltairine de Cleyre were either thrown out of their churches or voluntarily turned to atheism and freethought because they were smart enough to realize that conventional religion was their enemy. They were also brave enough to stand up and figuratively shake their fists in the face of the god that man had created in his own image. Because God has always been used against women as an instrument of male intimidation, those who rebel generally come to perceive God as imaginary. They ask themselves, "Why should I be intimidated by a figment of men's collective imagination?"

In persecuting such women, men once more demonstrated their odd conviction that their god wasn't able to take care of the matter by himself, without human help. But the women's minds had been opened. No amount of persecution could close them up again. In the late nineteenth and early twentieth centuries, there were many more women involved in the freethought movement than historians lead us to believe. Even today, believers tend to think of freethought (or rationalism, humanism, agnosticism, or whatever other label they may give it) as a small, aberrant minority ideology, but in fact it is extremely widespread, even among many who regularly attend a church. Most respectable American citizens maintain a pragmatic view of life and refrain from arguing about religion because they find it boring, irrelevant, or in bad taste.

Today, for the first time in two thousand years, it's possible for women seeking a more active spiritual life to find some manifestation of the new feminist ideology. As more and more women realize that the root causes of their oppression throughout European history lay in *theology* (God-lore), they may reject such religious sexism in favor of the new *thealogy* (Goddess-lore). There's a lot more to this than simply feminizing traditional images of God. There's a whole new worldview involved, and a new perception of humanity's place in the universe. There's also a completely new idea of the meaning of divinity.

As perceived by the new spiritual feminists, the Goddess is much more than a traditional Mother of God, or Mother of all the gods, as she was perceived in antiquity. She is not only Mother Nature, and the Mother Earth to whom we owe our being; She is also a spirit that each woman finds within herself and identifies with her own femaleness. Unlike our naive, scientifically uneducated ancestors, we don't postulate a literal humanlike entity sitting somewhere among the stars and watching our every move. The Goddess may not be transcendent, but She is the most meaningful metaphor for the life force that animates every creature on our planet.

We now know that the primary sex is the female one. Every fetus begins as a female, and it is the egg rather than the spermatozoon that truly embodies the mystery of ongoing life. We know that every young mammal depends on its mother for survival, and it is the mammalian female who inherits the genetic propensities for caring and sharing that created families, clans, and civilizations in the first place. We know it was originally the women who made laws, gave judgments, harnessed the forces of nature, and invented agriculture, shelters, pottery, medicine, calendars, writing, and other civilized arts. It was the women who communicated with the divine in ways that men couldn't understand. It was the women who brought forth new life in ways that men couldn't imitate, though Goddess knows they tried. It was the women who mothered both sexes and provided men with the sexual "bliss" that they considered their foretaste of heaven. It was the women who evolved ideas of divinity in the first place, by tracing their mother-lines back to a birthgiving Creatress of the Universe.

All this is part of our renewed perception of the Goddess, now that we can recognize Her as the most powerful symbol ever known of our planet's life-giving capacity. We know that no other planets in our solar system are capable of supporting life; probably we will never know whether there might be other life-supporting planets, in other solar systems circling other stars, unreachably far away as they are. But our own Goddess is here and now, immanent in every woman and in every man who recognizes his debt to mother, wife, lover, sister, daughter, and the feminine forces of nature.

Secretly realizing that Woman is the true foundation of the human family, and trying to lure vacillating women back into the fold, Christian fundamentalists today give a lot of lip service to "traditional family values." But this phrase is just a new code name for the male-dominated patriarchal family. It is heard most often from "fundamentalist and other religious groups who are still told by their leaders that the ranking of man over woman is divinely ordained."[12]

Serious difficulties with self-esteem are likely to be encountered by fundamentalist women who truly believe the biblical myth that only man was created in God's image, and woman was an afterthought. Such ideas sink into the core of one's personality and contribute to a lifelong impression of female inferiority. The feminists may joke that it was only on the second attempt that God finally got humanness right; but the woman who knows only a fundamentalist view can never take a strong stand against the myth that rules her.

Human history shows that the Goddess image helped to enhance human potential for peaceable cooperation, whereas the god image tends to enhance human potential for aggressive competition. As Ken Wilber remarked, "Testosterone has only two drives—fuck it or kill it."[13] A religion that is not only patriarchal but also based on a long-standing asceticism wherein sexuality was seen as just as sinful as murder, if not more so, was never a religion fostered by the nurturing, loving, sensual, body-centered, pragmatic feminine spirit. The new so-called cult of the Earth Mother has intrinsic appeal for women, as Marie-Helene Laraque said at a Canadian Women's Commission conference: "As women, we are particularly identified with our Mother Earth . . . we must respect her, care for her, love her. . . . The churches must respect our religions as we respect theirs. We have the right to practice our native beliefs, to have our sacred sites and our sacred objects. Instead of celebrating the 500 years [of Western occupancy] in 1992, the churches should ask our forgiveness."[14]

Arnold Toynbee observed the pious women of his day and remarked, "Religion and its practices have consistently been one of women's fiercest enemies. . . . The fact that many women do not realize this shows how thorough the brainwashing and intimidation have been."[15] Robert Ingersoll expressed similar opinions:

> Priests, theologians, have taken advantage of women—of their gentleness, their love of approbation. They have lived upon their hopes and fears. Like vampires, they have sucked their blood. They have made them responsible for the sins of the world. They have taught them the slave virtues—meekness, humility, implicit obedience. They have fed their minds with mistakes, mysteries, and absurdities. They have endeavored to weaken and shrivel

their brains, until to them, there would be no possible connection between evidence and belief—between fact and faith. . . . Superstition, the mother of those hideous twins, Fear and Faith, from her throne of skulls, still rules the world, and will until the mind of woman ceases to be the property of priests.[16]

To their credit, a few clergymen are beginning to admit the complicity of their organizations in the vast cultural tragedy of sexism. Father Leo Booth wrote: "All women have been sexually abused by the Bible teachings, and institutions set on its fundamentalist interpretations. There would be no need for the women's movement if the church and Bible hadn't abused them."[17] But there is a need, and the women's movement is present in the modern world, gathering strength with each passing year. In the course of a mere decade or two it has shown phenomenal growth.

The women who are breaking or have broken away from religious traditions have discovered a new freedom along with the history—or herstory—of the ancient Goddess and Her numerous manifestations.

Barbara Simpson says, "As women's minds are freed by education the church will disappear; and high time too. It is entirely a man-made institution, even if it is woman supported, and I think that in the future every thinking woman will congratulate herself that her sex had no finger in that pie."[18]

Every woman in our civilization has encountered some degree of prejudice, contempt, or victimization at male hands by the time she reaches adulthood. She has learned from her earliest years that all male strangers are untrustworthy and might hurt her in some terrible undefined way, just because they want to. Or she has learned the hard way that males who are not strangers can and will hurt her. She has been sneered at by male contemporaries, blocked from doing things she wanted to do, undervalued, underpaid, and/or sexually harassed. She has been mocked while walking on a public street, prodded and mauled by strangers in public places, treated as a sex object by acquaintances and dates. These kinds of indignities are suffered even by women who think of themselves, technically, as having never been victimized. Millions of women have suffered much worse, enduring rape, incest, battering, and many other kinds of abuse along with radical deprivation of self-esteem. They have learned not to hope for effective protection on the part of male authorities, because a patriarchal legal system is more concerned with protecting men's rights to women as property. They have been trained not to fight back. Their self-appointed spiritual mentors have counseled them only to beg mercy from a god who, according to his scriptures, cursed their entire sex and commanded them to keep quiet and obey their husbands (I Cor. 14:34).

Naturally inclined to be good citizens, interested in learning to do the right thing, women over the centuries have actually cooperated in their own oppression. Even today, "women fill churches, therapy sessions and self-help groups, inspecting their souls for trace elements of arrogance and power-tripping, when in fact they are the victims of that masculated behavior by husbands, bosses, schools, universities, businesses, governments, and other patriarchal institutions." As birth givers and nurturers, women are predisposed to giving to others, but, "What we don't see is that we are often giving in the wrong places, and on the wrong levels, and that we cannot do it effectively until it is validated socially as the Way to behave." Unfortunately, "the authoritarian image of God validates abusive patterns in men, and does not validate women's nurturing and compassion."[19] According to Elizabeth Cady Stanton, "There is nothing more pathetic in all history than the hopeless resignation of woman to the outrages she has been taught to believe are ordained of God."[20]

It is clear that some of today's women are profoundly disillusioned by the religion that was presented to them—at an early, unthinking stage of life—as truth and goodness, wherein they have discovered lies and evil. They criticize the oppressive, inflexible, punitive aspects of their religious training, as well as its harsh sexism. They feel that they have been wrongly denigrated and deprived of a sense of self-worth.

The fault is not in these women. The fault is in the religion itself.

Next to its generally harsh, unforgiving character, perhaps the greatest mistake of patriarchal religion has been its insistence on literal belief in mythical events and traditions that are essentially unbelievable. This error has not only maintained the faithful for centuries on a childlike level of credulity; it has also demanded increasingly absurd denials of plainly demonstrable scientific discoveries and poured forth rivers of hypocrisy from its own committed authorities, who are forced to lie routinely to their congregations under a shabby pretense of dispensing ultimate truth.

In the case of the Judeo-Christian Bible, it seems excessively silly to base any religion on a literal interpretation of a work—or, more accurately, a loose collection of works—now known to have undergone many centuries of mistranslation, editing and reediting, revision, plagiarism, interpolation, editorializing, and deliberately fraudulent doctoring of every sort. In hundreds of ways the Bible contradicts itself, and the exegists have been trying interminably to explain away these internal contradictions, without notable success. The science of "Bible criticism" or "higher criticism" is generally ignored by every religious community, because its findings are always at variance with the accepted canon, and what's more, they can be supported by the kind of evidence that believers are taught not to require. It may be a good idea for women disappointed by their traditional religious training to investigate this field of research, as well as the prepatriarchal world of Goddess religions now being uncovered by feminist scholars.

Ruth Hurmence Green declared that reading the Bible turned her into an atheist: "I had always been told the bible was a book about love, but I couldn't find enough love in it to fill a salt shaker. God is not love in the bible; God is vengeance." For this and similar reasons, many feminist thinkers have simply given up on any interpretation whatever of the biblical God, and declared with Annie Laurie Gaylor that "Repudiation of patriarchal religion is an essential step in freeing women." As Meg Bowman puts it, "Women will never have equal rights—will never be liberated—until either the major religions are abolished or women assume leadership and drastically change them."[21]

This is what breaking away is all about. Many women still cling to the faith of their "fathers" (literally) for the reason that spiritual life is important to them and they have been taught that Judeo-Christianity is the only possible spirituality. Even against all reason, people often cling to particular beliefs, particular myths, only because they have never heard of any alternatives. But there are alternatives to the Judeo-Christian mythos, alternatives that many women find much more compatible not only with their own feelings but also with external realities, both social and biological. What drives women to break, in the first place, with their traditional religious institutions? Different women answer this question in different ways, and it is instructive to pay attention to their answers.

MODERN WOMEN TALK ABOUT BREAKING AWAY FROM THE PATRIARCHY

The following pages present excerpts from interviews with modern women, aged from their mid-twenties to their mid-seventies, who express frustration with established patriarchal religions. All have broken away from their natal faith in one way or another, seeking a belief system more welcoming and comfortable for women.

🐚 🐚 🐚

Once I was a serious Christian. I was raised as a Lutheran and I took it very seriously. Even now it colors the way I look at theology. I can't accept a denomination that tells you something but doesn't really expect you to take it seriously, which is why I had real trouble with my religion. In my experience, it was "I, a poor miserable sinner," always feeling quite terrible about myself, never being able to find any joy in life. No matter what we did, it could never be enough. Just dying at the wrong time, unshriven, could get you consigned to everlasting torment. Getting a heart attack in the middle of a heated argument could condemn you immediately. It was quite distressing.

The Gospels didn't make much sense to me. Selling everything you have, as directed, would make a nice egalitarian society because no one would own anything. But with a society of itinerant preachers, who would be supporting them? It's not very good planning.

Western religions are extremely barren. Either the ritual is not explained, or on the other hand the ritual is cut out completely. It's very sad. Ritual is a thing of beauty, and it's always good to be crafting beauty. But without explanation or flexibility or choice, it becomes an obstacle, instead of a worshiping of the connections. A congregation begins to worship the person who is performing. That's very sad. It's a loss.

In the Lutheran Church, stripping everything down to the bare pews requires a lot of imagination to get a level of excitement up. The Catholic service is nice on some levels; it's very beautiful. When the eyes see something beautiful, it's easier to get the minds to link. I was made to feel guilty because I couldn't achieve a spiritual connection in Lutheranism. I had a tough time coming up with the correct penitential attitude. I had a hard time coming up with grief over my sins, or enough sins to confess. I was supposed to realize that I was eternally in a state of sin, never in a state of grace.

My older sister was a wonderful artist, but she was told to take art education, not just art courses, so she could teach art in a Lutheran school. Very sad. Naturally she would have to marry. Even though I was given advantages, still the boys were getting all the good things. The boys get everything. That's still true. They get more attention.

In church, it gets slapped into your face. You're insulted. Everything is Eve's fault. They forget about Deborah sitting under the palm tree dispensing justice. There's this male god who can say "Presto!" and overturn his own laws. There is no consistency, but you must abide by their inconsistencies. I find their theology very irritating. How can a several-thousands-of-years-old piece of literature be more important than my direct experience of what I perceive as divine? That gives me real problems.

When the men take over, they tend to exhibit a spirituality that is very rigid and structured, not a free-flowing thing of beauty. They don't quite understand that the reason we do rituals is to make ourselves happy. I don't think even an impotent male god would need all those people worshiping and singing to him to make him feel better. That's like a five-year-old, a real insecure god.

🐜 🐜 🐜

We've been so hurt by having a god that was outside of us, and elevated, and separated from the world. That doesn't work for me. As a child I perceived the deity as female, and then I thought that was all wrong and I tried to change it. It just made sense to me that She had to be a mother.

My family is Christian, and my father is reputedly very devout. I've never known what that means, except that everyone in the family has always said, "Oh, your father is very devout." I've never really seen it in practice. They're very conventionally Christian. No enthusiasm, no depth, just sort of surface. I tried very hard but it did not work for me. Also, it just inherently doesn't make sense.

I read a book on Catholic theology. The first two chapters were very difficult, and the rest of the chapters were very easy to understand. I realized that the reason was that, if you accept the premises of the first two chapters, everything follows logically and simply from there. But how can you persuade people to believe something that has no sense to it? The author worked really hard, and it was really good, but it didn't make sense. And this book is a classic. It formed generations of Catholics.

Patriarchy has sold us this line that we can't believe what we know. If we could believe what we know, we certainly wouldn't be doing patriarchy. I keep thinking about what Sonia Johnson says, if all the women stopped doing patriarchy tomorrow, we'd be done with it. It could be simple. The thing is, it isn't working for men either. So who's benefiting?

So much follows from not being able to believe what we know: not being able to believe what we know about what we're doing to the water, or how eliminating species is going to affect us, or forcing a woman to have children that she can't handle, all that stuff. We're living in a culture that has all of these institutions which prevent the accomplishment of the things for which they were ostensibly created.

🐜 🐜 🐜

My mother had stories about her Catholic upbringing in parochial schools in Brooklyn. They hit her hands with a ruler. She was force-fed milk one time, and never drank milk again since that day. I remember a confession I made around the time of my first communion, to a white-haired priest who was very nasty. I came out crying and feeling terrible about myself. I think it had to do with masturbation. He made me feel so dirty.

🐜 🐜 🐜

I grew up Jewish, but Judaism had never quite provided me with a sense of purpose. Being female, I lived with the resentment of not being able to fully participate as an adult in the Jewish community unless it was under certain restrictions. My own responsibility would be only to my home and family. While I don't find that repugnant, as an intellectual I felt very restricted. I could not read Torah. I could not practice Judaism in the same way as a man. A bat mitzvah has never been as significant as a bar mitzvah, the initiation of the boy into the community. The advent of female rabbis has not changed anything in the Orthodox or Hasidic communities. Hasids do not regard Reform Jews as Jews.

Of course, on the Sabbath the Shekinah fills the house. The female predominates. But it's not enough. The Goddess should play a much larger role.

Judaism is based on such a suspicion of the female. Its architects are willing to allot a certain amount to the feminine energy, but I do believe that mistrust of the feminine began with Judaism. I really impute that to the Jews.

My sister, who is a very bright woman, wanted to study at

Hebrew school and was kept from doing so. The rabbi said that girls shouldn't study.

Traditional theology is lists of thou-shalt-nots. Fundamentalists say in effect, "I'm going to pollute the earth, I'm going to stink it up as much as possible, because it's only a way station to the next world. Why should I bother to clean it up?" So we get this ecological disaster, with ecological uncaring on the part of a lot of people.

I left the Christian Church at fourteen, because it was full of "shoulds" and none of its "shoulds" seemed anything but condemnatory, punitive, and hatefully oppressive. Until I bumped into the Goddess, I was a wanderer in a wilderness of spirit, and I feel great hostility toward the institutions of the church that forced me to choose between angry, empty submission and angry, empty rejection.

Being a woman, growing up in this society, I learned to devalue myself. I was second-class because I was female. I learned that in my home. Males were more prized, and had more status. I was raised Episcopalian. My mother and her people were puritanical. The family left me with low self-esteem, hating myself on a deep level.

Patriarchal society devalues the female. Patriarchal religion is the power-over model, the ruling-from-above model, divorced from real involvement. I do believe there can be a transcendent aspect to divinity, but not in the form of a male god. The male god might be a symbol of transcendence, but gender exists only in living things and can only be immanent.

Patriarchal religion can be very exploitative. It doesn't trust humans. We have a society based on fear. That's the way we rear children. Things get distorted and lopsided under patriarchy.

I totally disagree with all the violence, corruption, power plays, hierarchies. About patriarchal religion, when I was younger I thought, "Why did they make this up? This is weird; this is cruel; this doesn't make any sense. What is all this killing?" I guess I was an unbeliever, even though I went through the motions in Catholic school. The religion is unduly cruel. In my church they had this very realistic Italian crucifix. I remember looking at the blood, and thinking, "Who made this one up? Couldn't they think of something better?" But I guess the patriarchs in power love it.

❧ ❧ ❧

I was raised Roman Catholic but I never could buy what they were saying. I was put out of religion class for heresy, and made to stand in the hall, because I caused trouble, they told me. What I did was ask questions. They didn't like that. I couldn't understand their god. I couldn't buy it all the way, though I tried.

I kept saying, on Saint Patrick's day, bring back the snakes.

Women have been under the control of males for too long. There has to be another way, and it has to be a good way. I don't think I will die if I say, "No, I don't believe in your god anymore. You can, and you can have him, but I don't believe in him."

When I had problems I went to the priest. What I found out was that he manipulatively and methodically used his position to set up a situation of abuse. Afterward, I found five other women that he'd done the same thing to. None of them would come forward, though I wanted to press charges. The church did move him to somewhere else. Apparently he had been moved before. There was a paternity suit against him in another parish. I went to the bishop with a fifteen-page report. He didn't want to be bothered.

The church will never relinquish its power. One chink in the armor, and they're gone. I think they're so afraid at this point, because there are so many people pounding on their door saying, "Hey, I'm not taking this anymore."

❧ ❧ ❧

I don't like all that duality, separation of the body and spirit. There is no duality. There is unity everywhere.

      🐌   🐌   🐌

If we were taught as little girls to love ourselves and honor ourselves, there would be no other way but to honor the Goddess. But we're taught that divinity or God is something other than us. It becomes something that we need to relearn. It's a foreign concept to most of the women who come upon the Goddess as adults.

I grew up Catholic but it never felt right to me. A few years ago I dug up an old paper that I'd written in my senior year in high school. It was a satire about the Catholic church, and about a priest's role in his relationship with the congregation. It was so bitter! I didn't remember feeling that way. But there was so much resentment and bitterness and mistrust. When I got a job in high school I had a valid excuse not to go to church, but for years I hadn't wanted to go.

      🐌   🐌   🐌

The patriarchal god is somehow a very nosy busybody. His nose is in everything. He knows what everybody does. I guess I learned about the patriarchal god the same way that I learned about Santa Claus— you've got to be very good or else he knows, and you'll go to hell. I wasn't taught the concept of hell, being Jewish, but you would get punished. Every time something happened, I would slip, and my mother would say, "God punished you."

I think if I still believed in the old concept of the patriarchal god, I would have major problems now. As a child I couldn't understand why my parents weren't getting together again, when I spent hours each night begging God for their reunion. He rejected my prayers, and allowed this terrible thing to happen.

Fear doesn't belong in a religion. It's so unspiritual. How can you be spiritual and be afraid? Fundamentalism fosters war. War is a part of its background. The Bible condones war. There have been many religious wars.

If women would just stop supporting the churches that are so antiwoman! We're the ones who educate our children in that religion. We're the ones who insist that everybody goes to church and Sunday school. We're the ones who do the bake sales, and we do a lot of the dirty work in keeping these religions going. If we would only just stop, and leave, and withdraw support! An individual woman can help by withdrawing support from patriarchy and becoming involved in women's circles.

🐾 🐾 🐾

One of the things that used to bother me about Buddhism was how Siddhartha gave up his wife and kids and wealth and princedom, and went off to get enlightenment. But what about Mrs. Siddhartha? What happened to her? And why wasn't she giving up everything to go off and get enlightenment? It doesn't tell you anything at all about footsteps for a woman to follow. If you don't have a female quality in your deity then there's nothing for women to model themselves on. A monotheistic god, being kind of an ethereal being off in the sky, doesn't tell anyone how to live. He just tells you how to follow orders. That's why I'd prefer a myth that has more family to it, a mother and a father, a male child and a female child.

🐾 🐾 🐾

When I was growing up, nobody thought religion was important. I was sent to Sunday school, but I never had a concept of a god other than one that I just wasn't much interested in.

🐾 🐾 🐾

Christianity never really worked for me. I've never been comfortable with how oppressive it is to women, gays, and lesbians. The concept of the Goddess is really important to me as a feminine image of the divine to counterbalance the masculine images that I was handed. I like to think that patriarchy as a social construction is more nurture than nature. I like to think that it's learned behavior. I hope men aren't naturally that way. I like to think they're not. So far, men have blown it.

I didn't feel that I needed Christianity any more. I saw the abusiveness in it. I got sick of having everybody appeal to a text and try to sock each other in the head by saying "I have the right interpretation!" "No, I do!" "No, I do!" I don't care what the text says. The text was socially and economically constructed out of a patriarchal agenda. So what the heck do we need it for?

During my first year in the seminary I sat in Bible classes hearing the very literal interpretation of what men and women should be doing, and getting really mad, and arguing with people over it. As soon as I started getting the solid academic knowledge, and realizing the implications of that, I started shifting. It was the out I was looking for. I became more and more liberal. After my first year, I realized that I didn't want to be ordained.

The real clincher was the summer after my first year when I went to Texas and did a chaplaincy in a hospital. I was the only woman in a group of seven men with a male supervisor. It was supposed to be a quasi-therapeutic process. It was terrible. There was no therapist there. You were supposed to be shredding your personality down. It was really destructive. I was furious the entire summer. I was so angry, I wrote this sermon about feminine imagery for God and preached it in the chapel. The next day the patriarch of the department stood up in the staff meeting and said, "We won't be using these chapel services for any kind of agenda." My service was connected to people's pastoral needs but I was doing it out of a feminine model. I was encouraging people to look at the feminine aspects of God which are in the Old Testament. I came in, I critiqued, and I was silenced; and other people were silenced. It was a terrible summer.

That pretty much clinched it for me. After I went through that experience I came back in the fall for my second year. I was supposed to go to my church and start the process. I just called up the minister and said, "I don't want to put my foot any farther in the door." I don't have the patience to deal with the churches' sexism.

There are many powerful, bright, committed women in the ministry now, and also men who identify with the feminist agenda. I have some male friends who are very liberal, very progressive, very willing to use feminine imagery for God. There are many people who are trying to transform it, even though there's still a lot of resistance.

Women need to be able to claim their power. So many women are just conscripted into the patriarchal system, which is intimately intertwined with capitalism. We have global capitalism, and no control over it.

I still believe in a higher power. I don't think I'll ever let go of that. My husband, who is also a seminary graduate, is an agnostic.

What I love about the Unitarian Church is that nobody ever tells me, "You can't ask that question." What always used to frustrate me in the seminary was being forbidden to color outside the lines. They'd say, "We can't talk about that." It drove me nuts. I don't want to have any boundaries about what questions I can ask, or what literature I can read, or what theories I can consider.

Why do patriarchal religions uphold the mainstream oppressive society? Because they don't teach people to think. They encourage people to accept the status quo. So the church, instead of being a transforming force, is typically just part of the status quo. That's a very disempowering and oppressive aspect of mainstream religion. The mystical traditions are not even very strong in today's theology.

What drove me to seminary was my own quest for some kind of mystical experience of the divine, communing or meditation or something. This is the experience of many seminarians: you go there, and you think you're going to have this nurturing theological awakening. But whatever illusion you have about how spiritually nurturing it's going to be goes out the window during the first semester. There's no time for any spiritual journey. It's just like any other school. But thealogy really honors the individual thought and experience, and nurtures and encourages that. Traditional theology does not do that. It's more spiritual when it comes from within, rather than being imposed from without.

☕ ☕ ☕

In churches I've heard so much bullshit. You're part of Adam's rib, and so on. They never follow or practice what they're always preaching in traditional religions. I can't accept their views. Why should I say that a man is better than a woman? They're not better. We're equal. We all have our abilities to contribute. Equality is important, but most religions don't practice it. I can't accept the idea that I should pay homage to a male god, and ignore the female. Why should I? It's not right.

In a patriarchal society, women can't reach their full potential. They're put down. Men might put down a woman for being too smart. What's wrong with being smart? It's better than being dumb.

They say, Thou shalt not kill. Well, whom shalt thou not kill? They claim it's okay if we go to war, that's legalized killing. If you mean, truly, Thou shalt not kill, that means on any level. Putting people to death is not a solution for anything. And to go out hunting, just for the pleasure of killing an animal—that's wrong. To kill animals just to wear their fur, and not use the rest of the body parts, is wrong. We shouldn't throw the bones and other parts away. The Native Americans used every part of the animal.

It's easy to go out and fight, but it's hard to sit down and talk through differences. The patriarchs never wanted to sit down and talk. It was either, "They'll do it our way, or let's kill them."

☕ ☕ ☕

I object to men's beliefs about their powers and abilities. There's a lack of reality in the perpetuation of such beliefs. They pretend that men have powers that women don't have, and therefore we should always listen to them, because they know.

I grew up with a father who was very religious, and I think he had a much easier life because of that belief. I am happy for him, but it didn't offer me the same thing. It didn't make me feel good. It was a punishing god. When I was growing up, I resented that. I don't look to religion for comfort. I look to people for comfort.

♣ ♣ ♣

What I believe now goes totally against the grain of everything I believed all my life. I was a Presbyterian and I was taught that there was only good and bad, and you were going to heaven or you were going to hell. As a kid I felt bad and guilty, because I am an incest survivor. Spirituality kept me alive through my teen years, when I thought I would kill myself. But the religion gave me a fearful god, a god who could destroy me. He was not loving or caring, or wanting what I wanted. So at eighteen I got pregnant and got married.

I still felt inferior. The marriage was abusive. Putting your faith in anyone outside yourself does more damage than putting your faith in yourself. I'm still angry. I grew up thinking that abuse in the family was normal.

I can't talk to a male therapist. I would feel very uncomfortable, because I would feel that they all take the side of men. They protect each other. To me, marriage is like a death sentence. You sign a piece of paper and sign your life over to some guy, and according to the law of this land, you belong to him. Love, to me, is equal to pain. To accept someone being kind is very difficult for me.

♣ ♣ ♣

When I was a child, I could never understand why people thought they had to go into a building to worship God. I didn't know anything other than the traditional god, but I thought if that god created the world, then why would one go indoors? Why wouldn't one be out-of-doors, celebrating all that he had created, and enjoying the sensual beauty, the sights, the smells, sounds, and feelings of it, feeling the sunshine? I had a difficult time with going to church and sitting on a hard wooden bench, listening to some man preach. That, to me, was not sacred. I felt much more spiritual outdoors, climbing a tree, sitting in the fork of a tree. What better thing to do than sit in the crook of a tree, feeling supported? Or digging in the ground, feeling its texture?

🐦 🐦 🐦

In my youth, my religion was based on fear. I don't think I ever prayed to God. He was too far above me. Priests were so awesome, with their dark clothing. I was afraid of the nuns. I didn't say boo. They were the authority. They dictated everything. They dictated how you could dress, and what you could think. What wasted lives.

I was a public-school child. They sat us in the back of the church. I never liked that. I had the feeling, when I was very young, that I was not as worthy as the Catholic-school kids. Children, seven or eight years old, take these things hard. Public-school children also had to go down in the basement for communion. It was very difficult for me.

When my mother was dying, she spent a lot of time holding on to the rosary. That was fine, but it wasn't helping her. Sometimes I'd say, "I'm a live person here with you; put down that piece of plastic." She professed to have this faith, which was supposed to be a comfort to her, yet she was so fearful to die! She was very afraid. I thought, her religion is really not comforting her. I can condone religion if it's helping you, but if it's untrue and full of fear, it's useless.

When I go to church now, I'm very aware of how they use the words "god" and "man." They never really introduce, or even mention, "woman." They're not open to change. They're going backward.

When my father retired, he decided to read the Bible because he was always a great reader. He got to a point where he said, "I don't believe that." When he came to God's orders about killing all the children, he put it down and never read any more.

🐦 🐦 🐦

I grew up Protestant, going to Sunday school every week. Somehow, male-dominant parts of the Bible weren't taught to us. The Sunday school teacher didn't teach the crucifixion story at Easter time. She brought flowers from her garden and discussed the life cycle of flowers. Eventually we did learn the Bible version. That version stunk.

When my family moved, it was traumatic. My father molested me that summer. There was nobody willing to hand me a book saying, "Here's the Goddess way." I went and got a Goddess religion book, to see how different it was. I found it incredibly similar to my own thoughts.

I was always told that my mother and grandmother were lazy, and worse. I watched my mother take beatings. My father was a monster, and his father before him was a monster.

I look back at my childhood pictures, and I look so old. And now I feel so young.

🐾 🐾 🐾

You have an entire culture so hostile to women that it makes eunuchs of the priests and then dresses them in dresses, and gives the priests all the qualities that in saner cultures are attributed to women: the nurturing, the blessing, the healing, even the burying of the dead. Those are all female acts.

I feel such tremendous hostility toward the Catholic Church in its aggressive state, because it isn't celebratory. It's eradicatory, if you will. It eradicates women from the world. Its perfect world would be a bunch of these faggy priests in dresses, nurturing each other with their moral Christlike hands. It makes me so angry that I can't listen to anything good about them. It always seemed to me that there's something fascist in organized religion. There's some dark seed in ideology that takes it so quickly from being a light in the world to a darkness, from being the hand that uplifts to being the fist that oppresses.

🐾 🐾 🐾

I'm not a Christian any more. I had to go the other way and really reject Christianity, though I think Jesus was an okay guy. Whether he was a god or not is not interesting to me.

I studied the Burning Times. I spent an Easter weekend immersed in reading about them. That summed it up for me—the evil that patriarchal Christianity perpetrated, and still perpetrates. Even though they're not torturing people, they still are damaging men's and women's sexuality. That's evil; it really is.

🐾 🐾 🐾

I didn't get anything out of patriarchal religion, try as I would. Nothing in that really spoke to me. What I became aware of was that the light was within myself. I had a dream where I was standing over a pool of water, and I could look up inside my body and see that the light was inside of me. It was like an epiphany. All of a sudden I realized that I was looking in all the wrong places. But it wasn't until years later that I started looking at patriarchal religion and realizing that this was a myth that men had created for themselves, to oppress women, and it had nothing for women in it. We need to start creating our own myths.

I knew early on that I couldn't rely on Christianity for nurture. I was searching for my spiritual identity. It was apparent to me that whatever I did would have to be balanced with respect to nature and animals—all of what mankind is working so hard to destroy. I also knew that whatever I was going to do had to further my own spiritual development. The idea that anything nonhuman was a lesser being turned me off. I felt that animals deserve respect. I had no respect for a religion or a god that would use fear to control behavior. I realized that I could not mesh with the religion, and rather than try to fit myself into a shape I didn't belong in, I separated from it.

When you start examining values, it's like peeling away layers of an onion. What we say our values are, and what they really are in terms of our behavior, are so incredibly different. For all our talk about family values, our society doesn't care very much about our children or our elders. I heard on the radio that one-quarter of all the children in this country live below the poverty level. That's obscene.

The church encourages men to think themselves the rulers of home and castle. A lot of the fundamentalists think the man has the ultimate say—right, wrong, or indifferent. This is the power authority, controlling by fear. Might makes right: That's how patriarchal religion operates. Churches say: We are a powerful religion, therefore we have control over you. You're going to burn in hell if you don't do what we say.

They created the structure of heaven and hell. They say if you're good now, and do what we say now, then somewhere in the distant future you'll get to heaven. Break the rules, or go against what we tell you to do, then you're going to burn in hell. That's the ultimate control over somebody's psyche.

Women have to be at a certain level of development, otherwise they buy into the whole patriarchal structure and look upon others as abominations because they don't abide by the rules of the church.

🐾 🐾 🐾

One of the things that bother me most about patriarchy is that they have no human values. There's the emphasis on words, and deception through words—the emphasis on goals rather than processes, seeing value only through the material things and social standing, the complete waste and pollution. I can't think of much good to say of it. There are a few good men out there who are working on it, and who know better. But the male idea of progress needs a female escape hatch.

🐾 🐾 🐾

I think we're at the end of a time period. We're at the end of religions looking to an afterlife. We're at the end of a culture that values what are our current values. I think the fact that it's ending is seen in this tremendous amount of violence everywhere, and we are both willing and unwilling, at the same time, to do something about violence. We say we should do something, this is terrible, and yet we don't really do that much about it. We're caught in the time warp. Violence is presented to us all the time, which means we really don't want to get rid of it. It's still serving its ends.

This is a dangerous time. Certainly not like the Burning Times, but it's unsettling. Everybody is very frightened about change, and the more frightened you are the more determined you are to hang onto the old, and not let anybody do anything different around you, if you can possibly help it. This is what our fundamentalists are doing: They're reacting to change.

🐾 🐾 🐾

I was raised a Catholic and went through all the traditional ceremonies. A whole bunch of things didn't make sense, in the context of what they were teaching me. The idea of God as a white man with a beard, sitting on a throne up in heaven, used to make me angry. So did the fact that the nuns were relegated to the sides of the altar, if they were allowed up there at all. The altar boys were there, but the nuns were forbidden.

I broke away from the Catholic church when I was about fifteen, when my father died. I had the excuse that if there was a god, he wouldn't have taken my father from me, so there must not be a god. Some of my friends tried to open me up to other religions, like born-again Christianity. Nothing really resonated with me. My religion was in the woods. That's where I would feel it most. It was only a few years, ago that I realized I was not the only person who felt this uplifting spiritual energy in the outdoors. I found that there were other people involved in the same pursuits, with the same beliefs. It was pretty exciting. The sensitivity had always been there, but not the knowledge that there are so many other people who think the same way.

In Christianity, a basic teaching is that we're sinners. We're not worthy, we're no good, and we're damned unless we do what that religion says to do. There's fear, and guilt, and shame. That's what I want to get rid of. One thing I remember clearly is singing the line, "Oh, Lord, I am not worthy." I can't remember the rest of it. I'm doing everything in my power to shift that thought. I always hated singing "Amazing Grace" where it calls the singer a wretch. Now I never sing it because I don't believe it.

They eradicated the Goddess. Just knowing that is a revelation. What is it with these men? They can't handle it. I think it's so great now that people are coming out about our real history.

Patriarchal religion certainly hasn't done much for us in the past. It's so domineering. They just want to control you. They want to control people, their thoughts, their actions. It's time for women to rule the world again. We used to rule the world, until we allowed men to co-rule, and then they took over. It's time we took it back, because they haven't done such a good job with it. Why should men rule everybody and everything? Religion shouldn't be something that's dictated to you.

Any male figure found by archeologists is still labeled "such-and-such god," whereas any female figure is labeled "such-and-such woman." There's only a little more awareness so far in the academic community, but there's much more popular awareness. When I talk with groups of women, I find that there's a whole challenging of the academic canon going on. A lot of ordinary people are reading books about these things that normally they would not be reading about. In popular culture, people weren't usually reading books about heavy mythological, anthropological, or archeological subjects until now. The fact of the matter is, the interest is out there. The popular strength of people investigating these things has circumvented the academic trails.

People in universities sometimes ask, "Why do you want women's studies? There should be men's studies." The answer is that we need women's studies because everything else in academia is men's studies.

A lot of Western religion insists that humbling oneself, submitting oneself, is virtue. Actually, when you think about it, this is not all that bad for male members of patriarchal societies, so they can learn a little humility. However, it's quite toxic for women, who have already been subjected to too much submission through society.

🐚 🐚 🐚

I grew up in a very evangelical situation, which I never had any problem getting rid of, because I never bought into it. I always felt that there was something wrong with this picture. Although there were things in the Bible that I liked, like psalms and comforting things, I have a really hard time even reading any theology that has the word "god" in it. I always associated that word with wrath and punishment.

I was always frustrated by the religion I was taken to as a child. It was a Swedish denomination that found Lutheranism to be too loose. If anything was fun, you weren't supposed to do it. Anything that called attention to yourself was wrong. There was no teaching of reason or reasoning processes. It was all, "Don't ask questions, just do exactly as you're told. This is what you're going to do, and this is what you're going to think, and this is what you're going to feel—and don't worry about feeling too much. If you want to have a feeling, we'll tell you what it should be." It was very unsettling, and I felt very much a loner. I was very repressed.

In my own family, only one of my sisters has managed to come out of this. One of my brothers became a minister in this denomination, and the other two are heavily invested in it. My father beat my mother. Things were really wrong, and the religion was not helpful.

You could never play cards. Drinking was beyond the pale; sex so far beyond what was allowed that there was absolutely no mention of it. Music was okay as long as it wasn't popular or suggestive in its lyrics. I remember being outraged that something like the Ice Capades was forbidden because the skaters wore short skirts. The minute I got to be eighteen and left home, I immediately started drinking and smoking with all possible speed.

Organized religion may be spiritual, but I haven't experienced it that way. I can see my own thoughts and feelings as spiritual. Traditional theology always seems to put women down, in a subservient position.

         🐜   🐜   🐜

I'm one of those recovering Catholics. When I thought it was time to start giving my daughter some sort of religion, I knew I didn't want to send her to a Catholic church. I asked her if she wanted to make her First Holy Communion, because my sister sends her kids to Catholic school, more as a practical thing than as a spiritual thing. My daughter said "No, I don't want to make my First Holy Communion. But does that mean we're still going to be Americans?"

My mother said to me, "You were such a good Catholic girl. What happened to you?" I said, "Mom, I'm just as good a pagan as I was a Catholic."

I remember having crushes on priests. That's the real reason why I liked to go to church. I wasn't listening to what they were saying; I was watching them say it. I liked the incense and the pageantry of it. But I knew once I went to high school I would stop going to church regularly. The nuns were not kind to me when they found out I wasn't going to a Catholic school.

I attribute my former lack of self-confidence to being brought up in a patriarchal society, a victim of emotional abuse from my father. Once women develop a feeling of power, it's a lot harder to buy into the bad things men have been saying. Women who buy into the patriarchal concept are probably going to be our worst enemies. It would be so much easier if all women were on our side. But there are many women who side with the old way.

My father said Hitler was good for the people, and for the economy. War is usually good for the economy, of course. But I don't like fighting or violence. It hurts me to see so much of it on TV, or in the news. It's so prevalent now.

&   &   &

My grandson is going to join the Jewish church and be bar mitz-vahed. It's going to cost my son over five thousand dollars, in order for my grandson to become a good Jew. The Catholic church also cons people when loved ones die. To get them out of their hell quicker, you give money to have a priest *maybe* think about them on the sabbath. It's a tool of greed. The Mother Goddess is so different.

&   &   &

Growing up Catholic, I knew something was not right there. I con-nect with the teachings of Jesus but I don't idolize him. What he taught was beautiful, but they have twisted it around. My mother is Catholic, but she understands my beliefs and respects them. She believes that the Bible is incomplete. She believes there were many women followers of Jesus who are not mentioned in the Bible.

Men try to be superior over women. I don't care for that. With a Goddess religion, we would be in a state of peace, instead of vio-lent. You don't see people giving their daughters toy guns. There wouldn't be war. With the Goddess religion, we would be closer to the earth. I feel that when you separate yourself from the earth, you are separated from your spirit. Everything is too materialistic in patriarchal society. We must get back to the earth, to more nat-ural things.

&   &   &

The female spirit has a bit of rebellion, and even in the most patri-archal religions the women gather together and reinforce their feminine strength. If they can't do it overtly, they do it in their harems or kraals. Women fight on different levels to maintain a female image. They may accept the established religion, whatever it is, but if it doesn't allow for recognition of the female, the women try to do it. The only other way women could fight back would be in small groups with the raising of the children. They should raise their male children to be respectful of the female, and of the Goddess concept. It would have to be almost a closet training program.

Patriarchal society's most objectionable traits are oppression and exploitation of the weak: mostly females, children, the poor, the sick. There's closed-mindedness and a "survival of the fittest" tendency in patriarchal society, also rigidity and stubbornness pretending to be absolute right. Most thinking people know there is never an absolute right, but patriarchal society says there is.

Because the Goddess worship is so very basic to the human female psyche, its establishment is bound to happen. It's like love: it's there. Given the opportunity to express itself and to be, it grows. It just has to take off, because it's a fundamental truth.

The primary thing an individual woman must do is get in touch with her own sense of being, and what she truly feels. She must discard all the concepts that she's been programmed with, and look at her inner self, her true self. Once she looks at her real self, then she has to look at her society. She has to ask, "Do these things go together?" She will probably say, "No, there's something very wrong here." Then she has to start looking for other women, like-minded women, and then she has to go out and have some kind of impact on her society, in whatever way she can. If she wants to organize a group dedicated to improving the earth or the lives of people on it, then she can do that. It's important for a woman to reevaluate her own place in society, and do good. It is not a new idea.

Often, our society doesn't let women do other than what society wants them to do. It's very bad, not only for the society, but for the woman herself.

We need to care for Mother Earth, and for humanity, as opposed to taking care of business: corporations, industry, and such institutions. Everything that patriarchal religion presents, the Goddess should be supporting the opposite. We should seek true spiritual experience as opposed to institutionalized ritual. Many contemporary religions have forgotten the spirit. They're like the army, or business.

We have no real evidence for any faith or belief system, except for what is felt by the individual. Is it in the mind, or is it something actual? Everyone has to answer that for herself.

🐜   🐜   🐜

I think the divine is beyond our human constructs. The Goddess can become a reified symbol just as the male god has in our society. But for me, the male aspect has been more negative. I'm not opposed to male qualities in the ideal form, but the Lutheran god that I was handed was a male who kills his son, who willingly gives this sacrifice for us, and that's supposed to make everything okay. This model of God is an abusive parent, who whips and scorns his son.

If you could distill it back to the original time, would you find that men would spontaneously create this? If men have aspects of male and female, yin and yang, and so do women, then if we were all whole and balanced we would come to some model that I think would be more feminine, because I think the feminine model is more empowering and more justice seeking.

🐜   🐜   🐜

Thealogy and theology are two different animals. The Goddess is so life giving, and the traditional theology that I was taught is so stifling. It was all "you can't" and "you don't." When prayers didn't work, I was told, "You didn't pray right," or "God sees it's not good for you." The Goddess says if you think you can, you probably will. She's encouraging. It's such a happy way to do things.

Traditional theology is just a means of controlling people. The Goddess is much more nurturing.

🐜   🐜   🐜

There was a study done where people were asked what religion they were. Half the people who were Presbyterian couldn't even spell it. They'd say something like, "I'm Pedestrian." That may not be too different!

🐾 🐾 🐾

I've suffered a great deal of abuse through the Baptist Church. My father was a Christian fanatic, a Baptist fanatic. I was sexually abused by him for years, until I got old enough to say no. I can remember going to the church for help—*his* church—and getting none. I've never forgotten, and I'm sure on some subconscious level I still think I'm guilty somehow. I wasn't taught a better way.

I absolutely believe in nonviolence. Even in my mother's family there was alcoholism and violence. I didn't want any of that for my own child. That was a major turning point. There comes a time when you have to realize that the change of spirit can't be put off; you have to make a time for it to happen. For a long time I was very distrustful of men, and I don't want to be that way. I was turned off Wicca because of the men involved. I don't want to be the opposite of male-dominant (i.e., female-dominant); I think domination is wrong, period. I'm looking for a mentor, a Crone.

🐾 🐾 🐾

I was raised an Episcopalian but my parents wandered about through many churches. Unfortunately, they have now gone back to an extreme fundamentalist sect and this makes for an unhappy division between us. Now they think I'm involved with devils. They know I'm very committed to the Goddess movement but they don't understand it at all.

I was visiting them when they had a meeting of the elders of their church. All the elders were men, and they sat around decision making while the women served them food and drink. I wanted to ask why there were no female elders. Christianity omits women, officially; but the women are expected to give and give to the church. Even when women are ordained, they aren't listened to very much. Once a woman minister told me that, in her experience, congrega-

tions wanted to be prayed for by a man. Female rabbis may get along
better than ordained women in Christian churches, but they still
have to deal with the vicious Old Testament god.

🐜 🐜 🐜

I read of a woman who said she wanted to be a church acolyte
when she was a child, but the minister said to her, "Now you know
God only wants boys to light his candles." She carried that rejection
with her all her life. On the very next page it told of the higher
number of women than men who are diagnosed with depression,
and I saw a connection right there. If you're told from the time you
can talk that you're always inferior to a male, or you are a rib,
there's no way that you can come to your full potential. You are
always second fiddle.

They put me in an Episcopal school that was all women. That
wasn't as oppressive to me as the Catholic teachings, all the
garbage about having to be confirmed, all the rote learning about
the Trinity and such. We were always singing hymns like "Onward,
Christian Soldiers": always there was violence in the name of religion. It was outrageous. Religious men seem to think it's okay to
slaughter others who don't believe their way. My son went to Bible
school and came home very depressed, convinced that he was a
sinner. I managed to convince him that children are not sinners. I
hang on to the idea that life is a blessing.

We should remember that the Bible was written by men, who
eliminated all mention of God as a woman over the years. There was
God the Father, and Christ the Savior, and the mother wasn't much of
anywhere. None of us could strive for a virgin birth. Once a nun said
to me, "*She* will rise," predicting the return of a Mother image. That
made a great impression on me, especially coming from a nun.

It's interesting that it took me forty years to discover the Goddess cultures, even though I have been to Crete; I never heard anything about the ancient religion. It amazed me that I could travel
and learn and read all these books, and not even know about the
Goddess culture.

🐿 🐿 🐿

My mother was a good Catholic girl. I went and did all the Holy Communion and so on. I enjoyed the incense and the rituals. Then when I was about fourteen or fifteen I heard about reincarnation, and I said, this is the first religious thing that makes sense. I was sitting in church one day, listening to what the priest was saying, and I told myself, this is a bunch of bullshit. And I never went back. I'm glad my mother got some peace out of her religion, but it's not for me. I realized that there are other choices that make more sense. Who needs all that guilt and sin and damnation? Mary was always over there on the side, but she wasn't a real part of the church. As I learned more about the effect organized religion has had on society, the more it appalled me. I didn't see a lot of good coming out of it, and I decided that it was not something I wanted to participate in. The directions our religions have taken for the past several thousand years are so far away from what's really important: nurturing and caring and loving, being in sustaining relationships with nature and the earth and future generations. It's the mothers who care about the future of their children. The men are not mothers and they don't think from that perspective.

🐿 🐿 🐿

In the Catholic Church there was no one for me to identify with as a woman. There was no role model for me. Mary was there, but she was incidental to the religion. When my daughter was about five, I decided that I really didn't want her to be raised Catholic. I wrote a letter to the priest, stating that I was not Catholic any more. He called me up and asked, "Why are you doing this?" I told him that I was going to join the Unitarian Universalists, and he cried, "Oh, my God, they're not even Christian."

I started going to the Unitarian Universalist Church, where they don't have a minister but instead have different speakers who come each week. One speaker came to discuss feminist spirituality and I took profuse notes. This was everything I wanted to know!

❦   ❦   ❦

The three worst things about the patriarchal fundamentalist Baptist church I was raised with were: (1) It gave the supreme being the male gender, a heavenly father, and therefore I did not feel made in God's image. It also confused me on the roles of mother and father because I didn't spend a lot of time with my father, so his role in parenting didn't seem as present to me as my mother's role. (2) The Bible seemed to blame and put down women because women were inferior to men morally. This "inferiority" required punishment and restrictions because women were naturally incapable of the intelligence and righteousness of men. That's why men did all the important stuff in the Bible. These things were made obvious to me by sermons and the Bible verses that we were told were the word of God. (3) This lopsided viewpoint couldn't be questioned or debated; obvious contradictions couldn't be pointed out without incurring the wrath of God for blasphemy, heresy, or irreverence. Since I was practically marinated in this thought system from a very early age it took me a long time to break completely free.

My inclusion of the Goddess image was at first an attempt to achieve balance with the male creative energy, sort of a yin/yang completion of the creative cycle. But as time went along I found myself very drawn to the female element. I was, frankly, sick of the male jargon, imagery, and myths. The Goddess got bigger and bigger and the god got smaller and tinier until the Goddess was the Flower of All Creation and the god was a few grains of pollen keeping Her fertile.

First and foremost, this new spiritual viewpoint made me feel safe. I never felt safe in the hands of the male deity; he was too violent and punitive. The Goddess was compassionate instead of legalistic. Instead of a final judgment, She just used what was as the fertile soil for what will be. It all made sense and I relaxed for the first time in my entire life. She made everything okay. I wept with relief. It was like coming home to a loving mom. I didn't feel like a motherless child anymore.

At last I can grieve for the loss of the Goddess in my formative years and see the wrath and hatred by which She was almost erased. I feel this same wrath and hatred is what is now being directed against women around the world. Although the Goddess has survived, disguised and trivialized, I cannot feel whole as a woman until She is placed back on Her throne of stars. She must be raised up in our collective consciousness to give women their place as equals with men in most things, and divinely gifted to bear life. Womanhood must be revered.

If enough daughters can be raised, like mine was, to know almost nothing about patriarchal religion and a lot about Goddesshood, they will naturally feel good about themselves. As the population of women so raised grows, an organized religion will also grow to meet their need for a spiritual community. These women, unencumbered by the awful esteem-crushing viewpoint of a patriarchal mindset, will work their way into every facet of government, media, and culture, changing the polluted stream controlled by a powerful few into a mighty river of sweet, clean, healing water, where all might come and drink freely. Women will make this planet a garden again for their children and their children's children.

4

What's Wrong with Patriarchy?

*A*LMOST ALL THE WORLD WE live in today is intensely patriarchal. Some people need definitions before they can understand what this word means. Our daily lives give us just the fact of patriarchy, without pinpointing any of its characteristics. Like birds raised in cages, women raised in a patriarchal system usually come to think of it as a normal way for human beings to live. They don't know anything else because they have never learned to picture any alternatives.

A patriarchy is a society where the moral and ethical codes have been created by men, with women having little or no voice in the process. Men are the primary lawmakers and religious authorities. Men govern and define the theology. Men control most of the money and property, earn more than women, demand attention from women and children more often than they give it, develop rigid sexual attitudes, and regard many forms of intimidation as permissible. Often there is considerable bigotry and intolerance.

Paradoxically, in a patriarchy men also do most of the lawbreaking, especially crimes of violence, which in our country run more than 90 percent male. When women become violent, more than half the time it is in retaliation against men who have abused them. Our male-dominated culture has a horrifyingly high incidence of father-daughter incest, father-child abuse, wife-beating, and rape. The most recent figures state that in America a woman is raped every four minutes. Nothing in patriarchal religious or moral standards provides much more than lip service to combating such oppressions. Frequently the oppression itself is simply glossed over with a euphemism, as when wife-beating is officially described as "domestic disputes."

Patriarchies are also typically warlike. Their religions may euphemistically preach peace, but whenever there is a war to be fought their gods are right in there leading the charge on the battlefield. War is an inevitable extension of the generally patriarchal combination of aggression, intolerance, and violence. There is little recognition of the majority opinion of women, who give birth and understand the long years of care and nurturing that go into the formation of each human life. To be able to snuff out life, human or otherwise, with satisfying swiftness is to many men the ultimate power trip. It is a godlike power.

To understand how patriarchies have developed their basically antihuman attitudes, we must return to times and conditions where patriarchy was not.

The human species is about three million years old, a very recent life form on a planet where other forms first began to appear some two billion years ago. Even among humans, patriarchy is the most recent of social systems, having existed in anything like a currently recognizable form only for about five thousand years, perhaps the last six-hundredth of the time that humans have lived on earth. Patriarchy, its social system, and its exclusively male gods, are only the newest products of a mere tick in geologic time.

Like other mammals, early humans knew only one parent, the mother. Paleolithic groups were based on mother relationships; tribes were composed of female ancestresses, their children, and their siblings. This basic human system is still reflected even in the Bible, where the lists of "begats" include mostly female names that were ignorantly copied from older records. For all but the last six-hundredth of the time humans have been on earth, fatherhood was unknown. For each child, the primary adult male relative was the maternal uncle, because the vital blood bond was perceived as passing only through the mother's line. This clan system was still to be found in Britain when early Christian missionaries first arrived there. The missionaries' writings state that the British tribes recognized no relationship with a father.[1]

Since the beginning, however, every person was intimately aware of the origin of his or her own life from a mother, who was not only birth giver but also nurturer, teacher, food provider, healer, and personal connection with spiritual forces. Each mother created life, and was in turn created by a mother, who was in turn created by her mother, so the natural progression in human thinking went back to an original creator of all life as a Great Mother, the primary Goddess. Few societies of the Stone Age envisioned male gods. Their artifacts show us only Goddesses and animal spirits. Their custom, as preserved in myth and folklore, show that men perceived their own connections with the divine as possible only through sexual and filial relationships with women. One of the reasons later patriarchies developed ascetic avoidance of sexuality was that nearly all people once considered female sexuality a manifestation of the Goddess. In a fully realized patriarchy such as the European Middle Ages, everything even remotely connected with the Goddess was diabolized into an object of fear and loathing.

The change began to take place between six and ten thousand years ago, more slowly in some parts of the world than in others. Some societies, such as the Trobriand Islanders, remained unaware of fatherhood even into the twentieth century. Early civilizations had temple complexes administered by women as agents of the Mother Goddess, where records were kept, calendars were devised, and careful observations of the heavenly bodies were made. In the Middle East, ancient societies usually had a high priestess who embodied the Goddess herself, and with whom the acting king had to have a sexual connection. Probably the general idea of fatherhood was first discovered by women themselves, through their recordings of lunar and menstrual cycles, for most early peoples had no idea of the exact length of a pregnancy, nor did they associate it with any particular sexual act.

Early mythical theories about men's role in reproduction were mostly absurd and crudely magical, like the custom of couvade (a woman's husband imitating her childbed labors), or the belief that men could become fertile like women if they could give blood from their genitals, like women. Many cruel practices of subincision and circumcision arose from this belief, because the first perception of the vital blood-magical stuff was menstrual blood, which everyone thought was what created a baby when it was retained in the womb, and also what made old women the wise rulers of the tribe when they passed menopause and so kept that miraculous blood within their bodies permanently.[2]

Many centuries passed before men understood the real nature of paternity. During that time they invented a number of male gods who were supposed to have created either life on earth, or eternal life for humans, by giving their blood and dying in the process. They could never quite manage the female trick of bleeding without pain or death, but they tried. From such myths arose the ubiquitous dying-god figures such as Osiris, Attis, Dionysus, Adonis, Kingu, Tammuz, Orpheus, Jesus, and many others.

Some peoples who discovered paternity before the others began to show the kind of aggressiveness that peaceful, egalitarian matriarchies had usually discouraged. When women made the ethical codes, children were gently raised and men were not trained to fight. Therefore, when the first violent patriarchs, such as the Indo-European Aryans, came down from the north into India and from the east into Europe and the Mediterranean, the peaceful agrarian peoples frequently were wiped out.

For thousands of years, various manifestations of the Mother Goddess lived on and were assimilated into the pantheons of patriarchal gods. Our classical mythologies took form in this period. Gradually, however, the god became more and more "jealous," exclusive, and antifemale, until we find the evolution of something like the violent, warlike biblical Yahweh preaching complete destruction of all the pagan Mother-worshiping peoples, and the wrecking of their temples and altars. The same kind of conversion by warfare took place in Europe after the Roman Empire turned

Christian under Constantine and his successors. It took more than twelve hundred years, but eventually two-thirds of all the landed property in Europe was in the hands of the church, Christianity was declared the only permissible universal religion, and the last shreds of paganism were destroyed in a five-century bloodbath now known as the reign of the Inquisition.[3]

Most Christian historians have been extremely euphemistic about the Inquisition, deliberately falsifying many of the records or, in the case of the Catholic authorities, quietly destroying them. Yet a few scholars like Henry Charles Lea, who went to the original sources, ascertained that this Christian reign of terror managed to torture and burn at least nine million people, 80 percent of them women, until in some European villages only two or three women were left alive. It was the ultimate triumph of patriarchy and the ultimate expression of misogyny.[4] We are still living with its echoes today.

As long as modern society continues to give official recognition to an exclusively male deity, and its moral standards are set by men who pretend to have been instructed by that deity, it will continue to be a patriarchy. Only women who are enabled to sense a female divinity within their own spirit can bring about the profound changes that need to be made if humanity is to last much longer as one of earth's life forms. Male aggression in the wild is created by nature to sort out the stronger, healthier males, to improve the breed, since weaker males lose their rutting battles and so never mate. Male aggression in civilized society is a useless anomaly, serving only to harm and to destroy. The survival of any species depends on the nurturing behavior of its females, not the aggressive behavior of its males. And even animals know better than our patriarchal gods, for among animals the males do not usually attack females or their young.

Thus it seems clear that the best hope for humanity is to return to its prepatriarchal ethic of male submission to the Goddess spirit, not in the hierarchical sense that men understand as power-over, but in the egalitarian sense of the ancient mothers who loved and comforted both their male and female children. Male-oriented societies are notoriously harsh in their treatment of children. They try to instruct by instilling fear. Naturally, this gives rise to traumas and tensions that produce more fear, eventually creating a cruel religion and a culture of violence. The violence of our patriarchal culture has perpetrated more persecution, aggression, and abuse than any other, all beginning in the home. Christian clergymen exhorted men from the pulpit to beat their wives, and wives to kiss the rod that beat them.[5] Children were to be brutalized by their father, according to seventeenth-century Anglican bishop Thomas Barlow: "Surely a father, by the right of God and nature, has the legitimate power . . . to use flogging and lashes to bring his children to do their duty and to obey his just commands."[6] Of course, the determination of how just his commands were was left entirely to the discretion of the man himself; and he, almost invariably, had grown up being brutalized by his own father.

Such Oedipal aggression by older males against younger males was certainly sanctioned by the Christian god, who was not only credited with creating the world's most sadistic version of hell, but also demanded the torture-death of his allegedly beloved son. Previous to this event, he sent all human beings to his hell. After it, he sent only most of them. With dogmas like these, his church mythologized Oedipal rivalry with a vengeance.

Under the modern Western form of patriarchy, a boy need not be personally abused in order to grow up violent. By the time he is in his mid-teens, an American boy's television and movie viewing will have shown him "at least 200,000 acts of violence committed by men. His sisters may have seen all this violence as well, but because the violence is committed by men, the girls do not relate to it as something they would do. The movies are telling boys, 'This is the way men act.'"[7] Children can watch hideous tortures on film, though our society is horrified by the idea that they might watch tender, sensual sex acts of mutual pleasure-giving between people.

Of course, the violence of patriarchal society has a purpose: preparation and readiness for war. Christianity has fomented more wars than any other religion over the course of its history. "Instead of diminishing the number of wars, ecclesiastical influence has actually and very seriously increased it. We may look in vain for any period since Constantine in which the clergy, as a body, exerted themselves to repress the military spirit, or to prevent or abridge a particular war."[8]

Margaret Mead wrote: "In every known society, homicidal violence, whether spontaneous and outlawed or organized and sanctioned for military purposes, is committed overwhelmingly by men."[9] It seems that men are easily corrupted by violence if the culture allows it; but there are other kinds of cultures in which violence is not considered a norm, and men are not given to it. Neolithic societies that respected women and revered the Great Mother seem to have been better at getting along without attacking each other.

> It is clearly not human nature that causes people to hurt one another. People of gentler cultures share the same human nature as we of Western civilization; it is our beliefs that differ. Tolerant and more peaceful cultures have respected both masculine and feminine faces of God, both heavenly and earthly representations of divinity. It is the limited belief in a singular supremacy and only one face of God that has resulted in tyranny and brutality.[10]

Early Christianity spread itself throughout Europe by means of violence and warfare. Later Christianity spread itself throughout the world by the same means; fanatical missionaries usually followed Christian troops who managed to wipe out vast numbers of indigenous peoples for having the wrong religion. Pascal noted that "men never do evil so completely and cheerfully as when they do it from religious conviction."[11] And yet, if religious authorities had been capable of rational thought, they might have preached tolerance out of a realization that all religions are the same at bottom. "The naked savage," says Ingersoll, "worshiping a wooden god, is the religious equal of the robed pope kneeling before an image of the Virgin. The poor African who carries roots and bark to protect himself from evil spirits is on the same intellectual plane of one who sprinkles his body with 'holy water.'"[12] Christians have always been amply supplied with their idols, fetishes, magic charms, amulets, and all other supposedly primitive religious paraphernalia.

Perhaps the saddest thing about Christianity is that it began with at least some potential for feminine input and, after five or six centuries had passed, betrayed and abandoned its women altogether. In the fourth and fifth centuries some sects had women priestesses, but early synods began to condemn this practice. Pope Gelasius (d. 496) said the women serving at holy altars represented "a contempt for the divine truths." In the middle of the seventh century, the Synod of Nantes recorded complaints that the practice was still going on. In the eighth century, the statutes of St. Boniface forbade women to sing in church.[13] Nevertheless, the medieval church had numbers of female bishops, functioning priestesses, and powerful abbesses before it was completely patriarchized and sealed against women.[14]

In 1917 the book of canon law stated that no woman may approach a Christian altar, not even a nun serving her sisters at chapel mass; and it is a venial sin even for a woman to give responses at a distance from the altar, if a boy can be found to do it. Pope John Paul II, in his instruction curiously entitled "A Priceless Gift," said that women must not be allowed the functions of a mass server. The now-canonized Pope Pius X reaffirmed St. Boniface's ban on women's voices in church choirs in 1903, stating that only boys could serve as sopranos. "The history of Christianity is likewise a history of how women were silenced and deprived of their rights. And if this process no longer goes on in the Christian West, that is not thanks to, but in spite of, the Church, and it certainly has not stopped in the Church itself."[15]

Christian churches claim to be the foundation of the human family, which is not only misleading but egregiously untrue from a biological point of view. Like other large-brained mammals, such as whales, dolphins, elephants, and wolves, human beings seem to have been genetically programmed for positions in the matrilineal clan. "The maternal totemic clan was by far the most successful form that human association has assumed—it may indeed be said that it has been the only successful one. . . . Social humanity has never succeeded in adequately replacing the primitive bond to which it owes its existence."[16] The support group provided by an extended family, living in physical proximity, seems the best means of developing well-adjusted individuals and productive citizens. Patriarchy has tried many modifications and substitutes to claim male authority in the family, but all have shown significant flaws. The fact is that Christianity was hostile to the family from its very inception. Jesus said no man could be his disciple unless he would renounce and "hate" his own parents, wife, and children (Luke 14:26). The early church insisted on the virtues of celibacy and the sinfulness of sex, marriage, and childbearing. St. Jerome said the destruction of the institution of marriage was the first duty of a man of God; St. Ambrose maintained that marriage was a crime against God.[17] Concerning that period of Christian history, Bertrand Russell says:

> It is strange that the last men of intellectual eminence before the dark ages were concerned, not with saving civilization or expelling the barbarians or reforming the abuses of the administration, but with preaching the merit of virginity and the damnation of unbaptized infants. Seeing that these were the preoccupations that the Church handed on to the converted barbarians, it is no wonder that the succeeding age surpassed almost all other fully historical periods in cruelty and superstition.[18]

Eventually the church allowed priests to marry and have families, but in the eleventh century it became evident that family life diverted both their loyalties and their bequests of property from the church. Accordingly, a series of papal decretals commanded married clergymen to cast their wives out on the street, sell their children as slaves, and disinherit all family members in favor of the church.[19] Ever since, the church has profited from its appropriation of all the worldly goods of those who join its ranks, as well as those who were destroyed as heretics.

To patriarchal thinkers, wives and children are not so much interbonded individuals as living raw material for the political power base, to function as breeders, workers, or soldiers. Women in patriarchal marriages have been exhorted to produce many offspring, at any cost to their own health and comfort, even at the cost of neglecting those already born. Today's antiabortion stand of religious fundamentalists shows a similar preference for quantity over quality of life, fostering ever more births of unwanted, unloved children, most of whom are destined to become wards of a state that can't care for them properly—a state against which many of them will rebel in criminal ways when they become adults.

Modern corporations also contribute to the breakup of extended family structures by constantly moving nuclear families to new locations, far from friends and relatives, taking no notice of children who might suffer from losing their sense of community, wives who might feel lost and isolated without their support groups, or husbands who take advantage of the family's isolation to allow themselves to become abusive. In antiquity, as women supported the family, clan, and village, so also the extended family supported the women against male aggression. In the absence of social networks, women are always at risk from uncaring or hostile husbands.

Deep in their hearts, many women feel that there is something terribly wrong with our system. They yearn to be a tribe. They yearn to keep their children near them, to watch their children's children developing through their own generations as an ongoing community of life. Male psychologists label such maternal feelings overpossessive, but animal behavior suggests that they are more natural than the separations and isolations that cause so much of our cultural anxiety. Women know it's wrong to break up families. They know that people generally have deep needs for the stability to be found in related groups who have known each other from birth.

Women especially yearn not to see their sons go away to war, where they stand a fair chance of being maimed or killed. Yet some sexist thinkers have even had the temerity to blame the patriarchal phenomenon of war on women. The pejorative term "momism" was introduced by Philip Wylie in his book *Generation of Vipers*, which actually claimed that the root cause of World War II was the heartless greed of American "moms" who demanded that their sons fight and die to win a more luxurious lifestyle for Mother.

Of course, the truth is that throughout patriarchal history, older men have taken sons away from their mothers and sent them into battle for the greater glory of the Old Boys' Club. War erodes the power of women and is a phenomenon of strictly male-dominated societies, not of the female-dominated societies of old, which showed greater respect for the living. A humane civilization would give nationalism a lower priority and institute cultural taboos against war and killing as strong as our present taboos against cannibalizing the dead (except, of course, for Christianity's cannibalized god). It makes little sense to respect a dead body more than a live one. It makes even less sense to neglect or ignore that vital blood bond that mothers feel in their very cores, and that all mothers' sons and daughters should consciously appreciate. That is the basic family value that the West has lost indeed.

Ever since the father god's all-too-successful suppression of the Mother Goddess, *man's* vaunted progress has included ever more sophisticated methods of killing ever larger numbers of his fellow creatures, both human and nonhuman. War alone has killed at least a hundred million people since the turn of the twentieth century. Responsibility for this slaughter rests on men, not women. No right-to-life scruples seem to deter men from exterminating full-grown human beings, often on a very large scale. And the men who do this continue to worship the god who allegedly condones and supports their efforts, even when both sides of the conflict have the same god. Thus the heavenly father looks rather like one of the more bloodthirsty Roman emperors, sitting back to watch his gladiators butcher one another.

Meanwhile, most women on both sides of men's crazy conflicts have felt within themselves an almost unbearable repugnance, a voice crying out against this so-called male morality of destruction—a Goddess spirit saying it is wrong and evil. If human beings could see themselves as children of one Great Mother, as they once did, perhaps members of the human family could become more like siblings together. Something like this should happen soon, before patriarchy brings about the destruction of our entire species and our planet as well.

"When I speak of God," said Ingersoll, "I mean that god who prevented man from putting forth his hand and taking also the fruit of the tree of life that he might live forever; of that god who multiplied the agonies of women, increased the weary toil of men, and in his anger drowned a world—of that god whose altars reeked with human blood, who butchered babes, violated maidens, enslaved men and filled the earth with cruelty and crime; of that god who made heaven for the few, hell for the many, and who will gloat forever and ever upon the writhings of the lost and damned."[20] Seeing the image of this biblical God in themselves has allowed men to believe for two thousand years that they are divinely empowered to act as the judges of women. Now, women are beginning to judge the society created by men, and to seek their own empowerment.

Aristophanes's *Lysistrata*, written in the fifth century B.C.E, was intended as a humorous farce describing how the women of Athens refused to have sex with men who took part in warfare, with the result that the war was soon stopped. The notion might prove to be something more than a comedy if women could get it across to men that they truly hate male indulgence in violent behavior of any kind. It might provide a step in the direction of a genuinely civilized world.

Mothers have the power to take dangerous toys away from little boys before they hurt themselves. The same power must be translated into adult terms. There is no power on earth so fit to call male establishments to account for their crimes against posterity as the bearers and nurturers of that posterity. That is, the feminine spirit is needed to embrace the humanness of all people. Left to their own discretion, few women would slaughter other women's children for the sake of an ideology—still less for economic profit, which is the real basis of any war.

Women are becoming less prone to feeling intimidated by the men's god into silence, obedience, and false guilt. They are beginning to speak out, disobey, defy, declare themselves spiritually and morally competent to judge the god who claimed to have given Adam the right to "have dominion over" and "subdue" all the natural world (Gen. 1:28). Women now know that men should not have that right.

Neither should men have the right to assault women or children in the ways that Western patriarchy has condoned or encouraged through its abusive antifemale theology. Though churches omit the fact from their histories, Christianity has a record of practicing and recommending wife-beating and other forms of physical abuse by men. Fifteenth-century ecclesiastical "Rules of Marriage" said that a man may beat his wife with a stick "out of charity and concern for her soul," so the beating would count as a meritorious act. In 1977, Ellen Kirby of the Board of Global Ministries of the United Methodist Church said: "The institutional church either through its blatant sexist theology, which has blessed the subordination of women, or through its silence, blindness, or lack of courage, has allowed itself to be one of the leading actors in the continuing tragedy of abuse."[21]

In nineteenth-century America, women were "treated like Negro slaves, inside and outside the home. Both were expected to behave with deference and obedience towards owner or husband; both did not exist officially under the law; both had few rights and little education; both found it difficult to run away; both had to breed on command, and to nurse the results." Karl Marx pointed out that in Western civilization generally, "Woman's true qualities are warped to her disadvantage, and all the moral and delicate elements in her nature become the means for enslaving her and making her suffer."[22] Contemporary theologian Mary Daly says, "The entire conceptual systems of theology and ethics, developed under the conditions of patriarchy, have been the products of males and tend to serve the interests of sexist society."[23]

What's wrong with the patriarchal mindset? Nelle Morton puts it another way: "In patriarchy someone has to get 'power-over' by putting others down; or have another globe to compare with our globe. See how we race to the moon and Mars before we can attend to world hunger, world poverty, world war, racism, sexism, classism, ageism, and colonialism at home.

"The result of patriarchal mindset for us educationally is parochial mentalities that consider others as strangers or enemy; territory-bound mentalities that cannot perceive the earth as the common home for us all."[24]

What's wrong with patriarchy? To Ann Oakley, it insists on, but often poisons, the marriage relationship. "Promising sublime intimacy, unequalled passion, amazing security and grace, men nevertheless exploit and injure in a myriad subtle ways. Without men the world would be a better place: softer, kinder, more loving; calmer, quieter, more humane. . . . Marriage for women is almost always a mistake. Married women without paid work are the unhappiest people in the world. But the mental health of men is improved by marriage. Why is this? It's easy to see why. If you're a woman, marriage promises everything and guarantees nothing."[25]

Some scholars claim that patriarchy began with the need for primitive men to "protect" the mothers and children of the tribe. But the laws, myths, customs, and histories of patriarchal cultures show quite the opposite effect. Patriarchal men don't protect women; they protect their own property (including women) from other men. In patriarchal terms, any woman not owned by a man is fair game. "The absence of respect for women's lives is written into the heart of male theological doctrine, into the structure of the patriarchal family, and into the very language of patriarchal ethics. This is the underlying deceitfulness and hypocrisy of the Catholic or 'Right-to-Life' argument against abortion . . . where 'humanity' and 'humanistic values,' are concerned, women are not really part of the population." Adrienne Rich points out that "it is not from God the Father that we derive the idea of paternal authority; it is out of the struggle for paternal control of the family that God the Father is created."[26]

Once he is created, what real human purposes (other than enrichment of the churches) are served by God the Father? His minions have provided the world with a well-nigh incomprehensible set of contradictory myths and irrationalities; a system of "salvation" that explains neither what the saving consists of, nor what one is to be saved from; a deity professing to be loving and merciful, while demanding atrocious cruelties to be inflicted by some of his "children" upon others of them; a set of scriptures so confused that, if they were indeed messages from him, it would seem that he either deliberately obfuscates or is incapable of expressing himself clearly; and a history of error and falseness quite out of place in an age when at least some people have finally acquired a better grasp of nature's truths.

Percy Bysshe Shelley tellingly summed up a number of the major problems with the patriarchal god: "If he knows all, why warn him of our needs and fatigue him with our prayers? If he is everywhere, why erect temples to him? If he is just, why fear that he will punish the creatures that he has filled with weakness? . . . If he is all-powerful, how offend him, how resist him? If he is reasonable, how can he be angry at the blind, to whom he has given the liberty of being unreasonable? If he is immovable, by what right do we pretend to make him change his decrees? If he is inconceivable, why occupy ourselves with him?

"It is no less inconsistent with justice and subversive of morality that millions should be responsible for a crime which they had no share in committing, than that, if they had really committed it, the crucifixion of an innocent being could absolve them from moral turpitude. Certainly this is a mode of legislation peculiar to a state of savageness and anarchy: this is the irrefragable logic of tyranny and imposture.

"It is sufficiently evident that an omniscient being never conceived the design of reforming the world by Christianity. Omniscience would surely have foreseen the inefficacy of that system, which experience demonstrates not only to have been utterly impotent in restraining, but to have been most active in exhaling the malevolent propensities of men."[27]

It may well be that what's wrong with patriarchy is its religious justification for sexism and many other social injustices:

Patriarchal societies are founded upon a crime. This crime is not the murder of the father, as Freud would have us believe. It is the rape and scorn of the mother. This is the unconscious horror that each girl-child inherits and, unlike male 'castration anxiety,' rape anxiety is all too often reinforced by the daily reality of the act and threat of rape. (Men's so-called 'fear of castration' is simply a fear of losing command over women in patriarchal society, which equates domination of women with 'manhood.' If Western males have any legitimate fear of castration, it derives from the act of circumcision, which is a terrible thing to inflict on a male infant; but this custom comes from the Father God of the Bible, it doesn't come from women or any Great Mother religion.) . . .

Until yesterday, women were policed by the professionals, also—gynecologists and psychiatrists who acted as cultural reinforcers of the rules of 'femininity'—who blamed our ills, like menstrual depression and pain, on our 'failure to be feminine.' How many men have grown rich, being in the business of telling women what we are supposed to be! Obviously, patriarchy wants us to be something that is not natural for us. . . . Until yesterday, 'once-a-month witches' were given drugs and electroshock treatment by the modern inquisition. [28]

One of the ways in which patriarchy puts down women most frequently is found in the choice of adjectives used to describe men and women. Lists of these adjectives can be compiled by anyone, and can go on almost indefinitely. The following is a sample comparative list; once any woman gets the idea, she can invent her own.

HOW MEN ARE DESCRIBED	HOW WOMEN ARE DESCRIBED
Intelligent	Smartass
Assertive	Aggressive
Ambitious	Pushy
Indifferent	Heartless
Tactful	Mealy-mouthed
Handsome	Decorative
Sensitive	Vulnerable, weak
Responsible	Controlling
Discriminating	Fussy
Indignant	Bitchy
Articulate	Mouthy
Well-dressed	Clothes horse
Learned	Pedantic, schoolmarmish

Dignified	Uppity
Shrewd	Scheming
Knowledgeable	Know-it-all
Unusual	Weird
Forceful	Castrating
Don Juan, stud	Whore, slut
Competent	Adequate
Absent-minded	Flaky
Quiet	Mousy
Hot-tempered	Shrewish
Bold	Shameless
Experienced	Over the hill
Orderly	Compulsive
Well-read	Bookish
Ascetic	Frigid
Commanding	Demanding
Emphatic	Strident
Lusty	Loose
Creative	Overimaginative

And so on.

Words become patriarchal weapons against women most particularly in the context of religion. Matilda Joslyn Gage noted nearly a century ago that "men have not yet learned to regard woman as a being of equal creation with themselves; do not yet believe that she stands on a par with them in natural rights even to the air she breathes. In order to secure victory for woman we must unfetter the minds of men from religious bondage." Anne Royall suggested that "all men wish others to think as they do on all subjects, but more particularly on religion; this is natural, and such is the nature of man, that he devises means to compel others to think as he does."[29] Genevieve Vaughan perceives a "legacy of masculation" in Western civilization generally, where "themes of male violence and domination pervade our imagination on television, in films, and in reality. Crimes of rape, battery and murder continue to be perpetrated against women and children. . . . Wars continue to be fought, devastating human lives throughout the globe. The environment is degraded daily by the long-term pollution created by business and war. Whatever the less masculated exceptions at the individual level, the great social mechanism of patriarchy is hurting everyone and must be radically changed."[30]

More and more frequently in recent years, radical change is being advocated not only by feminist scholars, philosophers, and historians, but also by average women in other walks of life. As the misdeeds of patriarchy become more widely known, women perceive the possibilities for revision of the social system that oppresses them and threatens the world of their children. While not yet formed into coherent doctrines, women's resentments of patriarchal injustice find ever-increasing expression. Revisions of attitude have already taken place here and there, but much remains to be done. When Freud asked, "What do women want?" he never dreamed that women could become so articulate about their needs as women are today . . . and tomorrow.

Modern Women Talk About What's Wrong with Patriarchy

Women's ideas about what's wrong with patriarchy are highly varied, but there is a recurrent theme running through all of them, a sense of enormous resentment at what the patriarchal value structures have done to both the natural and the human worlds. War, violence, exploitation, pollution, crime, and other evils are blamed on the generally patriarchal notion that men must dominate at all costs. Goddess-oriented women tend to reveal a surprising degree of cynicism about the hypocrisy of governments, corporations, male-dominated professions, and churches. The message that men should, perhaps, take from these revelations is that their supposedly hidden motives have never been quite so well concealed as they thought.

Because our culture has been patriarchal, it is easy—and maybe even correct—to say that everything wrong with society is wrong because of patriarchy. My guess is that that is simplistic, and probably not a complete explanation, but there do seem to be patterns associated with patriarchy—primarily the economic and political disenfranchisement of women, their resulting relative powerlessness, and the violence against women—which are apparently woven into its very fabric. I associate violence in general with patriarchy, and an impulse toward destruction: War seems to me to be the ultimate expression of patriarchy.

A second (but not secondary) objection to patriarchy is my objection to the hierarchical way patriarchies organize everything, an organizational scheme which has permitted the same rich mean old men to keep virtually all power in their own hands, and then hand it on to other rich mean old men. Periodically these same rich mean old men offer their own sons to the Moloch of their ambitions. We call that war. The rest we call society. Both seem to me to be the consequence of the terrible one-sidedness of patriarchy. Ultimately, it's that one-sidedness to which I object: It's not just that women are excluded, or even that women are devalued and—in the worst case—abused. It's that the values of caring, kindness, nurturance, creativity, sharing, healing, and respect for the natural world, for the earth and its fragile bounty, have been assigned to the women's sphere by patriarchs, and then denigrated and ignored along with the women. This is the great illness of patriarchy, that it is blind to the worth of the very things on which all life is, in fact, radically dependent.

I look at the human species and I wonder, are we fated forever to have strong men, who don't know how to listen to women, come and wipe out balanced societies where everyone knows how to give way at times? Fiction and history, as well as a lot of what goes on in industry, seem to state that. The corporate raider will win, not the balanced group. It's a pessimistic view, or maybe realistic. In that I see the end of our species. We will self-destruct. What I find objectionable is the lack of female representation in any influential way. A Goddess religion should teach respect for every individual.

贛 贛 贛

I work with men who are not always sophisticated or genteel in their manners. It puts me under emotional stress, trying to get along in this man's world. I do a good job, but I don't want to play put-one-over games. My new boss makes nasty remarks, like, "We never should have given them the vote." Then he says to me, "Come on now, lighten up."

I'm bubbling over with aggravation about job issues. I feel that I can't trust the men, or let them have the benefit of my expertise, which is what they hired me for. I want to work and have it be a clean experience. My integrity demands this. As I see it, we're here for mutual respect and a common goal. But the male agenda is different.

I feel really troubled about the attitude of manufacturers who think it doesn't matter what they advertise, and about the violence on TV. Somebody with a vested interest will say anything he needs to say, just to keep furthering that vested interest. They're not thinking of the whole or of the future. The world needs more respect and honoring.

When I became a mother, I was so focused on my son that I imagined the whole world focused on him. Then I woke up and realized that it wasn't so. Life goes on, but there is plotted harm in the world. We have to roll up our sleeves and get to work on it, which is a real challenge. We have a power source. Motherhood is a real good power source. Let's use it.

I want to live responsibly, pay my bills, *and* feel authentic about the creation of my life.

Goddess thealogy is win-win. More shared experience, respect, harmony, carrying the torch forward. Traditional theology is dominance over someone. Generally, women are more sensitive to others. We have that gift of sight. Men may have it, but they haven't tuned it up.

🐜 🐜 🐜

There are two basic modes of interaction. There's hierarchical, which is male, and there's teamwork and encouragement, which is female. What I find objectionable in corporations is that there's no room for the team and the female. There's lip service, but no true understanding of what a team is. I can approve of trying to strengthen everyone's weak areas so they become less unbalanced, but pounding on their weak areas so they lose self-confidence is not useful.

I've always thought that common courtesy is a most effective religious act. I've seen people be discourteous in totally needless ways. When I was in medical school I saw a surgical team treating a drug-addicted prostitute, being very condescending and mean and punitive to her. She didn't deserve that. She didn't need that. It was sad. Just a little bit of courtesy would have made a huge difference in her experience of medical care. I have lots of other examples, but that one seems pertinent because it shows the punitiveness of patriarchy. I don't think we're really motivated by punishment, but many men think we are.

🐜 🐜 🐜

Things I object to in patriarchal society: murder, rape, incest, child abuse, child molestation, eating disorders, pollution, deforestation, industrial stinks, car exhaust, barroom brawls, TV, news headlines, hostility, brutality, jealousy, and the pronoun usage in our culture. I object to the fact that older men own the magazines, the TV shows, the cosmetic companies, the fashion industry. Older men up at the top of the industries care nothing about individual people.

Also, the way men have to deal with their own manhood in patriarchal society is very unsatisfying. They have to play the game of not caring about women. Very often, when I'm talking to a man, he's looking at me and seems to be listening, but I know he's just waiting for me to shut up so he can make his point.

It's threatening to men when I don't play the flirtation game with them. The flirtation game is just ugly. After I've made eye contact and looked at him as if I'm his equal, if a man is cool with me then, there might be a chance for a friendship. But I've had to come to terms with the fact that some men will always find that straight look threatening.

🐾 🐾 🐾

Patriarchal religious expression excludes woman. As the church became more Greek-influenced and took on the values of the society around it, it excluded women more and more. In the Gospels, the actions of Jesus are welcoming to women. But that was forgotten.

I think secular patriarchal society is still using women to the nth degree: using women under the guise of liberating them. There are all those women who are working in the corporations eight or ten hours a day, having to manage a house, having children who are in substandard day care, all under the guise of being liberated and finding themselves! It's losing themselves, and for whose benefit? Certainly women don't benefit as a group. Individual women don't benefit. Children don't benefit. Who is benefiting? Corporate patriarchal society.

🐾 🐾 🐾

More women need to take a stand about their children and television. The single act of removing a television set from the house can mean everything to a child's social conditioning. When I think of the violence being portrayed in children's television cartoons as funny, I'm glad I don't have any such sense of humor.

🐾 🐾 🐾

Men and woman are socialized in such different ways. Young people have different kinds of masks that they use in order to belong. Masks for boys prevent them from sharing feelings. Girls' masks are different. I think girls are more honest because they learn to get in touch with their feelings. But boys often relish an opportunity to verbalize their feelings because so often they're not permitted to do it. It's not acceptable in many male groups.

When I was in Costa Rica I was advised never to ask a man for directions, because if he doesn't know them, he'll give wrong directions just to save face. He must never let on that there's something he doesn't know.

We have to deal with that kind of macho foolishness as well as teaching women to appreciate themselves as women. Maybe pendulums have to swing to the other side before they can rest in the middle. At some point the Goddess movement will have to address the problem of men.

ə ə ə

In business, if a woman changes jobs frequently she is seen as undependable and flighty, while if a man does it he is seen as getting on with his career. If a woman has pictures of her family on her desk, she's seen as unbusinesslike; but a man is seen as a strong family man, stable, dependable. It's hard to grow out of the ubiquitous stereotyping in the business world.

Control, power, dominance are the words for patriarchy. I've never been physically abused by a man, but mentally, yes. Dealing with men at work, I've had many different kinds of putdowns. Jokes, "Just kidding around." If they don't mean it, why do they say it? Or they'll say: "It's not a joke against women; it's just about my wife." There's that element of ownership. My wife, my son, my daughter, my car, my house. The family members don't seem to have names; they're property. When you work with someone for a while, you can remember that his wife's name is Sally, or Rhoda, and that he has three kids and what their names are; but still he doesn't use the names. He'll say "my house, my yard," instead of "our house, our yard." He doesn't even share with his spouse. It comes across as ownership, very impersonal.

I had a conversation with a male friend a while ago, and he said, "Well, I'll put you in your place." I said, "Where is my place? I'll put myself in my own place, and you'll have nothing to do with it." He said, "You'll have to accept me, I'm joking, you have to accept that I'll say things like that." I said, "No, I don't have to accept things like that. And if we're going to be friends, you'll have to accept the fact that I'll tell you so." Women have to tell them that their "joking" isn't funny or acceptable. Just not listening to them doesn't work.

Some people pretend that nothing ever happened during the witch-burning craze. They think the worst thing that ever happened in European history was the Holocaust. Somebody in public office made a comment that offended the Jews because he belittled the Holocaust; but you never hear of a comment that offended women because it belittled or failed to mention the Burning Times.

Men often fail to perceive victims as real people. It's like that in war. They don't think about killing someone's son or brother or mother. It's like Hitler saying "We are people, they are subhuman."

                            🐌 🐌 🐌

I wonder if Hephaestus, the power of making, the fire, the forge, isn't male, as if the power of male material creation has always been inimical to female creation. Tolkien had a thumb on the real pulse of human spirit in telling of the Ents and the Entwives, though I wouldn't necessarily make that a gender split. I think there are Entwife-people who put down roots, and stay, and generate life. And there are Ents who are journeyers, imaginative explorers. As a metaphor for how males and females differ, this seems to me more productive than, say, imagining a train on a track as male, and a woman in a garden as female. Rootedness can be true for both.

In the public domain, no female nurturing is allowed to participate. This is a great sickness, in America in particular. I don't want to think we're a terminally ill society, but symptomatically we seem to be that. We don't seem to find any place for male and female to coexist. Politically, it's winner take all, and the winner is usually male. We joke on the road about all those drivers that gun their cars and zoom past and cut you off. We say they're driving a dick shift. And they're allowed to do that in America.

American women seem visibly more successful in entering the male arena, but actually they've been less successful than in any European culture. Somehow, America seems set up to be confrontational. I don't know that we can ever get over that. It's very sad.

In America it is suggested that by buying, you are providing— that the purchase is as fulfilling as if you had made the object, or created it, or grown it yourself. The lie is in that suggestion that it will fulfill you.

Now we have shorthand, so that you can use a computer and access information, and doing it faster is equated with doing it better. I find that scary and really dangerously stupid. Doing things faster is not better, and not more thoughtful. In the old days, when you went to a library, you could thumb through a card catalog with each card hand-written or hand-typed. The card catalog had a life that was human. Thumbing through, you'd have serendipitous moments all the time, finding cards next to each other through accidents of alphabetizing. Now, when you go to the library, there is this much faster system on a computer, which saves you foot motion, but costs you all the serendipitous juxtapositions that were there before. You actually have to know what you want before you go to the library.

As libraries get bigger and have more and more closed stacks, you won't be able to browse, and you won't be able to make any more of the serendipitous connections that are actually the soul of scholarship. It will get thinner and thinner.

We're elevating technical competence to the place of wisdom because we're subtracting time. What has made a difference in my life is time, and I think it's a grave error to think that things will be better when they take less time. Culturally, women have been the keepers of time and the keepers of matter. Even though we might set up a political system that can put women in places occupied by men, the problem is that the matter and the time that women keep are not becoming integrated. Women can play the games politically and economically but they're still excluded. Essentially, they have to be like the men who are playing those games. "Affirmative action" has simply been to allow us to be pretend men, without shifting this terrible imbalance that I feel can destroy the world.

I see in my students that not having someone at home as a constant guide has made them stupid. It has never given them a model for the ways to organize time. It doesn't show them what they must do to be an integral part of a family. I've always been a very vocal, active feminist, and I think women should have the right to choose their lives, to choose to do things other than child-raising; but it hasn't worked out the way it should have worked out. There's something wrong with a world where women choosing to raise children are not valued, or celebrated, or economically supported.

Politicians throw God in every once in a while, to scare people. I saw a rally for Nixon, and everybody in the front row held signs saying, "God loves Nixon." How could they know?

Everything about patriarchal society is objectionable. I often get angry about it. What angers me most is that they're 45 percent correct, and 55 percent wrong. There's always an element of truth, but they look at it sideways. Men's need for wielding power-over, and their denial, brings the anger and misunderstanding.

When I was in school, there were two kids from the Indian reservation in the class. You couldn't talk to them, they were so angry. They had been so mistreated. Even their parents were mistreating them. The kids would get government checks for going to school, but the checks would go home for the father to drink. The only way they could get out of the trap was to learn the white-people's culture and play that game. They lost all their rights as Native Americans both in the government structure and on the reservation.

It's said that it takes a whole community to raise a child. But we don't have that kind of community any more. Kids in inner cities don't know what it's like to run free. How can they, when they're always fearing a stray bullet? That's so sad.

   🐾 🐾 🐾

One of the hardest things for me about this patriarchal society is that I feel that I was not educated up to my capacity. I remember wanting to take physics in high school and being told that girls couldn't take it. We were allowed to take chemistry, because you needed that if you were going into nursing. Some girls in a class ahead of mine insisted on taking higher math, but it was remarked about. Only the very smartest girls got to do that.

Later, when I was teaching, it was at the beginning of the second wave of the women's movement. There was a lot of discussion between the principal and the teachers, who were women. We would go to him and point out that in textbooks, even the spelling book, boys were doing all the active things and girls were being passive. He said it had no meaning, we were just looking for problems. He would listen, then tell us we were crazy. But it was important. What goes into children's heads is what becomes internalized. So when I was dictating spelling sentences, I simply changed the sexes around.

My strongest objection to patriarchal society is the war mentality: raising young boys to fight in armies. It doesn't help to have women integrated into the armies, too. I think it's disgusting that our representatives in government are so overwhelmingly male. I was outraged when Anita Hill was defamed by all those senators who didn't really know what she was talking about. It was a travesty of justice.

   🐾 🐾 🐾

Men: They're all Hitlers, even though they knock Hitler. They insist on being right even where no one knows what's right or wrong.

Their notion of superiority is ridiculous because in my estimation the people who follow the patriarchal religions are the most mediocre souls on this planet. They're little minds all tunneled into themselves. That's a bad generalization, but in many ways the Christian religion teaches people to tunnel into themselves and their god, yet it doesn't teach them how to live.

It's the basic philosophy of Christianity that bothers me the most: A father loves his son so much that he's willing to let him die! That's our Christian example of love. I find that very difficult to understand. A good father should teach his son how to live kindly and givingly, how to live with others and with all living things—not make him die to prove how much he loved him. That's one thing I have against the Christian religion. Another is that it has enslaved half the world, the half that holds up the sky, as the Chinese say.

There are many people who pretend to be Christians but aren't, because it's not personal with them. It's a dictated philosophy and theology that has not kept up with modern times. It doesn't provide anything real for its believers. Some people think that what they do for their church is going to get them somewhere, but most, deep down in their hearts, are only hoping. Their minds can't comprehend what the church claims to be truth.

When I grew up, mothers were in the home. I'm not saying that's where mothers have to stay, if they're inclined to be scientists or some other kind of workers. But it would be nice if mothers could stay home and their position would be valued by society, as it should be, and paid for by society. Then maybe the moral tone of society would change. We need to prioritize the most important thing for a woman to do, raising her family. If that isn't honored, we're not going to change anything in the culture as we know it.

🐝 🐝 🐝

I feel left out because I spent years living in a rural community where things were very old-fashioned. All the guys wore flannel shirts and drank a lot, and had abusive relationships with their wives and girlfriends. I was stuck in that rut.

☙ ☙ ☙

Sports are wonderful. They helped discipline and enrich Greek and Roman civilization. But competition today has nothing to do with the real soul of sport competition. It has everything to do with commercialism and it's a lot of bullshit.

Football is like the whole concept of taking somebody's land and knocking their skulls in. O. J. Simpson is a prime example of the gladiator gone wrong, the male principle run amok. Even tennis, not the most macho of sports, has assumed horrifying importance in our society.

Through science and technology, we have ravaged nature. What kind of a society can exist by "conquering" nature, having its technology based on an image of rape? We need Goddess worship to stimulate the reserves of mercy and compassion in people.

☙ ☙ ☙

I spent many years being controlled by a man. It had to stop, or I would have gone to a mental institution. My husband beat the children for no reason except that he was unhappy about something. I started to ask the questions. Where is the money going? Where have you been? It wasn't adding up. I went for help to a man in the church, and the man in the church abused me. I wasn't getting anywhere.

Finally I got some help for myself and my children through Al-Anon. I went back to school, and picked up an R.N. and another degree. I started to work toward separating from my husband, so I would be able to support myself. I had to get him out and keep him out, which was harder. He'd go, but he'd always come back, more and more aggressive. I had to get restraining orders. I learned to get support from the group, the kind of support that I couldn't get from my family. My relatives were raised to make men think everything has to be their idea.

The judge said clearly in court to my husband, "Both of these children have been abused by you." We won the case, and I think this was some kind of expression of Goddess worship. I couldn't have done it without some kind of a belief that something was going to help me. It's hard to find other women who are supportive. They don't want to lose their own security.

I'm not out to save the world. I know what I can and can't do. I've worked with kids most of my life, so I worked on a children's crisis unit. Sometimes I get a chance to teach the kids. There was a little girl who had been burned by her father. The mother couldn't do anything about it. They're Muslims, and the mother wouldn't dare say anything against the father.

I try to teach children to take care of themselves. It was important to me not to sacrifice my children. I tried in the beginning to have their father come to the house and watch them on Saturdays while I worked, but he wouldn't show up. He didn't care about them.

The men in my mother's family were very nice, gentle men. But my father's family called them a bunch of sissies. They took care of the women almost as if they were pets. In my father's family, the women worked. My paternal grandmother worked all the time, sewing all the time for the garment industry. I remember her sewing in the evenings, making frogs for jackets. She supported the family, because my grandfather wouldn't work.

I don't think women tend to divide work into "my work, your work." They just see that there's work to do. In systems that are all male-run, the men can say, "I don't do that. That's women's work." Men's egos demand that they have someone below them. I find that objectionable, and women shouldn't tolerate it. The essence of patriarchy is absolute, downright lies to control people.

So much troubles me about patriarchal society, especially the fact that women are subjugated and made less of, in politics, in the business world, in their own homes. There are even women who are against women, because of their patriarchal training.

I dislike the dictates, the rules and regulations, the things you have to do and the things you're not allowed to do, all impractical, unnecessary rules. I'm thinking of the fundamentalist religions; I grew up in one. I found it tremendously obnoxious. I couldn't imagine a fundamentalist Goddess. I don't think she'd approve of the rules and regulations.

🐞 🐞 🐞

There was a time, during the '60s and '70s, when mothers were portrayed as villains, the ones who destroyed families and drove children to ruin. They were caricatured and trivialized, and even made grotesque. That's one of the things that happen in patriarchal society. Women—and what women do, and who they are—have been trivialized. So much of what their voices could say has been silenced.

The worst thing is that they take our young sons and send them to war, and they make our daughters feel bad about their bodies. You try to support your daughter's feelings about herself, but patriarchal society tells her that her body is never going to be this or that. I don't know one woman who really feels good about her body.

Perhaps even worse is the fact that everything that happens on this planet comes out of a sense of competition for resources, money, power. They ask, "Do you think it would be any better with women in power?" The answer is no, not if women have to play in that ballpark. There will be women who will learn to play by those rules. This is not going to change until the spiritual aspect of our lives changes.

At the heart of patriarchy is the desire to keep life linear, like a series of victories; the desire to see life dualistically, to pit the body against the soul or spirit. It's transcendental, in the sense of having to get away from the body and from nature. Traditional theology is hierarchical, not egalitarian. That's a very big difference. These are issues that mean something to me, that I can become impassioned about. I feel them creating unhappiness in my body.

& & &

According to the Sufis, the relationship with a lover is the same type of relationship you have with God. There was Christ-and-his-church, bridegroom-and-bride. On your wedding night Jesus gets his rocks off by raping you. The ideas of royalty and kings are degradations of the ideas of clan mothers, grandmothers, great-aunts and such, who used to administer community properties. A lot of our problems started when people stopped seeing the wealth as belonging to the clan, and began letting individuals have it exclusively. Most of patriarchy's problems are rooted in greed, the desire to have everything at the expense of others, even at the expense of our own families. Patriarchy takes over when men want to make sure they're not giving their money away to people who are not under their control.

I felt quite left out of all the images when I was sitting there in Christian churches. I put a female image on things because I'm a woman. My parents and early teachers thought I was rather bright, so I was able to get a few more opportunities than if I'd been just a run-of-the-mill kid. I was supposed to make something of myself. My parents encouraged me to do things, to study hard, to have a career, perhaps become a doctor. Still, my family chores were always cleaning and doing the dishes and helping with the cooking, and my brother got to do all the fun chores like working in the yard, mowing the lawn. My mother wouldn't let me do any of that. She was afraid I would wreck my hands. She was shocked when I got a car and I really loved tinkering with it, changing the oil myself and such. Even though I was supposed to have a career, to do something important, my "proper role" was being a home-maker, which was not considered important. I never wanted to be a boy, but I always felt that boys had it better.

& & &

The nastiest things about patriarchal society are power-over, competition, greed as the highest value, and the accumulation of wealth. This is such a consumer society! Look at fashion, for instance. How many clothes do you really need? People don't even use their clothes until they're worn out. If they're out of style the next year, they have to go out and buy more clothes. Everyone is encouraged to spend money, so that somebody else can make money, so that somebody else can be financially higher than others. It's a me-first mentality. There's a vicious circle where you accumulate all these things, then you have to work harder to support what you've already accumulated. The person who has the most money when he dies wins.

Work, per se, is not one of our highest values. People work because they have to, to pay for everything. People get caught in the cycle before they realize it. How do you get out of the cycle? Work itself is good. To work at something you love and enjoy is good. But I don't think people get to do that. People are exploited by those who hire them. All the employers care about is getting as much work as possible out of the employees.

I took two days off and stayed home from work, and watched daytime television. Truly, it is a pollution of the mind. It's absolute garbage. Watching that kind of stuff on television all the time would be like going out and eating whatever you find in a garbage can. It's unbelievable to me that people do that every day. We should be a lot more selective, because you are anything you take in, as in the computer programming term, "Garbage In, Garbage Out."

It's difficult to challenge patriarchal values because they're so firmly entrenched. Consumerism is out of control. We don't take care of people, or of the world around us. Many people feel that they're not acceptable for reasons of looks, age, weight, race, all kinds of things like that. Some of the more liberal ideas are in line with the Goddess movement, though liberalism is somewhat out of vogue these days.

We're at a point now where self-empowerment is a biggie. That's a drawing into yourself, self-nurturing. Once you're empowered, then it's time to go out and work on changing some things. You have to have your consciousness raised. You have to realize that you've been oppressed by this society. If you have not had your consciousness raised, the women's spirituality movement is not going to appeal to you.

♣ ♣ ♣

Because I'm over sixty, what I find most objectionable about patriarchal society right now is ageism. That's my ox getting gored. My only defense against it is simply to be as outrageous as I can. Any time I can get men to look me in the eye, I do. But why should we have to be shocking? In a way, it's marginalizing yourself. You have to be careful how you do that. If you go too far, or do the wrong thing, you're discounted. They say, "That's a crazy lady, don't pay any attention to her." I think we have to tread a fine line.

♣ ♣ ♣

In Japan, linguistic differences between the sexes can be seen even in young children. A boy will look outside on a sunny day and remark, "It's a beautiful day, I say." A girl will say, "It's a beautiful day, don't you think?" When I find myself doing this kind of thing, I really try to correct it. If I say to my husband, "Don't you think we ought to do so-and-so?" it's really rhetorical, because I'm going to do it anyway. I catch myself, and think I should be more definitive. Sometimes I feel like an adolescent who's just learning who she is.

Women are conditioned by our society to be patient in enduring lack of power, lack of autonomy. Most women in a condition of helplessness, as in a hospital, would accept it. They can even enjoy staying in bed all day and being waited on. Men tend to chafe more, because they hate not being in control.

♣ ♣ ♣

It's been a struggle for me, wanting to believe that humankind is a positive force, but having to look at the incidence of war and so much destruction. It forces us to look at the world as a dichotomy, with positive and negative poles. I don't necessarily like that dual-istic view. It's hard to accept the inhumanity of man; why should we have to?

When I talk to people with a patriarchal point of view about matriarchy, they seem to feel that matriarchy would be simply a reversal of patriarchy, with the men as second-class citizens. They can't perceive it as a way in which all life is nourished. Women can understand it because they treat their sons and daughters together as loved children. In the patriarchy it's all power-over and issues of control. The power that I feel, particularly in my moon times, is power to support. It has nothing to do with gaining control. That's a hard concept to get across. We need to open ourselves up to trusting one another.

My experience with women bosses in the corporate world is that they have bought the patriarchal line, from the suits and close-cropped hair to the power ties and wielding power-over. That was one reason why I had to get out. I couldn't bear to turn into that, or live under fluorescent lights in buildings with windows that don't open.

I hope to get some of the maintenance people that I know to stop poisoning the environment with the chemicals they use to keep the lawns on industrial campuses. Some days when I was going to work, I would become totally choked up because of the pesticides and herbicides they used. I'd like to see them create gardens around corporate buildings, so people would have an opportunity to get back to the earth. They should have the opportunity to work the soil. Many of these buildings have been built in the middle of some of the most fertile ground.

Insults have been given to our planet by the agribusiness. It's really scary to hear of the things they're planning to do. Those of us who have opportunities to make money shouldn't run from it, as long as we're not hurting anyone else; but we must be responsible. We should be like the Seneca, and always consider the seventh generation from our own, not do things just for short-term gain.

Our system allows some men to think they're here to legislate or decide what's best for the rest of us, without even knowing who we are. A large flaw in the patriarchy developed in the Middle Ages, when doctors were thought responsible for health problems, priests for spiritual problems. A mechanistic view of the world set in, men thinking they were here to rule over nature instead of working with nature. We still think a magic bullet or a pill will make everything better, instead of asking, "What is going on in my life?"

There are seeds of hope in the Goddess movement, even though people seem to fear what we're doing. It's up to each individual woman to show care and trust for other women, and show the men in their lives what the possibilities can be. I think the biggest issue we need to work on is overcoming fear.

🐜 🐜 🐜

The Goddess movement has completely changed my viewpoint on women and myself from filtering everything through a screen of male opinion, male approval, and appeasing powerful males, to thinking of women as complete, powerful, beautiful, and magical. I also see the victimization of women, their impoverishment and lack of good choices as the direct result of a patriarchal culture based on a patriarchal religion. Once I became aware of the treatment of women in patriarchal societies, I was horrified to see the amount of violence and abuse women were subjected to with little or inadequate protection. Through reading books . . . I became aware of thousands of years of feminine history and female spirituality that had been omitted or obliterated by patriarchal religion.

I was astonished to see that the original face of the Divine was female. Through a process that I call Goddesscide, the Great Mother was systematically wiped out and replaced by God the Father. The natural order of things, in which the woman gives birth to the man, was turned upside down and backwards, and the man gives birth to the woman. I felt robbed of something vitally important.

5

PHYSICALITY

*T*HE SEXISM THAT DISFIGURES OUR society today had its roots in early Christian horror of sexuality in general and of female sexuality in particular. According to St. Jerome, everything bearing a seed of sensual pleasure should be regarded as "poison." Augustine and others said that even within marriage, sex is sinful and obscene. St. John Chrysostom declared that a Christian man "cannot endure" looking at a woman. Tertullian insisted that death first came into the world when Eve taught Adam about sex, and all women are to blame for this forever. St. Odo of Cluny said a woman is nothing but a sack of dung. St. Thomas Aquinas wrote that every woman is birth-defective, born female only because her father was sick, weak, or in a state of sin at the time of her conception. However, true freaks were born as a result of their mother's "heated and obstinate imagination." According to the Gospel of Thomas, St. Peter said women are not worthy of life, and Clement of Alexandria added that "Every woman should be filled with shame at the thought that she is a woman." These teachings and thousands more like them have had their impact.[1]

Naturally, along with determined diabolization of formerly sacred sexual customs went even more intense diabolization of the formerly sacred harlot and her pleasure-giving social role. Prostitution continued to flourish, because men continued to want it and reward it financially, but an enormous campaign of hypocritical denunciation blamed the women instead of their customers for this "sinful" practice. Men abused the same women from whom they received pleasure as a means of assuaging their own religion-engendered guilt feelings about their own sexual enjoyment. Often, prostitutes were (and still are) beaten, mutilated, or otherwise mistreated by male customers unable to sort out their confused notions of pleasure and punishment. The sadistic mistreatment of wives or girlfriends has similar foundations even today.

In seventeenth-century England it was a Shrove Tuesday custom for gangs of men to break into whorehouses and beat the inmates or hamstring them by cutting the tendons behind their knees.[2] A victim of this jolly sport would never walk again, but would have to crawl around on all fours for the rest of her life. Of course she could lie in bed well enough, her only real purpose as far as men were concerned.

Customs involving physical mutilation or handicapping of women seem characteristic of patriarchal societies, as we know from studying such matters as infibulation, Chinese foot binding, medieval corseting and chastity belting, and even our modern modifications like hobble skirts and spike heels. Some seem to expect that women must endure pain in order to be sexually attractive—as in the case of unnecessary cosmetic surgery—while men can get along with whatever nature gives them and are not expected to modify themselves to any great extent.

Extreme sexual repression in a society often breaks forth with extreme sadism directed against women, as our history tells us happened in church-dominated, guilt-ridden Europe during the centuries of witch-hunting. Some nine million died the most painful possible death, after days, weeks, months, even years of the most fiendish tortures, primarily because they were women. The Inquisition's official handbook, the *Malleus Maleficarum*, declared all women more guilty than men of the sin of carnal lust, which makes them all witches, and "all wickedness is but little to the wickedness of a woman," because of her "many carnal abominations."[3]

The bitterness of sexually repressed men against the other sex was literally boundless, even though the repression came from their own kind, not from women. Men didn't seem to have enough insight to figure this out, nor did they have enough moral courage to challenge their God's purported rules. In its ascetic derogation of sexuality, Christian Europe transformed the original aims of patriarchy—control of motherhood and eradication of the Goddess—into a whole civilization of perversion that frustrated men as well as women. In this respect, patriarchy failed to achieve what men really wanted. It resulted in a civilization so full of violence and pain that it may be stretching a point to call it civilized at all.

In its early centuries, Christianity reacted against sensual pagan practices by turning to a rigid asceticism, in which the body was despised as an imperfect, unholy, earthbound vessel, generated through sin and full of obscene urges. Sexuality, to St. Augustine, meant only "diabolical excitement of the genitals."[4] To St. Thomas Aquinas, it was filthiness, staining, disgustingness, shamefulness, disgrace, degeneration, sickness, corruption of integrity, and a reason for "aversion" and "loathing." To churchmen generally, "no sexual lapse could ever be trivial." For a man, the light touch of a woman's hand could be a mortal sin, "if it occurs with impure intent," and kisses on the arm are "regularly mortal sins."[5] To Calvin, human beings are "nothing but mud and filth both inside and outside," and to the Calvinist New England theologian Jonathan Edwards, a human is "a little, wretched, despicable creature; a worm, a mere nothing, and less than nothing; a vile insect." A Catholic sermon written in about 1700 says that one should "treat one's body as a sworn enemy, and subdue it through work, fasts, hairshirts, and other mortifications." Indeed, mortification of the flesh was almost always perceived as particularly pleasing to the Christian god. Antoine Godeau preached that "suffering is the badge of a true Christian."[6]

Pleasure, on the other hand, was regarded as spiritual poison, wholly in the realm of the devil, from Christianity's earliest years.

"If any man love the world, the love of the Father is not in him. For all that is in the world, the lust of the flesh, and the lust of the eyes, and the pride of life, is not of the Father" (1 John 2:15, 16). St. John Chrysostom actually believed that the real sin of Adam and Eve was sex. Because they had "forfeited the heavenly jewel" of their virginity, all humanity was subject to "the destruction of death, the curse, the pains, and a laborious life," along with "that mortal and slavish garment," marriage. St. Bonaventure (d. 1274) stated that original sin rendered the sexual act corrupt and "stinking," and that the devil had power and authority over human beings because they are "too lustful."[7]

The Council of Trent ruled in 1564 that anyone claiming that virginity or celibacy are not more blessed than marriage was to be anathematized by the church.[8]

Peter Damian called women "Satan's bait, poison for men's souls, the delight of greasy pigs, inns where unclean souls turn in."[9] According to St. Magnenn of Kilmainham, no priest should ever have anything to do with a woman: "To be familiar with her and to know her is a thrusting of the head into mire; and a renunciation of baptism, of faith, of piety; a pact with Lucifer, with Satan and with Abiron; with Pluto and with Beelzebub; with the swart sow, and with the chief captains of Hell's host." A tenth-century German church council decreed that priests' wives and mistresses should have their heads shaved and be lashed. Pope Leo IX ordered that such women be arrested and given as slaves to the nobles. Many of them committed suicide.[10]

The Gregorian Reform movement of the eleventh century forced clergymen to cast off their wives and children, on pain of fines, public ridicule, prison, loss of salaries and benefices, and physical harassment. The children were declared illegitimate, disinherited, and sent away to live homeless in exile; many were murdered. Those men who refused to abandon their families were disgraced along with them, and "confronted the horrors of starvation, prostitution, servitude, murder, and suicide." The ex-wives were reduced to slavery by Pope Urban.[11]

So much for family values.

The imposition of clerical celibacy harked back to the asceticism of the primitive church, which taught that complete renunciation of sexuality would be essential for admission into heaven. To this end, Christian men had themselves castrated in such numbers that the emperor Domitian finally forbade the practice, which was one reason why Domitian was vilified through the centuries as a persecutor of Christians.[12] The women couldn't be readily castrated, but absolute, immovable virginity was urged on them until many learned to despise their own bodies. St. Jerome recommended that a grown woman should not take baths, that she should "blush and feel overcome" at the sight of her own nakedness, and that she should ruin her good looks by "a deliberate squalor," so as not to distract men from their pursuit of saintly purity.[13] Female "anchorites" were praised for living day and night loaded with heavy chains, "for the sake of penance," meaning that they were supposed to repent being women and sexual creatures.[14]

The later church blamed women, not men, for the very existence of human carnality, which was viewed as the major impediment to spirituality. John Scotus Erigena insisted that the end of the world would eliminate dual sexuality because the female sex, "that imperfection, that stain on the purity of creation, would be no more." Walter Charleton, founder of the British Royal Society, addressed all women as "clogs to virtue, and goads that drive us all to Vice, Impiety, and Ruin. You are the Fools' Paradise, the Wiseman's Plague, and the grand Error of Nature."[15] Of course it was Mother Nature, not God, who was responsible for the error.

A twelfth-century jurist wrote, "The image of God is in man . . . woman is not made in God's image."[16] This was generally believed; and yet, despite all their woman-hatred, monks and priests were always eager to appropriate the imagery of motherhood. Bernard of Clairvaux wrote to a departed brother, "You were torn from my breast, cut from my womb." Bishop Anselm of Canterbury talked about Jesus "giving birth" and "nurturing sons. . . . Christ is the mother who dies in giving birth to the soul."[17]

From the thirteenth century onward, "women were confronted with the closed ranks of a masculine society, governed by a thoroughly masculine theology and by a morality made by men for men."[18] Phyllis Chesler describes a patriarchal civilization as, essentially, "a male homosexual civilization. Women are valued only for their reproductive capacities. In all other areas, men prefer to remain separate from women, and in close contact with other men. A culture that covets such separatist all-male control of religious, military, economic, and political institutions is, psychologically speaking, a homosexual culture."[19]

The male dread of femaleness, notable in patriarchal systems, dates back a very long way, to the time when all life-magic was supposed to inhere only in women, specifically in women's wise blood. Female menstrual cycles, thought to have been established by the Moon Goddess, displayed that essence of life each month, but kept it hidden when it was occupied with creating a baby, or with providing an elder woman with her mysterious, wisdom. There is no stronger taboo in human history than the taboo that forbade men to touch or even look at this awesome blood. In fact, the very word *taboo* originally applied to menstrual blood and meant magical, sacred, wonderful.[20] In their efforts to imitate feminine life-giving, men of early civilizations tried very hard to approximate its magic in their own ways.

The name of Adam, "man made of bloody clay," harks back to the life-magic of the Mesopotamian Great Goddess who formed the first humans out of clay and brought them to life by anointing them with Her own moon-blood. This was actually practiced by primitive women in many parts of the world as a conception charm. The Babylonian god Bel pretended to bring forth living beings by copying the Goddess's clay sculptures and anointing them with blood from his "head" (penis).[21] The biblical God also copied such clay magic, but changed the feminine blood essence into one more readily available to males; air, or breath (Gen. 2:7).

Later patriarchs intensified the fearful *taboo* on women's blood, which the Bible calls the "flower" of the womb (precursor of the "fruit"). Any man who touched a menstruating woman, or who even sat where she had been sitting, became ritually unclean (Lev. 15:11–24). And yet the custom of circumcision and other kinds of male ceremonial bloodletting—including sacrificial killing—began as men's attempts to usurp that same female magic. The Jewish custom of circumcision originated in Egypt, where it was performed on pubescent boys at the same age as girls' time of menarche; and each boy was dressed as a girl for the occasion.[22]

Anthropologists have found similar customs all over the world. In the South Pacific, a boy newly circumcised was described by the same word that applied to a girl at her first menstruation. In Australia it was believed that menstrual blood, though normally feared by men, was a powerful life-giving charm that could cure diseases.[23] One Australian man confessed that the men's coming-of-age blood rites were stolen from the women. "It all belongs to the women . . . the baby, the blood, the yelling, the dancing, all that concerns the women; but every time we have to trick them. " The women, however, were not tricked. When they initiated their daughters, they told them what the men were doing and laughed at them in secret .[24]

Many Middle Eastern myths indicate that the original object of "holy dread" was menstrual blood, especially that attributed to the Goddess, the earliest symbol of life-giving and redemptive power.[25] Blood was the essential soul stuff, even according to the Bible (Lev. 17:14). Priestesses of the Goddess at Eleusis mixed their own menstrual blood with the seed corn, believing that there could be no better fertilizer. "Since the men had no magic blood of this kind, they could not grow corn as well as the women could, any more than they could grow babies."[26]

With the rise of linear masculine mythologies, and the corresponding decline of cyclic feminine ones, the power of menstrual blood was diabolized into an object of intense fear, a petrifying Medusa, a deadly witch-charm. The Zoroastrian Zend-Avesta taught that food within three steps of a menstruating woman is poisoned, and that she can "smite" the sun, animals, plants, and men just by looking at them; even hands ceremonially cleaned by holy water become unclean by her merest glance.[27] The taboos became even more stringent as time went on. The Bible reinforces an extensive set of taboos against male contact with menstrual blood, and Pliny wrote that any man who lay with a menstruous woman during an eclipse would die of a deadly disease. St. Jerome wrote: "Nothing is so unclean as a woman in her periods; what she touches she causes to become unclean." St. Augustine said any child conceived during a menstrual period would be defective. Isidore of Seville repeated Pliny's claims that a menstruating woman could damage fruit trees by her glance, and that dogs who licked menstrual blood would become rabid. Beginning in at least the eighth century, Christian churches forbade menstruating women to set foot on their premises. As late as 1684 it was still commanded that such women stay outside the church door.[28]

Throughout the Middle Ages, in most areas of Europe it was strenuously forbidden for menstruous women to take communion, though Canon Matthias of Janow wrote in the fourteenth century that priests should never ask women in the confessional whether they brought their menstruous selves anywhere near the church, because such a question was itself indecent. Thirteenth-century theologians such as Albert the Great, Thomas Aquinas, and Duns Scotus made sexual intercourse with a menstruous woman a mortal sin. This was still the church's position in the seventeenth century, though in the nineteenth and early twentieth centuries it came to be regarded as a venial sin.[29]

The blood of childbirth shared similar taboos in Christian culture, which is why canon law forbade women to receive communion until forty days after childbirth, lest some vaginal blood might still flow.[30] "In the Bible we can see the original Orwellian Newspeak occurring, in which false male imitations of menstruation and childbirth (the circumcised foreskin, the wounds of Christ) are made sacred and holy, while the real thing done by women is made filthy, sinful, and bestial. . . . The very religions that have turned human sexuality into pathology and nightmare should not be allowed to determine how public school children learn about sex! Most of our American misogyny, especially ideas about menstrual 'uncleanness,' comes from the Bible; for this reason alone the Bible should be kept from public schools, as a major source of the cultural defamation of women."[31]

Churches' rules forbidding a woman to touch or even approach the altar are based on the ancient menstrual taboo: a curious confession that even the power of God can't overcome the power of woman's physicality. Of course it's all superstition and nonsense, but it has had dreadful impact on the psyches of both women and men.

> Warlike, aggressive male societies are in rivalry with women over which sex sheds the most sacred blood. War is men's response to women's ability to give birth and menstruate; all three are blood-shedding rituals. Women's blood rites give life, however, while men's bloody rituals give only death. To compensate for this, such authoritarian societies culturally repress and degrade women's blood functions, while elevating murderous war to a holy act. . . .
>
> At her first menstruation the young "modern" girl is abandoned by her culture. She is made to feel that her body and its rhythms are a biological impediment to "freedom" and "fun." The subliminal message she receives from her culture is that a properly functioning body is male and noncyclic. . . . If she wants to be "equal" at work she must function like a male, i.e, noncyclically. (All legal and cultural disputes about women being pregnant or nursing at work, or nursing in public, derive from the fact that all workspace, all public space, in the West is defined in terms of the noncyclic male body. Women cannot "enter the workforce," or "enter public life," unless they agree to act as though their bodies were functionally male also.) To act as though one could function like a male is to suppress the fact that one is actually female.[32]

At the physical core of patriarchal attitudes is the implicit assumption that women should function according to men's sexual specifications, rather than to their own. Chesler says, "About 'sex' men do not easily think beyond their own bodies . . . men do, in a defensive and unconscious way, often project their own sexual feelings onto women and then judge women harshly. Despite professedly great interest in 'sex,' men traditionally have acquired very little genuine sexual knowledge—certainly no knowledge about what pleases other, female human beings."[33] Victorian doctors regarded female sexual feelings as pathological, likely to interfere with the all-important reproductive function, and even "unwomanly," their favorite phrase for anything about women that they didn't like. Doctors were especially alarmed by female masturbation, which was viewed as a disease. The recommended treatment was clitoridectomy, on the ground that "the clitoris serves no purpose for procreation but only rewards lust."[34]

Naturally, men were not punished for masturbation by having their penises cut off, even though comparable operations were performed on women many times throughout the nineteenth century in England, France, and other European countries, as well as in America. Male doctors imposed on women the punishment that they perhaps wished to absolve their own secret guilt.[35] "A childhood of sexual frustration has been transformed into an erotic style that remains explosively and uncomprehendingly selfish, guilty, and defensive. Few men seem to have recovered from male childhood's enforced sexual distance from forbidden others and from the shame and habit of secret, fantasy-driven masturbation."[36]

In 1882 a doctor wrote in a French journal: "It is reasonable to concede that cauterization with a white-hot iron gets rid of the sensitiveness of the clitoris, indeed that with repeated cauterization one is able to remove it completely . . . it can be readily seen that children, after they have lost feeling through cauterization, are less liable to sexual excitement and less inclined to touch themselves."[37] Repeated torture with a white-hot iron? You can just bet they were less inclined to touch themselves—and less inclined to get anywhere near a doctor, too. One can readily picture their desperate panic.

It is curious that only in recent decades has the clitoris been recognized as the primary female sex organ. Patriarchal society has always endeavored to ignore it, even to keep men ignorant of the fact that it exists.[38] "The propaganda for femininity (femininity being the apparent acceptance of sex on male terms with good will and demonstrable good faith, in the form of ritualized obsequiousness) is produced according to the felt need of men to have intercourse. . . . The propaganda for femininity teaches women over and over, endlessly, that they must like intercourse; and the lesson must be taught over and over, endlessly, because intercourse does not express their own sexuality in general and the male use of women rarely has anything to do with the woman as an individual."[39]

In patriarchal society, men constantly focus attention—either negative or positive attention—on the physicality of women, but so objectify it that they usually fail to understand even a little of how women feel about their own bodies. The female body is every man's first home, to which he yearns to return in some sense, but under patriarchy he is taught to despise what he desires, and to despise himself for desiring it. The strain of asceticism that runs through Christian history from its beginning has probably done more emotional and physical harm to both sexes in Western civilization than anyone has ever fully assessed.

Here and there, one can find a few indications that certain Christian authorities have become aware of the problem, and of the responsibility of Christian tradition in creating the problem. This happens most often when churches notice that the former faithful find their teachings distasteful enough to cause widespread desertions, especially desertions by women who are the most reliable pillars of the church. In 1991 the Presbyterian General Assembly issued a report on "Presbyterians and Human Sexuality," which represented some attempt to modernize the theology and, without frankly admitting guilt, to claim "leadership" in following a grassroots movement that they used to condemn. Former errors have been glossed over and a new attitude is supported by new biblical exegeses, since the Bible can be used to support any point of view whatever, ranging from charity and love all the way to war, racism, child abuse, witch-hunting, and sexism. Notorious biblical self-contradictions are now described as "richness and diversity within Scripture." After having declared the opposite for hundreds of years, the church now declares that sexism is not divinely ordained, and that Bible-based subordination of women was "misuse" and "distortion" of biblical texts. (Actually, the biblical wording was quite unequivocal.) Curiously, the report contends that "the ability of any community to guard against narrow, overly biased readings depends . . . on how diverse and egalitarian that community is able to be." In other words, the moral code is determined by the community, not by the Bible.

This seems a radical viewpoint, but it pales beside some of the report's other inadvertent admissions. The following are some sample remarks:

- "Sexuality is foundational to Christian spirituality." Since when?
- "The good news is that God has created us as sexual persons." This may be good, but it's hardly news; and the majority of Christian authorities over the centuries have considered it very bad news indeed.
- "Christianity has been misinterpreted into a system of Western male dominance." Well, not exactly *mis*interpreted, since Christianity was the basis of Western male dominance.
- "Men need Christian education to deepen respect for others and especially for women." In view of the fact that Christianity was the major influence in destroying cultural respect for women, this remark seems quite incomprehensible.
- "A reformation of sexual ethics is called for precisely because social conditions have changed." In other words, the church doesn't lead; it follows.
- "A patriarchal sex ethic argues that good sex (and proper social roles), require men to stay on top and in control of their women, and for women passively to accept such arrangements as inevitable. This ethic of control is wrong, dehumanizing, and unchristian." Wrong and dehumanizing, yes; unchristian, no.
- "One message the church must communicate is that a Christian sexual ethic cannot be patriarchal and remain authentically Christian." If this message is successfully communicated, it can only mean that there has never been any such thing as authentic Christianity, since Christian sexual ethics have never been anything but patriarchal.
- "Christians have internalized powerful verbal and visual images that women are not fully human and not fully cre-

ated in the image of God." True. And why not, since this is precisely what their Bible teaches?

- "God's call to gays and lesbians is to live responsibly in sexual, as well as nonsexual, relationships." This remark is amazing. After centuries of the most profound hostility toward homosexuals, God is now "calling" to them?
- "It seems particularly hard for male clergy to realize that women (clergy or laity) may find their off-color jokes and innuendoes unwelcome." Are clergymen in the habit of making crude sexist jokes?
- "Charges of sexual harassment and abuse are surfacing throughout the church at every level. . . . It is time for the whole church to reconsider its incarnational theology." This tacitly admits a connection between theology and sexual harassment.
- "The failure of the Presbyterian church to name the issue, to define clergy sexual misconduct, and to provide clear structure and procedures for seeking justice for victims is related to the extent to which the theology of the church is influenced by the social conventions of a patriarchal culture." The lie here is inherent in the little words "is" and "by." It should read: "the theology of the church *influenced* the social conventions of a patriarchal culture."

The material quoted above indicates that at least some Christian authorities are beginning to realize that a problem exists, in regard to their received views on women and sexuality; but they don't really understand what to do about it. The Presbyterians certainly are not the only ones with the problem; they just serve as an example of the kind of evasive, self-protective language that churches use to gloss over their culpability. But many women are already too enlightened about their own history ("herstory") to be fooled by such trivial playing with words.

Male eschatology is built on negation of the mother. Rejection of sexuality and procreation is not merely a function of prudery. Or, rather, antisexual asceticism is itself based on the

fantasy that, by escaping the female realm of sexuality and procreation, one can also free oneself from finitude and mortality.
The escape from sex and birth is ultimately an attempt to
escape from death for which women as Eve and mother are
made responsible. Male eschatology combines male womb
envy with womb negation.[40]

Why else, indeed, would men turn against the very thing they
most enjoy and crave, namely a warm, loving sexual relationship,
and load it with guilt, terrors, fears, threats of hell, ridicule, shame,
imputations of dirtiness, and even a complete obliteration of its
pleasures in God's heaven? "The only thing that makes life
endurable in this world is human love, and yet, according to Christianity, that is the very thing that we are not to have in the other
world."[41] The so-called god of love has never been anything like the
very physical Goddess of love, in Her Aphroditean aspect, all sensuality and sweetness. Even when it comes to visions of an afterlife, it has been reported that "males are concerned about their
own immortality, while women think little about it, except in the
context of relationship—they would like to be reunited with loved
ones. Males want their own self-perpetuation."[42]

Patriarchal religion might be summed up, then, as the ultimate
expression of selfishness: the glorified male ego rejecting relationship in order to concentrate on itself. But, as Ingersoll said, if there
were a God who could make people happy in another world, "it
will be more than he has accomplished in this." Paradoxically,
man's divine image of his own ego has only betrayed the foolishness of his pretensions; for "Think of the egotism of a man who
believes that an infinite being wants his praise!"[43] Surely, the central concept of any religion ought to be bigger than that.

MODERN WOMEN TALK ABOUT PHYSICALITY

*One of the things many women resent most about patriarchy is its tra-
ditional denigration of the body. Sexuality, the comforts of the flesh,*

*and normal physical processes have been greatly deplored, even diab-
olized, in Judeo-Christian culture. Indeed, during the "Age of Faith"
everything that was of the flesh was supposed to be simultaneously of
the devil, and pious folk were expected to despise and abuse their
bodies for the greater glory of their souls. In the official view, female
bodies were particularly obnoxious and shameful. Part of this attitude
undoubtedly stemmed from older pagan views of the female body as a
life-giving essence of divinity and a prime symbol of love and nurture.
Women rediscovering the Goddess are also rediscovering those ancient
principles of respect for their female selves and turning away from the
traditional patriarchal separation of body and spirit.*

🐾 🐾 🐾

It's important to honor women's bodies, including the right of
women to satisfy themselves with masturbation if they want. In a
man, that's not even questioned, so in that sense men are more in
touch with their sexuality. Birth control, family planning, and all
such information is important for women.

Although I believe in the image of the Goddess taking many
forms, I grew up in a society that says if you don't look like Barbie,
you're not okay. I bought the whole idea. I had a mother who struggled with her weight, and thought she was appealing to my father
only when she was thin. She would gain and lose, gain and lose,
over and over. And she's still doing it even though my father's dead.

On an intellectual level I understand the body-image issue, but
it still comes up on an emotional level. I think the women who are
growing up with Goddess worship can be free of that. My biggest
hope for Goddess worship is that we can change the way adult
women feel about themselves, starting in childhood with their
daughters. Even liberated feminist women who are in their power
in all other ways have trouble with the body image. I can see that,
even though I grew up with that set of beliefs and have changed my
beliefs as an adult. It's still with me. The only way for women to be
really free is to start with each brand-new little soul who can be
told not to belittle her body: "That's just what *they* say. It's not true."

❧   ❧   ❧

When I first started learning about the Goddess in the "Cakes for the Queen of Heaven" course, the image that really grabbed me was the Willendorf Venus. They were talking about body image. Being a large woman, I was delighted to encounter that celebration of a large woman's body. It took my breath away to think, "You mean, I can like my body?" It was a revelation. That's how I started coming to the Goddess.

One thing I learned through Goddess-oriented women is that sex gets better with age. Society tries to make us think we're in the prime of female life when we're twenty-one, and it's all downhill after that. But I spent time sitting with women who couldn't decide whether sex was better in their forties or their fifties. Even a few voted for the sixties. My jaw fell to the floor. I said, "You're kidding! No one ever told me that before." It's a secret that patriarchy wants to keep from us. Woman-loving men don't want to keep it a secret, but patriarchy does.

So part of my understanding of the Goddess is that getting older means getting better. Many of my friends are older women. When they get around menopause, it seems they're going to Alaska's north coast, or they're heading out west to study the Anasazi. When I took a vacation, all I wanted to do was go to a resort and lie on the beach. I felt guilty about that, when my friends are off hiking the Brooks Range or something. What patriarchy really wants us to miss is the realization that getting older is a good thing.

❧   ❧   ❧

I "see" the Goddess in the moon—and in the way my body's tides ebb and flow with the moon's cycles. Night skies are songs of our bodies. I think that is why we have always told stories about the stars.

❧   ❧   ❧

Probably, Goddess myths were developed originally to explain what happens in nature. Women are particularly attuned to what happens in nature because so much of what happens in our own bodies corresponds to what happens in nature. The rhythms of the female body correspond to the rhythms of nature. In looking at images of the Goddess, we look at what happens with us. It's not all sweetness and light, either. There's a wide variety of emotion. Anger and rage are incorporated into Goddess images as well as love and nurturing. It's a hand-in-hand relationship. There's Kali, the destructive force, as there is in nature. The Goddess image is in tune with nature rather than trying to have power over nature.

"Goddess image" implies pictures of women. My favorite kind of Goddess image is a photograph of a real person. Idealized women don't do anything for me. Ordinary women have personality, life, their own wishes, their own ways of doing things. Sometimes, in public places, I get fascinated by faces. I like seeing the divine aspect in real life. I appreciate the beauty in what I look at, and the spiritual has a strong tie to beauty. But idealized images don't strike me as being spiritually moving. In every woman there is something inexpressible. That, I think, is the spiritual.

Prior to my enlightenment, my moon time was my enemy. I always had horrible cramps, and would throw up, and was debilitated for a couple of days at a time. I never had the benefit of women around me, telling me what a sacred event it was. It was always a struggle, until I read books about its powerfulness, very positive interpretations of menstruation. Now I have been involved in creating rituals, and some women I know have been open to the idea of celebrations for their daughters' menarche.

I give my blood to the earth. We had a wisteria bush that hadn't flowered in fourteen years, and after a year of giving it my blood, it flowered. House plants, outside plants, vegetables—they all seem to thrive on it. And the blood is there, every month, to nurture them. I don't consider it a waste product, but rather a nutrient-rich source of natural fertilizer.

The most powerful thing has been finally having some connection in my life for the idea of a Crone. Society doesn't support that. Patriarchy has always said that when a woman is past childbearing age, she's disposable. But now I have these wonderful older women as models, that give me something to look forward to. That's exciting. I'm looking forward to becoming one who holds her wise blood inside.

🐌 🐌 🐌

I wanted to honor my daughter in the circle when she got her first period. We need to acknowledge these milestones in our lives. About a year earlier her friend had gotten her period and we did a circle for her. We all brought her gifts. I made her a talking-stick. One part of the ritual was that everybody told her menstrual story.

My story was that I had never been told about it, so it came as a big surprise to me. I had a stomachache. I stayed home from church. My mother came home from church and I showed her my underwear. I didn't know what the hell it was.

Now that I think of it, that was really mean, not to tell me what was going to happen to me. So my daughter has known about it since she was six or seven. For her tenth birthday, I bought her a facts-of-life book, which she took out into the neighborhood. The girls giggled over it, and all that. But I thought it was very important for her to know what was coming. I'm very proud of the way she's been handling herself ever since she got her period. I bought her a little red purse from Tibet, and told her I would save it for her, for when she got her period. When it happened, she said, "All right, Mom, give me that purse."

The Goddess movement has really helped a lot in how I raised my daughter.

🐌 🐌 🐌

Somehow we have cooperated in forging ourselves a new set of chains.

In the dentist's office I was thumbing through *Glamour* magazine. I thought, thank Goddess I am not between twenty-five and thirty-five any more. I couldn't possibly live the life that this magazine is promoting. The amount of energy that you are supposed to expend, keeping yourself fit, finding the right clothes, paying attention to your sexual life, finding the right condom, making sure your man is sensitive and caring and that you invest your emotional time well—it's all very well but this is totally exhausting. I don't think we're helping young women by selling them into the same bondage. I don't know how you get out from under this obsessiveness about appearances, but maybe Goddess is an influence that can say, "Stop, slow down, make more considered choices, don't buy into everything that's being tossed at you."

🐝 🐝 🐝

The worst thing Christianity did to our civilization was to criminalize sexuality—to make everybody feel bad about feeling good. That religion has taken away from us many different kinds of happiness that nature has provided, at least potentially. Now the puritanical types are going around saying that AIDS is God's judgment on the promiscuous generation, that they all deserve to get sick. I'd say, if it were not such a misuse of the term, fuck him. If God created AIDS, for any reason whatsoever, he's a lot more sinful than we are.

Puritanical religions always foster sexual ignorance and sexual abuse, which leads to self-hate for many people, who can't help being sexual creatures because that's their genetic nature. Religion feeds on people hating themselves. I know because it happened to me, and I'm angry about it. I wasted a lot of years believing in that punishing god. Now he's out of my life for good. Or I should say, for the better.

6

REPRODUCTION

*P*ATRIARCHAL RELIGIONS HAVE NEVER CONCERNED themselves about moral control of violence or crime in society with any-thing like the ardor they bestowed on control of sexuality—specifically, female sexuality. This is quite comprehensible when you know the bottom-line reason for instituting patriarchal religion in the first place: to allow men to claim the honor of parenthood, and to enjoy postmortem deification brought about by the worship of many descendants. This was what the biblical God promised his patriarchs in return for their obedience: "I will make thee exceeding fruitful, and I will make nations of thee, and kings shall come out of thee" (Gen. 17:6).

During the first 2,995,000 of humanity's 3,000,000 years on this earth, people lived without a concept of fatherhood and children belonged to their mothers. They believed the life-giving power was a gift from the creative Goddess to women only, and men undoubtedly envied it. Female ancestors were deified, with the passage of generations of people who owed their existence to them. Sexuality was not a religious issue, because nobody knew that children were begotten as well as conceived. Therefore there was no monogamy, as it came to be practiced during the patriarchal fraction of human existence.

Since only women can produce children, men's new claims to ancestorhood had to depend on strict control of women's sexual activities. The traditional casual promiscuity of prepatriarchal ages had to be condemned by the new gods, so that each woman could be sexually bound to just one man, to whom she would "give" *his* children. And since firstborn children were especially important, bearing the primary responsibility for father-exalting rituals, it was essential that young women remain virgins until marriage.

Therefore we have the Bible, for instance, ordering the death penalty not only for adulteresses but also for every girl found not to be a virgin on her wedding night. If her bridegroom fails to make her bleed, God says she must be stoned to death at her father's door by the men of her village (Deut. 22:21). Out of such prohibitions arose a thousand sly folk customs involving, say, the use of chicken blood, or the public display of bloody sheets on the day after the wedding.

Under Islam, one of the world's most intensely patriarchal religions, this was carried so far as to institute hideous customs of female genital mutilation, in which prepubescent girls are literally sewed up, leaving only tiny holes for the passage of urine and menstrual fluids, and are cut open on their wedding days and again at the birth of each child. Such an operation, known as infibulation, involves amputation of the clitoris—euphemistically misnamed "female circumcision." The victim will never experience orgasm and will always associate sex with pain, from undergoing agonizing genital operations performed without anesthesia.

A nurse working in a hospital near a large Muslim community here in the United States recently told me of seeing many terrible cases of infection and other complications from such crude tortures as infibulation and clitoridectomy. Yet nothing is done by American law to stop these brutal customs, because they are "religious" and U.S. authorities prefer not to interfere with what are called religious beliefs—or so they say.

In 1993, there was a case of similar brutality committed against a man. It became a national cause célèbre when Mrs. Bobbitt (of the singularly appropriate name) cut off the penis of her battering, rapist husband. Doctors hastened to sew the thing back on, and were delighted to make it work again. Yet women have their organs of sexual pleasure permanently cut off by the millions throughout Africa and the Middle East, and by the thousands right here in the United States, and no one protests. If foreign beliefs had to do with ritual castration of men, it's entirely possible that steps would be taken to stamp out the custom without delay.

In India, the terrible practice of *suttee*, or widow-burning, was established to make sure that no women could bear another man's children even after her husband's death. All her children were to be devoted solely to the perpetuation of his name and the pious propitiation of his ghost. Once men decided that their hope of ancestral immortality lay in rigid control of women's sexuality, there was no limit to the ruthlessness by which such control was enforced. Even in our own culture, centuries of patriarchal training have given many men the idea that wives who show even the slightest indication of lusting after other men, or daughters who seem to be growing up to be sexual creatures, may be beaten, tortured, or even killed under traditional, God-endorsed, "unwritten law."

Ideally, from the patriarchal point of view, every woman would be sexually bound to one man for her lifetime, and every man would have unrestricted access to any woman he wants—ergo, a double standard. But since it takes two to tango, obviously this is unworkable. Promiscuous men would be constantly trespassing on one another's turf. So certain groups of women were set aside to service all men who wanted sexual variety. These women constituted an underclass of whores, not expected to attach themselves to any single man or to bear children. Of course, unattached women did bear children from time to time and patriarchal society burdened such children with the heavy social stigma of illegitimacy, and their mothers with the name of whore whether they were professional prostitutes or not.

Professional prostitution has an interesting history. In ancient oriental countries, when there were still temples everywhere dedicated to the original Goddess, priestesses were sacred harlots, revered rather than despised for their sexuality. One of their holy functions was to provide men with a foretaste of the bliss of heaven, as it was long believed that every orgasm was a brief sample of the ecstasy in which gods and other divinities lived. The beneficent Great Goddess allowed men to contact this divine power through physical union with women: a belief that is still extant in such theologies as Tantric Buddhism and various Polynesian, Melanesian, sub-Arctic, and Native American traditions.

The Goddess disliked both monogamy and restrictive virginity. For many centuries Her temples perpetuated the custom of prostituting every girl in the temple once before her marriage, so she was deflowered either by a priest or by the first stranger to offer her money. Her firstborn child was thereafter properly known as virgin-born or god-begotten.[1]

Often, young women served in the temples as promiscuous priestesses until the birth of their first children; then they entered secular life and married. Such women were known as *horae* in Greece, *virgines* in Rome, or *kadeshas* in Palestine. Several traditions hint that the Virgin Mary served as a *kadesha* during the time when the angel Gabriel—whose name means, literally, divine husband—"came in unto her" in the temple, the biblical phrase for sexual intercourse (Luke 1:28).

Greek and Roman classical paganism is packed with gods who were frequently divine husbands to mortal virgins, upon whom they begot a host of legendary heroes and saviors. A divine father and a virgin birth were de rigueur for any spiritual leader in those days; so earthly illegitimacy, far from being a stigma, was a definite asset.

An early Greek myth about father god Zeus gives us a revealing insight into the concept of the jealous god, so familiar in our Bible. This earlier myth strongly suggests that God's problem was specifically sexual jealousy. It seems that in the lost Golden Age—corresponding to the biblical Eden—human beings were first created androgynous, female and male in the same body, just like the primal Androgyne of Hindu iconography, or the primordial Hermaphrodite who combined the god Hermes and the Goddess

Aphrodite in one person. These two-sexed humans lived in a perpetual state of bliss, like the gods themselves.

Zeus became intensely jealous of their pleasure, feeling that it ought to be reserved only for deities like himself. So he ripped the humans apart, separating their female halves from their male halves, condemning them to live in constant yearning for reunion with one another. Incidentally, the word religion by derivation means exactly that: "relinking" or "rejoining."

Father Zeus made a mistake when he separated the human halves. In careless haste, he tore away a piece of flesh that properly belonged to the female, and left it stuck to the male. Consequently, every woman has a hollow that bleeds in memory of her loss, and every man has an extraneous piece of flesh that fits her hollow, and is not under his control, but is controlled by Woman because it belongs to her.

This myth ingeniously explained the origin of human sexuality. Certain Gnostic and rabbinical traditions assigned much the same story to the jealous god of Eden, declaring that Adam and Eve once lived as an androgyne and were torn apart when God "took Eve out of Adam" to end their life of togetherness, peace, and pleasure. Cabalistic Judaism of the twelfth and thirteenth centuries insisted that all the world's troubles arose from this separation of male and female, and that even God needed to be reunited with his female half, variously called Shekhina, Sophia, Astarte, Baalat, Malkuth, or Anath.

The myth also helps explain the peculiar and paradoxical love-hate—or rather lust-disgust—dichotomy that patriarchy has developed in its profoundly confused attitudes toward sex. In early days, men so feared invoking the displeasure of jealous gods that they feared their own sexual enjoyment as a possible crime of *hubris*—that is, usurpation of a god's prerogatives. They also feared women's apparent control of male sexuality, in addition to their already intense envy of women's physical control of life-giving and life-sustaining functions. As a result of such fears, patriarchy sometimes took the ascetic route to denial of female powers. declaring all sexual or sensual enjoyments sinful in the god's eyes.

This attitude came down to us through Zoroastrianism, Essenism, Manicheanism, and early Christianity, more or less in that order. It is still quite comprehensible in our own time, though it certainly represents an unnatural and perverse confusion of pleasure and pain responses. Beginning with St. Augustine, Christian fathers were so terrified of sexuality that they declared it the source and means of transmission of original sin through all generations: the sin for which God condemned the entire human race to eternal torture after death. They revered ascetic saints for renouncing sexuality altogether. Some churchmen, like Origen, had themselves castrated in order to follow Jesus's recommendation: to make themselves eunuchs for the sake of a blessed immortality in heaven (Matt. 19:12). Together with many of his contemporaries, Origen renounced the very idea of marriage as "something unholy and unclean, a means of sensuality." Eventually, of course, the church was forced to accept marriage and even to dignify it with the term "holy matrimony"—provided it was maintained in a condition of sexual inequality. Pope Pius XI ruled in *Castii Connubii* that "married life presupposes the power of the husband over the wife and children, and subjection and obedience of the wife to the husband."[2]

Christian fathers emphasized this aspect of marriage above all, even when they denigrated it as an unworthy and polluted state. St. Augustine said, "Nothing so much casts down the mind of man from its citadel as do the blandishments of women, and that physical contact without which a wife cannot be possessed."[3] But women's blandishments didn't seem to earn them much respect from husbands; Augustine further ruled that every wife must be her husband's servant, and a marriage contract was a legal guarantee of servitude. Wives should "remember their station and not set themselves up against their masters." He presented his mother, St. Monica, as an ideal wife, slavishly obedient to her bad-tempered, unfaithful, domineering husband who, though generally violent, never had occasion to beat her because she was so quick to obey his every order.[4] The church that canonized her never abandoned this Augustinian view of a wife's role. Gratian declared that every wife is a slave because man, not woman, was made in the image of God.[5] Through the centuries, confessors were told that the most important question they must ask married women was whether they had "obeyed their husbands in all things."[6] Augustine stated unequivocally that "Man was made to rule, woman to obey."[7]

Equally patriarchal Islam reduced woman to the status of slaves or domestic animals. The Koran says that disobedient women must be scourged and sent to "beds apart," and any wife, mother, daughter, sister, aunt, niece, or female cousin may be killed with impunity by any man who believes her guilty of adultery.[8] This ruling was a law passed in 1991 by Iraq's Revolutionary Command Council.

Even when there was no question of adultery, male control of women's sexual and reproductive lives was supposed to be absolute under patriarchal rules. The Christian church officially frowned on marital sex for pleasure alone; every sex act was to take place only with the expectation of begetting more children. A leading theologian of the seventeenth century, advisor to bishops, declared that the cause of the biblical flood was "the defilement, the pollution, the desecration of the conjugal bed" when people were using it for "the evil of sexual pleasure." St. Bernardine of Siena had ruled that wives should be willing to die rather than give in to husbands who wanted only sexual enjoyment. And yet other theologians insisted that a wife must yield to her husband's every demand for sexual services, in order to "avoid adultery" (his, that is), even when she was too poor or too overburdened or too ill from excessive childbearing to support any more children. "Catholic sexual morality is largely a master-race morality and a pitiless exploitation of women."[9] Riane Eisler notes: "The rules designed to strictly control women's sexuality were not devised to protect morality, but to protect men's ownership of women's sexual and nonsexual services, as well as of any children they bore."[10]

Despite all the rigid insistence on making women into breeding machines, the church gave them little support or respect in that role. Biblical authority ruled that a birth-giving woman was unclean and must stay away from the god's temple, lest she pollute it (Lev. 12). The medieval church forbade new mothers to enter church buildings until forty days had passed since their deliveries (sometimes it was eighty days if the child was a girl, which made the whole process automatically even dirtier). Women who died in childbirth were often refused burial in consecrated ground, on the theory that they and their offspring belonged to the devil at that period in their lives. They could not be laid out in the church, as men were. The Jesuit Peter Browe wrote as late as 1938 that married women were not to be allowed to take communion frequently, because they were impure and might soil the sacred host. In view of such precedents, there seems to be little point to the statement of Pope John Paul II in his 1979 General Audience: "I want to remind young women that motherhood is the vocation of women."[12] According to the tradition of his church, it is a vocation with little honor.

One of the holiest images in ancient paganism was the Goddess Giving Birth, an explicit depiction of a child emerging from its mother's body. To Christian authorities, such an image was the ultimate obscenity. To see a woman in the act of giving life is still considered unfit for the eyes of children, whereas to see a man in the act of taking life is a daily occurrence for every child in our media-centered society.

Far from revering women for choosing the vocation of motherhood, the church consistently demanded that it be forced on them whether they wanted it or not. Even a rapist had the right to force a woman into motherhood, according to theologian Thomas Sanchez, who said a raped woman must do nothing to remove or injure her assailant's semen, on the ground that it would do "injustice to the human race, whose reproduction would be impaired."[13] This policy of according more tender respect to a rapist than to his victim seems not to have changed. "Pope John Paul II's response to the mass rapes of women in Bosnia was not to back those who are today working to have mass rapes finally recognized as war crimes. Rather, it was to pray that the violated women not have abortions."[14]

Of course, abortion has been a particularly sore issue in recent years, thanks to fundamentalists wishing to reverse the law of the land that made it legal. However, the churches' claims to have "always" considered it a crime are quite false. Abortion was recognized as legal up to the nineteenth century, as long as it took place before the eightieth day of pregnancy.[15] The Catholic church originally held that the fetus was soulless before quickening was felt. Only after God had given it a soul would it begin to move in the womb. In 1869 Pope Pius X announced in effect that the church had been mistaken about this, or else God had misinformed his vicars on earth, and lo and behold, the soul was inserted into the fetus at conception, after all.[16] The purpose of this revision was to begin opposing abortions, which had become a little less dangerous for women than they used to be.

Pursuant to this comparatively new policy, Bishop Leo Maher of San Diego wrote in 1975 that every member of "an organization that promotes abortions, such as the National Organization for Women, must be refused the Sacrament of the Eucharist by priests, deacons, and extraordinary ministers for they ignore God's law."[17] Presumably this blanket excommunication would apply also to every member of the United States government, which declared abortions legal, and of the American Medical Association, which teaches and practices the techniques.

The church has been a little more consistent in opposing birth control, the original motive of which was to prevent married couples from indulging in sex for fun. St. Augustine said a marriage bed is a bordello and a wife is a harlot unless marital relations were undertaken only to beget children. In the thirteenth century, William of Auxerre said a godly man can have carnal knowledge of his wife only if it is devoid of enjoyment, because the sinfulness of the act increases in proportion to its pleasure.[18] Clement of Alexandria declared that a man commits adultery with his own wife if he doesn't intend every sex act to beget a child, and that "feelings of sensual pleasure such as those had in the embraces of a harlot are damnable in a wife." The Jesuit Father Gury, the most widely read Catholic theologian of the nineteenth century, wrote that a woman commits a grave sin if she "leads her husband astray, even indirectly and tacitly, into the misuse of marriage," by which he meant birth control, by complaining that she has too many children, or that she will die if she has another pregnancy. According to Catholic doctrine, women were expected to accept illness or death in pushing their motherhood beyond healthy limits. In 1930, Pope Pius XI said all people who practice birth control are pursued by God "with the highest degree of hatred," and in 1980 the papacy still described birth control as a man's "adultery with one's own wife." Contraception was classified as a mortal sin without exception; up to 1917, canon law labeled it murder. Penitential books show that "anal and oral intercourse . . . were often punished more severely than abortion, indeed more severely than premeditated murder . . . in its struggle against the sexual realm, the Catholic Church to this day displays more commitment than it does against taking human life in war, mass murder, and the death penalty."[19]

Creative or alternative sexual techniques, which might be suspected of preventing conception, have always aroused the bitterest anathemas of churchmen. St. Thomas Aquinas stated that any deviation from the missionary position is a worse crime than incest, rape, or adultery, while the worst sins imaginable are non-conceptive sex acts such as masturbation, homosexuality, oral intercourse, and coitus interruptus. It was the duty of a wife to resist any sexual deviations on the part of her husband, and if he tried to use a condom, to resist him "as she would a rapist." Theologian Arthur Vermeersch (d. 1936) insisted that a wife must fight a condom-wearing husband until he beat her into submission or she sacrificed "a fair equivalent to life," because "marital chastity, like all Christian virtues, demands its martyrs."[20] The Catholic *Codex Latinus Monacensis* 22233 declares that any woman's desire to deviate from missionary-position sex is as serious a sin as murder.[21] And as late as 1926, the Catholic Index of Forbidden Books included *Ideal Marriage*, the only unorthodox part of which was its acceptance of alternative copulatory positions.[22]

Pope Leo the Great stated in the fifth century that all conjugal intercourse is a sin, and Pope Gregory I also said, "Sexual pleasure can never be without sin." On such grounds, marital relations were forbidden on Sundays, on numerous feast days, for twenty days before Christmas and Pentecost, through all of Lent, throughout pregnancy, during all menstrual periods, for forty days after child-birth, and in all periods of penance. In effect, the days when god-fearing Christian men were permitted to "sully themselves" with their wives, as the clergy put it, were few and far between. A twelfth-century theologian directed that if a woman wants sex during one of the forbidden times, her husband must "keep her impudence down with fasts and beatings."[23] But nothing was said about a wife punishing her husband for wanting sex at a wrong time.

The early church had tried to wipe out sex, on the ground that the end of the world was imminent and it was futile and sinful to produce more children. Jesus cried woe on pregnant women or nursing mothers in the last days (Luke 21:23), which was taken to mean that women should stop giving birth. But as the years went on and no apocalypse occurred, church authorities soon found that it was necessary to keep up the numbers of the faithful; so the original rule was countermanded. The church has gone to the other extreme, an enormous disservice to the human race in these days of out-of-control overpopulation, which will soon strain every resource of the planet and lead to misery for many. "The only life many of the leaders of the anti–family planning movement seem to care about—indeed obsess about—is life *before* birth and *after* death."[24] In between, the living seem to get little consideration.

At bottom, patriarchal callousness toward the problems of posterity or of women seems to hark back to that ancient, primitive jealousy that made men yearn to usurp the female magic of repro-duction, to command the loyalties of their own tribes, to be revered as parents and founders of clans. Through the manipulation of reli-gion, they did succeed, although the process took thousands of years and a complete restructuring of natural social bondings.

Best of all from the patriarchs' viewpoint, they didn't even have to go through the inconveniences and pains of pregnancy, birth giving, and child care. All they had to do was enslave women and force them to do the real work. Fathers could sit back and receive the glory, being designated the true parents by religious authorities who claimed that women were only passive vessels for the lordly male seed. To this day the Catholic Church has not really assimilated the implications of the discovery of the human ovum.[25]

A sure sign of a fully developed patriarchy is a system of patrilineal nomenclature, with complete suppression of the matronymics that older civilizations used. In ancient Egypt, for example, each child was given its all-important soul-name or *ren* by its mother when she first put it to her breast. It was said that even the gods required mothers to give them names, or else they would waste away and die.[26] The Great Goddess Kali was supposed to have created every life form by speaking its name in Her primordial language of Sanskrit—a very ancient idea that was copied by the biblical God and became the basis for the mystic doctrine of the Logos. As human beings evolved language and gave names to things, they seem to have developed the notion that the names they gave were essential qualities of the things, and essential souls of living beings. In Gen. 2:19, God deputizes Adam to give names to the animals, and throughout the Old Testament the all-important father-names appear in endless lists of patrilineal "begats," while the names of maternal ancestresses are quite forgotten.

So, under patriliny, women's names vanished with their own generation, and their surnames vanished with their marriages. The all-important male descent was the only one to be remembered and passed along. English surnames (or "sir-names") even today show the centuries-long effort of men to claim for themselves alone the honors and privileges of parenthood and/or ancestor worship. Such names indicate that the son is the father's possession and all male posterity will continue in the same way. For example:

Aarons, Aaronson, Abrams, Abramson, Adam, Adamson, Alberts, Albertson, Andrews, Anderson, Arnolds, Arnoldson, Bennett, Benson, Bernards, Bernardson, Charleson, Carlson, Clarkson, Daniels, Danielson, Davis, Davies, Davidson, Dawes, Dawson, Denis, Dennison, Dicks, Dixon, Dickinson, Donalds, Donaldson, Edmunds, Edmundson, Edwards, Ellis, Ellison, Ericson, Evans, Evanson, Fergus, Ferguson, Fredericks, Frederickson, Hanson, Harolds, Haroldson, Harris, Harrison, Henrys, Hendrickson, Howards, Howardson, Humphries, Isaacs, Isaacson, Jacks, Jackson, Jacobs,

Jacobson, Jamison, Jimson, Jeffries, Jefferson, Jones, Johnson, Johannson, Josephs, Josephson, Lewison, Manns, Manson, Marks, Markson, Martins, Martinson, Masterson, Matthews, Matheson, Michaels, Michaelson, Morrison, Mortonson, Nels, Nelson, Paulson, Peters, Peterson, Phillips, Philipson, Reynolds, Reynoldson, Richards, Richardson, Roberts, Robertson, Robbins, Robinson, Rogers, Rogerson, Samuels, Samuelson, Sandys, Simons, Simonson, Stevens, Stevenson, Thomas, Thomson, Williams, Williamson, Willis, Wilson.

All these names and others like them indicate claims of paternity. There are no similar surnames to honor mothers. An even longer list may be compiled in which last names are simply repetitions of men's first names, indicating that there is an implied "son of" appended to the family name. The following, for example, are common English surnames:

Abel, Abner, Adolph, Allen, Alexander, Alfred, Ambrose, Amos, Angelo, Anthony, Archibald, Arthur, Ashley, Aubrey, Austin, Baldwin, Barry, Bartholomew, Barton, Basil, Baxter, Bayard, Benedict, Benjamin, Bertram, Boris, Boyd, Bradford, Brian, Bruce, Bruno, Byron, Calvin, Cameron, Carrol, Cecil, Cedric, Charles, Chester, Christian, Christopher, Clarence, Clark, Claude, Clement, Clifford, Clive, Clyde, Conrad, Constantine, Cornelius, Craig, Crispin, Cuthbert, Cyril, Cyrus, Dale, Dean, Dexter, Dietrich, Dominic, Douglas, Dudley, Duncan, Earl, Edgar, Edwin, Egbert, Elliott, Emery, Emmet, Ephraim, Ernest, Errol, Ethan, Eugene, Eustace, Everett, Fabian, Fairfax, Felix, Ferdinand, Floyd, Francis, Frank, Fraser, Gabriel, George, Gerard, Gifford, Giles, Glenn, Godfrey, Godwin, Gordon, Graham, Grant, Granville, Gregory, Griffith, Grover, Gustave, Guy, Harvey, Hector, Herbert, Herman, Hilary, Hiram, Homer, Horace, Howell, Hubert, Hughes, Humphrey, Ingram, Ivan, Jason, Jasper, Jay, Jerome, Joel, Jonathan, Jordan, Julius, Kean, Keith, Kenneth, Kevin, Lambert, Lawrence, Lee, Lennox, Leonard, Leopold, Leroy, Leslie, Lester, Lincoln, Lionel, Llewellyn, Lloyd, Lorenzo, Ludwig, Luke, Luther, Lyman, Lynn, Magnus, Malcolm, Marshall, Marvin, Maxwell, Melvin, Meredith, Miles, Millard, Milton, Mitchell, Monroe, Montague, Morgan, Mortimer, Morton, Moses, Murray, Nathan, Nicholas, Nigel,

Norman, Norton, Ogden, Oliver, Orville, Osbert, Oscar, Osmund, Oswald, Otis, Owen, Patrick, Percival, Perry, Philbert, Quentin, Randall, Randolph, Raphael, Raymond, Roderick, Rodney, Roland, Rolfe, Ronald, Roscoe, Ross, Roy, Rudolph, Rupert, Russell, Saul, Schuyler, Sebastian, Seymour, Sherwood, Sidney, Sigmund, Silas, Solomon, Spencer, Stanley, Stewart, Sylvester, Terence, Theodore, Timothy, Tobias, Valentine, Vaughn, Vernon, Victor, Vincent, Virgil, Wade, Waldo, Wallace, Walter, Ward, Warner, Warren, Webster, Wendell, Wilbur, Wilhelm, Willard, Winfred, Xavier.

There are no women's names in comparable use as surnames.

We can, however, find numerous examples of daughters who were given patronymics with some sort of feminized endings, to show that they too belonged to their fathers and not to their mothers. A few such names are:

Alfreda, Andrea, Augusta, Carla, Claudette, Edwina, Ernestine, Francine, Fredericka, Gabriella, Georgette, Georgina, Geraldine, Henrietta, Jacobina, Jean (John), Jeanette (John), Joan (John), Joanna (John), Justine, Leona, Martine, Maxine, Michaela, Nicolette, Paula, Pauline, Roberta, Theodora, Thomasina, Victoria, Willa.

We do not find any similar examples of mothers' names given to sons with a masculinized ending. In Scandinavia, some surnames have "daughter" appended to them for women, instead of "son" or "sen," but they are still called daughters of their fathers, not their mothers. "Kristin Lavransdatter" is the daughter of Laurence (Lavrans); her mother's name is lost.

Most mammals know only one parent, the mother. The natural preeminence of mothers in bearing, feeding, nurturing, and socializing the offspring is the central fact of mammalian life. When men began to arrange human societies to what they thought was their own advantage, they had to establish for fatherhood a recognition that had belonged previously to motherhood. When father gods were invented, priests and kings claimed to embody them; family trees were traced through males; children had to be taught to obey fathers instead of following and imitating their mothers like every other young mammal. This was usually accomplished by violence. Tribal cultures that restrict the freedom of women and children, and threaten them with physical harm, are typically warlike and violent.[27]

Western civilization has lived for a long time with radical patriarchy. Still, the system continues to fall short of its aim to deify the paternal principle alone. God the Father is only a concept constructed of words and learned habits of thinking. Motherhood continues to be the natural basis of acculturization and family solidarity for most human beings. Women do by far the largest percentage of child tending and child teaching, hold the families together, maintain contact with relatives, keep in touch. Every infant recognizes mother as the birth giver, nurse, stimulator, comforter, and source of life's necessities, by inborn instinct older than the human race. Father-reverence must be learned; mother-reverence is inherent.

Perhaps one of the silliest things Father Freud ever said was that every woman wants to have a child largely because the child is a penis substitute in her penis-envying unconscious mind. The truth is rather the reverse: Men's envy of motherhood brought about the creation of patriarchy, a less satisfactory imitation. Not even subconsciously does a mother think of her child as a penis. Her child is a whole person, whom she loves as she will love few other creatures in her lifetime. Freud's excesses of phallus worship have brought his entire body of work into disrepute as women have begun to understand more about the machinations of the patriarchal mind.

Instead of women afflicted with penis envy, our society seems to have more indications of men afflicted with womb envy. The trend toward husbands' participation in the birth process shows that many fathers want to claim some part of the natural parent-child bonding for themselves, even though they can never feel the gut experience or the hormonal response of maternity. At times the father in the delivery room is designated the "coach" or "manager" of his wife's birthing, another verbal euphemism that recalls old customs of couvade, when men pretended to give birth, or pretended to give the newborn its soul by breathing on it.[28]

Men's participation in the birth process is thought to increase the father's capacity for caretaking and loving his child. Perhaps it does. But giving birth is still a strictly female function to which males are necessarily peripheral. Despite the male takeover of the obstetrical profession at the beginning of the twentieth century, birth is still the primordial female Mystery, source of life, and archetype of creation.

No doubt there are good fathers who genuinely love their children and are capable of bringing them up well; but they are statistically less evident than good mothers. Divorce courts tend to favor fathers, which sometimes presents the absurd spectacle of divorced fathers being granted visitation rights even when they have been proven to be wife beaters or child abusers. When mothers are not allowed to take their father-abused children to a different state, out of the unworthy father's reach, this can only be viewed as a miscarriage of justice.

Further degradation of motherhood takes place in a patriarchal society when it is casually imposed on many individuals who aren't prepared to handle it: young teenagers, drug abusers, prostitutes, homeless or indigent women, or those who already have too many children. Even with the best of intentions, such women are not likely to live up to the standards of good mothering; moreover, it is certain that they will be personally blamed for any failure, although the real failure is that of a society that imposes motherhood without supporting it.

In John 7:38, Jesus is made to say that when a man believes in him, "as the scripture hath said, out of his belly shall flow rivers of living water." No scripture is known to say this, but the metaphor of the living waters emanating from the belly was a symbol of the waters of birth.[29] All the living waters of the earth were supposed to have come from the belly of Great Mother Tiamat, according to Babylonian myth, when the god Marduk divided her so as to isolate the "waters above the earth" from the waters below, the seas and rivers. The god of Genesis emulated Marduk's feat (Gen. 1:7); but the original spirit of the deep (*tehom*) that existed before him was female. She was Tiamat to the Babylonians, Temu to the Egyptians, Themis to the Greeks, and out of her all life arose. She didn't speak it into being; she gave birth to it. The Bible draws a veil over her original identity, but like the women in a patriarchal society that conceals them from view, she is still there.

Motherhood is all-important; it is *the* instrument of continuation for any species on earth, and for our species in particular because human infants are born more helpless than any other creatures except the marsupials. Human mothering is much more than birthing and nursing. It is also years of teaching, interaction, communication, demonstrated affection, and social guidance. Men can do it, but in the contexts of a patriarchy, usually don't.

And after all the trouble, anxiety, and emotional investment, all the love and caring, mothers are frequently expected to let the almost finished product go off to fight patriarchy's wars, to be killed in some particularly unnatural way. An analogy comprehensible to men might be an inventor who spends twenty years of his life perfecting an extremely complex machine, one of a kind; then he is expected to hand it over to a psychopath who will set an explosive charge under it and blow it to smithereens. The warlike society is always concerned about the next generation of cannon fodder. Charlotte Perkins Gilman wrote: "All this talk, for and against and about babies, is by men. One would think the men bore the babies, nursed the babies, reared the babies. . . . The women bear and rear the children. The men kill them. Then they say: 'We are running short of children—make some more.' "[30] One might suspect that this is one of the secret social motives behind the actions of men who take an antiabortion stand, while the secret psychological motive is that they identify with the fetus rather than the mother.

It is also typical of militaristic societies to emphasize an afterlife, because if men believed that their personal deaths would be final, they might be less willing to risk death on the battlefield. Warlike cultures in general belittle the life of the flesh and glorify the hypothetical afterlife for this reason, like the ancient Druids who were said to teach the doctrine of rebirth to their warriors to make them braver. Islamic soldiers were told that if they died in battle, they would go directly to the best of all heavens, where—significantly—they would be forever tended by beautiful, sensual, complaisant *houris* (sexual angels). Such teachings may have made men more willing to die, but they also extracted a terrible price of neglect, discomfort, and misery in the only real life that humans know. Christians followed the classic pattern in this respect, celebrating saints whose tortures were described in lip-licking detail by writers who, centuries later, simply imagined them; and postulating Valkyrie-like angels to carry Christ's warriors to a delicious immortality, the exact nature of which was never made clear. Cyprian wrote that the martyrs had "delighted" their Christian god with "the sublime, the great, the acceptable spectacle" of their tortures and painful death, accompanied by "the flow of blood which quenches the flames and the fires of hell by its glorious gore."[31] The church was so pleased with these gory spectacles that it spent most of the ninth and tenth centuries inventing them, for most of the saints' biographies are entirely fictitious. The church today admits as much, but still takes its profits from their fraudulent relics, and calls their sadistically imagined life stories "edifying."[32] So far, not one single account of a martyrdom has been found that can stand up to the doubts of scholars and historians.[33]

Marilyn French wrote: "To create symbols that suggest that some people live forever, is to implant in human experience a falsehood so profound as to distort it utterly. Life carries sorrows for all creatures; sorrow and deprivation are not escapable. But it is possible to live with an eye to delight rather than to domination. And this is the feminist morality."[34]

Ruth Benedict believed that there is no such thing as a biological need of man to go to war. "The havoc," she said, "is manmade."[35] As an anthropologist she studied societies unlike our own, some of which showed the pattern known as "life-affirmative," which characterized the ancient matriarchates:

> There is a minimum of hostility, violence, or cruelty among people, no harsh punishment, hardly any crime, and the institution of war is absent or plays an exceedingly small role. Children are treated with kindness, there is no severe corporal punish-

ment; women are in general considered equal to men, or at least not exploited or humiliated; there is a generally permissive and affirmative attitude toward sex. There is little envy, covetousness, greed, and exploitativeness. . . . There is a general attitude of trust and confidence, not only in others but particularly in nature.[36]

Therefore it is essential for the survival of a decently human humanity, in a satisfactory way of life, that women receive more respect and mothers receive more support. For too many centuries, women have struggled to give their children healthy, happy lives while patriarchal mores and customs have blocked their efforts, poured contempt on their nurturant qualities, robbed them of their children's allegiance, and punished them for the very tenderness that spells survival for every young human. John Knox in 1560 condemned all women as "impatient, feeble, foolish, unconstant, variable, cruel, and lacking the spirit of counsel."[37] The terms might better be applied to the patriarchal males who have so unwisely created a culture of violence, ignorance, bigotry, and injustice. The true spirit of counsel is, and always has been, Mother.

According to Andrea Dworkin, this is "the simplest revolutionary idea ever conceived, and the most despised": it is, for men, the idea that women are not defined solely by sexuality and reproduction.[38] It is the idea that women know, better than most men, what is right, what a viable morality should be, and what kinds of behavior can foster the best possible lives for the most people. Women know these things because, as mothers or potential mothers, they are sensitive to the needs of others. Thus women naturally oppose what might be called the sadistic model of society. "For the sadistic character there is only one admirable quality, and that is power. He admires, loves, and submits to those who have power, and he despises and wants to control those who are powerless and cannot fight back."[39] This character can be seen as the central model for an entire culture when that culture submits to an authoritarian, dictatorial image of the male god, and the countervailing image of the Great Mother is lost.

"As we have listened for centuries to the voices of men and the theories of development that their experience informs, so we have come more recently to notice not only the silence of women but the difficulty in hearing what they say when they speak. Yet in the different voice of women lies the truth of an ethic of care, the tie between relationship and responsibility, and the origins of aggression in the failure of connection."[40]

What, really, is the reproductive role of the male, who has in the human species assumed a right to control the whole process, even though his part in it is relatively minor? In other species there is no question of any such male usurpation. Reproduction is entirely under female control.

> Males may well be an evolutionary dead-end that will be abandoned when another system, less parasitical on and wasteful of female energies, appears. But there are other possibilities, and these can be summarized by saying that males might make sense if they allow the needs and desires of females to control their actions. . . .
>
> Among species with genders, it is the females that have control over the reproductive cycle; the males appear to be virtually irrelevant. The single-parent family is the rule in nature and that parent is almost always female. It is the female that watches the environment to clock the arrival of favorable conditions, secure the food to make and nourish her eggs, find and/or prepare a proper place to lay her eggs or leave her young, and incubate, nurse or feed, train, and protect them. By and large males take no part in these activities. . . .
>
> When one looks at females in nature one sees industry, progenitiveness, and efficiency; when one looks at males one sees the most amazingly elaborate forms of wastefulness.[41]

"Nurturing," says Genevieve Vaughan, "is the origin of our species—not competition and hierarchy or the survival of the fittest. Human mothers ensure the survival of the unfittest—infants."[42] True human lives are created by the long, arduous, many-faceted processes of mothering, not by the mindless momentary act of begetting, which men share with the males of all other species, even down to worms, fish, insects, and other invertebrates. Human mothers raise human beings.

In the light of these insights, we can perceive how vile is the ruling of the seventeenth-century saint Jean Eudes that pregnancy is a "humiliation" to all women, "to know that while they are with child, they carry within them an infant . . . who is the enemy of God, the object of his hatred and malediction, and the shrine of the demon."[43] Such doctrines could never have been evolved by mothers; they could only be elucidated by shriveled, bitter, resentful celibates who had never experienced human love. What mother could look into the face of her baby and reflect that God hates this child, who is really a demon? Such pronouncements surely indicate how far from the basic human realities a patriarchal religion could stray.

And even in spite of such obvious contempt and dislike of woman's inimitably vital part in human reproduction, patriarchal religions still try to hand it over to male control. *Men* have the effrontery to try to deny women their choice in their unique function of motherhood, although the modern world desperately needs to control its exploding population, and male rules force many women (or too-young girls) to bear babies whether they can adequately nurture them or not. Thus the world is filled with unwanted children for whom adoptive parents cannot be found. Sherry Matulis writes: "The Anti-Choice concern is not for that tiny little couplet of sperm and ova; not for the zygote, nor the blastocyst, nor the embryo, nor even the fetus. The concern is for the status quo of the Patriarchy."[44] But the patriarchy does not love or raise the unwanted children; it simply uses them as another inconvenience imposed upon women, then abandons them to an indifferent fate. Good mothering is the last thing any patriarchy is able to do; therefore one might think that it should keep its hands and its mouth off the subject of mothering altogether.

MODERN WOMEN TALK ABOUT REPRODUCTION

Women who are concerned about reproductive rights usually feel a deep concern also for the environment, the planet itself, as burgeoning human populations overrun the continents and outgrow available resources. Ecclesiastical opposition to birth control and abortion, they feel, has never given consideration to increasing the quality of human life, but only its quantity. We overreproduce ourselves at a severe cost to our Mother Earth, to other species, and ultimately to our own posterity. The Goddess movement naturally takes the question of human reproduction very seriously.

🐞 🐞 🐞

One of the things Goddess religion would do would be to reinstitute the idea that women have the right to make choices about life and death, which is really a revolutionary idea. Right now men have the choices over life and death, and only certain men, and over only certain people. But when I think of the number of people who are opposed to abortion, on the one hand, but yet are in favor of the death penalty, or of going to war in mass numbers to slaughter millions of people—I just don't get it. It makes no sense to me at all.

Women need to take that responsibility on, and we must trust ourselves to do that. Good mothers are not only sweet. Good mothers know when to kill, too. A friend of mine used to say that she thinks men should have no part in child rearing for three generations. There would be three generations of children reared only by women, so they could get the right attitudes. Then the boys would have the right attitudes. I think it needs to be something like that. There would be a lot of things that I hope would go out the window, like rape and incest and pornography and war.

Goddess religion should address the whole issue of our relationship with our bodies—not only in terms of contraception and abortion, and things like in vitro fertilization and messing around with genetics—but also just the concept that our bodies are okay, that we can live safely and happily in our bodies.

    🐜 🐜 🐜

A woman has a right to her own body. A man can't tell a woman how to handle it. It's her right to ignore any man who tries to tell her what to do. We're going through a big controversy with a lot of people being intimidated or hurt or killed because of men trying to tell women what to do with their bodies.

I used to get the labels "pro-choice" and "pro-life" mixed up, because pro-life means being in favor of life, and that's what I'm for. But you just don't bring a baby into the world for no reason. It has to be wanted, and it has to be taken care of. To give birth and then abandon a child is antilife.

    🐜 🐜 🐜

There's a strong instinct in a mother bringing home a baby. I know how I felt toward my babies. Nothing else mattered. I was tuning out the rest of the world. But some mothers are so battered by the patriarchal world that they just reject their babies. And the pope still says no birth control!

Their birth-control issue is just a ploy to control women. I see that also with the Arab women and Turkish women, the Muslims. They come in to the hospital with four or five little kids climbing all over them. These women are so burnt out. They very often ask, "How do you not get pregnant?" They have no idea.

    🐜 🐜 🐜

The abortion issue affected me. My parents were very involved with the church's view of right-to-life. So when I became pregnant and decided to have an abortion, it felt really shameful. It was something I thought I'd have to take to my grave, an ultimate sin. I still haven't told my mother. There are still scars. I want to be free of all that, because I did the right thing.

❦   ❦   ❦

In my first marriage, I couldn't get pregnant. I went to the doctor about it for years, and then my husband finally went once for a sperm count. It turned out he had a really low count, and he got very depressed and wouldn't talk to me for a whole weekend. Then I kept on going for more tests. We ignored the fact that he was the one with the problem! He couldn't face it. He had to deal with it through me, as if I could change his sperm count. We ended up separating, and I got pregnant by a new lover within the first two months.

I couldn't deal with that, so I had an abortion. I talked to a priest who asked me to appear in an interview with him on public-access television. It was the most disgusting experience. I came off that interview at the TV cable station feeling so used! That priest kept asking me how I could have done such a thing, and didn't I feel bad about having an abortion. He was like a destructive force. I walked out of that room feeling low and disgusted. I wasn't strong enough to tell him how he made me feel. I was too trusting, because I had generally looked up to men, like my father and the priests.

Men like that shouldn't be claiming to represent a religion. I wonder what he did to other people.

❦   ❦   ❦

We must feed the planet and take care of the children, so they have proper nurture. Antiabortionists are killing the doctors, so even though abortion is legal they hope to have everyone afraid to do it. The whole thing is getting worse.

❦   ❦   ❦

People who put their lives on the line to counsel women in Planned Parenthood, or make any of those efforts to better the lives of others, are like Goddess worshippers. I always thought of Planned

Parenthood as a moderate, benevolent sort of organization, but now the radical Right is trying to discredit it. I know that women who work there are getting discouraged. Only a short time ago everyone was rejoicing and saying that finally their ideas have gotten across; but it was a short-lived victory.

🐑 🐑 🐑

My sister just had a baby and has to do everything by herself. She's still with the father, but he's not nice. She wants to leave him, but she's afraid. He hasn't so much as changed a diaper or offered to feed the baby. We need a different worldview that would help mothers more and make fathers take their share of responsibility.

🐑 🐑 🐑

For all living things to survive on this planet, we have to stop that dominance craziness. We have to start thinking logically, as China has, about overpopulation, which is going to be the downfall of the planet. As we overpopulate it, we lose more and more other species. We lose the trees, the land, the animals. We have to start thinking logically about what tomorrow's life is going to be like. We have to think of the planet as a living being, our Mother Earth. Rather than trying to dominate her, we have to learn to share. We have to create something that's going to last for all living things into the future, until the planet itself ends its existence. We shouldn't allow it to end because of our stupidity. Our primary problem is population control.

🐑 🐑 🐑

I feel that if someone believes abortion is murder, I must respect the fact that they believe this. I wouldn't want to take away their right to refuse an abortion. But I don't share their view, and no one should legislate my right to my own differing opinion. An abortion is an unfortunate thing, but we should not be deprived of our choice when the alternative is even less fortunate. Our daughters and granddaughters should have this choice.

It's not a frivolous decision. It's serious. Nobody is going to get up with that baby in the night, or educate that baby, or clothe that baby, but its mother. Before people have children, they should ask themselves whether they can be the kind of parents the children should have. For someone to call you selfish because you decide not to have children is as stupid a misuse of words as there ever was. It's nobody else's business. It's a very personal decision. Surely the Goddess religion should address that issue.

♣ ♣ ♣

The worst thing is "pro-life," and the fact that there is absolutely no legal obligation on the part of the father to make life possible for the kids. We have confused ovaries with reproductive power and responsibility, and have created this immense subculture of female parents, who are not mothers, because they're really children themselves, and have no model for mothering. They can't mother.

There's a huge new continent of female parents with children who can't possibly ever make it in anything that we know as society. They reproduce because they're so uneducated, so powerless. They give us this population of people that we can't look to for anything.

It might be a less competitive world if the model were circular instead of hierarchical, and we might be able to discover new ways of marking excellence—perhaps by joyous inclusion, a celebration of good things shared. It might also be a world which valued creation, rather than destruction, and one which found creative ways to resolve differences. It would certainly be a world in which children were chosen, cared for, nurtured, and cherished—not a world which transforms them into the majority of the poor, the disenfranchised, the ignorant, the hungry, and the abused. It would not be a world where violent men picketed abortion clinics in the name of "life," and went home to do nothing about the numberless, nameless, homeless, uncherished children born into intolerable lives every day.

On a socially conscious, socially active political level, I would like to see women's bodies legally inviolate. There are far too many human beings in the world for the health of the planet, so, as a first step, I wish there would be developed a safe and effective method of birth control. Furthermore, until education can really take over, I fantasize that all girls, upon reaching puberty, would be given a birth control device that would prevent conception until the age of twenty-one, at which time each woman, now educated and better able to be responsible for her own life—and therefore more likely to be able to provide for a child—could choose to have it renewed, and choose for how long. I would pour a much greater part of our taxes into developing a really fantastic network of day-care and young-child-care facilities—the only thing more expensive than education is ignorance; and if ignorance isn't attacked young, it can't be corrected.

I would make parenthood legally a matter of equal responsibility—and I feel absolutely fascist about this. Fathers legally should, at the very least, be financially responsible for their offspring. Once a child is born, his/her parents' names should be recorded on the birth certificate, and for the next twenty-one years, the father's as well as the mother's wages should be garnished, if necessary, to pay for the child's care and education. It enrages me that most of the people who live below the poverty line in this country are women and children.

I don't think childbearing should be a right—particularly because so many of those who exercise their "right" to have children do not take any responsibility for them. I think it should be a paid-for privilege. Children need a great deal of care, especially in the early years. Under patriarchy, this incredibly skilled and time-consuming care has been arbitrarily assigned to women and to the home, regardless of whether or not the "home" can provide the care; and both have been denigrated and unpaid. Nowadays most women, single and married, must work in order to shelter and feed their families. Society—especially American society—has been very slow to respond to this change. Yes, women have been burdened by this ridiculous double expectation that they "bring home the bacon" *and* care for the home and raise the children. But the ones who suffer most are the children.

The answer is certainly not (as the awful right-wing would have it) to close the public world to women, and force them back into their kitchens and bedrooms, utterly dependent on the goodwill and talents of men. Even if that weren't cruel and stupidly wasteful of human talent, it's hardly practical. Not everyone is suited to motherhood or child care, and no one should be forced to spend her life in service to a ruling class distinguished only by the need for front zippers on their trousers.

I actually think it inevitable that America will have to make child rearing a national responsibility. I think there are humane Goddess-centered ways to deal with that responsibility. At the same time, I think that if we Goddess worshippers are not "proactive," that is, if we don't seize control of this issue (and if we don't wrest control of reproduction away from men), society—and perhaps the earth itself—cannot much longer survive patriarchy.

But I'm not inclined to believe that we can do this by "becoming a mainstream sect." The right-wingers in this country have done it by becoming politically powerful. Goddess worship would give us the base for such power by providing the beliefs and the network. But the exercise of power would be political, not religious.

🐝 🐝 🐝

My mother was a teenager when she became pregnant with me. She was forced to have me, because that's what one did. You get pregnant and you pay for it. I didn't come into the world celebrated. I was her punishment.

🐝 🐝 🐝

Many adults who now intellectually understand the need for birth control in an overpopulated world, and use it, still feel immense guilt. Part of my understanding of the Goddess is that sexuality is a very important part of life, and pleasure is okay. "All acts of love and pleasure are My rituals," the Goddess says. That is a most profound statement. It took me a long time to come to understand it.

My mother bore her last child at forty, and-almost died. The doctor told my *father* that she would die if she had another baby. I asked her, "What did you do?" She said, "We were Catholic. There was only one thing we could do, to be absolutely sure that I never got pregnant." They stopped having sex.

🐞 🐞 🐞

A priest once told me angrily that there is no such word as birth control in the Catholic Church. Then he stormed out, giving me no chance to reply. They never seem to face anything.

🐞 🐞 🐞

Having midwives attending the home birth of my first child opened me up to the realization that I had missed something by spending little time with women. At first I didn't connect it with anything spiritual, but I felt a warmth and caring that men are seldom capable of. I saw that I had been missing something from not being around other women.

My involvement with the midwives helped me to see that women have a whole different energy, and it's good to celebrate those differences. For me, it feels really natural to put a feminine personality on my spiritual ideas. Motherhood began my path to the Goddess, that special wonderful thing of women. My birth experience was the first time I had ever done anything that important. To see a baby thrive and grow on nothing but my breast milk was very important to me, a deep connection with the life force.

The Goddess movement can be a vehicle for ecological understanding. I don't see anything like that in patriarchal religion. Our lives are only a flicker: birth, life, and death make a cycle. We have to make the world better for the next generation. Goddess religion emphasizes the cycle of life, the renewal of life. It gives us the capacity to influence the world and do the most good we can. That's worth protecting.

7

DOCTRINES

*M*OST RELIGIONS PROFESS SOME KIND of adherence to "good" as opposed to an avoidance of "evil." But what is good, and what is evil? Few terms in any language are more relative than these. People tend to define evil as anything that harms, or might harm, themselves, their loved ones, their community, or—in a broader but by no means consistent sense—humanity in general. Yet humanity itself is evil to other species, whose very existence is threatened by humans. A hunter is evil to the hunted. A meat eater is evil to the meat animal. An army is evil to the opposing army. Humans are evil to other humans. The definition is always arbitrarily based on one's point of view.

Some people also call evil certain relatively harmless things that other people embrace, enjoy, or actively seek. Many of us cling to our own vices even when they are demonstrably harmful to ourselves or to others. Conversely, there are things widely regarded as evil that really harm no one. A number of sexual practices fall into this category, having been condemned for centuries by Christian ascetics. For example, masturbation has long been defined as a sin, and as late as 1975 Pope Paul VI declared that anyone who masturbates "forfeits the love of God."[1] The pope pretends to know

God's opinion on such matters, but many other people have quite different opinions. Is anyone so naive as to imagine that clergymen never masturbate?

Christianity has always had trouble dealing with its own definitions of evil. From century to century and from sect to sect, its lists of wickednesses have been continually altered in the effort to absolve the Christian god of ultimate responsibility. Even though God openly declares himself the creator of evil in the Bible (Isa. 45:7), this passage has been studiously ignored by theologians who want their deity to represent only good, even though his world obviously contains much evil.

One solution to the problem has been to attribute everything evil to the disobedience of human beings, starting with Eve and the unnamed fruit now envisioned as an apple. The Eden myth with its Satan-serpent is crucial to Christian belief, which is why many theologians remain committed to its preservation, even in the face of all rational and scientific evidence to the contrary. Fathers of the church founded cultural sexism by insisting that Eve's disobedience brought death as well as sin into the world. Were it not for her and her temptation of Adam, they said, men could have lived forever. All her female descendants must suffer to pay for this unforgivable crime, which necessitated even the death of Christ. As Tertullian said to Woman, "The sentence of God on this sex of yours lives in this age; the guilt must of necessity live too. You are the devil's gateway. . . . You destroyed so easily God's image, man."[2] The fathers failed to realize how inconsistent it was to impute such casual but irresistible power to the "weaker" sex.

Churches purport to disseminate the knowledge of good and evil, yet still incongruously view Eve as the proto-sinner for having craved this same knowledge. Martin Luther wrote, "God created Adam master and lord of all living creatures, but Eve spoiled all."[3] The hidden implication here, of course, is that Adam was not master and lord of Eve. St. John Chrysostom said, "Among savage beasts none is found so harmful as woman."[4] Tertullian declared woman "the obstacle to purity, the temptress, the enemy . . . the gate of hell." The Shi'ite scripture *Omm-Al-Kitab* similarly affirms that "women are created from the sediment of the sins of demons," and that they have no souls. In 1890, the Reverend Peter Z. Easton concurred with such beliefs, answering in the negative his own rhetorical question "Does Woman Represent God?" by calling her "an incarnate demon . . . a creature of unbounded lust and merciless cruelty."[5] Martin Luther explained away the faster development of female children by saying that "girls begin to talk and stand on their feet sooner than boys because weeds always grow up more quickly than good crops."[6] John Wesley, after damning "The Monstrous Regiment of Women" as the source of all sin, even made such sin responsible for so-called acts of God like storms, floods, and earthquakes.[7] Albert the Great, teacher and mentor of St. Thomas Aquinas, asserted that "woman is a misbegotten man and has a faulty and defective nature . . . one must be on one's guard with every woman, as if she were a poisonous snake and the horned devil. . . . Her feelings drive woman toward every evil, just as reason impels man toward all good."[8] Aquinas was entirely in sympathy with such sentiments. His god gave him to understand that girl children would never be born at all, were it not for the fact that at the time of their conception their fathers were somehow weakened, ill, or in a state of sin.[9]

Actually, the unnamed biblical fruit dispensed by Eve was later interpreted as an apple precisely because it used to represent a blessing, not a curse. It was through apples that the ancient Goddess bestowed Her gift of life on both gods and men, according to numerous mythic traditions. The Eden scene could have been mistakenly deduced from a Canaanite icon showing the Mother of All Living (the Goddess Astarte) presenting Her life-giving apple to a man or a god.[10] The serpent in the Tree of Life commonly represented the Goddess's first consort or totem, a worldwide symbol of immortality based on the snake's periodic skin-shedding rebirths.

The Goddess's apples kept all the gods alive, according to Scandinavian mythology. Without them, the gods would grow old and die. Apples were placed in Scandinavian graves as charms to secure rebirth or godlike immortality.[11] The Greek Great Mother Hera kept the magic-apple-bearing Tree of Life, guarded by Her sacred serpent, in Her magic paradise-garden in the far west, recalling the Bible's derivative description of mortal lands as lying "east of Eden." Similarly, the Celtic paradise for immortal heroes lay in the far west, ruled by the Triple Goddess. It was named Avalon, "Apple-Land."

Just as patriarchs converted the Mother's gift of the life-giving magic apple into a gift of death, so also they turned the primary divine function of woman into a curse. Birth was called a "sorrow" imposed as punishment on women by the biblical god (Gen. 3:16). To carry out God's will by making women suffer was so important to nineteenth-century churchmen that they opposed the use of anesthetics in childbirth; God should not be deprived of women's agonized cries.[12]

The underlying psychological reason for the myth of the curse on women's birth giving was that the life it gave was not, and is not, eternal. Each mortal life carries the seeds of its own death because every living form is self-limiting. Every life in Mother Nature's world comes to an end and by its death nourishes other life. Some men wasted much of their precious life-spans in vehement resentment of their own mortality, which they tended to view as an ultimate evil. It had to be blamed on someone, apart from their purportedly all-good god. Hence the devil, the serpent, Eve, and poor weak-willed Adam.

The myth set up a situation that theology has not yet managed to clarify. Innocent humans stumbled into the temptation that an all-knowing, all-creating, all-good god had somehow arranged for them, while he foresaw the result perfectly well, yet chose to blame them for their inevitable, preordained fall. Clearly, this solution was of little use, because the responsibility for human sin still devolved back upon God, who knew all about it and did nothing to prevent it. Therefore, he couldn't be both all-good and all-powerful.

A parent who deliberately allows a naive child to misbehave, in order to inflict punishment afterward, certainly deserves little respect. It was hard to see how such a father god could deserve respect—let alone worship—from his unjustly manipulated children. Moreover, the implication that human beings could so easily deny God's will made God seem considerably less than omnipotent. Indeed, this god seemed self-contradictory to the point of foolishness, having made himself a world that didn't suit him, and having demanded unconditional obedience (on pain of eternal torture) from people created with the will to disobey. He further contradicted himself by saying the sins of the fathers should not be visited on the children (reversing one of his earlier rulings), yet he held the whole human race responsible for the misdemeanor of one ancestor.

A partial solution for the patriarchs was to invent a devil whose power would be greater than God's, at least some of the time, to oppose God's will whenever evil needed to be explained. "The devil made me do it" has been man's favorite evasion of personal responsibility. Though it was the handiest excuse ever devised, it was severely flawed by having to subordinate the will of an allegedly omnipotent god to the will of his adversary.

On the other hand, if God created the devil and allowed him to work his evil without serious interference, then God must again bear ultimate responsibility for the world's wickedness. Christians implicitly recognized this in a number of doctrinal opinions. Natural disasters that cause widespread suffering are still called acts of God. With or without a devil, the Judeo-Christian deity has never been philosophically absolved of criminal negligence, or deliberate mischief, or helplessness before a human or demonic entity capable of defying or overruling him.

The people called witches, either by themselves or by others, have been frequently accused of devil worship. The accusation was absurd during the Burning Times, when it slaughtered millions of European women, and it is still absurd today, for a very simple reason. Modern witches can hardly be devil worshippers, because they don't believe in a devil. The devil is a Christian concept; therefore, only a Christian can be a devil worshiper. Pagans don't envision a devil at all.

A curious paradox of devil belief arose from the fact that Christian salvation is dependent on it. If there had been no devil to initiate an original sin, then there would have been no fall, no loss of Eden, no hell to be saved from, no need of a savior, and no purpose to the complex edifice of Christian theology. That's why believing Christians can't free themselves from the idea of the devil. Without him, the faith becomes futile. The true Christian trinity must consist of God, Jesus, and Satan.

The vexed problem of fixing blame for evil has given rise to numerous odd examples of theological doublethink. When a bad thing threatens to occur, and is averted, those who prayed to avert it will thank God for having listened to them. When, despite all prayers, the bad thing happens anyway, its victims are commanded to call it God's will and resign themselves to it, without blaming its divine perpetrator. When one's efforts are crowned with success, it is said that "God helps those who help themselves." God is always placed in a win-win situation, but is made truly responsible for nothing.

Thealogically, the problem of evil is summed up by its classic dilemma: God can't be both all-good and all-powerful. If he wants to prevent evil and can't, he lacks power. If he can prevent evil and doesn't, he lacks goodness. Therefore, there must be a devil to play the role of God's dark twin. Otherwise one is led to the inescapable conclusion that God is evil, or partly evil. Another way of putting it is that if God can make everything good and won't, he is not good; and if God wants to make everything good and can't, he is not God. Not even the most tortuous theological casuistry can escape this dead end of either-or thinking.

Thealogically, the problem evaporates in the naturalistic and sensible concept of the Goddess with Her intrinsic dark side, as both creator and destroyer. She ruled all the cycles of life and death, waning and waxing. The Hindu birth-giving virgin mother Maya was also the death-dealing Kali Ma. The Greeks' summertime maiden Kore was also the wintry underground queen of the dead, Persephone, whose name means "Destroyer." Birth-and-death pairs of Goddess images are found everywhere in ancient mythology: Isis-Neith, Inanna-Ereshkigal, Hebe-Hecate, Athene-Medusa, Astarte-Anath, Brigit-Morgan, the Mother Earth who gives birth and takes back the dead flesh, the joyous Flora of spring and the grim Halloween Crone. Just as Christianity's trinity had its origin in much older Goddess images, so also the whole idea of theological dualism may have developed in the first place from ancient priestesses' vision of the turning karmic wheel, the alternations of days and nights, seasonal changes, growth and regression, seedtime and harvest.

With the advent of patriarchal societies, the dark side came to be improbably perceived as somehow avoidable, seeming even darker as it was relegated to masculinized forms of the underground Crone. The formerly neutral realm of the dead began to take on a more frightening hellishness, while the gods of light became the adversaries of the gods of darkness, instead of their natural alter egos in time, as was the case with the Goddesses. Virgin and Crone, two phases of the same entity, evolved into angel and demon, forever in conflict.

Doctrinal dualism reached a peak in the teachings of Zoroaster, whose universe was sharply divided between the forces of light under the god Ahura Mazda, and the forces of darkness under his equally powerful twin brother Ahriman, also known as the Great Serpent, who lived underground with armies of demons. Early Christianity was deeply influenced by Zoroastrianism and its offshoot Mithraism, finding there the original notion of a final battle between the light and dark spirits at the end of the world, and a "Son of Man" who would be sent to save humanity. This Persian religion was one of the earliest fully patriarchal belief systems, and its attitude toward women reflected intense fear and hostility. The Zoroastrian *Vision of Arda Viraf* asserted that those women permitted a place in heaven were women "submissive to control, who had considered their husbands lords." But in hell, women who talked back to their husbands were forced to lick hot stoves with their tongues, while those who had been untrue were hung up by one leg while scorpions and snakes crawled in and out of their bodies, or their breasts were torn by iron combs.[13]

It has been commonly claimed in patriarchal societies that women who live in abject obedience to men will be treated well, both in this life and in the next, whereas women of rebellious spirit will be severely punished. In practice, of course, nothing works quite that way. Abject obedience to a bully only escalates the bullying, as many battered wives have learned to their sorrow. During the medieval period when European women were almost completely enslaved, the all-male church's bullying of them escalated to amazing heights of cruelty, outdoing even our twentieth-century Holocaust in Hitler's Germany.[14]

During the so-called Age of Faith, spiritual leaders of western Europe developed a horror of everything female, blamed the transmission of original sin on women's bodies, and abhorred the natural impulses that draw the sexes to each other. We still carry the legacy of those perverse misapprehensions. Despite the silly claims of modern televangelists that there are real demons in the air all around us, the only real demons we need to exorcise from our world are the man-made demons of violence, greed, intolerance, and ignorance. These are the forces that make it impossible for women and children to live safely in our cities and for different groups of people to understand that they are all brothers and sisters, children of the same Mother Earth.

Just for a moment, imagine a world in which any woman or child might walk alone on any street, back alley, lonely road, woods path, waterfront, or any other place at any hour of the day or night, and encounter a strange man or men without even a momentary sense of threat. That would be a civilized world.

Our "civilization" is actually so savage that we can't easily envision this. Our women and children have to learn that every man must be feared until he is proven innocuous. We've come to a terrible pass when all men must be routinely suspected of criminal, sadistic, or homicidal tendencies. The male violence occurring daily in American cities and towns is encouraged by the violent fantasy world shown in the male-dominated entertainment industry. Television and movies incessantly present women being terrorized, raped, beaten, or murdered by men; and this primary means of acculturization purports to be entertaining.

Patriarchal morality, or lack of morality, is less a theological issue than it is a daily problem of male-dominated society gone astray, threatening its own females and young, and placing every man under suspicion whether he deserves it or not. What the society needs is a way to exorcise hatred, war, cruelty, and the kind of "amusement" that presents senseless brutality as somebody's fun. We need to exorcise the artificial barriers that our religion has set up between male and female, body and spirit, good and evil.

Thealogical perception of the relativity of good and evil does not mean abandonment of moral codes. On the contrary, it requires not less but more sensitivity to the needs and feelings of others. On the ground that whole groups of strangers could not he regarded en masse as evil, war would be unthinkable. As an everyday behavioral guideline, the witches' credo works fairly well: "Do what you will, provided you harm none." It is a simple restatement of the Golden Rule (which originated with Buddha, not Jesus) that might lead to a more civilized world.

If the doctrine of original sin and its transmission through Woman and through the flesh seems absurd, perhaps even more absurd in a scientifically enlightened age is the doctrine of the resurrection of that same sinful flesh. This incongruity is the result of unthinking accretion, two unenlightened views of the physical body having been arbitrarily combined by churchmen who failed to perceive that they contradict each other.

Patriarchal ascetics despised the fleshly body as the source of all sin, lust, filth, and corruption. Christian women especially were taught to think of their bodies as irredeemably unclean, "formed of foul slime" as the Rule for Anchoresses put it.[15] Nevertheless, the corrupt corpus had to be treated with some respect if the church was to profit from funerary rites. Therefore, Christian funerals came to present the paradoxical preservation and presumed imperishability of the despised body, while Christian teaching made the embalming and careful entombment quite unnecessary.

Embalming was a legacy from ancient Egypt, where the doctrine of resurrection of the flesh was taken for granted through thousands of years. Bodily preservation through mummification had become a fine art because the Egyptians believed that, by the magic of the savior Osiris, the dead would rise and walk again in a material afterlife where they would require the same physical comforts and amenities that they enjoyed on earth. The embalmers tried to make sure that the corpse wouldn't decompose, and that all its parts would remain available. Brains and internal organs were carefully packed away in canopic jars. The body was pickled in brine and treated with resins to retard spoilage. After a fashion, it worked. Egyptian mummies managed to resist normal processes of decay for millennia, though Egypt's dry climate may have contributed at least as much as the skills of the ancient embalmers. Still, what survived was not an ideal body in which to be reanimated, unless one expected to star in a horror movie.

Most people today have ceased to believe in the resurrection of the flesh as an article of faith, even when their church commands such a belief. Nevertheless, even when rationale may be lacking, modern corpses are still carefully mummified, deodorized, cosmetized, stuffed, glued, and sewn together with taxidermal cleverness, and rendered relatively immune to decay so they can be displayed to mourners, who dutifully remark how natural they look.

Actually, they don't look natural at all. The natural appearance of a dead body is gray, distorted, shrunken, or bloated; its natural odor is bad, a fact that gave rise to the custom of smothering caskets in banks of flowers to mask the corpse's stench. Through most of the history of Western civilization, undertakers knew much less about preservative methods than the ancient Egyptians, but recent scientific methods work better.

Today, dead bodies can be kept fairly recognizable for many years, as they are not only mummified but also packed away in airtight, watertight, expensive metal containers, wasting Nature's resources on an industry of enormous profitability and astonishing pointlessness. If the time and money spent on preserving the dead were applied instead to assisting and educating the living, the environment might be better served.

Funerary customs continue to imply that the dead are somehow aware of their bodies' disposition, and might feel insulted if they were allowed to rot away as Nature intends. The modern mummification industry is based on implicit assumptions just as profoundly superstitious as those of the Egyptians, as are many related notions such as the legends of vampires, zombies, liches, the efficacy of saints' relics, and the doctrine of the resurrection of the flesh.

Superstition continues to imply that it may be dangerous as well as impolite to betray indifference to the departed. Well-attended funerals are considered significant, as if the corpse requires an appearance of tumultuous popularity, even though the majority of attendees really don't care very much. Formal attentions to the dead still carry the primitive implication that in some undisclosed antechamber of the beyond they are still able to see and hear, even without the organs of seeing and hearing. All is based on the typically patriarchal reluctance to recognize the natural inevitability of death, to believe against all evidence to the contrary that death might be as harmless and survivable as sleep.

For a long time, early Christians claimed that their dead were not dead at all, but only sleeping. They believed the claim of Jesus, that some of his own generation would be still alive when his Second Coming and the world's end occurred (Luke 9:27). Therefore, as that generation died away, it became necessary to assume that they had not really "tasted of death" in order not to contradict the Messiah, who should have known what he was talking about. He didn't know, as it turned out.

The part played by religion may be the most profoundly cynical aspect of the modern mummification industry. For a price, any ecclesiastic will stand over the mortal remains and declare them now happily alive and well and living in heaven—even if the remains in life had no interest in religion and no convictions about heaven. For a price, any ecclesiastic will even relegate a demonstrably evil person to "sure and certain" blessedness, without checking into the corpse's moral qualifications. The gates of heaven are opened to those who can pay. High-ranking mafiosi and some of the world's most brutal tyrants have been accorded some of the world's grandest funerals. Furthermore, outmoded superstitious cant will not provide much real comfort to those who are seriously grieving, and whose feelings should receive more respect than can be found in such traditional twaddle.

Unfortunately, the mummification industry now has a legal stranglehold on society. It has been made unlawful for families to bury their dead privately, or for a dead body to fulfill its natural destiny and decompose as quickly as possible, to feed bacteria and other organisms, to fertilize the soil, to send its elements back to what Lucretius called the eternal drift, and what pagans symbolized as the Goddess's ever-stirring cauldron. Morticians often take advantage of their customers' grief, embarrassment, or fear, by hinting that survivors must be ashamed if they don't buy the most expensive attentions. Some squeeze all the money they can even out of poor families, or sick, lonely, destitute widows, to prettify the dead at the expense of the living. An industry that feeds on human sorrow, gouging profits from people at their most helpless and vulnerable, treats genuine mourners as an exploitable resource.

The doctrine of the resurrection of the flesh is essential to a church that still asserts it on behalf of its savior god and his divine-but-not-divine mother. The ascension of Jesus was supposed to have been quite literal. His body left its tomb and levitated up to heaven. He even came back down to earth and did it again (Luke 24:51). Early churchmen claimed that he came back yet again for the express purpose of visiting his mother's tomb—variously located in Ephesus, Bethlehem, Gethsemane, or Josaphat—to reanimate her corpse and escort her into heaven in her own original body.[16] For two millennia the church fathers debated about whether Mary's "assumption" should be made an article of faith. It was finally made so in the year 1950 by Pope Pius XII. Neither he nor anyone else knew it for sure.

Ancient, crude ideas about the location of heaven, somewhere vaguely up in the sky, produced these improbable visions of material bodies floating upward. Today, with the understanding that "sky" is only a thin shell of atmosphere around our planet, these doctrines become impossible to sustain.

Where is heaven?

It is provable that no material body can ever travel at anything like the speed of light, which can span about six trillion miles in one earth year. This distance is called a light year. All the stars perceptible to the naked eye are within our own galaxy which measures approximately one hundred thousand light years in diameter. Even if Jesus and Mary were miraculously able to move their physical bodies through space at the speed of light, today, after two thousand years, they would have covered only one-fiftieth of the distance across their home galaxy, let alone have approached any of the enormously distant other galaxies in the universe, of which we can detect no end. Where, then, would these divine bodies be going, and how long might it take them to get there?

Indeed, the doctrine of the resurrection of the flesh forces us to wonder where any of our physical bodies might be going. What we now know about the universe makes the whole question meaningless. We can locate neither heaven nor hell.

Resurrection of the flesh was a necessary corollary to the hypothesis of hell as well as that of heaven. If the body couldn't live on, with all its nerves and perceptions intact, how could it properly suffer the promised agonies of hell? And how could the blessed souls in heaven enjoy watching the damned writhing in their eternal pain, as most of the more sadistic Christian authorities claimed they would?[17] Hell was the stick that accompanied heaven's carrot. It was generally assumed that without the fear of hell, no one would bother to become a Christian. Certainly the notion of salvation would be meaningless if there was nothing from which to be saved.

The ancients firmly believed in an underworld populated by the dead, though it was not necessarily a place of torment. They even identified specific entrances to this underworld, located in certain caves or clefts in the earth. Persian mythology provided the underworld with its sulfurous fumes and rivers of fire, doubtless deduced from observation of volcanoes, and made it a place of torment.

The ancients were naturally ignorant of geology. They had no conception of the nature and structure of what lies under the earth's crust. What they knew of caves encouraged them to believe that a whole world of hollow, air-filled spaces might exist below. Christians were no wiser. God's allegedly "infallible" vicars on earth were just as hopelessly misinformed about their planet's deeper layers as they were about the universe surrounding it. Consequently, we have the absurd spectacle of millions of people even today believing that frail human bodies can continue to exist forever in conditions of such pressure that *rocks* are reduced to a red-hot soup; or, alternatively, in conditions of cold near absolute zero, without air, water, means of locomotion, or the force of gravity that caused human bodies to evolve as they have. Neither the underworld nor the overworld shows any sign, to humanity's newly opened eyes, of resembling those crude old-fashioned concepts.

George Smith writes: "Hell stands as a constant reminder of the essence of Christianity: God is to be obeyed because, in the final analysis, he is bigger and stronger than we are; and, in addition, he is incomparably more vicious."[18] Nowadays there are many who would like to remake God in a kinder, gentler image, doing away altogether with what Madalyn Murray O'Hair characterized as the five "insane" ideas of Western civilization: slavery, racism, sexism, violence between individuals and countries, and the idea of "a god that gives punishments and rewards in the afterlife."[19] Attempts to do away with the concept of hell bring additional problems for the liberal theologian, however. "If the liberal denies hell, he must explain why Christianity is important, because there is no longer anything to be 'saved' from. If he admits the existence of eternal torment (which is unlikely), he must reconcile vicious cruelty with what is represented as a religion of love and compassion. Typically, the theologian says as little as possible on this subject—which is incredible when one considers the importance of hell as a historical teaching and a religious concept."[20]

Not only that, but the restructuring of God to a less vindictive model does away with more than the brutalities of hell. "There is no element of good or beauty in [Christianity] unless one is able to see worth in the idea that a father would dictate execution of his child as the only means of softening his own heart. God says to man: I am angry at you, but after I make you torture and kill my only son, I will not only find it in my heart to patch-up a longstanding feud with you but will actually reward you by letting you move in with me forever."[21] Obviously the whole premise is devoid of reason. Christianity's hypotheses about the reasons for Jesus' death, as well as those about the nature and ultimate disposition of anyone's death, cannot be supported except by the most tortuous circular arguments that leave rational thought far behind.

Indeed, rational thought is the last thing that Christianity requires of its adherents. Martin Luther warned that reason is God's worst enemy; "there is on earth among all dangers, no more dangerous thing than a richly endowed and adroit reason . . . for reason must be deluded, blinded, and destroyed." According to Luther, the man of faith must trample all reason underfoot, and "wish to know nothing but the word of God." A modern critic calls it "a fundamental and viciously destructive teaching of Christianity: that some beliefs lie beyond the scope of criticism and that to question them is *sinful*, or morally wrong. By placing a moral restriction on what one is permitted to believe, Christianity declares Itself an enemy of truth . . . Reason becomes a vice, something to be feared."[22]

Despite two thousand years of theological effort, the Judeo-Christian God still fails to alleviate the basic fear of death. Patriarchal writings deny or distort the processes of nature, claiming for example that a male (Adam) can give birth, or that menstrual blood is poisonous, or that all women are inferior to all men, or that the human species, alone among all other living things, might be somehow exempt from death. Our world has been enslaved by notions like these, left over from primitive patriarchy.

The image of the Goddess as Destroyer, Crone, Mother Death, was the most thoroughly suppressed, not only because She was horrifyingly realistic, but also because She represented a doctrine that would have deprived male religious authorities of their power to threaten hell or promise heaven, to manipulate human fears to their own advantage, to wield the theological carrot and stick. It has long been a patriarchal premise that men will not behave themselves unless they are threatened with terrible punishments. It would be sad indeed if that were true.

Tantric worshippers of the great Hindu Crone Goddess Kali Ma had quite a different view of the matter. They saw Her as an ugly, ferocious ghoul as well as a loving Mother and a beautiful mystic Shakti; but they said Her hideous death aspect was most essential to enlightened comprehension of her. The sage's knowledge of his Goddess "is incomplete if he does not know Her as his tearer and devourer."[23] She stood for death viewed head-on, face to face, without evasions or denials: a female force overriding every man's will.

Attitudes toward death present a decisive difference between worshippers of the Goddess and worshippers of male gods. The latter assumed that salvation from death could be achieved if one made the right moves, worshiped the right deity, and preferably made him and his immortality part of one's self by regularly ingesting his sacred flesh and blood. Then one could become transcendent like the transcendent god, removed from the ordinary cycles of germinating, growing, fruiting, decaying, and rotting. Stasis could be achieved, either as perpetual happiness in heaven or perpetual agony in hell.

The last possibility was unattractive, to be sure, and untold millions have been tormented into severe neurosis by contemplating it. Still, clergymen considered it necessary to strike terror into the laity. Punitive fatherhood was carried to a logical conclusion, mightily developed and made graphically explicit throughout a long span of centuries, culminating in the most sadistic fantasies of the afterlife that have ever been envisioned.

By contrast, Goddess worshippers saw humanity in the context of nature, part of the natural cycles of living and dying, like all other creatures. They were embedded in the living world without either the abject fear of special sinfulness or the arrogance of special soulfulness, subject to the same natural laws and seasons of flourishing and decline as every other plant and animal. In Hindu iconography, ugly Kali as Mother Death still teaches nature's lesson of acceptance to those who can understand. She was not understood by Europeans, who labeled Her "destroying demon" or "Goddess of disease."[24]

Though Goddess worshippers were realistic in their acceptance of death, they didn't believe that death should be premature or violent. Rather, each life form should live out its natural span and reproduce its kind. Reaping should take place in the season of harvest, not in the season of sprouting. This philosophy needs to be rediscovered in a world that seems to have forgotten true reverence for life: a world where nonhuman creatures are unthinkingly slaughtered, and men even talk in war rooms about "acceptable" millions of human fatalities.

Any vision of life after death in the father god's heaven remains forever unverifiable, no matter how many struggle to describe it in rivers of words. No two descriptions agree, for the good reason that this afterlife has never been seen anywhere but in the human imagination. Men secretly know this but do not want to admit it. Even those who profess unyielding confidence in a blessed immortality seem to fear death as much as anyone else. Even those who proclaim heaven an eternal, ineffable bliss seem oddly reluctant to make the trip.

Conversely, those who frankly acknowledged the inexorable power of the Crone seemed less afraid and more inclined to enjoy their span of conscious existence, unburdened by the guilty sense of sin. When death was envisioned as a return to the womb of earth, "elements of inner-world mythology continued to wrap themselves around the archaic myth of the Earth Mother. All the talk of gaining the paradise within the earth reduces . . . to the longing to return to the total protection of the womb. . . . In many descriptions of the paradise within the earth, the writers express a strong desire to return there, as if the inner world had been humanity's first home."[25]

Such comforting ideas were certainly denied and obliterated by Christian churches. "The ancient concept of an underworld where one would go after death for rest and rejuvenation became the frightening Christian idea of hell, a place filled with fire and brimstone where one endures eternal pain and agony."[26] The agony was not to be evaded even by innocent babies, or even fetuses, according to the teachings of churchmen, who were perhaps particularly jealous of beings still not quite separated from the real uterine paradise. Their spite was obvious in declarations like that of St. Fulgentius: "Little children who have begun to live in their mother's womb and have there died, or who, having just been born, have passed away from the world without the sacrament of holy baptism . . . must be punished by the eternal torture of undying fire." The Puritan theologian Jonathan Edwards called such children "reprobate infants" and "vipers of vengeance, which Jehovah will hold over hell in the tongs of his wrath."[27]

There can be little doubt that the Christian doctrine of hell was a fantasy built out of hate, especially the hatred of clergymen for anyone suspected of disagreeing with them. Tertullian frankly expected to "laugh and be glad and exult" when he saw "the wise philosophers," who dared to talk about alternative gods, roasting over hell's coals.[28] Pope Innocent III set a durable policy for his church by insisting that "anyone who attempted to construe a personal view of God which conflicted with Church dogma must be burned without pity." The twentieth-century pope Leo XIII, perhaps yearning for a return to the glory days of the Inquisition, agreed with his predecessor: "The death sentence is a necessary and efficacious means for the Church to attain its end when rebels act against it . . . especially obstinate heretics and heresiarchs. . . . it can and must put these wicked men to death."[29]

It is clear that such doctrines effectively undermined any attempt on the part of less vindictive clerics to present their god as a deity of love. As the inimitable Robert Ingersoll said, "Theology makes God a monster, a tyrant, a savage; makes man a servant, a serf, a slave; promises heaven to the obedient, the meek, the frightened, and threatens the self-reliant with the tortures of hell." Voltaire pointed out that "the man who says to men, 'Believe as I do, or God will damn you,' will presently say, 'Believe as I do, or I shall kill you.'" Joseph McCabe expressed a similar opinion: "Any body of men who believe in hell will persecute whenever they have the power."[30] The Bible commands that any disbeliever in Yahweh must be killed (Deut. 13:8–9).

Founding fathers of the United States of America insisted on rigid separation of church and state for good reasons. They rejected the god of old Europe, knowing all too well his history of persecution and violence. Thomas Jefferson wrote: "The Christian God is a being of terrific character—cruel, vindictive, capricious, and unjust. . . . We discover [in the Gospels] a groundwork of vulgar ignorance, of things impossible, of superstition, fanaticism and fabrication. . . . In every country and in every age the priest has been hostile to liberty; he is always in allegiance with the despot, abetting his abuses in return for the protection of his own. . . . On the dogmas of religion, as distinguished from moral principles, all mankind, from the beginning of the world to this day, have been quarreling, fighting, burning and torturing one another, for abstractions unintelligible to themselves and to all others, and absolutely beyond the comprehension of the human mind."[31] In direct contradiction of modern fundamentalists who claim that the United States was established on "Christian" principles, George Washington himself wrote in 1796, "The government of the United States is not, in any sense, founded on the Christian religion."[32]

The founding fathers knew all too well how evil a politically dominant religion can be, how readily it can strangle individual liberty and freedom of thought, how harshly it can punish, and how unjustly it can condemn. They wanted their new nation to tolerate divergent opinions, rather than hunt down heretics as the Old World had done. They were still just as sexist as their forefathers, but they took the first steps toward rejection of the Judeo-Christian doctrines that lay at the roots of sexism. They were critical of patriarchal religion's greatest doctrinal mistake, namely its tendency to insult human reason by demanding literal belief in unbelievable things.

This mistake had maintained Western civilization at a childlike level of credulity for centuries, and also necessitated increasingly absurd denials of demonstrable scientific truths as the Age of Enlightenment gathered momentum. Church authorities were beginning to pour forth rivers of hypocrisy in attempts to maintain their status as repositories of ultimate truth.

Any religion that insists on belief in a factual basis for its most improbable doctrines is decayed at its core. Inner insecurity is the real reason behind the extreme hostility of fundamentalists toward liberals, frank nonbelievers, and objective scholarship. They think their own secret doubts (perceived as sins) can be absolved by attacking all other doubters. Their impossible goal is to clear the world of all people whose opinions differ from their own, so there can be no hint of disagreement anywhere to threaten their faith.

Many believers dare not subject their beliefs to rational discussion. They are enraged by the mere existence of rational, grown-up people who find their doctrines silly or pointless. If one's peace of mind depends on maintaining an irrational belief, then any questioning of that belief is perceived as a threat. That is why atheism, literally "absence of god," is seen by the theist as an ultimate threat, to be subjected to merciless attack even when no provocation has been offered.

Nevertheless, it becomes ever clearer today that traditional religious doctrines can and should be questioned, especially where they have led to oppression, injustice, and sexism. The nineteenth-century pope Gregory XVI wrote: "It is in no way lawful to demand, to defend, or to grant unconditional freedom of thought, or speech, of writing, or of religion, as if they were so many rights that nature has given to man."[33] Of course, the United States was founded on the theory that these freedoms are indeed lawful, even mandatory, for an enlightened, progressive nation; and the writers of the Bill of Rights said so quite openly. Judeo-Christian tradition stands in opposition to what Thomas Paine's classic treatise designated *The Rights of Man*. The Bible accepts and even endorses slavery (Lev. 25:44–46; Eph. 6:5; Tim. 6:1; Titus 2:9–10, and so forth), puts down women and orders their subjection to men (1 Pet. 3:1; 1 Tim. 2:11–12), and, in the Old Testament, again and again directs that all people of divergent faiths, men, women, and children, must be slaughtered. This is hardly an adequate foundation for an enlightened spirituality.

The "Syllabus of Errors" issued by Pope Pius IX (1864) insisted that the church has the right to perpetuate the union of church and state, to require that the Catholic religion be the only one allowed, to prevent free expression of opinion, and to prevent the state from granting freedom of religion.[34] Thus Catholicism, at least in its nineteenth-century guise, seems adamantly opposed to American freedoms; and since the Catholic Church claims infallibility and perpetuity for papal pronouncements, one would assume that it would not readily reverse itself.

American thinkers, therefore, have included many who confessed to active dislike of religious doctrines. Ralph Waldo Emerson said, "As men's prayers are a disease of the will, so are their creeds a disease of the intellect." Robert Ingersoll said, "It seems almost impossible for religious people to really grasp the ideas of intellectual freedom. They seem to think that unbelief is a crime; that investigation is sinful; that credulity is a virtue, and that reason is a dangerous guide. They cannot divest themselves of the idea that in the realm of thought there must be government . . . rewards and punishments, and that somewhere in the universe there is a penitentiary for the soul."[35]

Certainly religious doctrines that demand the sleep of reason are not likely to help solve the many severe problems facing people in the modern world. Neither are religious doctrines based on lies, plagiarism, or tampering with texts. The people who claim their religion is Bible-based seem to have little notion of how baseless their Bible is. New Testament manuscripts that theologians call original are nothing of the sort; they are copies of copies, no two alike, about fifteen hundred of them with more than eighty thousand variations. More than 150,000 contradictions and discrepancies are found in them. A modern scholar says, "The Christian community really continues to exist because the conclusions of critical examinations of the Bible are largely unknown to it." And the secret revisions, omissions, and updatings go on with every new translation. In 1893 Pope Leo XIII said in an encyclical that "although there can be no error of any sort in the sacred books, it was important to adjust scriptural statements to scientific facts."[36] If there were no errors, why were adjustments necessary? Fundamentalists also ignore the apocryphal scriptures that were arbitrarily omitted from the canon although many of them were equally revered in past times. The Gnostic gospels mention female disciples as well as male disciples of Jesus; it has been suggested that there were twelve women corresponding to the twelve men. Certainly women figured more prominently in early Christianity than is now admitted. Two learned ladies, Paula and Eustochia, collaborated with St. Jerome in writing the Vulgate Bible; but later scholars erased their names and wrote instead "venerable brothers."[37]

Joseph Campbell writes: "It is never difficult to demonstrate that as science and history mythology is absurd. When a civilization begins to reinterpret its mythology in this way, the life goes out of it.

. . . Such a blight has certainly descended on the Bible and on a great part of the Christian cult."[38] It is generally understood by thinking people that laws are not divinely ordained, and that clergymen can't claim total authority for anything, least of all the self-contradictions and unscientific mistakes in the Bible. Campbell also comments: "Is it not ironic that our great Western civilization, which has opened to the minds of all mankind the infinite wonders of a universe of untold billions of galaxies and untold billions of years, should have been saddled in its infancy with a religion squeezed into the tightest little cosmological image known to any people on earth?"[39]

Not only the cosmology, but also the daily practice of Christianity has been squeezed into a doctrine of the crudest naivete: the doctrine of transubstantiation, whereby congregations were taught that their eucharistic bread and wine was not bread and wine at all, but the actual flesh and blood of Christ. It was theologically affirmed that the cannibalistic rite was real, not symbolic. It is still so affirmed. "Contemporary Christian thinkers who have sought to interpret the Eucharist as a symbolic event have been rebuked *ex cathedra* by the Pope." The 1965 encyclical *Mysterium Fidei* insisted on "the marvelous change of the whole of the bread's substance into Christ's body and the whole of the wine's substance into his blood."[40]

Such insistence on literal cannibalism was the central premise of the Christian cult from its inception, when it copied its Holy Communion from other popular mystery religions of the Roman empire, notably those of Osiris, Dionysus, Adonis, Orpheus, and Mithra. Such saviors were eaten by their worshippers, sometimes in the form of a sacrificial animal whose blood would carry away their sins, but more often in the less expensive form of bread and wine. The basic theory was one of sympathetic magic: to share in the god's immortality, the worshipper had to make the god's body part of his own body. Thus human flesh could be transformed into divine flesh. A follower of Osiris, for instance, believed that he would become "an Osiris" by eating the holy bread, made of special wheat that sprouted on the god's sarcophagi. Then he would be recognized as Osiris by all the beings of the afterworld, and would be freely admitted to the blessed realms.[41] Similarly, Dionysus's wine-blood gave immortality, and so on throughout all the communion rituals of savior gods in general. To be killed and eaten was the fate of sacred kings, impersonating their gods, from the earliest cultures in which men began to try copying the life-giving blood-magic of women by shedding male blood in solemn sacrifice.

"The idea of consuming the human body is often viewed as the most profane act imaginable. Consequently, all over the world, the fear of such a possibility is commonly used to express the most basic form of malevolence. However, by the paradox which is religion, in the sense that it often demands a suspension of everyday reasoning and standards, the very same notion of eating human flesh and blood is transformed into the most sacred of all acts." Having adopted this sacred act and made it central to Catholic worship, church authorities nevertheless inconsistently condemned the same ceremony performed by others. Sahagun thought it shocking that converted Mexican Indians continued to observe in secret their "great heresy and abominable sin," which consisted of "creation by the Aztec priests of dough images of their god which were distributed and eaten."[42]

Cannibalistic communion is not really such a paradox, when we consider its original crude rationale: to join the god in his immortality, one must make him part of oneself. The idea was so commonly accepted in antiquity that Christians saw no reason to question it; nor did they ever question it since. The Virgin Mary was assimilated to the role of the Goddess, which was also vital to the performance of the sacred drama. "It is the function of the male god of fertility to die for the land and for his people, while the Goddess never dies. Her function is to weep over him, perhaps to help bring about his return, or to give birth to the divine child who is to take his place. The world first weeps with her and then rejoices at the renewed promise."[43] When it was keyed to the seasons, the sacred drama was performed in the same way each year. It is still performed, in essence, at Christmas and Easter, but its deep, primitive connections with the year's cycles have been severed. The god was born of the Goddess, or Her virgin surrogate, at the winter solstice with the rebirth of the sun. The god was slain at the spring equinox so that his body and blood would fertilize all creation in the season of planting. The modern name of this festival, Easter, is one of the old Saxon names for the Goddess Herself, Eostre.[44]

In India, the communion wine was viewed as Tara, the Earth Goddess Herself, in liquid form. According to the Mahanirvana Tantra, She was "Mother of enjoyment and liberation," and in the guise of Her holy liquid, She "burns up the heaps of sins, and purifies the world."[45] Christian missionaries were naturally inclined to perceive Her as a demon, as they perceived everything female, divine, and not of their faith.

It is the nature of religious concepts to slide rather easily between the holy and the forbidden. The word *taboo* means both "sacred" and "unclean," in the sense that anything supernatural is likely to be dangerous. Cannibalism took on this aura of taboo in Judeo-Christian culture, quite possibly because the eating of human flesh was presented as a sacrament, to be undertaken with "holy dread," only under ceremonial conditions. The ancient Hebrews had much the same attitude toward the eating of pig's flesh, because the pig was formerly a sacred animal eaten only for special occasions; in Egypt, the savior Osiris was himself incarnated in the pig. Swine were commonly sacrificed in the cults of Adonis and Astarte, as well as in the Eleusinian Mysteries.[46]

However irrational it may be, the Jewish taboo on swine's flesh is still extant, and so is the Christian taboo on cannibalism. Christians have always been willing to kill their fellow humans, sometimes in very large numbers, in wars, crusades, holocausts, witch-hunts, and the like. "From Sweden to Italy, from the Danube to Massachusetts, the church murdered more people in the name of Christian orthodoxy than any tyrant, or indeed any succession of tyrants has ever done in the name of Empire."[47] The taboo applied to eating, not killing. Yet surely, to torture or murder living, feeling bodies is a much greater crime than using them for food once they are dead.

Of course, the doctrine of transubstantiation contradicts the other doctrine of the resurrection of the flesh. If Jesus's body went whole into heaven, every atom intact, how were so many tons of his flesh recreated to serve eucharistic needs throughout the centuries?

It would be difficult, if not impossible, to list even half of the absurdities that have passed as doctrines and articles of faith under Christian auspices. For example, St. Ambrose declared that daylight and sunlight are completely different, from separate sources. Pope Paul V "infallibly" asserted that the earth does not spin on its axis, and does not orbit the sun, because this is "entirely contrary to Holy Scripture." Martin Luther pontificated: "We know, on the authority of Moses, that longer ago than six thousand years the world did not exist."[48] He also insisted that children born handicapped are obviously soulless demons and should be drowned. Many theologians maintained that the deaf and mute are automatically damned, because they are without the faith that can only come through hearing. Yet a pastor of Hamburg thundered against "the irreligious arrogance of wanting to get the deaf and dumb to speak."[49]

As the Protestant churches drew away from Catholic doctrines during and after the Reformation, each developed its own set of doctrines and denounced the others as false and deluded.[50] Their sectarian battles betrayed a curiously mistrustful underestimation of their own god, for they credited their rivals with the power to rob him of his glory in one way or another. The English Parliament of 1653 forbade any publications that might deviate from standard Anglican doctrines "to the great dishonor of God," as if his honor were extremely fragile. To say that Jesus was not God was a capital felony in seventeenth-century England. It was claimed also that the Quakers were "deposing the majesty of God himself" and "ungodding God."[51] To those who made such claims, God must have seemed very feeble and vulnerable.

The majority of modern churchgoers don't know the doctrines of their sect. Exactly what beliefs their attendance supports, and how they differ from the beliefs professed by other denominations, remain matters of indifference—and clergymen would just as soon keep it that way. Too much intellectual probing might reveal too many holes in the doctrines, and perhaps in the mental powers of the clergymen themselves. Reverend Kirsopp Lake wrote that the modern clergyman "is apt to have a lower standard of intellectual honesty than would be tolerated in any other profession."[52] Like politicians, clergymen dare not say what they really think, but instead must say only what they believe their audience wants to hear.

So the Western world has been saddled with centuries-old doctrines that few people genuinely believe, but are alleged to be so sacred that they are beyond challenge. Yet the scientific method should have taught us, by now, that the only way to find out the truth is to challenge the hypothesis, to see if it can stand up to criticism. Science discovers the truth because it is willing to be objective and to abandon any theory not supported by the evidence. Religion does the opposite: It invents evidence to prop up the untenable theory.

Catholicism long affected the power of God himself, omniscience, by its doctrine of papal infallibility, claiming that the pope was never wrong because God would never allow him to make a false statement. During the Age of Enlightenment, when God allowed the pope to state that the earth is flat and does not orbit the sun, and other similarly egregious mistakes, the doctrine was revised to say that the pope is infallible only when speaking *ex cathedra* on matters of faith and morals. At such times he is "possessed of that infallibility with which the divine Redeemer willed that His Church should be endowed for defining doctrine regarding faith or morals."[53] But the scriptures, on which all such doctrtries are supposed to rest, say not one word about this. One may safely assume that it was not the divine Redeemer who willed anything of the sort, but rather worldly men who took upon themselves the divine right to tell other people what to do, and have profited by it ever since. Despite the fact that Jesus never mentioned any such thing as infallibility, these worldly men still presume to control women's bodies, dictating what women shall or shall not do with their own sacred capacity of motherhood—which, by natural law, belongs to each female, and no male has the right to interfere with it. Nonhuman males recognize female autonomy when it comes to sex and motherhood. It is only the human males, political animals to the core, who do not.

Because Judeo-Christian "morality" is still tied up with dogmas that will not bear examination, its ethical teachings are weakened.[54]

There is an enormous hubris connected with religion's assumption that all the universe—or at least, all the planet—is organized around the existence of human beings. Richard Leakey points out that the average life-span for vertebrate species is about two million years, and six thousand primate species have lived since the time of the dinosaurs; only 183 of those species still exist. We happen to be one of them. "*Homo sapiens* was one of a range of possibilities in the evolution of the hominid group, not an inevitable product of that process. . . . Because we find it impossible . . . to imagine a time when we will no longer exist, we naturally equate the future of *Homo sapiens* with the future of the planet. But . . . we are not stewards of the Earth, forever and a day. We are merely short-term tenants, and pretty unruly and destructive ones at that."[55]

When gods were invented, no one knew the true extent of the universe. Indeed, no one knows it yet, for we can find no limits to the space in which galaxies seem to be scattered. But a humanoid god seems exceptionally trivial in the light of present knowledge. As Etta Semple said, "Why not study Nature, and cease to worship a myth which ignorance and superstition have placed behind it?" Susan B. Anthony declared, "I know there is no God of the universe made happy by my getting down on my knees and calling him 'great.'" Matilda Joslyn Gage remarked that "Possessing no proof of God's existence, the church has ever fostered unintelligent belief.' " It is all very well to say that faith does not require proof; but to believe the patently absurd In the face of overwhelming proof against it is not so much faith as folly. "Beliefs must be consistent with each other and not obviously in conflict with fact."[56] Judeo-Christian doctrines do not meet this standard. Many women are now, understandably, seeking a new definition of religion and a new way of looking at human existence.

MODERN WOMEN TALK ABOUT DOCTRINES

Theorists have argued forever about the relationship between religion and morality without reaching any real conclusion. Does religious faith create morality, or is the religion itself created by a prevailing ethic? Studies have shown that incarcerated criminals profess proportionately more religious faith than the public at large, which seems to argue against those who claim that only the "fear of God" can make a person behave decently toward others. Atheists, on the other hand, tend to be law-abiding, tax-paying, responsible citizens, not inclined to criminal behavior. Certainly Judeo-Christian patriarchy has been the most violent culture to appear in its two thousand years of history. What religious doctrines say, and what their adherents practice, seem to have little correlation. However, doctrines seem to be necessary, and the Goddess movement therefore considers how they may be evolved.

🐾   🐾   🐾

On a logical basis, I don't believe in life after death. We tend to believe in it when a person dies who has affected us strongly. People we cared about live on in our thoughts and actions. That has a tremendous influence. But belief in life after death is really unimportant. It's what you're doing right now that counts.

To me, afterlife doesn't make any sense. There's a continuation, in the sense that when the body decays, it becomes part of the earth, the plants, and the animals that live on the plants. Molecules continue. That's the only life after death that makes sense.

🐾   🐾   🐾

Many times I've gone into churches, just to sit and meditate and be—certainly not to get in touch with any god, but just to be with myself. There's a comfort in beautiful surroundings.

As an atheist, I don't believe in a god. But I don't turn away from people who do believe. I've had people putting me down for being an atheist. One woman told me how sorry she was for me, how much I was missing in my life. I didn't need her pity or her putdown of my belief system. If your belief system works for you, then why not follow it? So I don't put down others' belief systems even when I think they're potentially dangerous. I accept their choices. Judging other people only detracts from me. I have a lot of trouble with all groups that try to tell other groups what to do. I don't want to be a part of that.

For a large part of my life, it was important for me to be right. But it's not even an issue now. If I can connect with people at a level that's comfortable for me, and their belief system doesn't intrude on mine, then I can be comfortable with them. I avoid people who won't let me be part of their world unless I buy into their beliefs. I choose people who let me do what I do. If we happen to overlap and share some experiences, so much the richer.

Often, people want to believe misinformation even when they're offered real information. Most belief systems are myths, and most people find it easier to stay with the familiar myths, erroneous though they may be. Truth used to be very important to me, and I was shocked when I found out that other people didn't need to *know*. Many people even deny demonstrable truth. When you give them a fact, they'll say somebody made that up, it's all phony. Yet they'll believe the most incredible stuff.

I don't think many people even are able to separate what's comfortable in their lives from what's uncomfortable. They just live, without tuning into what doesn't feel good or make sense. They play the role of victim and don't realize it.

🐾 🐾 🐾

The moral values that I have seen enacted in Goddess worship, if generally held, would produce significant changes in the patterns of society as we know it. For one thing, responsibility would not be hierarchical. There is presently no dogma, no set of things that Goddess worshippers must believe or do. I am struck by the resemblance (except for ecological issues) of Goddess values to some of Christ's preaching; but what Christ had to say and what the Christian Church has done with it are shamefully different. Goddess knowledge is about doing. And the Goddess never crucified Her only child to make a point. Nor am I aware that any war was ever begun in Her name, not that She was ever an excuse to persecute others. The Goddess has many children, and we are all they.

&&&

The doctrines never made any sense to me. The virgin birth, the body-and-blood thing, the Second Coming, the one-way trips to heaven or hell, all that hoo-ha. It's so childish. I mean, we're grown up now, it's time to stop looking for Santa Claus.

It would be just silly if it weren't so serious, when you consider that millions of people have killed and millions more have died over nonsense like these doctrines. Who could possibly care that much about what brand of garbage somebody else chooses to believe? Even it it's not your own brand of garbage, they have a right to think whatever they want, as long as it doesn't contradict provable facts.

We ought to chuck all the doctrines and concentrate on improving our own world and the lot of all the people in it, and all other creatures too. It makes me furious to see the churches raking in all that tax-free money, and only a tiny trickle of it ever goes out to help somebody. Religion causes so much misery. Even those who have religion and say that belief in their doctrines makes them happy—very often, underneath, they're miserable. Why else would they be so mean to others? It makes them crazy, this sustained effort to take old fantasies and fairy tales literally and confuse them with historical reality.

&&&

I don't believe in God or Goddess as people but as powers. The Goddess is a feminine, nurturing power; she is Love. Christianity is fire and brimstone and wars and crusades. The feminine power is nurture, life—the other side of the balance, that's been so long lost. We need the nurturing rather than the controlling power.

8

THE GODDESS IMAGE

*U*NLIKE THE GOD, WHO WAS devised only in a late period after men
came to understand their part in reproduction, the Goddess
was there from the beginning: birth giver to the universe; source of
women's maternal magic; maker of sun, moon, and stars; and death
bringer, also, in a world where every form of life is temporary and
fated to cycle into other lives. Human religions began with the Goddess because human emotional attachments begin with Mother.

> We human beings are helpless, utterly dependent creatures for
> years and years. Because of this there develops in us a deep psy-
> chological need for an all-protecting [Parent] or, depending on
> what culture we are in, some other cosmic assurances. It is nat-
> ural enough for human beings to thirst for such security, but there
> is not the slightest reason to think that there is such security. That
> we have feelings of dependence does not mean that there is
> something on which we can depend.[1]

Such qualities as hairlessness, lifelong learning capacity, and
ubiquitous ideas of deity in all human cultures indicate that the
description of a human being as an infantilized ape is essentially

correct. Psychological as well as physical dependence on a larger entity is characteristic of the infant; and psychological dependence may persist throughout life even though physical dependence is outgrown. In nature, that larger entity is a mother. Though later human cultures became patriarchal and changed it to a father, the replacement was never truly adequate.

> As all schools of psychology agree, the image of the mother and the female affects the psyche differently from that of the father and the male. Sentiments of identity are associated most immediately with the mother; those of dissociation, with the father. Hence, where the mother image preponderates, even the dualism of life and death dissolve in the rapture of her solace, the worlds of nature and the spirit are not separated; the plastic arts flourish eloquently of themselves, without need of discursive elucidation, allegory, or moral tag; and there prevails an implicit confidence in the spontaneity of nature.[2]

Campbell says that in every patriarchal mythology "there inheres an essential duplicity, the consequences of which cannot be disregarded or suppressed. Mother Nature, Mother Eve, Mother Mistress-of-the-World is there to be dealt with all the time, and the more sternly she is cut down, the more frightening will her Gorgoneum be."[3] Certainly the death-dealing Crone forms of the Goddess frightened men to the point where they denied Her altogether; yet their jealous, punitive, irritable, warmongering, lightning-hurling, hell-creating father gods surely were no better. To substitute a patriarchal image of destructiveness for a similar image drawn from the natural processes of life and death is not an advance but rather a retreat into nightmarish fantasy.

The ancients addressed their Goddess images with a reverence entirely equal to, if not stronger than, that expressed by god worshippers. The great Crone Goddess Kali Ma was told by Indian scriptures that: "Thou art the Original of all the manifestations; Thou art the birthplace of even the gods; Thou knowest the whole world, yet none know Thee. Thou art both Subtle and Gross, Manifested and Veiled, Formless, yet with form. Who can understand Thee? . . . Thou art the Supreme Primordial Kalika. . . . Resuming after dissolution Thine own form, dark and formless, Thou alone remainest as One ineffable and inconceivable . . . though Thyself without a beginning, multiform by the power of Maya, Thou art the beginning of all, Creatrix, Protectress, and Destructress."[4]

In the original matrilineal social organizations, "Headmen, who made up the council or assembly of elders of a tribe, served as the governing body for a Divine Woman or Queen, who personified the Great Mother and presided over a matrilineal society. The early king of such cultures ruled, not in his own right, but in his capacity as consort of the Divine Woman." Rome's legendary founder-king Numa was said to have been the consort of the Goddess Egeria, by whom he acquired his "blessedness" and "divine wisdom," as well as the rules and rituals of religion in general. In China, the Mother of All Things gave the original laws to the god of heaven, who passed them on to earthly rulers and humanity.[5]

Kings of the ancient Middle East attributed their right to rule to their official marriage to the Goddess. The Sumerian king Shulgi declared that his spouse was Inanna, "the queen, the vulva of heaven and earth." Kings' wedding hymns carefully described the physical union of Goddess and consort: "Oh my queen, queen of the universe, the queen who encompasses the universe, may he enjoy long days at Your holy lap. The king goes with lifted head [i.e, phallus] to the holy lap, he goes with lifted head to the holy lap of Inanna."[6] All of ancient Mesopotamia revered the Goddess under the name of Mammetum, "maker of fate, She who decrees the fate of the men and gods." In Canaan, She was called Lady Asherah, Progenitress of the Gods, whose sacred groves were so often attacked by Old Testament fanatics. Under the name of Ishtar, She was fulsomely praised in Akkadian hymns:

> Praise Ishtar, the most awesome of the goddesses, revere the queen of women, the greatest of the deities. She is clothed with pleasure and love. She is laden with vitality, charm, and voluptuousness. In lips She is sweet; life is in Her mouth. At Her

appearance rejoicing becomes full. She is glorious. . . . The fate of everything She holds in Her hand. At Her glance there is created joy, power, magnificence, the protecting deity and guardian spirit . . . Ishtar—to Her greatness who can be equal? Strong, exalted, splendid are Her decrees. . . . Ishtar among the gods, extraordinary is Her station. Respected is Her word; it is supreme over them. She is their queen; they continually cause Her commands. to be executed. All of them bow down before Her.[7]

In the Greco-Roman world, the Mother of the Gods had an assortment of names and attributes evolved from combination and syncretization of early tribal religions. She is familiar under such designations as Rhea, Demeter, Aphrodite, Hera, Juno, Venus, Ops, Themis, Ceres, Minerva, Diana, and many other titles derived from classical revisionist mythology. During the early centuries of the Christian era, She was fervently worshiped in Rome as the *Magna Mater* ("Great Mother") called the "August One" (*Augusta*), the "Nourishing One" (*Alma Mater*), and the "Most Holy One" (*Sanctissima*). Phrygian Cybele identified with Celestial Venus, Juno, and Minerva. The emperor Augustus regarded Her as the national Goddess and his wife Livia as Her embodiment on earth. The emperor Julian wrote reverent hymns to Her:

Who is, then the Mother of the Gods? She is the source of the intellectual and creative gods, who in their turn guide the visible gods; She is both the mother and the spouse of mighty Zeus; She came into being next to and together with the great creator; She is in control of every form of life,. and the cause of all generation; She easily brings to perfection all things that are; She is . . . in very truth the Mother of all the Gods.[8]

Our Christmas tree was derived in part from the worship of this Goddess, whose temples featured sacred pine groves called *pinea silva*. At the festival of the Goddess and Her consort, Attis, priests called "tree-bearers" (*dendrophori*) would cut one of the pine trees, decorate it with ribbons, and solemnly bear it into the temple where it was set up as a holy image. The high priestess presiding over these rites was Sacerdos Maxima, assisted by other priestesses known as *ministrae* ("ministers").[9] Tree worship was common also in northern Europe, where Germanic tribes venerated the Goddess in conjunction with sacred groves, and suspended all warfare and hostility during Her festival times, every individual maintaining the Peace of the Goddess no matter what the provocation.[10]

The Round Table, representing the zodiac, was another popular image of the Goddess and Her influences in antiquity. According to Petronius, the temple and altar of the Great Mother symbolized all of reality: "Mother Earth lies in the world's midst rounded like an Egg and all blessings are there inside Her as in a honeycomb." Wall paintings surrounded her with other Goddess images: "Fortuna stood by with Her flowing horn of plenty and the Three Fates spinning Their golden thread." Doorposts were painted with "the Moon in Her courses and the likenesses of the seven stars." Such imagery descended later to representations of the Virgin Mary. According to Plutarch, the Round Table stood for Mother Earth because "besides feeding us it is round in shape, it is fixed, and very suitably it has been given by some the name of Hestia"; that is, Hestia-Vesta as the central hearth and heart of the world. Anaximenes likened the whole earth to a table, and the emperor Justinian possessed a Sacred Table made of all known metals, stones, and woods, representing everything produced by Mother Earth.[11]

Hundreds, even thousands, of Goddess images became absorbed by Christian syncretism in the early Dark Ages, even while Christian authorities were anathematizing the Goddess and all Her consorts as several varieties of devils. The great temple of the Virgin Goddess Athena, the Parthenon ("Virgin-House"), was rededicated to the Virgin Mary at some point in the late fifth century. The church of Panaghia Blaslike ("Virgin of Fecundity") was based an the old shrine of Aphrodite Ilithila, "Mother of Fecundity." Ilithiya Eleutho, the Goddess as "Liberator" of the child from the womb, invoked by women in childbirth, was masculinized as a mythical St. Eleutherius; but under the name of St. Venere, Venus as the marriage Goddess is still invoked by Albanian girls preparing for weddings.

Peasants at the old shrine of Eleusis continued to crown the ancient statue of Demeter with garlands "in the hope of good harvests," all the way up to the nineteenth century, when the statue was finally removed to a British museum.[12]

Christian Gnostic literature retained surprisingly frank references to the Goddess and several of Her traditional symbols, such as the serpent. Gnostic versions of the creation myth combined the Teacher, the Serpent, and Eve, or Hawwah, the Aramaic rendering of Her name. She was called Hawah, Mother of All Living; and *hewya*, "serpent," derived from *hawa*, "to instruct." She existed before Adam, and called upon him to "arise" into life. "And when he saw Her, he said, 'It is You who have given me life; You shall be called Mother of the living—for it is She who is my mother.' It is She who is the Physician, and the Woman, and She Who Has Given Birth. Then the Female Spiritual Principle came in [the form of] the Snake, the Instructor, and it taught them, saying, You shall not die. . . . Rather, your eyes shall open, and you shall become like gods, recognizing evil and good."[13]

On the Origin of the World, another Gnostic gospel, named the Goddess Sophia, or "Wisdom," and Eve Zoe, or "Life." Eve Zoe commanded, "Adam, live! Rise up upon the earth!" This text echoed the traditional command of Isis who brought the dead Osiris back by saying, "Osiris, live! Stand up thou unfortunate one."[14] The Gnostics maintained that God was able to create a world only because his Great Mother Sophia gave him the idea, "infused him with energy," and instructed him out of Her own knowledge. Later, out of hubris, he imagined himself to be the sole creator. "He was even ignorant of his own Mother. . . . It was because he was foolish and ignorant of his Mother that he said, 'I am God; I there is none beside me.'"[15] He was so full of his own importance that "he boasted continually, saying to the angels, 'I am God, and no other one exists except me.'" His Mother saw that he was impious and condemned him for his conceit. She told him, "You err, blind god. An enlightened, immortal humanity exists before you."[16]

Among Jewish Gnostics, this Great Mother Sophia became Hokmah, "Wisdom," described as God's cocreator in Proverbs 8. The *Wisdom of Solomon* explained:

Her bright shining is never laid to sleep. But with Her there came to me all good things together. . . . And I rejoiced over them all because [Hokmah] leadeth them. . . . She that is the artificer of all things . . . there is in Her a spirit quick of understanding, holy, alone in kind, manifold, subtle, freely moving . . . all-powerful, all-surveying, and penetrating through all spirits. Yea, She pervadeth and penetrateth all things. . . . And She, though but one, hath power to do all things; and remaining in Herself, reneweth all things. . . . For She is fairer than the sun, and above all the constellations of the stars; being compared with light, She is found to be before it. . . . She reacheth out from one end of the world to the other with full strength, and ordereth all things well.[17]

One of the Hebrew names for the Goddess was Shekina, whose splendor "feeds the angels." It was written that "Her radiance is so great that even angels must cover their faces before Her. Her body measures millions of miles." A third-century Galilean rabbi repeated the Gnostic claim that She had to admonish God for being too self-important and vengeful. To the people, She was "a great heavenly reality whose shining countenance shoved the theoretical doctrine of the Oneness of God into the background."[18] She was identified with each of the Old Testament matriarchs as "power sources" for their consorts, and with Lilith who was originally the lily-symbol of the Sumero-Babylonian creatress, and, according to some texts, an archaic wife of God.[19]

"Every one of the secret texts which gnostic groups revered was omitted from the canonical collection, and branded as heretical by those who called themselves orthodox Christians. By the time the process of sorting the various writings ended virtually all the feminine imagery for God had disappeared from orthodox Christian tradition."[20] Nevertheless, her multifarious images persisted, not only in the complex iconography of Mary, but also in their own pre-Christian forms. The Saxon Goddess Wyrd, or "Fate" (origin of Shakespeare's trinitarian Weird Sisters) was presented in Old English writings as holding superior power over God; the Gnomic Poems said, "The glories of Christ are great; Wyrd is strongest of all."[21]

Numerous surviving inner-world myths demonstrate that "the image of the all-protecting, all-nurturing Earth Mother, shoved underground (as it were) by a patriarchal, urban, achieving culture, insists on appearing wherever feeling and intuition are allowed to dominate. It appears to be the time, in fact, for the Earth Mother to return to the stage of human culture. The growth of feminism has brought with it the return of Goddess worship alongside the mono-theism of Christianity, Judaism, and Islam."[22] In addition, native peoples insist on clinging to their Goddess even in the Christianized twentieth century, as a Hawaiian writer says: "My mother and grandmother raised me in the Pele religion. . . . We would go to the volcano and to places in the forest to pray, and people still do that. We hear people say the old religion is gone but it isn't. . . . Pele is all the land. She's the volcano and everything that grows there is Her. The steam and the vapor and lava are all parts of Her body, and Her family is all the forest plants and the life of the sea. . . . The whole island of Hawaii has been made by Her lava. You can't drill geothermal anywhere and not violate Her sacred body."[23]

To sum up:

> That societies in the past have arranged themselves on the prin-ciple that woman is the superior sex, we know well: in fact, it seems likely that until men found out their power of fertilization, woman was always regarded as superior. . . . About the eastern shores of the Mediterranean there had lived peoples who from the mists of antiquity were accustomed to look to women for the shaping of their society: here, the social order was based on the principles of the wife's being permitted more than one husband, and succession in authority and property passing from mother to daughter. It is a natural state of affairs arising from a primitive ignorance of the part played in procreation by the male.[24]

Now that the Goddess seems about to reemerge into popular consciousness, some patriarchal authorities are trying to make room for a feminine image within the context of their own philos-ophy. Christian Science speaks of a Father-Mother God, and many mainstream thinkers now envision a genderless deity or else a god who is both male and female. However, many feminists object to these palliative measures that try to make a virtue of necessity. Nelle Morton wrote: "It is not my purpose to argue that God has a maternal side or that the nature of God is both male and female. . . . To argue such, I am convinced, serves to keep women shortsighted and the Goddess suppressed."[25] The fact remains that "god" is a masculine noun, and is understood as such even by those who offer to read something feminine into it. Moreover, it continues to represent a masculine mindset.

> It is too late for authoritarian patriarchy to turn the tide. It is too late for the rulers—those in control—to remedy the world's ills, even if they wanted to do so. They are too close to the causes of world disorder to have any kind of global perspective beyond saving their own skins and "inheriting the earth," which image the Bible keeps alive for them. . . .
>
> This mind-set spawns dualisms that split the self, alienate one people from another people, and prevent a worldwide common access to knowledge and the reverent uses of the resources of the earth now available.[26]

For such reasons many women now feel that a return to the ancient concept of Goddess supremacy is essential to the process of healing the wounds of the modern world—not a return to literalism particularly, but a resurgence of the reverence for "motherness" and the reestablishment of feminine values under the Goddess symbol. The literal belief in father god has produced many social evils: wars, pogroms, crusades inquisitions, fanaticism, exploitation, slavery, greed, fear, and rigid asceticism. Surely the world would be well rid of all of these.

Home is Mother. Hestia, Goddess of the hearth. Mom and apple pie. Women make homes; men do not. When George Gilder wrote a book about men and their gods, he called it *Naked Nomads*. When Nelle Morton wrote a book about coming back to the Goddess, she called it *The Journey Is Home*.

Even people whose biological mothers were somehow unsatis-
factory, unwise, immature, rejecting, or downright cruel still
cherish an inward vision of home as an idealized mother: the
devoted, warm, unconditionally loving mother that every child
deserves. It is a social truism that even grown men require a certain
amount of "mothering," but it is hardly recognized that women
require it too. Psychologists today tend to recommend that women
learn to mother themselves, but few recognize the real need for a
Mother Goddess image that facilitates the process.

Women speak of finding the Goddess within themselves, and
within the minutiae of daily experience, and within other women,
as a result of "coming home" to the circles where Goddess energy
is accepted and celebrated. There are several important differences
between these circles and the temples, churches, and mosques of
patriarchy. Perhaps a most important difference is the form of the
circle itself, where each participant has her own radius no closer
to, nor farther from, the central altar than anyone else. There is no
hierarchy. There is no audience passively watching a specially privileged person perform, or inertly listening to instruction by
someone "holier." On one occasion a single person, or several persons, may lead the group; on another occasion, others will do it. No
one claims special authority. For women who have spent years
feeling that they must always defer to special authority, someone
stronger or wiser or more powerful or more spiritual, this comfortably democratic atmosphere is a revelation.

Furthermore, there is no dogma. There are no rote-recited creeds
declaring "I believe in. . . ." Participants are not expected to express
belief in anything whatsoever. Traditional Judeo-Christian doctrines
such as original sin, body/soul dualism, heaven and hell, dependence
on a savior, or the pyramid of supernatural hierarchy with God at the
apex all have been rejected by the majority of women, but each individual may believe or disbelieve whatever she pleases. There is a realistic perception that personal belief systems can—and probably
should—change as one progresses through one's life stages.

Like the ideal mother, women seem to understand better than
men how to extend unconditional acceptance to others. Perhaps

this is genetically programmed. Female mammals extend such acceptance to their young; the offspring doesn't have to do anything but exist. As reflected in father religions, father love is far more conditional. Heavenly fathers love only those who act in a certain way, fulfill certain duties, refrain from certain behaviors. The heavenly father has always been a harsh judge, but the Mother Goddess accepted all that emanated from Her womb. Her moral codes tended to deal sensibly with how people treated each other, rather than with how they treated Her.

Another attractive aspect of women's circles is that they always make room for humor and playfulness. Jokes are acceptable; laughter is frequent. This makes a strong contrast with the solemnity that most people are raised to think "religious." There is ancient precedent for this, too. Priestesses of Demeter at Eleusis used broad humor at public ceremonies such as the Thesmophoria; female clowns imitated the Baubo Goddess with her absurd face painted on her belly. Joy and merriment were considered an integral part of fertility festivals. Throughout the Middle Ages, men of the church were constantly railing against pagan rituals for their "female levity" and constantly hostile toward women who laughed. Why, light-minded laughing women might even—unthinkable thought!—laugh at the pretentious solemnities of men!

> Male public culture gets caught up with machines and puts emphasis on things, that are not alive. The decision-making of males in power tends to happen in a vacuum with little reference to the needs of life. Paradoxically, the public leaders who are supposed to help us deny death become increasingly oblivious to life and show increasing contempt for it. We have a civilization in which males in high places imitate a male god in heaven—both think themselves above the petty concerns of simple nurture and delight in generative life.
>
> Because men are raised to feel themselves removed from the needs of human babies, they are often insensitive to the seriousness of initiating enterprises which make the planet toxic and create machines to exterminate life altogether.[27]

Male public culture in religion or business—which are really the same thing—tends to ignore basic human warmth to the point where the men involved in the enterprise feel the lack and depend on women to fill the vital holes in their personal lives. It is a cliché of human society that most men need wives and children to make them complete human beings. Unfortunately, patriarchal society also teaches that some men may abuse those wives and children to make up for any trauma they may have suffered in their own childhoods. This sort of thing has been tolerated and even condoned by male-dominated religions for many centuries, in the guise of "corrective discipline," and is just now becoming recognized as a crime against humanity.

Theology has never made any significant contribution to human comfort in general, or to human beings' tolerance of each other's differences, let alone unconditional acceptance. "Through hundreds and thousands of generations men have been discussing, wrangling and fighting about theology. No advance has been made. The robed priest has only reached the point from which the savage tried to start."[28] The gentler elements within Judeo-Christian tradition have tried to teach that God is love, but somehow this tenet is seldom carried out in practice. On the contrary, God seems both vindictive and greedy. The central doctrine of Christianity depends on the cruel death of Jesus. When pagans asked the early Christians why this cruelty was necessary, "the deranged reason of the little community found quite a frightfully absurd answer: God gave his Son for forgiveness, as a sacrifice. . . . The sacrifice for guilt, and just in its most repugnant and barbarous form—the sacrifice of the innocent for the sins of the guilty! What horrifying heathenism!" was the comment of Friedrich Nietzsche, who didn't realize that heathen religions were often kinder.[29]

The Goddess as death-dealing Crone came to each and every life form in the inevitable course of time, but not in punishment for guilt or sin. There was no place in Goddess religion for absurd thoughts like theologian Carl Rahner's "Death is guilt made visible."[30] Followers of the Goddess generally recognized, realistically, that both life and death are part of existence and are to be simply accepted.

This was the opposite pole from Christianity's theological denial of death, coupled with its actual infliction of death as punishment, often for such "crimes" as not believing the Christian myth.

Coming home means coming to a place where one feels comfortable. For many women, patriarchal religion has always been uncomfortable. There are too many improbabilities demanding belief, too many contradictory rules demanding obedience, too many unworthy people demanding reverence. There is too much sexism, elitism, bigotry, anti-intellectualism, avarice, and hubris. From time to time, patriarchal reformers try to remedy some of these ills, but the system tends to overwhelm their efforts. Men in religion engage in power struggles just like men in any other male-dominated hierarchy.

Once the women have come home to their own kind of organization, their own brand of religious consciousness, will they create something radically different? Only time will tell.

MODERN WOMEN TALK ABOUT THE GODDESS IMAGE

Just as the "thousand-named Goddess" has appeared in many different guises to many different peoples over the past half-million years or so, she is also seen in many different ways by women today. Yet there is a kind of consensus to be seen in their impressions, which overlap at many points to provide an image that seems more agreeable to women than any god has ever been—even to women who have no particular urge to believe in a deity at all. The following selections illustrate the feminist consensus.

🐜 🐜 🐜

The first time I saw an art exhibit with images of women as Goddess, I laughed out loud, I thought it was so funny. I have since changed my mind. It's become something very real to me. At first I thought it was simply the idea of finding divinity within oneself. These images made life so much richer, and much more worthwhile, and I liked them, and they were basically literary.

Women come to the Goddess through one of two paths: through experience or through reading. I came through reading, so I got to know Her gradually. As I began to accumulate a little information about Goddess images, and to know more about them, I thought them nice metaphors for experience.

I used Goddess names to characterize various facets of the personality. That's valid; that's a good way to do it. We all incorporate Hecates and Aphrodites at different times and ages, depending on the state of our stomachs. I think a lot of women relate to the Goddess that way. It's the idea of self-worth plus the recognition of the variety of their personalities.

My image went from metaphor for spiritual experience to Truth, to the idea that this force does exist, with recognition of the force as feminine, beyond the little names that we give Her. Of course, we image the things with which we're familiar. I've had one or two experiences when She was there. Probably twenty years ago I could not have said White Buffalo Calf Woman was there, or I could not have said Hecate joined us. But I really do feel that those powers, when spoken of by those names, were there because that's what they feel like.

                                                🐜   🐜   🐜

For me the Goddess image must include the ugly parts, just as Kali is the destroying monster sometimes—because she isn't "true" otherwise. Nature is a nurturing Mother, sure, but Nature is also barren deserts, predatory animals, killing diseases, blizzards and tornadoes and volcanic eruptions. The Mother has her fits of destructiveness and it's all part of recycling everything in that ever-boiling, symbolic cauldron. Those terrible occurrences that we call "acts of God" would make God seem like a pretty nasty character if he really did make disasters just to watch people squirm and die. But somehow the image of Kali as death bringer seems more true to life as it is, like the one who gives birth to everything in also naturally the one who gives death. We are children of the earth, and in the end Earth eats us all. That's not only a religious truth, it's a scientific truth also.

I'm a gardener and so I know the value of rotting things and compost. Freshness and new shoots can't survive unless there is decaying matter to feed them. The Native Americans had the right idea: We must all decay in order to feed the world of the future. What's the point of mummifying our dead like the ancient Egyptians did? Where did that ever get them? There isn't going to be any resurrection of the flesh, so we should quit using all that embalming fluid; and even if our flesh did come back to life, what kind of life are you going to have with your veins full of formaldehyde?

The Goddess image has to encompass both the upward and the downward arcs of the wheel of life. That imagery is the most intelligent I have heard. Christians had to invent the devil to account for the downside of everything, but that only caused ever more confusion and fear.

There was a time when I would look at images of Goddesses from other cultures only in an artistic way. But then I began to see the spiritual side of them, I had an entirely different reaction to the physical images of the Goddess. I'm drawn to them now. There's a truth, a core in there that I recognize and acknowledge. I feel it. There's a link that I find very interesting. I think every female has her own universal image that reflects the female experience.

Women, who create life and nurture it, have to look at the divine aspect of their being. In many cultures it's seen as just what the cows and pigs do, too; but we know that we're responsible for bringing life into the world. Regardless of what our society says, this is a basic truth. A woman who's in touch with herself does see it as divine.

Women should relate to the Goddess idea for the sake of their own self-esteem. They should acknowledge the basic tenets of the Goddess religion, because they're good, and they would sustain and nurture life and improve the earth. I think women should relate to the Goddess image because it would create a balance in a male-dominated world with male-dominated philosophies. We need the yin and the yang. We need just what women are doing now: an underground movement. It shows women how to increase their own self-esteem and self-worth through small gatherings. Women should be able to meet and gather and reinforce one another in this grassroots type of movement. I don't think it's going to be done in highly oppressive societies where males have all the power and money and means to suppress it. It's very frightening to see our society swinging back in that direction.

      🐚 🐚 🐚

I don't really have an "image" of the Goddess, per se—I am always moved by the way ancient cultures have imaged Her, but some considerable power of those images over me derives very much from their age. Things that have survived the erosion of time seem almost magically to carry the past forward to us. I am also imaginatively stirred by the idea of whole cultures worshipping the Goddess, particularly in the ways that such worship must (I imagine) have made people respectful of the earth and of living things. People who saw themselves as Earth's children, it seems to me, are connected to its beauty and its fruitfulness in ways that we have lost. So I "see" the Goddess most clearly in my garden, because that is where—physically—I have the most direct contact with the earth and with growing things.

      🐚 🐚 🐚

Many women think the image of the Goddess is important because so much of what's come down to us, from the Bible and from history, is so male-oriented. From that male point of view, women are chattel. A woman must cleave unto her husband, and follow him, and this and that.

I feel very strongly that the Goddess image embraces all people. Men also benefit from it. We are not a we-hate-men group. We believe in the Goddess image because we are going to empower ourselves. Women need to be empowered because of the position they find themselves in sociologically.

🐚 🐚 🐚

I think of the Great Goddess, prior to the Goddess being broken down into specific aspects. I relate more to the ancient Goddesses by way of an image. In my personal experience, I relate to the Goddess as nature: animals and plants and earth and everything, the soil, the grass. All of that is Gaia, the Goddess.

We all have a different perception of the Goddess. We probably relate differently to what we know about the Goddess. Much of it is based on knowledge and experience and actually reading about Goddesses. I meet people who don't have any understanding of Her and who ask, "Where can I learn about the Goddess?" I tell them there are lots of books that they can read. One has to read them and then assimilate the information in order to come up with knowledge of the Goddess, as opposed to feeling alone, without the benefit of knowledge.

🐚 🐚 🐚

The Goddess image represents female power. It's getting in touch with things within yourself, rather than looking to things outside. It's also very representative of nature. Goddess worship is acknowledging the forces of nature. I think most real things are sacred, the things in and of nature, rather than all this transcendent stuff.

🐚 🐚 🐚

In my own personal life, I'm cognizant of the ancient images of Goddesses from classic cultures as powerful female images of divinity. But those are less meaningful for me than the concept of Goddess as earth spirit, life spirit. I find that I interchange the words "Goddess" and "spirit." In a yoga class recently I was meditating on the green earth and the life force, having a feeling of oneness with everything: the gift of the earth and the universe. To me, that's more Goddess, more spirit than anything else. However, I still find the statues and the archeological finds very intriguing.

🐝 🐝 🐝

The Goddess is intertwined with nature. I should make a distinction between nature and ecology. Both are important. Ecology is humankind, working with the world around us, sometimes working for the world around us, where we have trampled it in the past and now need to defend it. That's an important dimension of being a Goddess person. Nature is something else. Nature is you, the individual, being the subject of this wonder that is around us. The Goddess speaks to you through that. The only way we have to know is through the experience of our senses. Nobody is going to write it all out for us and drop it out of the sky. It's not going to happen that way. It's going to happen by coming in through the senses and then being processed.

The decision that each person has to make for herself is: is the Goddess a metaphor or a reality? This was something that I struggled with. Is the Goddess real? How do I know? Was She something that women made up to make themselves feel better?

One day it came to me that there is no way of knowing. The "leap of faith" applies to the Goddess too. I could make the decision that, yes, for me She is real, bigger than me, other than me; or I could say no, it's only a nice metaphor for all those things that I believe. It's something that each individual person has to come to on her own. For me, She is a loving, caring presence that is within me but beyond me, bigger than me but also within. That affects what I do and how I think.

Because I am a woman who has grown up in this skeptical age, the age of psychology, I think there could be other kinds of reasons for my experiences. There are the mundane experiences, like when I'm in the parking lot and there is no parking space, and I say, "Mother, if I'm going to get this errand done I must have a parking space," and the next thing you know, this guy pulls out right in front of me and I pull in. And there's wrestling with a problem, wondering what I'm going to do about it, and saying, "Okay, Mother, I've got to come up with an answer," and later on in the day having it come into my mind, obviously the best way to handle it, a solution I hadn't even thought of. In all the things that I was considering, that one didn't even enter my head. Is it the Goddess or the subconscious at work? Who knows?

🐝 🐝 🐝

I see the Goddess within myself. It's a part of myself that's been suppressed for many years. I also see Her in cultures throughout the world that have worshiped different Goddesses. I've learned a lot from history books and mythology.

Right now, She's growing inside me. I'm learning to accept the feminine part of myself. I can be freely feminine without having to be defensive against the masculine part of the world. This is very controversial, compared to what I grew up with. I try to find balance in which I feel about myself and what I feel about other women. My experience of the Goddess has been positive and uplifting. I feel safer. I can be myself.

I was really connected to nature from an early age. The safest place I felt was near nature, enfolded by it. I would play with trees. As a kid I was never allowed to fly a kite; I'd like to do it now. It was Mother Earth who kept me alive.

🐝 🐝 🐝

Part of my understanding of the Goddess is that She's everywhere, even in the names of cars, or little things people say, like "Bless you"—little superstitions. I like finding things like that. When I look at superstitions, or power words in our culture, just a little bit under the surface I see matrifocal or Goddess-oriented things. That's a really big deal for me.

I even saw the Goddess images in a Catholic church, even though they want to call it Mary. The voice of the Goddess has always been with me, but it's only in the past four or five years that I've understood what it is. I realize that it's a long hard road before people will recognize it generally, and that makes me feel frustrated. I can't point it out all the time to all of my friends.

❧ ❧ ❧

I sort of flowed into Goddess worship. It's quite unformed, even now. I read about the great myth of the Mother Goddess who has a son, and then marries the son, and then kills the son. I have the feeling that there's something basic in human experience there. I don't like the myth but I think it expresses reality in a certain way. When we get back to acknowledging it, we'll be better off.

I think the Goddess accurately reflects the awesome power of birth and death. What I'm clinging to right now is the Virgin, Mother, and Crone as a model for female existence. I like what Merlin Stone said about wondering how it would feel to read a whole book in which She, Her, and Goddess were all capitalized, and he, him, and god were not. I think that's an important experience for women in the world today, to sense female ways of being spiritual and powerful. I think that's a greater need than anything else. I don't know where the fundamentalist women get their image of holiness that is female.

I think religion is the expression of what human beings yearn for. More and more of us yearn for a relationship that is in balance with the earth and can go on indefinitely. Out of that may come a morality of respect for other living creatures, or even nonliving. If we're mining out all the minerals, or they're spread out in too thin a concentration across the surface of the earth, that also is wasting, as much as tearing down whole forests and polluting whole oceans. However we end up restructuring the religion to express that yearning, the morality must be one of respect for the earth and the environment. We have junk littering the summit of Mount Everest, and junk littering the orbits, and junk littering the moon. We really have not picked up after ourselves.

❧ ❧ ❧

It feels as though I'm connected with something larger that is directed, that has purpose, intelligence, a plan; that sees the big picture that I can't see, and is reliable—and I'd do well to rely on Her. It's different from the conventional image of God because there is no sin, no judgment. I don't have to live up to Her. It's simply a question of to what extent do I want to cooperate with something that's ongoing. I don't believe in reward or punishment after death. That never did make any sense to me.

Ever since I was a small child I felt that there was a power greater than myself, and that She loved me. Where I went wrong was in trying for a long time to be a Christian, denying what my original feelings and perceptions were, trying to be something different to match the mold that was out there for me to fit into.

I also think the Goddess is funny. She has a lot of humor. And I think She is a well rounded figure, not only the nurturing, motherly, loving, sweet, gentle kind of figure, but She does take Her power to end life as well, to destroy things, to make changes, and to look you right in the eye and tell you the truth. I loved the description in *The Crone* about the evil eye being the one that could see through illusions. I think She's got that kind of eye. I also think She is self-sufficient. She creates for Herself.

    🐜 🐜 🐜

For me, the Goddess image is the feminine aspect of the divine, the part of the divine that is nurturing, empowering, not oppressive. It teaches us to work together in the world for justice, right relations, economic justice, social justice. I really feel that the divine is beyond gender, though when I was a seminarian it was always "he," except for the radical feminists and liberals who were critiquing that. The Goddess became important to me because I needed an image of the divine that I could identify with as a woman.

Even if I'm not talking about the Goddess exclusively in terms of what I'm doing, I feel that it's tapping into the feminine energy of the universe. One should judge the spiritual journey by whether or not it furthers justice in one's own life and the lives of others. I feel that feminine divinity is in everything. Ethics, even when not articulated, can constitute Goddess worship. Mutuality, right relations, and justice very much reflect the feminine, the Goddess energy.

❧ ❧ ❧

I guess if I had to claim a spiritual entity for myself, it would be Mother Nature, or the feeling I get from music and art. It's vague to me. All I can say is that it gives me a lot of feeling of potential in my life, and patriarchy doesn't. I feel as if my life is opening up as a result of it.

❧ ❧ ❧

I couldn't see much difference between God and Goddess until I read a book about Goddess culture. Then I thought, "Wow, this is so true." We think things have to have a beginning and an end, but they don't. Goddess religion is like a circle looked at from the top, so everything is included in it. But the patriarchal god's view is from the edge of the circle, so it's like a table at eye level, and all you can see is a line, with a beginning and an end. Nothing's in it, everything's on it. I learned principles in Sunday school, but they're all distorted by priests and Bible readers. It's frustrating.

I had a dream about all people in a huge circle, and everybody fit in, and everybody moved, intertwined. It was a universal image, something that transcended the patriarchal world. I think embracing the Goddess religion would bring it about.

❧ ❧ ❧

I see the Goddess as every conceivable character: Maiden, Mother, and Crone. I see Her as the formidable huntress, like Artemis and Diana, and as the virgin Kore, and Maya, and the sexy nymph and the pure madonna. I see Her as Mother Earth, who had so many names in every culture of the world. I see Her as the dangerous death-dealing Crone, who was also the midwife and the wise serpent and the healer and the queen of the underworld, and all those other powerful images that Western civilization chose to suppress: the Full Moon, and Hecate, and the witch, the owl, the she-wolf, the bitch, the Valkyrie; Kali the corpse eater and Kali the flower maiden. I see the Goddess as every woman, because we all have bits and pieces of those characters in us, always.

I think the wonderful thing about Goddess images is that they *are* so human, and yet all-embracing and universal and applicable to the way we perceive all of nature around us. Sometimes in a fit of universalism the mainstream religionists will say God created the stars, the sun, the moon, the earth, the sea, the mountain, the wind, the whole green world and everything else that we can perceive; but the neat thing about the Goddess is that She *is* all those things, and She created God, as well—or so the older myths say. She is a far more encompassing image than he is, just because she has all these characters.

What's more, we're not restricted in how we can envision the Goddess. We don't see Her as a skinny hollow-eyed man dying on a cross, or as a white-bearded patriarch in the sky and that's all; no, we can even see Her in a fiery underworld with horns on Her head and a pitchfork in Her hand, if we want to. We can see Her as a slender crescent-moon lady or a fat Willendorf Venus, a kindly maternal Virgin or an awful dispenser of mortal diseases. Any way you want to see Her is all right. Yes, we have seen the Goddess, and She is us!

That's really something to think about—that the Goddess represents everything our imaginations are capable of.

🐝 🐝 🐝

My personal understanding of the Goddess is as my mother. My physical mother was a remarkable woman, but she turned herself off in a lot of ways. Though I loved her deeply, she was silenced long before I was born. The patriarchal takeover long ago forbade such women to exhibit or practice spiritual knowledge.

I view the Goddess as mother of all. I respond to the American Indian tradition of Spider Woman, or Thinking Woman. It's really refreshing to think of the Goddess as a Thinking Woman who brought the world into being. I tried to draw on that idea while I was growing up in a patriarchy. Throughout my school years I was considered trainable rather than intelligent. I'm not brilliant, but I can think. Looking upon the Goddess as a Thinking Woman is something I can really hang on to.

I find that when I try to talk to other women about the Goddess, at first they seem to find the idea very strange. But if it's connected with motherhood, they understand. I have a personal beef about what's been done to motherhood. I'm a member of La Leche League, which tries to help mothers. I think mothering is so important. I see the Goddess as a metaphor that combines mothering, nursing, and nurturing. This is what we are not doing for ourselves. For other women to relate to the Goddess idea, motherhood is a good start. When you begin to nurture another woman, she becomes willing to listen.

🐾 🐾 🐾

I was trying to reach back in my memory to the farthest-back Goddess image that I had. When I fell asleep at night, I would think of snuggling myself as a baby into the arms of a very comfortable woman with large breasts and large arms that circled all around me. It's as though she didn't exist from the waist down, because all she was was the place where I could rest and be safe and warm. I felt very loved, putting myself in that place. My Goddess image might have had a bandanna or perhaps tied her hair back. I don't remember any hair. She had a loving expression, even with closed eyes. I remember the very heavy, encircling arms and very heavy, soft breast. I called her Suroume. If I were going to attach a person to it, I think the idea came from my mother's mother. I stayed with her a lot, and she was a woman who liked to hold babies.

I didn't realize until I tried to emulate it in my own life what I thought of the Goddess. I didn't realize that this person I had in my mind was probably my primitive image of Goddess. At a later date I was able to say that Goddess is divine, and everyone has a piece of that. I can strive toward those attributes because I have a piece of the divine in me. The only way I could imagine that was to say to myself that deity is a Goddess. I'm not sure how men would relate to that, but I think they could relate to Mother as Creator. I haven't troubled myself too much about what men might think of it.

I think we all carry a piece of that divinity, which might be what Jung calls the higher self. I relate personally to Demeter because I am quite maternal. I was the oldest of a large family of children, and I started my own family when I was only twenty. I still think of myself as the provider and grower of food, so that myth is close to my heart. When my daughter moved away, I really felt that I was going through the Demeter-Persephone story. I felt very abandoned, just as the Goddess must have felt. And in the spring she is coming back.

My daughter gave me a plaque of Demeter for my birthday.

I also relate to the character of Atalanta, running from suitors. Any heroine appeals to me. When I was a child I felt very sympathetic toward Joan of Arc. In Norse mythology I read about Loki, who was full of mischief and a troublemaker; but the Goddesses straightened out the mischief that he had done. I like having heroines who straighten things out, and comfort other people, and take care of peace, and order and harmony. They give people models to emulate. That's how I understand the Goddess image.

If girls were conditioned in youth to emulate, or at least know the stories of, Goddesses, and to think of Goddess as Creator, that would give them a better image of themselves, and let them place more value on what they do.

The Unitarian Fellowship has a course unit on Goddess worship, more or less integrated with the pagan unit and tied in with environmental issues—people relating to divinity as other than God; there's not a lot of relating to God there to begin with. "Cakes for the Queen of Heaven" created a big response. Even so, women's spirituality seems rather suspect even in this congregation. The denomination is very inclusive, and contains many people who are secular humanists and don't think we should be relating to any kind of divinity. Those are people who object to the Goddess.

I relate to Tara as a meditational figure. She is compassionate and all-seeing. For an individual, the best thing to do is incorporate the Goddess into your own life and let it radiate outward from you. Thealogy can express divinity with the feminine being just as important as the masculine, if not more so.

     🐒 🐒 🐒

I think this society needs to bring up the divine feminine for balancing and healing ourselves. I hope our society will evolve that way. I see the Goddess in the Jungian sense, as an archetype of the divine. I see Her as a female image, or a feminine divine immanence, a sacred Beingness with a capital *B*, as opposed to the transcendent. Some might see the Goddess as transcendent, but I see Her as in the real world, not as ruling the world. She is in you and me and the physical world. I see Her as the many in the one, or the one in the many. There are all these statues and icons, so I see them as multiplicity in the oneness. I got the concept from reading. It made a lot of sense to me.

     🐒 🐒 🐒

I see the Goddess as a big woman, a voluptuous woman, very round, open, an inviting, voluptuous female body, with no barriers; a big fat woman, very well endowed. That was always my personal image of Goddess.

I can't deny that the Goddess is a real entity. I can't deny that anymore. I can't even make believe. I truly believe in Her. She was taken away from us. That She was taken from us, and we couldn't have Her, was a bad thing. Women should keep practicing Goddess religion and passing it on. With little girls, plant the seed in their minds that there is a Goddess.

After my mother passed away, I was very upset. I was very close to her. I remember being up on a mountain, where we had paid for skiing, but I was so off balance that I couldn't ski. I kept crying and crying. Then I saw a vision, not outside me but inside me. I saw my mother with my grandmother and my great-grandmother, and then a river of women that went on and on in both directions. I realized that there is a spirit that goes on. That was what I saw as the spiritual part of the women—the spirit of the Goddess that's given to each woman. I thought it would be nice if I had a daughter. But it was okay because the river went on. It was all women. I had been closed off from other women. I was literally afraid of women. But at that point I realized that it was okay to relate to other women.

The moral tone of society will have to change with Goddess religion. It would make it okay for women to be on their own, to support themselves and not have to be dependent on males.

🐝 🐝 🐝

I relate strongly to Hecate. She came to me as a patch of mugwort outside my back door, several years ago. I felt a need to investigate this plant. Hecate just kept coming to my mind. I asked for Her advice in dealing with problems. I just think of Her, and there She is. I see her as a Crone, always dressed in black. I have a great garage-sale find: a plaque that shows Her as the Triple Goddess.

🐝 🐝 🐝

My idea of the Goddess varies. Sometimes I think of Her as a huge, benevolent-looking woman. I never really put a face on Her. Though She's not faceless, I never thought about what Her face would look like. My idea is that She is the deepest part of myself, very much within me, that part of my mind that creates dreams, and is all-knowing, or knows a great deal more than I do about myself. It's the part that knows when I'm going to make a faux pas, or a Freudian slip. It does it on purpose, so I'll understand.

She's also, in a sense, cosmic. She's outside of the universe, but not in control of the universe, the way you're told the patriarchal god is in control. Of course there isn't an entity that looks like a woman out there in space anywhere. Whether She exists at all outside of my imagination is a big question mark. I'm using Her image as something to hang on to, something to pin a label to, a concept.

If anything exists, I want Her to exist. I want Her there. So in a sense I create Her for myself, to fill in the blanks of what I don't know. I understand that I'm filling in the blanks, that there might be nothing out there at all. But there has to be something that started things, and I think of Her as that energy. And She is also within me, more than just outside myself.

Most women who've been brought up to think of a god as an old man with a beard may have an easier time identifying with a Goddess image, a physical picture. But maybe women are brighter than that. Given the concept, they can accept it without comic-book pictures.

        🜚 🜚 🜚

My understanding of the Goddess image is mostly my understanding of my life as a woman. I see Her in human form every day, though images from other cultures and images from other forms of life resonate Her energy in a visible way. Usually I see Her in the women I'm acquainted with, but sometimes also in women I just happen to see. I feel a certain presence that reminds me of their divinity: a glow, a smile, a knowing look, or something that reminds me of the wisdom that women have. A woman who happens to recognize her self-worth is someone in whom I see Goddess energy. If she recognizes herself and loves herself, it's easier to see her. There's less to look through, fewer walls. The divinity just shines through.

        🜚 🜚 🜚

My concept of Goddess has been the woman in all of us, the woman who has strength, who has her own power. I value the woman who knows that she has choices. For me, the Goddess is not a deity. I don't relate it to images or idols. It's a feeling of appreciation for women, sharing a common experience, coming into this world as women. I don't know very much about Goddess in historical terms. I come to the circle just to share that feeling of women being women and feeling good about it.

After my consciousness was raised, I realized some of my own prejudices against women. I have looked down upon women who were "only" homemakers, or only living for somebody else. I realize that, as the years have gone by, I've learned to value women for whatever their choices have been. Now I have pride in being a woman, whereas when I was raised there wasn't any such pride. I value what women have to contribute to each other, and I realize how essential their occupations are. Goddess is permitting me not to have to know anything. I can dance around and just feel, and value women for what they have to share.

        🐝   🐝   🐝

I'm enrolled in a priestess-training program, and in line with that I've been thinking, What is the Goddess in my life? It's more empowering to think of the Goddess as being solely inside us, as being some force or power or connection with the rest of the world that resides inside of us. I'm thinking that the Goddess is that universe-sized being of which each of us is a cell.

It's very important to me to have a being to whom I can turn when things are hard, to whom I can return thanks when things are good, who is a greater source of knowledge than I am, from whom I can learn, and who loves me—which is not to say She doesn't love everyone else, but She has to love me personally—and who I feel is trustworthy and powerful.

In my experience I've found that it has become possible for me to stop trying to create all the circumstances in my life, and rely on the flow of this force, power, energy, whatever it is, to guide the direction of my life in the way that it's best to go. In fact, the more I try to get in there with my little meddle-fingers and try to create things for myself, the less smoothly things go; and the more I remain open to perceiving and responding to the evolution of my life, the more smoothly it goes. That's not to say I don't do anything. I do a lot of work, because that response makes a lot of work. I may be simply relying on a form of intuition that is inside me.

I'm not sure that if I were going to make a figure of Kali, I would have her dancing on Shiva and sucking up his entrails. That's not exactly the image that I would come up with; but I can understand it. It makes sense to me. And in my own life, and my own practice, I'm really drawn to the Death Goddesses.

The Goddess that speaks the most to me right now is Inanna, with that journey through the underworld, through the seven gates, and the giving up and giving up to get the transformation at the end. It makes perfect sense to me.

My cofacilitator in "Cakes for the Queen of Heaven" is a much younger woman, and in many ways she fits into the norm. Yet for her too, this way of looking at the world and this connection with the divinity is radically different. It has clearly empowered her. It has clearly made her more. If women leave that group with anything, I hope it will be the feeling that they can be more.

      🐝 🐝 🐝

To me the Goddess is the feeling I have when I'm troubled or confused and I keep quiet for a minute, and then another voice comes into me. It's my own voice, but I feel it's also another. It guides me. It gives me some specific action to take. That's my personal understanding of the Goddess. The voice is always female, and totally loving, warm, caring, and understanding—motherly, sisterly. Whenever I feel hopeless about this world, it comforts me.

      🐝 🐝 🐝

I don't really envision the Goddess idea as much as feel to the marrow of my bones that I *am* the Goddess idea. The Goddess groups I have participated in made me feel like I was celebrating womanhood, finding the moon magic we all share, increasing our wonderfulness, and undoing all those hours I sat on a church pew being told that I must suffer the curse of Eve. I also like the subversive feeling that I can now do openly the same thing for which I could have been burnt at the stake a couple of hundred years ago, and the Man can't touch me.

& & &

It's interesting to me, how women get on the quest for the Goddess. I studied mythology in school but had absolutely no identity with the Goddess. It didn't make a lot of sense to me. Then I stumbled across a Goddess ritual. It was like: This is what I've been looking for.

The witches' creed is, if you don't find it within yourself, you're not going to find it anywhere else. This is very illuminating. I think many women have the feeling that they're not getting their spiritual needs met, and they're looking for something else. When they get exposed to the Goddess, it feels like coming home.

One thing I like about the way we do Goddess religion is that every woman is equal to every other. It's not hierarchical. People are not elevated to positions of power. Anyone who wants to can put on a ritual. No one has to achieve some lofty position in order to lead a ritual. We acknowledge that although we are all different, we are all equal. One person is not more valuable than another. Each person brings something of value to the circle.

When you have that model in your religion, you carry that model out in your daily life and acknowledge that everyone has equal value, even though people function in different roles. We're so into hierarchy that making the most money tends to determine how valuable a person is. One may covet what another has. Any time you set up people to be unequal, you create an atmosphere in which war is possible. A major key to the Goddess religion is that it encourages a belief system where every person is sacred in her own right.

& & &

The Goddess led me to the Goddess religion. I started going to the Unitarian Church, because they're pretty liberal. I looked at it as going to a lecture every Sunday. I thought, hey, this isn't bad. You spend an hour, and you get to meet people. But I think there was a higher purpose.

There was an announcement that a "Cakes for the Queen of

Heaven" course was being offered. For some reason it just clicked. That was something I wanted to do. From the first session I just loved it. I loved being in a group of women and discussing these things. I was upset when I had to miss a session because of sickness. I just got the Goddess fever.

The group I was in was mostly mothers and young women. It was a really nice cross-section. But of all those people, I think I was the only one who caught fire. The moment it happened was when we digressed from the course and did a ritual. We were chanting: "Isis, Astarte, Diana, Hecate, Demeter, Kali, Inanna." I found that to be so powerful! From then on I was just enchanted by this whole Goddess thing.

That summer I went to a Goddess convocation in Massachusetts. Five or six of us made a little procession on the way to dinner, beating drums and shaking rattles as we walked up to the dining hall. It was such a powerful thing! Everybody in the camp stopped and looked at us. But it seemed very natural.

Some people at work are really scared of what I'm into, and they don't want to know about it. But others hear it. I give them little bits here and there, and they know there's nothing to be wary of. The scared ones are usually the devout Catholics who do things without thinking of why they do them.

Ever since I started following the Goddess path, I've done things that I just knew were right. I've started tapping into that intuition thing. I never did before. I was always an intellectual person.

In the beginning I kept thinking, Wow, all these people have been in this for so long! Where the hell have I been? Well, I know where I'd been. I was busy raising a child and working, and that took all my energy. But as my daughter grew, I had more time.

It blows my mind that in the circles, I would be in the same room with such wonderful people. Then I realized that I'm one of them. I'm special, too. Sometimes I'm not sure if the Goddess is out there, or in me, or both. I'm not sure I can define it. But I know I've been following Her with my heart. She never steers me wrong. I now feel very holy, whereas I never did before.

The thought has crossed my mind a few times, that maybe this is just a phase. But I look at people who have been into this for so much longer, and I figure it's not a phase. Even if I go on to something different, it will always be part of me.

I realize that it's a popular trend. It's something that's happening. All paths lead to the same place, to self-enlightenment. I know from the variety of things I've tried, that the Wiccan way is the one for me.

The coming-back of the Goddess was meant to be. I believe things happen for a reason. Sometimes I'll be working, and I have a question, and a book will come across my desk that has the answer. Even though the Goddess is within me, I think she's also another force outside that's guiding things. I think of her as a Gaia figure. What the Goddess religion has done for me is it has given me a lot of self-confidence.

I was in college before I finally realized that there were different religions, and each religion thought it was just as right as another. I took a history of religion course. I don't remember the Goddess being mentioned in the course, but it was a good background for me. I went to a Buddhist chanting session. It was nice, but it just didn't speak to me.

I've been following my heart, seeing where it leads me. I've been to a lot of different places. The monthly circles really nurture me. I never know what the topic will be, but it doesn't matter. Going there is like a ritual in itself.

When I brought a friend to a circle in a different town, she said, "I feel like this is home. These are my people." That's how I feel, too. I never thought that, at this time in my life, I'd be getting into new things. When I was in college I was interested in many things. But after child rearing, I never thought I'd get into a whole new realm. I have, in the Goddess movement.

My library at home can top any library in the county as far as books on the Goddess go. I really thought I had nothing more to learn, but the Goddess showed me that I have a lot more to learn.

      🐾 🐾 🐾

I think the women's circle is a wonderful thing. I just love it. Being in a male-dominated society, you start to think at times that there's something wrong with you, but you don't understand what it is. You try to place it. If you're not subservient, they say you have something physically wrong or mentally wrong. My abusive ex-husband used to say, "I'm trying to temper you." I wasn't tempered. I didn't fit. In finding the Goddess, I found that I was okay.

The first time I went to the women's circle, I just sat and watched. I felt as if I had been there before, as if I had seen it before. I saw women dance. It was the most beautiful thing. I love to dance, but I thought it wasn't okay. I thought my arms were too fat. But I saw women there, and their arms were like mine, and their bodies looked like mine, and it was okay for them to be that free, to go and dance and play the drum. The more women find that kind of freedom, the easier it will be for them to feel more powerful.

When I take it back with me to my everyday life, there's a power that comes with me. There's a definite lack of fear that comes out of Goddess ritual. It will pick up its own momentum and keep moving, because more women are coming to these events. The women I've brought with me want to come back again and again. My girlfriends drive a long way to attend the women's circles. They think it's great. They look forward to it.

&   &   &

I've participated in full moon and new moon ceremonies, and I've learned from them. The Goddess image frees me up to see the female form as valid, uniting two polarities as a spiritual source. Lately I've been calling it "The Force." I'm enjoying the sense of freedom I get from looking at divinity as the Goddess.

Some of my male friends are put off or upset, thinking this movement is going to make all women alienated from men. They feel threatened. They think we might become a little bit militant. Even some very nice men I know are fearful, cautious, uncomfortable, especially when a number of Goddess women get together. It's almost like we're too powerful. But maybe it's a justified backlash. There's

been so much attention paid to the male god. Isn't it natural to discover the potentiation of the female Goddess? The pendulum swings.

When I interpret the Goddess, I give myself a voice. I feel like
I'm just coming into my adulthood. I feel centered, empowered. It's
very healing to incorporate the Goddess into my life. I don't know
that I believe in either God or Goddess too literally, but I feel good
about growing in my life according to my own individual female
choice, to be a human being to the best of my ability. Goddess circles are beyond judgment. They're just joy. It feels really earthy.

I love the Goddess stories. We learned about Brigit, and the Candlemas hearth fire being ritualistically put out and relighted for the
next year. The stories are rich and beautiful. Paganism was such a
natural, earth-connected way of doing things.

Respecting the Goddess is valuable for all society, because it
means respecting ourselves and respecting life. We should be
banding together to relate to Mother Earth, and instead we've got
all this internal fighting, Nazi stuff, terrorism. There's so much fear!
Instead of expanding, our society is shrinking spiritually. So we
need to speak out and share our vision. We don't always know the
difference we might make.

I like having my little altar, set with whatever is precious to me.
I like calling in the four directions. Spirituality is what it is to feel
alive and connected, every day. It's with me always.

Part of the beauty of women's moon circles is that you know
it's happening at the same time in another state, another town,
another country. It's happening all over the world. Though there's
an awful lot of fear and violence, still there's this grassroots God-
dess-Earth-consciousness that's gaining. It's like a fire under the
hay: you won't see it until it pops up. But it's going to be widespread and make a big difference. Men are being called upon now
to question themselves in a good way, to rethink who they are.

        🐾   🐾   🐾

I feel privileged to be here at the beginning of something that's
starting up. In a hundred years somebody's going to be looking

back at what we're doing now. I feel like one of the fortunate ones, because at a young age I was able to hear the whispers and went seeking something that I knew was in my heart. I was seeking something I didn't have a name for, and didn't know where to find, but I knew it existed. I knew I had to meet with other women who called themselves witches, though I grew up with Hollywood witches as my only models. Something in my being said no, that's not right. I'm grateful that I heard those whispers and started looking, asking the universe to guide me.

I started reading many books on witchcraft. I asked myself, how am I going to become a witch? I couldn't tell anyone; it seemed too weird. Then I read about herbs and healing, and thought, that's not so weird. Maybe if I just start to ask questions about herbs, I can find the magic in that and start to learn.

I got an herbal catalog and it had information about herbal teachers. I sent away for information on becoming a green witch, and realized that I could do that. I dove right in and took a month-long course. I was initiated, and came back completely changed.

I met with women who were practicing all-woman circles with other women. I had been reading mostly about mixed groups, but that was a scary thought, having to be that open with men. My relationship with men had been either brother, father, or sex partner. But when women came together it seemed very safe. I could be vulnerable, or strong, or ugly, or fat, and I was still accepted and loved. For the first time I experienced life outside the patriarchal world. I thought this was the best of all my dreams come true. Here's people who don't know me, but love me, just for being here and wanting to participate. There was so much unconditional love that I experienced from the other women! I've experienced so much during rituals that have made changes in my life. There's nothing else that deserves so much credit for my personal growth.

What I liked about my first Goddess ritual was that it gave me a tremendous sense of peace, without anybody telling me right or wrong, you have to believe this way or that way. It honored the real, natural things in life, the natural forces. I find that very important and satisfying.

There was no hierarchy. I liked the fact that all kinds of women came, from every walk of life, and each one was accepted on her own level. You could contribute as much or as little as you wanted. I like the rituals. They're very peaceful, and I always feel good when I leave.

What I like about the Goddess movement is that we can admit that we create our own images, that the supernatural is something we create in our minds. Traditional religions do it but don't admit it. You have to believe the way they do, or not at all. People in the Goddess movement believe in peace. They believe in women's rights. They believe in ecology. And they work for many of the issues that I'm for.

In a Goddess group, you feel more a part of something. Women seem to be more generous, more giving, more encompassing. Each person can be her own individual. You don't have that in a patriarchal religion. It's very sad, because I think they miss a lot.

Sociologically, Goddess religion works toward peace, toward stopping wars, and toward supporting women's rights, abortion rights. The idea of sitting down and talking together, passing the talking stick, is great. Everybody has a point of view. You don't have to agree with it or condone it, but you don't have the right to condemn people. The whole group has a right to speak, and that's good.

The Goddess movement makes women feel stronger, more empowered, more confident. There will be big changes, and the Goddess movement will reinforce them. We need better schools, not bigger prisons. Women are more nurturing and more sensitive to these issues. Women need to work together.

🐾 🐾 🐾

What I found for myself with Goddess religion was being able to step up for myself and claim my own power. I feel like a stronger individual, and a lot more directed. I didn't know where I was going with my life, and now I feel that I have a direction. I want to help promote the Goddess religion and help other women recognize their own power. I feel very strongly that women have to do a lot of changing. We've got a long way to go before we develop an egalitarian society.

      🐚 🐚 🐚

It's difficult to explain in words what the women's spirituality movement has done for me. It's like a radiance that starts within and goes outward. I used to be afraid of other women. I thought everything I was doing was wrong, and other women were too critical. But I've been growing up. I've found that other women are supportive and nurturing. Today we've missed the kind of interaction women used to have when they all went to the watering hole to do their wash together. In this society you can go to the laundromat, but no one talks there. This spirituality thing has opened my eyes, allowing me to learn more about other cultures and other women. It's like being awakened.

      🐚 🐚 🐚

I was thrilled to discover the Goddess, and to learn that there were Goddesses whose religions went on for centuries. I'm now well aware of what life might have been if there had not been the male hierarchies. The church kept all that such a secret! It was almost like a taboo. Why not have some discussion of it? But many people don't want to know. They're in their own little packages, and they don't want to hear anything else. They don't want to be uprooted or disturbed, to have to change their thoughts.

    The moon meetings are great. The first time I went there by myself, not sure what to expect, I felt right away that this was the place for me. Through the Goddess image, however I see it in myself, I feel that I am capable of doing, experimenting, achieving. It's within me, part of my life experience. It builds confidence.

In my youth I was always praying to something outside of myself, and I was afraid. I got rid of the fear. The sense of the Goddess is much more peaceful, because you're not always looking for help somewhere else.

I think people are becoming more educated, and there is a great yearning among women, the awareness has grown so much. Women seem to come together from all over. We should make more women aware of the history of the Goddess. I found that intensely interesting. I was very excited to find out about it. People need to be made aware of that history, and how it was kept down.

Goddess awareness emphasizes your own spirituality, your own inward being, so you really feel good about yourself. It reinforces the connection with the Goddess as Earth, through the rituals. I don't want someone preaching at me and making laws. I want the coming together of earth and people, without a lot of rules and regulations. There's much more explanation to the Goddess rituals, and you feel good about them. It's much more positive than the traditional religions that promote fear. Patriarchal religions always want to keep you in the dark. They really don't want you to know what something means. They don't want you to find out on your own. The Goddess religion is not dictated. People come together voluntarily. The Goddess is much more approachable on the human level.

                                                    ❧   ❧   ❧

As far as I have pursued the Goddess, it has been immeasurably empowering for me as a woman. I don't see the Goddess as female so much as I see Her whole. I imagine this as a healing journey, so I like that Jungian anima-animus.

Of all the creation myths that I responded to powerfully, it was always the one where somehow there was an accident in the beginning that divided us into genders or races. I think the right ending would be wholeness and healing, and recognizing the way things come together, so they meet and match and make a new thing. I don't want the end result to be that one gender is less than the other, even though, myself, I'm so angry and frustrated by the way males have defined things and limited things and chopped and cut and excluded.

Patriarchy has been totally oppressive. I understand that I can't necessarily even imagine a world where the two come together, but the right ending seems to me to be that, because the imbalance over so many centuries has been so destructive. It would be a mistake for women to think that woman-ness could make up the whole universe. Any time feminism seems exclusionary, I think that's wrong. But in my own development, I'm still so needy to celebrate femaleness that I can't yet embrace maleness.

One night, there was this incredibly bright full moon. I got up and took off all my clothes, and went out in the yard, which was encircled by trees. There was the moon directly overhead. I remember raising my arms in a gesture of worship. There was nothing in my immediate life to cause that except the moon. Eventually I picked up my nightgown and went inside. I thought I ought to feel dumb, but I didn't. Seven or eight years later, I realized that there was an informal or intuitive or emotional connection between myself and the moon.

Finding the Goddess made me feel proud of my female presence in the world, whereas before I was proud of things that I accomplished but not necessarily as a female presence. As a result of finding the Goddess, I see myself more as part of the balancing of energy. I feel that what I do is more important.

It seems to me that one of the things we learn from sitting in circles and listening to each other is that we are responsible for ourselves. When I leave the moon circles, I am refreshed and ready to go home and try to be better at what I do. I am ready to try to be kinder to myself and to others, to be more patient with myself and others, and to be more honest with myself and others. A life of Goddess worship seems, for me, to be intensely private, personal, moral, celebratory, and noncoercive.

None of these qualities has been part of traditional worship as I knew and experienced it. So a world in which Goddess worship prevailed would be one in which women's bodies, for example, would no longer be the grounds on which society literally and figuratively makes war. Nor would it be one which obsessively ranked things. There might be a range of possible "goods," instead of the dogma of lists.

I think of Goddess worship as subversive, as grassroots, as underground. This is an aspect of it that I value very highly. The joy that I have found in it has been taken in small groups, in dark rooms, in womblike and very private spaces. While this may change for me, right now the only kind of Goddess group to which I would willingly belong is this kind and no other.

🐾 🐾 🐾

We need to bring the feminine back, to honor it. That's something we have to create. Using the Goddess image or the Goddess archetype is helping to make a balance. Those things speak to me, resonate with me. For the Goddess is living, not just some kind of intellectual enterprise. The Goddess images have helped to heal me, to honor my femaleness, to help me connect with my body.

I was raised to devalue my body. I had some sexual wounding. I was taught that the body is evil, wrong; sex is evil. The Goddess has helped me reclaim those denied aspects of myself. Embracing the Goddess helped me into an ongoing process, embodying the archetype, where I feel and sense within myself that my body, as well as the earth's body, is the Goddess body. Doing rituals with women, using these symbols that came from all traditions, helped me. It's a transformational process. I can't tell you how much I've been changed by it. Growing up in a female-hating family, I learned to despise myself. The Goddess helped me to love myself.

At a crucial time, I was going into an underworld phase—I like that metaphor. I went to a Woman-Wisdom school. Over a nine-month period, we reenacted the "going into the underworld" with Inanna. The group was loving and compassionate. I wasn't judged;. I could cry or laugh or whatever. It began in October, and by the spring I had a different kind of feel about my body. I felt Her within me. It's hard to explain. It's something you experience.

That healing process involved my body with the Goddess

archetype. It expanded me in many ways. When I was growing up, everything was contracted: you don't do this, you don't do that, you don't express yourself. Incorporating the Goddess into my life has helped to bring out my creativity. I work with clay. I have an altar that is my own creation, most meaningful for me. It's a labor of love. I understand the ancients and what they were doing, expressing love of life, love of being. On the psycho-spiritual level it has been a very radical change for me.

🐜 🐜 🐜

My experience of Goddess thealogy was a long time coming. It's only now, at the age of forty, that I realize how many events led up to my recognition of my intimations of the Goddess—this A-ha! experience. Finally I understood that there is feminine energy trying to push its way through to me.

Since I've become a full-time devotee of the Goddess, the synchronicity in my life has been incredible. It's the first theological concept that really meant something to me, that resonated with my spirit.

I began to attend more and more rituals. I began to read. I began to realize that the force that was moving into my life was the force of the Goddess. While the male force may be important, I saw that the Goddess was what was missing from my life, what had been missing from Judaism and other avenues that I had explored. The concept of God the Mother made absolute sense. Things seemed to move into alignment for me. From then on, my life has been very different.

🐜 🐜 🐜

Goddess worship, as I have experienced it in the early full moon groups and in the dark moon circle, has been one of the most profoundly important experiences of my life. It is in these circles that I have been voiced and validated as a woman, where I feel both powerfully myself and powerfully female. While I never before felt apologetic about being a woman, either in my personal or in my professional capacities, I never felt celebratory either—as if my gender had nothing to do with me. So the circles have brought me to consciousness of myself as a woman, and to celebration of women and their relationships; and neither of those, I think, might have become available to me in any other way. Based on my own experience, I can imagine that other women could relate to the Goddess idea the way I have. And, since it has made my life much richer, I can imagine that it would theirs, too.

Home has historically been where most women have spent most of their time. So, in inserting myself into the unbroken female heritage, I have necessarily joined history's women at home. In my studies, and in my public and professional lives, I have always been surrounded by, taught by, and mentored by strong, talented women—so in those realms, I have had the blessing of taking women's excellence for granted. To find it at home as well feels like a healing, a bringing together both spheres of my life in one celebration. That has been the particular gift of the Goddess to me.

🐾 🐾 🐾

Organized religion is not pertinent. It's not part of my daily life. I prefer the spirituality of women's groups. For me, spirituality means learning more about myself, becoming more aware of what I am. If other people don't agree with what I'm doing, that's their problem. I'm picking up on something that I lost through the years. I thought it was dead, but it came back.

Religion and spirituality are not the same thing at all. Organized religion has its spiritual side but it isn't based on what the majority of women need. It's too dominating over women.

🐾 🐾 🐾

It's a relief to say, "This is who I've been all along. I'm pagan. I want to run around the woods; that's the way I am." I like it. All my life I was so bored, I thought nothing had any color. Nothing had a soul. I was estranged from my world. I couldn't communicate with it.

During my Buddhist period I sat for four days in a yogic position and got a hip problem and a sense of feeling worse than ever. I can't deny the fact that I come from a Western tradition and I'm very involved with the material universe. While I'm here on this planet, I like touch and smell and taste. I don't deny my animal base, or my base animal. Paganism allows you to revel in that rather than deny it.

There is the famous Charge of the Goddess: "All acts of love and pleasure are My rituals." What's wrong with that? When they take out the "shalt nots" you can relax a little. The great thing about Goddess worship is that it does not have a doctrine of self-abnegation.

       🐸 🐸 🐸

For me, Goddess spirituality is the deeper well from which to continue to draw the power that we need to live our lives with integrity and authenticity in a world that is encouraging us to do differently. My well is shallow. I run out of that pretty quickly. I need to be connected to something much more profound.

For many women, what's most attractive is the idea of the Goddess as a nurturing mother, a loving mother. We evolve from that point if we can take that first step. If there's anything I have been spending my life encouraging people to consider doing, it's taking that first step. When I used to organize people to get arrested in the desert to end nuclear testing, I would say, "Take that one step across the line." Just one step, and it opens the world up.

Goddess worship is life, living life, being as authentic as possible, refusing to back down from what you know to be true, and self-investigation. I believe, as the Gnostics did, that self-reflection is a spiritual act. And there are all those wonderful things that nature-oriented people like me are learning as part of Goddess religion: the changing of the seasons, watching the moon, feeling connected to other life forms. Celebration of those things in a group I find to be very powerful.

My most powerful work, however, I do alone, because I always agree with what I want to do, whereas a group may have problems with that. Celebrating the events of life—not just the events of nature, but also the events of our lives—is so empowering for women, and so seldom done in our culture, or done in such an eviscerated way. I find, in the group that I meet with, that we are really sharing those things that are difficult for us, and also those things that are wonderful, and are able to celebrate and support one another. That makes a lot of sense to me. I really am powerfully drawn to the idea of women in community, not living together but having that commitment to one another, particularly women who have children.

I think thealogy is based on real life. It's based on what we know in our bodies to be true, on what we see around us to be true, and it's an extrapolation from that. It's not a theory that we impose on our lives. I think theology is a set of concepts about God that we impose on the world, no matter how crazy they seem, no matter how much we have to deform the world to fit into them. My thealogy doesn't have a male divinity in it. I think there is a presence for that, for people who want that. But it doesn't feel necessary to me.

🐜 🐜 🐜

I have trouble with any kind of religion. The part I like about Goddess groups is recognizing women as valuable, giving them credit and appreciation. I like the idea of choices, another option for women, instead of a patriarchal-type religion that's all about revering the man at the top. I like the idea of the circle instead of the pyramid: a leveling. That's very comfortable for me. I like the idea of women finding commonality and sharing. I was very happy with what I was experiencing in women's circles, not looking for anything more.

I hear of the Goddess movement in other states, very widespread now. I also hear it put down as "a bunch of witches" in an attempt to take away its power. But I think it will spread by word of mouth, as more and more people become aware of it. There's an increase in credibility as women within the movement are seen to be mainstream women, women working in corporate America. A lot of women in the movement are very bright, well educated, not looking for strictly mystical answers. They perceive reality. That has made a difference. If I thought the group was all mystics, that would have turned me off. My friends know me as a woman who has lived a sensible life, not flitting around. I've certainly been very responsible in my behavior. That lends credibility. The Goddess religion will spread by word of mouth, and by attracting mainstream women who have the willingness to be open.

If people could understand that Goddess religion is such a three-dimensional thing, they'd know that you can't really teach it. It has to be absorbed. It's more a metamorphosis than a conversion. For me it's probably basically emotional, though I try to be a rational person. I come at Goddess religion from the heart. It makes me more aware of religious experiences, the kind you can't talk about. I had an experience like that, dancing under the moon. People need to get out of the two-dimension lazy, conditioned responses.

My introduction to the Goddess was when I showed up at a circle group, when it was small. To me, the divinity that is the holy spirit, that energy, whatever it is out there, in here, is everywhere the same. That's what I call Goddess. It's part of life, and I'm the voice of that. That's what I talk about in my conferences, even though some people get freaked out by it. But that's my Goddess worship, and it's really very mainstream. I don't think of God/Goddess as male/female when I do meditation. It's just energy. But it manifests as female because the earth, as all-producing Mother Goddess, was so significant in the past.

Four thousand years ago most men had no idea that there was such a thing as fatherhood. When that idea got into the consciousness of people, the shift in power began. I understand that before that power shift, it wasn't women dominating men. They were more like equal. I can definitely dig going back to that. A lot of men feel threatened when you start talking about Goddess, because they think it's patriarchy spelled with a capital *M*, instead of a religion of equality.

🐝 🐝 🐝

What touched me most deeply was what I learned about witches as a child: that they were persecuted and killed for sharing their herbal knowledge. I always identified with the witches. All they were doing was healing people. I realized that these women were good, and what they were doing was right.

As I get more in touch with my own Goddess nature, people comment that I look beautiful, innocent, young, sexy. At thirty-seven years old I'm asked for my ID when I go into a bar. And It all has to do with accepting the beauty within me and all around me.

Goddess worship means moving toward right living, maintaining our connection with the earth. Goddess worship is the ability to be in nature, to be at peace with nature; to recognize the life force that's all around us, our connection with plants and animals and each other; to take steps toward ecological preservation; to educate people about the need for us to preserve the environment. This is homemaking in the broadest sense of the word.

🐝 🐝 🐝

My personal experience with the Goddess movement is the feeling that I had come home. Even those words are not really sufficient. When I started attending the circle, I felt things going on there, a tremendous amount of good energy. Call it love, though that's a word that doesn't really convey it properly. I felt so much acceptance.

Later I found myself saying, "Let's see, what should I wear tonight?" And then I'd think, it doesn't make any difference what I wear to the circle. It was a wonderful feeling: I'm going to go, and I'll wear whatever I want, depending on what kind of a mood I'm in. Sometimes I like to dress for a particular celebration. If the theme is black, or white, maybe I'd like to wear those colors. I can wear my pentagram if I want to, but I don't have to. I can come dressed any way I please. It was nice, and fun, to see a certain number of people dressed for the seasonal occasion. But there was never any feeling of "Come and see my designer clothes."

I felt a lot of unconditional acceptance. I heard other people expressing what I feel—if they haven't been to the circle for a few months they miss it, and they're happy to get back to it. When I can't go, no one says, "I took roll, and you weren't there." It's my loss if I can't get there. I'm not answering to anybody, whether I'm there or not. I go when I can, because we want to do the things that feed us. I've found the women's circle a very feeding experience.

I liked seeing in the Goddess circles that there was an attempt— I think a successful attempt—to keep free of any little clique that would make all the decisions. I heard it stated more than once that when a decision was to be made, all who were interested could meet, and anyone was welcome.

I have brought other people with me to the circle, because it's something that I want to share. If it speaks to them as it speaks to me, fine. If it doesn't, that's all right too. When you find something that you think is quite beautiful, it's natural to want to share it.

My husband teases me. He says, "Is this the night that you go howl at the moon?" I laugh and say, "Yeah, this is it." He's not threatened by it. I'm very suspicious of any man who's so chauvinistic and afraid that he has to hang on to his masculinity by fearing women's freedom.

The Goddess religion is very personal. You bring to it whatever you want to bring, and you take away what you are ready to take away.

🐾   🐾   🐾

I didn't really start to be aware of the Goddess image until I started to attend a full moon circle, where we talked about the different Goddesses. When this happened, something that was suppressed in me started to come out. I feel like a Goddess when I dance. I chant to the Goddess and do affirmations in the mirror, and I get empowered and charged. It's a strong female-feminine surge that I get. It's a form of freedom.

🐞 🐞 🐞

When I was going to the university, one night I got on an elevator in the library, going up to the stacks on the third floor, which was deserted. I walked down a corridor and all of a sudden came face to face with a painting that had been done by a student back in 1876. It was an image of Joan of Arc. I thought I'd never seen a face as beautiful as that. It hit me like a ton of bricks. Perhaps it was the quality of the painting, or the technical virtuosity. I don't know what it was. I looked at that face, and I was infused with a mystical sense. It was almost as if a shaft of light went through my body. I didn't know what the heck I was experiencing. It was only years later that I realized I was having a Goddess experience. The image had nothing to do with St. Joan, particularly. Maybe it was an embodiment of the Goddess represented by St. Joan, the radiance that flowed through her, and the fact that because of that radiance she was burned as a witch. The experience was so powerful that I couldn't speak about it for years. Any mystical experience is usually ineffable; you just can't put it into words. It was pretty amazing.

Several years ago I met a woman who was a member of a druid grove. Of course the minute she mentioned that, I became terrified. I had visions of human sacrifice, or Goddess knows what. She invited me to one of their rituals. I didn't even know what Beltane or Samhain was. I didn't know any of the old Gaelic names for the holy days or the old religion. But I went.

I remember humming a tune in my head before I walked into that first ritual, and when I arrived the stereo was playing the same tune, some kind of old Celtic country tune. I think my first ritual was the autumn equinox. I was fascinated and began asking a lot of questions.

The Goddess religion would naturally appeal to someone like me, set apart by a Jewish background; and then female, which of course brands you immediately; and now pagan; and left-handed to boot!

I think women should relate to the Goddess in any way that

feels right. It's an intensely personal experience. One woman's perception may be different from another's. I don't know that a particular liturgy would work for everyone.

There's a very famous speech in *Strange Interlude* by Eugene
O'Neill, the "God the Mother" speech. Where the heck did that
come from? It startled me when I read that play. It speaks about the
idea of dying being not so terrible, if we go back to the bosom of
God the Mother. I think everybody's stupidity in established religion is motivated by the fear of mortality, anyway. "Rage against
the dying of the light." The concept of the Mother taking us back
would do a lot to shift consciousness immediately.

If the Goddess religion attracts men and women both, it might
temper the testosterone mania and be of the utmost value to
society. We should keep practicing, learning, developing our understanding, and keep working in groups. I don't have any really
broad-based visions for Goddess worship. One attracts people to it
by allowing, with an open hand. Networking is very important. I
like to get to know all the pagans I can, in whatever city I'm in, and
familiarize myself with all the pagan organizations. A good way to
meet pagans is to go into the shops they run. You network, you find
out what other people are doing, and you expand.

Goddess thealogy is predicated on being born into the universe,
loving the material world, loving your body, loving the physical
sensual existence, not denying it but reveling in it. It's based on the
idea that you should enjoy the earth while you're here. No self-
abnegation.

The Goddess-directed idea is that you're on the breast of the
Mother all the time. You're in Her bosom, or Her womb. How are
you going to conduct yourself? How are you going to act? There are
men who strut around being macho testosterone cases, and yet
when it comes to their mothers, you say one word against their
mothers and they'll kill you. It's the same principle. When you're
with your Mother, the one who birthed you, how are you going to
conduct yourself? It's a very different mindset.

What's missing from patriarchal religion is the immanence. That is what has been denied and devalued: woman, earth, physical reality. We need to revalue them as feminine or female. Men might want to think of divine immanence without putting a female aspect on it, but I think it's very important in a patriarchal society to bring the feminine back and honor it.

The Goddess helped me to reclaim my life on a deep level with the images, the mythology. The Goddess encompasses the totality of the person: psychological, sexual, the whole thing, not to denigrate any part of it.

When I learned about Wicca, that was intriguing to me. I wasn't comfortable enough with myself to accept being skyclad, though. That wasn't for me. A friend introduced me to women's spirituality, and I was looking for that before I met her. It was something I wanted to do. Then, here she came into my life to show me Goddess rituals. We formed a group. It coincided with things in my outer life. I think the Goddess movement is diverse enough so that you can do a lot of different things with it. Each person needs to do it according to where she's coming from, and she may take from it whatever she finds meaningful.

       🐀 🐀 🐀

I resent not being able to have rites of passage to every stage of life. After I read a lot of information about the three stages of Virgin, Mother, and Crone, I thought back on my own life. We all make it through the Virgin part, because we're expected to be that. But Motherhood is being usurped now, especially by the medical profession, and there are not supposed to be any Crones at all. We're all supposed to be Virgins forever.

Among the women I work with, there is a little power struggle now and then, but that's mainly due to the patriarchal system we've gone through. For the most part, women's groups are sharing. Women are happy to contribute.

Now I'm glad to know that the Goddess movement is taking shape. I really feel that there's been a shift. There are no hierarchical steps that you have to go through in order to be something. Women accept each other the way they are. I think it's the end of an era that everyone's talking about.

🐚 🐚 🐚

For years and years I had a kind of diffuse animism, which probably was my basic religion. I'd appreciate and acknowledge the deity in a rock or a tree or a stand of mushrooms. I think we should treat all of nature with more respect. Like the ancients, perhaps we should ask permission before cutting down a tree, and acknowledge that we've changed it, and thank it for what has been provided for us. We should balance the need against the cost in a different way.

For years, when people asked me what my religion was, I'd say I was a druid, though I didn't know there were existing druids. I had a vague sense that they were people who had had a connection with nature. My questioners would recognize and yet not recognize the term, so they would back away and not press me. It worked very effectively.

I find the myth of Inanna to be most powerful. She was and is revered as an adolescent, preparing for her power and her marriage. Then, as a married woman, she consciously gives up everything to descend into the underworld. Then, having been transformed, she comes back even more powerful. She retained the loyalty of everyone except her husband, who seized her power.

I love the Triple Goddess concept—the Goddess as a young girl, a mature woman, and a crone. That's the death and rebirth cycle. I don't know how it speaks to men, who are half the population, even though they won't acknowledge that we are the other half. Not acknowledging half the population doesn't work.

If we reverenced the life force in the young, think how much healthier our teenagers would be. We don't hold up a rich and nourishing image of what youth can be. We stereotype them as destructive.

The Goddess Gaia is a powerful symbol for the modern world. The earth as an entity can be, and is, speaking to us. I don't know of anyone who thinks of the earth as not female. Care of the earth, respect for the earth, leaving things the way you found them: that's the irreducible minimum of Goddess worship.

🐜 🐜 🐜

When I feel stressed, if I go outdoors to the trees and stream I feel healed in about ten minutes. I spent most of my childhood on thirty-five acres with a brook and woods. When I go into the woods, I feel the connection I have with mother Earth.

I'm excited about watching my son developing. He doesn't get stuck in male or female stereotypes. He's interested in many things, including knitting. When I see my son as potentiation coming forward, to add to humanity, being a woman and bringing forth life feels so affirming to me. I think men don't feel as closely connected to the processes of fruition. When I see my son in the springtime of his life, with budding joy, I feel celebratory about the Goddess.

🐜 🐜 🐜

One thing that I think is useful about crosscultural investigation of other cultures and other perspectives is that it's a mind-blowing experience. We see that in many of these cultures that anthropology and sociology and Western academia have deemed primitive or undeveloped, people are often less childish than we are. When a Lakota saw the buffalo being killed and left to rot on the plains, he said the white men were like children, to kill for no reason and let these animals rot. We constantly say that the primitive cultures are like children. There's this Freudian notion of a progression from the childlike primitive all the way up to us, who are of course the most advanced and developed, and we're adults who don't have these childlike neuroses that tribal societies have.

When I read about people who believed the dolphins were their brothers and sisters, and the Lakota who believed the buffalo were their brothers and sisters, I see there's not this two-legged/four-legged separation. From our culture's viewpoint, that's a childish

way of looking at things. But really it's a very profound, sophisticated way.

A lot of the crosscultural analysis that's been done lately is
enormously useful. It makes us, as Westerners, rethink everything
that we've long accepted. It makes us question all these assumptions that we've grown up with. I think it's very important for us
culturally to be aware of the fact that there is a multiplicity of ways
for us to conceive of deity, and that it hasn't always been this male
monotheistic groove that Western culture has gotten into.

I was sitting on a balcony with an oblique view of the ocean. It was
a rather ordinary balcony, not the most "spiritual" setting. At my
back was Granny's Wild West Pizza and Beer with its accompa-
nying obligatory miniature golf range. This one featured an incon-
gruous giant Viking. Across the street a family was out on their balcony and snatches of music and laughter drifted over to me.

I was wearing a very full, very old mud-colored skirt and a
baggy black cotton top. I sat hugging my knees. and staring at my
bare feet. I decided I liked my feet.

I felt like a rock, compact, solid, connected to the earth even if
I was three stories up. I looked out to the ocean. I experienced my
surroundings and myself and decided that I was very happy. It was
a spiritual moment.

But I do not believe in Spiritual Experiences or in a Spiritual
Life. I do not believe in a duality of body and spirit or a dual life,
mundane and spiritual.

We have only one life. It is the totality of our person, body,
mind, and experiences. Each day we arise and live that life. Each
day we have within us the power of the god/Goddess. Each day we
know the world around us through our senses. Each day we confront the realities of our world. This is the life that has been given
to us to lead.

Each day our life has great beauty. Each of our senses affords
us moments of intense joy and pleasure. My eye sees a color of

such intensity that I must stop and stare. My ear hears a particular piece of music or the voice of a loved one saying that which I so much need to hear. The smell of the damp earth, the touch of the sun-warmed fur of a pet make me aware of these senses.

And then there is the glorious treat of taste! There is the wonderful combination of sensual stimuli: the smell of garlic, the brown of the bread and gold of the butter, the warmth and crunch of it. Imagine the smell of freshly brewed coffee and its heat and taste on the tongue. What wonders and beauty our everyday life holds.

The problem is that life has not only the wonder of my coffee in the damp mists of early morning, but also the heat, smell, noise and stress of the traffic jam in August when I am already twenty minutes late. How do these things relate to Spiritual Experience?

There may be truly transcendent experiences. People say they have these intense feelings of being one with the world, of unity with the god/Goddess. I know nothing of these experiences. I do not expect to have them. I expect only to have my everyday life and its common experiences.

But I think these everyday common experiences are little epiphanies. The dictionary defines epiphany as the manifestation of a god. The word's origin denotes a showing forth. Common experiences can show us the beauty and wonder which is the sacredness of our lives.

Access to this sense of the sacred is through awareness. It is not easy to be aware. It is all too easy to be unaware of the richness around me, to drink my coffee with my mind on other things. The heat and stress of traffic can dominate my life and close me to other impressions. It is easy to let anger, frustration, or negativity overcome my awareness.

All of life is sacred. It is filled with small beauties and large ones which are the manifestation of the god/Goddess. There are the joys of the senses. There are the gestures of love and regard, shared laughter, the opportunity to give a kindness. These are my Spiritual Experiences. My life is enriched each time I am aware of the beauty which is present. For me, these beauties are the Goddess making Herself known in my coffee cup.

🐞 🐞 🐞

The first inkling I ever had that people had worshiped a Goddess was when I saw pictures of the Venus of Willendorf: a dear little thing with the exaggerated bosoms and stomach and hips. I was drawn to that figure without knowing why. I continue to be, today. At first I didn't realize that I was seeing a concept expressed in stone. As the years passed, I became increasingly dissatisfied with the paternalistic idea of a male god who had to have his boots licked and his cheeks kissed on a regular basis. He never answered *me*.

I drifted into a group that ceremonially hailed Mother Earth, then everyone bent down to touch the ground. This grew on me. Mother Earth was the only tangible spirit. It was borne upon me that we really are a part of this marvelous planet. Something created us and sustains us, and that something is called Mother Earth.

I began a habit of lying down in the grass in my front yard, to touch the ground firmly. One day when I was lying down there I said within my mind, "Is there really a Mother Earth?" A voice answered me and said, "Yes, I am here." If I hadn't been lying down, I would have fallen down. To this day I don't know if the voice that answers me is my own subconscious, but the answers to problems that I bring to Mother Earth are always common sense. I'm encouraged to find my own solutions. I'm told that I am responsible for all of my actions. But at the same time Mother comforts me.

I went on a vision quest, a twenty-four-hour period of solitude. I felt an intense wordless communication with Mother Earth. An umbilical cord was formed at that time. I have been given to know —though that's an odd phrasing—that Mother does not expect active worship. She knows who She is; She doesn't need to be worshiped.

Mother Earth cares about us, but does not know us as individuals until we introduce ourselves to Her. At that point comes a personal relationship with the Goddess. I feel inextricably linked with Mother, and I feel that it shows up in all of my relationships with everyone, overflowing into my everyday life. One day in the car I had an overpowering urge to find a place on wooded land where nobody has walked or camped: a clean spot to talk to Mother. She answered immediately in my mind: "Child, everything around you was made from My body: the concrete pavement, the steel in your car, the rubber in your tires. You are at home anywhere on Me. I am always here in everything."

I was not a nurtured child, and to feel the love and care and nurturing of Mother Earth is an ineffable joy that permeates every day, every minute. Now that I feel a recipient of love and care, I'm also able to give it in heaping buckets full. I see women differently, because now they are echoes of Mother Earth, not echoes of my flesh mother. I'm no longer afraid of women. I welcome their company; I enjoy it enormously. They're individuals who are just as loved and cherished by Mother Earth as I am; there's no competition for it. We all sit in the Mother's lap and She loves each of us individually. It's an astonishing concept that doesn't exist within patriarchal Christianity.

I found my way to the Goddess movement slowly, by studying all the various religions of the world, and many ancient societies and cultures. It's interesting to me that each civilization had some concept of a religion, and that most present ones are patriarchal. None of those held any answer for me. I couldn't feel comfortable with the male deities. The religions are very didactic. It wasn't until I got back beyond the Greek religion, where the change took place from the Goddess to the god, that I began to find some answers that were more satisfactory. I see no transcendent deity. The Goddess is within.

9

RITUALS
AND PURPOSES

*I*N ITS EARLY YEARS, CHRISTIANITY had no rituals. It was simply a sect preaching millenniarism and the imminent end of the world. Rituals were pagan; they celebrated the seasons, the passing points on the wheel of time, the plantings and harvests, the annual rebirth of the sun, the phases of the moon, the couplings of Goddesses and gods, the periodic honoring of the dead, the weddings, and the birthdays. Pagans didn't believe in the imminent end of the world. They thought all the cycles of life would keep recurring as usual, provided the right rituals were performed with due propriety to maintain the cosmic order.

The central Christian festival of Christmas was never Christian at all in its origin. The Jerusalem church refused to accept Christmas into its calendar until the seventh century C.E.; there was no tradition of Jesus' solstitial birth in the Holy Land. Armenian churches continued into the present to ignore Christmas and to celebrate the Nativity on January 6, which used to be the festival of the Virgin Kore. In Rome, the midwinter solstice was designated the Birthday of the Unconquered Sun (*Solis Invictus*), a title later reapplied to Jesus. During the later empire, the festival had been instituted in honor of the Syrian sun god, called Baal or Adonis, usually identified with Mithra.[1]

251

Church fathers were much opposed to the trappings of this pagan festival. Tertullian claimed that it was sinful to adorn houses with green boughs and lights in honor of the solstice. "If thou hast renounced temples," he said, "make not a temple of thy own house-door."[2] Of course the pagan customs continued nevertheless, and were eventually assimilated to the Persian myths of the sun god's birth, attended by his three Magi and marked by the appearance of his star (originally Sothis, or Sirius, indicated by the three "wise men" stars in Orion's belt). When the gospel canon was chosen about four centuries after the time of Jesus, the book of Luke won acceptance by only one vote. Without this bit of luck, today there would be no Christmas creches, no shepherds watching their flocks, no annunciatory angels, no star in the east, no stable or manger or any nativity story at all.[3]

Christmas continued to be recognized as pagan, and therefore sinful, as late as the seventeenth century in England, where it was still associated with old heathen tree worship and solstitial magic.

> In 1647 the English Parliament ordered that Christmas, along with other pagan holidays, should cease to be observed. A 1652 Parliamentary act repeated that "no observance shall be had on the five-and-twentieth of December, commonly called Christmas day; nor any solemnity used or exercised in churches in respect thereof." Market was to be kept and stores were to remain open on Christmas day. In New England, where celebrating Christmas was considered a criminal offense and remained forbidden until the second half of the nineteenth century, a person caught celebrating Christmas was liable to end up at the stocks or the whipping post. Factory-owners changed starting hours to 5:00 A.M. on Christmas day and threatened termination for those who were tardy. As late as 1870 in Boston, students who failed to attend public schools on Christmas were punished by public dismissal.[4]

People who bewail the "commercialization" of Christmas might reflect that it is precisely that commercialization that finally assured its popularity and established it forever in the mercenary heart of Western civilization as God's most blessed orgy of shopping.

Again and again the fathers of the church outlawed and excoriated pagan rituals, without notable success. St. Eligius, bishop of Noyon, wrote in 640 C.E.: "Let no Christian place lights at the temples, or the stones, or at fountains, or at trees, or enclosures, or at places where three ways meet . . . let no one presume to make lustrations, or to enchant herbs, or to make flocks pass through a hollow tree or an aperture in the earth; for by doing so he seems to consecrate them to the devil." Pope Gregory the Great wrote to the bishop of Alexandria in the early seventh century that "The English Nation, placed in an obscure corner of the world, has hitherto been wholly taken up with the adoration of wood and stones." In the tenth century, British clergymen were ordered to "totally extinguish every heathenism; and forbid well-worshipping and necromancies, and divinations . . . with various trees and stones." Egbert's Penitential said it was "great paganism" for any woman to cure her infant's illness by "sorcery," which usually meant application of herbal remedies on the advice of a wise-woman, instead of prayers purchased from a priest. In 1035, King Knut tried to forbid "worship of stones, trees, fountains and the heavenly bodies."[5] None of this had much effect. Some of the temples, stones, and sacred fountains mentioned by Eligius are still standing and have even been incorporated into the very fabric of churches.

A Christian preacher wrote: "Service of Satan is everything dealing with paganism, not only the sacrifices and the worship of idols and all the ceremonies involved in their service, according to the ancient custom, but also the things that have their beginning in it. Service of Satan is clearly that a person should follow astrology and watch the positions and motions of the sun, the moon, and the stars for the purpose of traveling, going forth, or undertaking a given work, while believing that he is benefited or harmed by their motion or their course; and that one should believe the men who, after watching the motions of the stars, prognosticate by them."[6] Yet people pray to idols still in most churches, even though they are euphemistically called holy images instead of idols; and astrology is obviously alive and well and flourishing in all media of communication.

Probably these "paganisms" and "services of Satan" became acceptable, along with idolatry and Mariolatry, when churchmen realized that the people craved them and would pay for them. "The church," as Robert Ingersoll remarked, "has always been willing to swap off treasures in heaven for cash down."[7] The observation that rituals could and would be paid for led to a conviction that rituals should be paid for. Funerary rituals, for example, were performed in England only in return for the heriot, a special tax laid on bereaved families for something of value that had belonged to the deceased. Each dead parishioner, no matter how poor, was expected to contribute the best of something from the estate: best cow, goat, garment, bed, or anything that would bring in money. Some abbeys claimed up to one-third of the deceased's goods, and withheld burial until the goods were handed over. In 1515 it was written that priests "daily refuse to fetch and receive the corpses . . . but if some best jewel, garment, cloth or other best thing as aforesaid be given to them."[8] Marriages, baptisms, churchings for postparturient women, exorcisms, prayers for the dead in purgatory, and all other ecclesiastical services turned out to be valuable commercial enterprises, all with price tags.

Four important pagan rituals that were not readily assimilated by the church were the four turning points of the year: Imbolg, or the Feast of Lights, at the beginning of February; Beltane, or Walpurgisnacht, at the beginning of May; Lammas, or the Feast of Bread, at the beginning of August; and Samhain, or the Feast of the Dead (All Hallows), at the beginning of November. These four dates have been reclaimed by women's groups as their own Goddess-centered holidays, comparatively free of Christian contagion because they were observed throughout the centuries in ways that retained the pagan connotation.

Imbolg used to celebrate the making of new fires in honor of the Mother Goddess who brought "light" to the eyes of newborn children. The Romans named Her Juno Lucina, and Christians later converted Her into St. Lucy, whose emblem was a pair of eyes. In Sicily, her Festival of Lights originally took place at the winter solstice, when the light of heaven was symbolically reborn. In Sweden, She was represented by a girl wearing a crown of candles, the Lussibruden (Lucy Bride).[9] The Christianized version of Her feast day became known as Candlemas. In Ireland, it was identified with the Goddess Brigit, later St. Brigit, whose formerly pagan shrine at Kildare featured a sacred fire tended by nineteen priestesses, for the nineteen-year coincidence of solar and lunar cycles.[10] The canonization of the ancient Goddess Brigit took place because the church could not eradicate Her. She was once the Triple Goddess of the Celtic empire of Brigantia, source of all the "fires" of passion, poetry, inspiration, technology, fertility, and agriculture, which were supposed to be intimately connected with the rituals at Her central hearth-shrine.[11]

Beltane, Walpurgisnacht, May Eve celebrations were particularly abhorred by churchmen because they initiated the Merry Month of the "wearing of the green" in honor of Mother Earth's new green garment; the month when marriage vows were laid aside, and sexy fertility rituals were supposed to accompany the planting of the crops to insure a rich harvest. The festival's German name derived from the ancient May Queen or Fertility Goddess Walpurga, who like St. Brigit was spuriously canonized in an attempt to bring Her devotees into the church.[12] However, the sexual nature of May Eve rituals seemed ineradicable. "Young fellows and maids . . . fall into ditches upon one another," said one critic. Another spoke of the Maypole as a *herm*, that is, a phallic pillar that long represented the erect organ of the god Hermes in his annual mating with Aphrodite, as the Goddess Maia, Virgin of the Flowers. Romans sometimes identified Her with the spring-flowering Flora, and according to Douce, "There can be no doubt that the Queen of the May is the legitimate representative of the Goddess Flora in the Roman Festival." Even as late as the eighteenth century it was recognized that Lincolnshire Maypole dances were keeping up "the festival of the Floralia on May Day."[13] May was the month of sexual license, and it still bears one of the names of the Goddess Herself, Maia, Mother-Bride of the phallic Hermes just as Mary was the Mother-Bride of God. Interestingly enough,

Buddha was born of the same holy virgin Maya under Her flow-ering cherry tree.[14] Her name in Sanskrit meant "magic," perhaps an original reference to the magical return of young green life to a world depleted by winter.

Lammas was the Mass of the Loaf, or Feast of Bread, celebrating the death (by reaping) and resurrection (by sprouting) of the grain god, who was known as Lug or Lud in pre-Christian Britain. The festival used to be called Lugnasad, and Ludgate Hill was one of its ancient shrines. August was the harvest month, sacred to Juno Augusta in Rome, and to Her grain-producing, crop-tending coun-terparts: Ceres, Demeter, Ops. Essentially, Lammas was a festival of thanksgiving to Mother Earth for Her gift of food, and the ceremo-nial eating of the bread-flesh of Her consort represented a hope of abundant supplies for the coming lean months of winter. All the seasonal festivals at specific points throughout the cycle of the year were addressed to various aspects of the "thousand-named" Great Goddess, who changed as the earth changed, and whose rituals were invented in a time before history by Her priestesses in their longing to control the processes of nature by sympathetic magic.

Samhain, the Eve of All Saints, All Hallows, Hallow-Eve, or Hal-loween, was the pagan Feast of the Dead, once thought to open a crack between the worlds, so that necromantic priestesses ("witches") could summon the ghosts of honored ancestors to com-municate with their descendants and share their harvest feast. In some traditions, notably the Celtic, actual skulls of tribal ancestors were preserved and brought to the table as ghost-guests (Germanic *Geist* was the root of both words).[15] Sometimes, an appearance of light and living warmth was provided by a candle inside the skull— hence the modern jack-o-lantern, originally the "death's head at the feast." In some areas the annual Feast of the Dead still involves feeding children the candy *memento mori* in the shape of sugar-paste skulls or skeletons, and the decorating of ancestors' graves. Giving treats to children was supposed to show the ancestors that the tribe would continue, and that the young ones were in need of ongoing nourishment.[16] We still give Halloween candy to children, but we have forgotten why.

Patriarchal religion tended to avoid Halloween, which was primarily the festival of the Goddess as Crone, the death bringer, Her fearful persona living underground as Queen of the Dead. In Scandinavia She was Hel, or Nifl, ruler of Niflheim, the underground land of souls. The Sumero-Babylonian underground Goddess Eresh-kigal is familiar to us as the dark twin of Inanna or Ishtar. In Egypt, Neith or Nephthys was the similar dark twin of Isis. The Celtic Morrigan, or Cerridwen, Goddess of Fate, was sometimes incarnate in the corpse-eating White Sow, who recalls the divine Diamond Sow of Buddhist Tantra. Similarly, the Finno-Ugric Goddess Kalma, ruler of graveyards, probably was yet another offshoot of the all-pervading Indo European Dark Mother, Kali Ma, who is still worshiped in India every November during the high holy days of the Kali Puja. Southeast Asia also still feeds the ancestral spirits at the harvest-time Feast of the Hungry Ghosts.

Three names from classical sources in Europe survived long enough into the Christian era to become designated "Queen of Witches," in whom the church seriously believed, up to the nineteenth century. They were Hecate, Persephone, and Lilit: one Egyptian, one Greco-Roman, one Hebrew.

Hecate is familiar in Greek myth as the underworld third of the female trinity, along with Hebe the heavenly Virgin, and Hera the earthly Mother. However, Hecate was a late Greek version of the Egyptian Goddess Hekat, a wise Crone associated with traditional priestesscraft (or witch lore) of midwifery and magic. There is some indication that medieval European midwives did include prayers to Hecate among their procedures; and as churchmen wrote in their vile *Malleus Maleficarum*, "No one does more harm to the Catholic faith than midwives." In Her original Egyptian persona, Hekat was an amalgamation of the seven obstetrical Hathors, daily delivering the newborn sun, and also a divinization of the old tribal matriarch known as *hek*, the wise-woman who understood all *hekau* or magical Words of Power. The term "heck" as a euphemism for "hell" may have been derived from underworld Queen Hecate, just as the word for hell itself was the name of Norway's underworld Queen Hel.

The Greeks adopted Hecate and married Her to their underworld god Hades, by way of a very labored story about Her having been carried underground in the river Acheron, where the fearful gods dumped Her to wash away the contagion of the birth chamber for they, like all patriarchs, dreaded such intimate female mysteries. However, other mythological sources indicate that Hecate was sometimes viewed as the whole female trinity. She was Hecate Selene, the moon in heaven; Hecate Artemis, the spirit of nature; and Hecate Persephone in the nether regions. Porphyry said Her triad represented all phases of the moon and governed the fertility of crops throughout the earth.

Hecate was worshiped everywhere in the Roman Empire at three-way crossroads as Hecate Trevia, "Hecate of the Three Ways." Her images stood at crossroads to receive the offerings of travelers and their gifts of gratitude for safe journeys. Here is a hint of the original purpose of crossroad burials as a pagan custom, later much vilified under Christianity. Those who believed in the pagan underworld Goddess would have wanted burial near one of Her images, rather than in the churchyards of the new foreign deity brought by missionary priests who said the Goddess was a demon.

Another name for the medieval Queen of Witches was Proserpina, the Latin form of Etruscan Persipnei and Greek Persephone. Her classical myth confuses Her with Kore the springtime Maiden, wedded perforce to the underworld god Pluto (Hades), while Her mother Demeter grieved for her. This myth bears the marks of extensive reworking, for Persephone's name means "Destroyer," like the title of Kali Ma. She was undoubtedly a pre-Hellenic title of the famous Black Demeter who lived underground and received the dead. Pluto, meaning "abundance" was probably one of the earlier names for Demeter Herself. It was common for patriarchal revisions to masculinize female deities and forebearers, as in the biblical "begats" which are largely feminine names.

Gnostics taught that newly dead souls would meet Proserpina in the underworld as soon as they crossed the River Styx. She would care for them and teach them the Words of Power and the magical gestures they would need to know, to ensure a comfortable afterlife. Knowledge of these matters was a primary purpose of

Gnostic initiation, even among Christian Gnostics—whose ideas, of course, were officially declared heretical in the fourth and fifth centuries. Nevertheless, the traditions persisted in secret for at least a thousand years, until the fully established church commenced its all-out campaigns of persecution and witch-hunting.

The third Queen of Witches was Lilit, or Lilith, known in apocryphal Hebrew writings as the first wife of Adam. This version claimed that She disobeyed God and sneered at the angels he sent to control Her; She rejected Adam because he was too bossy and too crude in his sexual techniques; She defied both Adam and Yahweh, and went to live by the Red Sea where She found sexually compatible male spirits by whom She conceived thousands of children. This detail identifies Her as one of the primary Earth Mothers, having the title of Mother of All Living, which was later transferred to Adam's second wife Eve.

Lilit was addressed in prayer on a four thousand-year-old tablet from Ur, and was known in Sumeria and Babylon as Belit-ili or Lily Goddess. The lily or lotus was a fundamental Asiatic symbol of the divine yoni: cosmic female "gate of life" from which all things were born in the beginning. In Egypt also, the lotus was defined as the female Gate that gave birth to the sun in the first dawn of creation.

Suggestions of female sexual power were enough to turn Lilit into a dangerous she-demon of the succubus variety in the view of rabbinical scholars and their Christian successors. Succubae came to be known as *lilim*, or Daughters of Lilit, who coupled with holy men to create the inadvertent sin of a wet dream, drawing out some of men's souls along with their semen. Christian monks were told to sleep with their hands crossed over their genitals, clutching a crucifix, to ward off the lewd attentions of the beautiful Night-Hags, or Night-Mares, as they were sometimes called. (It didn't work, of course.) "Hag" originally meant a holy woman, whereas the original Night-Mares included black mare-headed underground Demeter, and in northern Europe the witches known as Volvas who could turn themselves into mares between sunset and dawn.

Traditions associated with Lilit gave rise to some of the church's crudest ideas about witches, such as typically male fears of their

sexual insatiability, their occult powers over men's genitals, and
their knowledge of charms to induce impotence or sexual enslavement in men. Indeed, these unmentionable sexual fears lay at the
root of witch-hunting terrorism in general, just as today they still
lie at the root of many forms of male violence against women.

The owl was another sacred totem of Lilit, who appears in
ancient bas-reliefs with bird feet and probably was embodied in the
owl-eyed "Eye Goddess" statuettes of ancient Mesopotamia. Owls
represented Crone wisdom also in the Greek cult of Athene and the
Welsh legend of Blodeuwedd; the "wise owl" was the official totem
of both Goddesses. The Latin word for "owl," *strix*, evolved into
Italian *strega*, "Witch." Night-flying witches were often depicted
with owl wings.[17]

Other notable pagan seasonal festivals were taken over by the
church and converted into spurious saints' days, like the Mid-
summer Solstice, which became St. John's Day, and the Spring
Equinox which was subsumed by Easter. This "movable feast," still
determined by the moon, was named for the Saxon Goddess of
spring, Eostre, and assimilated to the Christian crucifixion because
it was an ancient tradition to set up effigies of the slain-and-resur-
rected vegetation gods in fields to fertilize the soil in preparation
for planting. The modern scarecrow descends from such customs.
Easter's symbols include the egg, emblem of potential life, and the
moon-hare, now known as the Easter Bunny. In the beginning it
had nothing to do with the legend of Jesus, except insofar as the
deaths and resurrections of many pagan savior gods seem to have
taken place in the spring.[18]

In addition to seasonal festivals, there were always rituals for
individual life passages such as birth, marriage, and death. For girls,
there used to be menarche rituals, and for women, menopausal
celebrations of the passage into cronehood and its ultimate
achievement of wisdom. The church took over baptism and forbade women to name their own children, as they had formerly
done by baptizing them with breast milk, or to dedicate their children to the Earth Mother, as they used to do by placing them on the
ground at crossroads. Yet the French still speak of a baby's mother-

given nickname as a *nom de lait,* "milk name," and pious tradition still avoids crossroads as the favored locales of pagan spirits.

Marriage used to be so pagan a ceremony that it was kept outside of the church until Renaissance times. "The very suggestion that marriage should be regarded as a sacrament would, to the Christian Fathers, have been gross blasphemy."[19] Early versions of the marriage ritual, adopted in the sixteenth century, show that the church had not yet managed to make it a male takeover of female assets and services. The bridegroom pledged his property to the bride, saying, "With this ring I thee wed and this gold and silver I thee give and with my body I thee worship, and with all my worldly chattels I thee honor." The bride answered, "I take thee to my wedded husband, to have and to hold, for fairer for fouler, for better for worse, for richer for poorer, in sickness and in health, to be bonny and buxom in bed and at board." A curious note in the margin, made at a later date, stated that "bonny and buxom" meant "meek and obedient."[20] It was only later that the bride was made to swear obedience to her husband. In the Russian wedding ceremony, the bride's father presented the bridegroom with a symbolic whip, with which he tapped the bride while she kissed the shoe of her new master.[21] In 1640, English churchmen ordered that a bridegroom should ceremonially plant the sole of his foot on his bride's head.[22]

Thus we see that rituals serve political purposes, and women's groups recognize the need to devise new rituals that elevate and dignify women, to replace the traditional rituals that either degrade or ignore them. Why, for example, should women attend a "communion" in which they symbolically consume the body and blood of a male god, when they have within them just as much claim to sacredness as any male, however enlightened? Ingersoll wrote, "Who can imagine the infinite impudence of a church assuming to think for the human race?"[23] Humans have always created their own rituals according to their own needs and perceptions. In view of the new recognition of women's right to continue such creative ritual making, their new rule seems to be: If it doesn't feel right and good, don't do it, don't say it, don't watch it or listen to it. Even though feminist political pressure has taken "obey" out of the marriage service now, there is still a long way to go.

MODERN WOMEN TALK ABOUT RITUALS AND PURPOSES

Different women bring different kinds of expectations and appreciations to their spirituality meetings, and view the goals of such activities in different ways. Some enjoy being involved as facilitators; others prefer to participate as an approximation of the Greek chorus. Each woman interprets the meaning of it all in her own way, as can be seen from the following remarks.

🐝 🐝 🐝

I see Goddess worship almost like revolutionary cells operating in the basements of society, subtly undermining the accepted way of looking at things. I tell some of my male friends that in every county, in every state, once a month there are groups of women getting together, reordering society, and there's nothing you can do about it. We're going to change the way our children think. The terrorist way of changing the world is not going to work. The world is always changed by ideas, by people being free to think new things.

A Goddess religion will have to do something for the men. Many men don't seem to understand the idea that separate forums would be a good thing. Their own existence is so barren that they need women to bring spirit into their lives. Without women, I don't think men would even think about it or make the time for it. It's very difficult for them to rewire the way they've come to understand theology. Women need a space of their own, so it's good to have separate-but-equal concepts; but men need something too. They're not going to come up with it on their own. They're not going to reinvent it on their own. Their dog-pack mentality is so hard-wired into them that they can't do it. So we have to figure out something to do for the men.

At least with mainstream religions, men can be dragged kicking and screaming on the leash of guilt into the churches. But we don't want to do guilt, because that's not a good motivation. We have to make what we do more public, to expose or demonstrate ritual better.

Men are attracted to certain expressions of spirituality. They like watching the Tibetan monks draw sand paintings. They like Native American spirituality. We have to let them know that we're not sitting around once every month bashing men. They have this fantasy of us all talking about how terrible our men are, whereas in fact we tend to talk more about how terrible our parents were. They don't quite understand what's going on. It's difficult, in a confidential situation, to let anyone outside know what actually goes on. Knowing that it's going to be open always changes what we're going to be saying.

There are groups that contain men, but it's difficult to find an open one. In such groups, too often the men seem to take over, and the women aren't getting their feminist forum.

Our expressions of joy are things of beauty, experiences of love. Those are for us, for the people, not for the gods. That's where thealogy differs from theology. Our acts of worship are done to benefit the celebrants.

🐝 🐝 🐝

I had my Crone ceremony with other women. We made a beautiful shield with parrot feathers and crystals and shells, a little face mask, and a Zuni fetish. I went and did a ceremony in the woods, with a peace pipe. I made a little fire, and I didn't talk. I had a silent day. It was a beautiful ritual, and I feel that I gave myself that. I know that by honoring myself, I can honor others.

🐝 🐝 🐝

There's something very special about Goddess religion at this time. It is underground—I don't want to say secret, because it's not secret; but it is among women. It's special because it's something that we do, that not everybody does. That makes it even more special. I don't want to lose that specialness. Once you get to be an established religion, then everybody's doing it. Then you want to go off and do something else that not everybody is doing. There's something nice about being one of the initiated.

ॡ   ॡ   ॡ

I think women should relate to the Goddess by openly worshipping the Goddess. Your whole life becomes a different kind of life, though the spirit's still the same. It's okay to be attractive, to be pretty. It's okay to put down the chainsaw and not drink with the boys. It's okay to be as female as you're supposed to be, and be respected. I'm glad I found Goddess. I think planting flowers, or doing anything inspired from within, constitutes an expression of Goddess worship. It's always good to create pretty things. Though I have two sons and deal with males in my life, they no longer squash my creativity.

ॡ   ॡ   ॡ

I like very much having Goddess images to look at, feel, and touch. They put it all together into something real. I like having something tangible. That's what I enjoy about owning Goddess images that I can hold. I like seeing the many feminine forms, being able to accept their variety, in our society that tries to dwindle every woman down into one feminine form that's thin and shapely and rounded in just the right places. We don't all come in that form. Only a very few, very young women fit the image.

I don't really think of worshipping the Goddess. It's just that the Goddess is all around me. I appreciate the beauty of this earth. That's probably the most worship I feel. Some of our rituals are indoors, in artificial surroundings, though we try to bring in plants. I feel best when we can do rituals outdoors. I'd like to run barefoot through the grass and splash in the puddles, and try not to make it serious. I love it when our rituals break down into giggles. One of the reasons I love that so much is that I couldn't do it in church. It was a definite no-no. You couldn't laugh and giggle and relax and be yourself and have fun.

I've heard people say, "Why don't you have workshops for men and women? Men need it too." I've drifted in that direction, but then I have to go back because I still see the need for women to support each other and grow in themselves. There'll be plenty of time to bring men in at some point. It radiates out. The stronger a woman feels, the more impact she'll have on those around her.

An individual woman can learn as much as she wants to about the Goddess, and accept whatever works for her. That's another beauty of Goddess spirituality. There is no doctrine associated with it, no set list of rules. It's just learning and growth. I don't even want to put it forth that everybody who leads a ritual has to have one central altar, or must call the four directions. People should be allowed to have their differences, and to be appreciated for their differences. Don't force everybody into the same mold; know that some people are skilled in one way and allow them to flourish in that way; if they want to change, allow them to change.

The urge to dominate is a social problem that we have. Managers shouldn't dominate just because they're in a control position. They shouldn't think they have all the answers. Hierarchical levels are another ill of patriarchy.

Women see differences and say, "Oh, that's different; let me learn about that," rather than seeing differences as bad. When I think of dominant religions today and the way they've been forced on so many indigenous peoples, and are continuing to be forced on people, I am appalled. They say, "If you don't change and believe my way, which is the only way, you are evil." They make no effort to learn about what the other people's lives are. Women that I meet through the Goddess religion are so much more accepting of other people's religions and feelings of spirituality. They're willing to listen.

🐝 🐝 🐝

Women need to learn about their own lives by breaking down all the preconceptions. Women are too separated. They need to fuse themselves together in their minds, to stop thinking all other women are out to get their husbands. Women are taught to be competitive with each other in too many ways. Love yourself, whoever you are. Then you can look at other women differently. Stop watching TV. Stop reading fashion magazines or buying food that isn't healthy. Get a good book, look at the moon, hug a tree. Simple things. Look around the world and see things for what they are, instead of for what you've been taught they are. It's hard, but it's also really simple. It can lead to a woman waking up every day and looking in the mirror and saying, "I love you." That's Goddess worship.

Traditional theology comes from the external and is put into you. It's pounded into your head. Goddess knowledge comes from inside. It never has to be written down in words. There are no words to say you must do thus-and-so or you will die. Traditional theology is intrusive. Goddess knowledge is inclusive.

🐚   🐚   🐚

Rituals are Goddess worship. Women gathering together, sharing experiences—that's Goddess worship. I do chanting. I like the idea that in each group there are women of all ages. I attended a really good ritual honoring aging and the Crone. Women's worship is coming together for the rituals and the sharing. We connect through our experiences. It gives you peacefulness.

Goddess worship starts with women in a circle, having some commitment to each other, honoring our bodies and honoring the earth. Anything that comes out of that is almost by definition ritual.

🐚   🐚   🐚

Everything I do as a woman is a Goddess worshipping, a celebration of the Goddess. The Goddess coming into my life meant not that I did things differently, but that I saw what I did as a different thing. I often believe that just by being a woman in the world, and making female ethical choices, and sometimes to say, "This is not good enough," I am connected to Goddess. I don't think it should be a woman's burden to say, "Whoopdedoo! Every crappy thing is worthy of celebration." We should choose: I'll give my energy to this, and not to that.

To meet in a ritual circle is one kind of celebration, an affirmation of the sacred that is shared, and an acknowledgment of the Goddess that is public. These meetings water the roots of my "faith."

I think, though, that where I really celebrate/worship the Goddess is in my life at home. Much of its daily minutiae has taken on a holiness—when I set the table, I recognize it for a reflection of the altar. When I set my house in order, I understand it, in its repetitiveness and necessity, as something of universal ordering, and I see that my labor has value and beauty, as well as necessity and repetition. When I sew, as when I clean, I am aware of the many women who are occupied with these tasks—and of all the women who have taught me to do these things, and of all the women who have done them before me. And I feel connected to meaning in my life, and meaning in others' lives, and I feel connected, too, with the dead. So there is a wholeness in what I do with my time and my labor, where before I found only irritation and boredom.

Goddess worshippers gather in circles, not in pews. We speak of the Goddess as She is made manifest in our lives. We don't get preached to, and we don't preach to others. Our circles aren't organized to produce "experts" or to talk about how right we are and how wrong everyone else is.

Goddess knowledge centers on health and on healing, and on this world, not some "next." Western religions center on death, and the absurdity of an accountant God who keeps a tally, and who rewards and punishes. This has not prevented the things people do in the name of Western religions from being violent, vile, and cruel. I except from my tirade Buddhism and its cousins, the life-celebrating and peaceable religions of the East. The native peoples of North America truly know that they are Earth's children, and it is their sense of the sacredness of the world itself and our kinship with all living things to which we must return if the planet is to survive.

Goddess knowledge does not include a system of rewards and punishments, or reward in and after life. This life is the blessing.

We live in the lap of the Goddess, and we return to Her when we die. All that we are returns to Her, and in our dissolution, our bodies become one with Hers.

Under the light of the moon, all Her children are equal. Life is celebrated and nurtured. Children are precious. Under the moon, a woman's body belongs to her. Love is the source of the sacred, and men and women are no longer afraid of each other.

🐿 🐿 🐿

The thing I love the best, my favorite ritual, is the blessing. It's just so great that anybody can bless anybody, and we don't have to go to some male priest. I've come up against resistance to this. I ask someone, "Would you like a blessing?" and she says, "Oh, no, I have to go to a priest for that."

I give people fairy blessings, which are similar to Goddess blessings. It's fun, and it's a game, and joyous; but I'm dead serious about it, too. When I say "Thou art Goddess," I'm telling each woman that she is divine. I'm giving everybody blessings and telling them they're divine children of the Goddess. I sing about it, I talk about what we do in our circle, how we invoke the four directions, and how we use the Native American traditions, which are sort of in vogue at this point. If I can use that to help elevate the idea of the Goddess and make it more acceptable, I'll do that.

I object to being told that because I'm a woman, I'm not allowed to do this or I'm incapable of that. I think that's ridiculous. People first started to relate to the Goddess because of the earth. The earth gives birth, and so do women. I think it's important that people honor that divinity in the fact that women give birth. The female was long considered divine. That's how it should be.

🐿 🐿 🐿

There is value in taking time to go inside oneself. I get so much energy from the things around me that I may forget to go within. But the more I do, the more balanced I feel. I do simple rituals, focusing on something specific that I'd like to bring about. Most of it is just a feeling of completeness that wasn't there before. I look at women's circles as a way to contact the energy that I, as a woman, and women as a whole put out.

๛ ๛ ๛

When I think of worship in general, I think of ritual. Worship is an act of honoring, which may or may not be incorporated into a religious system. Worship is wherever women gather to honor the Goddess concept, wherever they openly express the Goddess within, the feminine strength within, wherever they actively live their philosophy.

Individuals should incorporate the philosophy into their lifestyle. The whole psychology of the circle, the lack of leadership, is different from the typical patriarchal religions and authoritarian religions. It is a much more accepting and warming growth area. The logistics of the rituals themselves recognize the individual and recognize the equality of all beings. That's just wonderful. It's a clear statement of the lack of strata or hierarchy. Goddess groups really incorporate the individual into the worship itself.

How would a Goddess religion change the moral tone? Wow! Accepting, loving, forgiving, nurturing, caring, earth-oriented, nonaggressive, nonprejudicial. It would really enable the world to be as it is meant to be, with people caring and nurturing and protecting each other, whoever they are, all beings. Most religions do not do that in any way, shape, or form. They may verbalize it, but their words are hypocritical. They're not inclusive; they're exclusive. You cannot have a unified humanity with all this exclusiveness.

The Goddess philosophy accepts all in love and honesty and truth and openness and caring, and I think that's wonderful. It would make such a difference, not only in the moral tone but in the lifestyle of humanity. We wouldn't be materialistic. We wouldn't be destroying the earth. We wouldn't be making war on each other. I think the Goddess presents a religion that is the true religion for humanity.

☙ ☙ ☙

Goddess worship is acting on your own conscience, making sure your beliefs are your own choice, as opposed to adopting the beliefs of others or going along with whatever your family has done. I think service is important. If I do different kinds of service, I can experiment and do things that I like to do. Goddess worship can be anything that you love to do, and that you do well, to help others.

I think a Goddess religion would need to be coed, but I'm not sure. There are male feminists out there. There is a such a thing as a cultural elite which is very profeminist. The artistic, intellectual imagination of the society, the so-called higher culture, creative people have been looking for this kind of faith.

☙ ☙ ☙

Nature love is Goddess worship. I've come to believe that if we all had a Goddess religion, certainly women's self-esteem would be raised a thousand percent. After such empowerment, there's no way that patriarchs who are causing all this war and destruction would be allowed to go on. They would be made to stop.

Sharing at the grassroots is important, and really touching people. In this society we rarely touch. But once you actually do touch, both hands, there's an emotional connection.

Goddess thealogy differs from theology in that it's warmer, more nurturing, less hierarchical. It's direct, it's here, it's accessible. The Mother is the accessible, nurturing sustenance all around us.

☙ ☙ ☙

People who are into their bodies are worshippers. People can define it in the way they want to. You can use the images any way you want. You can redefine them, reconstruct them. You can use the myths and add on. What's appealing about it is that it's a living thing, it isn't rigid. You can use your creativity.

Part of the Goddess is being creative, in a psychological way or a more activist way. You can be solitary or communal, as required. Goddess religion can deal with everything from child rearing to morality, psychology, health, and how we interact with nature. It really can go into all fields. How we are born, and how we die. It should go through the life cycle and honor all phases and aspects of the life cycle, from infancy to old age and death.

🐞 🐞 🐞

Goddess worship ranges from just an informal recognition of a strong female divine presence in one's life, to doing rituals alone as a solo witch or joining a full-moon group. I found out when I was studying for my master's degree that in New England there are many groups of women who just gather to meditate silently together. I like to check out various things, where people seem to have something creative going on. I'm interested in studying various aspects of religious experience. Even when I'm not interested in a certain group, I'll attend their meeting just to see what those people do. I visited a Pentecostal church and found it very interesting.

I've never felt that Goddess spirituality is a proselytizing practice. Nobody goes door to door saying, "Hi, can I talk to you about Goddess religion?" But a significant number of women I've talked to do believe in proselytizing. I expected them to say, witches don't do that, Goddess worshippers don't do that; you need to find your own path. But I was surprised to hear some of them say, "Sure, of course I go out and talk about it. *They* (fundamentalists) are going out and talking about *their* side. "

There are people who really believe that Goddess worship is a positive transformation for society, and they feel that more people should be aware of it. So conscience dictates that they let others know about it. This is not dissimilar to the salvation argument: This is important for the salvation of society from patriarchy, and for the salvation of the earth. So, some do go out and make converts. Others say no, pagans don't do that.

One thing that can constitute Goddess worship is political

action. Most feminist spirituals are very active politically. A lot of political elements in various groups are integrated into rituals.

In New Hampshire there was a case of a woman being stalked by her ex-husband, and the courts wouldn't put an injunction or a restraining order on him. The courts did nothing until finally this woman was killed. In groups around the area, women did several rituals to protect other women from being battered or stalked. Rituals would be done, and then there was a letter-writing campaign or a voting-registration effort. Political activism can constitute Goddess worship. One witch has said, "We know what every good witch does: votes."

From a Protestant-culture point of view, we tend to define religion as a conversion. You become such-and-such a religion. People ask, "What religion are you?" as if you're supposed to have one set of beliefs or practices. But when you ask people in real life what they do to express themselves religiously, well, they pick a little of this and a little of that. I can see people incorporating Goddess ritual and different philosophies into their lives along with other stuff. Many women do the Goddess stuff and their more mainstream religious stuff too. Many Jewish women are Jewish and Goddess worshippers. I know of a Lutheran woman who is very active in her church but also goes to a Goddess circle and is very active in that as well.

Some people who have grown up with a particular religion still consider it their heritage even though they don't find it particularly fulfilling. Rather than reject it completely, they'll say they're ethnically Catholic, or Protestant, or whatever.

Many of the pagan festivals or Goddess spirituality festivals have wonderful programs for children. The kids have fun because so much of it involves play. But you never know—having been in this very accepting, nonhierarchical faith, where there isn't any strong orthodoxy, will these kids grow up and become fundamentalists? Will they react against their upbringing? Could they suddenly become very conservative?

Goddess religion can't be divorced from feminist issues. It's feminist by nature. There are also issues of social justice, racial equality, and environmental problems that are very important. All the colonizations of women's bodies, of nature, of darker-skinned people, of all the native peoples of the world, are definitely related. Issues having to do with protection of children, social violence, and such should be addressed by Goddess religion. I think it's really about giving women a vision of the possibilities of their power, and what they can accomplish.

It's not so much about male patriarchal gods having ruled long enough, and now it's time to go the other way. It's more about creating a balance. Often, people have said that having a single Goddess would be just as bad as having one male god. But Goddess worshippers feel more that this female divine presence has been suppressed and taboo for so long that She needs to be present in a much stronger way than the male for a while, to redress what has happened. I think eventually there will be a balance.

There was one instance where male imagery was brought up in our group, and that was really offensive to a number of women who thought of the group as a safe sanctuary where female energy could be celebrated. They feel that all the rest of the world is a patriarchally dominated world, and this little microcosm is insulated from all of that. They worship the Goddess so prominently because everything else is patriarchal or, in effect, men's studies.

I don't think there is one Goddess thealogy. I think there are thealogies. They differ from traditional theology by espousing more of a partnership model of power, rather than a power-over. Goddess thealogies emphasize greater agency on the part of women: a more active will, a proactive approach to their spirituality, their worth, and all their relations with the community. I don't mean just a community of women, but the community of life, of the whole planet. There's more active participation. There's more emphasis on the stories that include women. Women are not only participants; they play key roles in those stories. They provide a mentoring function too, to advise other women about their paths and decisions.

We need more gynocentric narratives in sacred stories, and a yin-and-yang harmony rather than this constant combat, pitting differences against each other.

🐾 🐾 🐾

Goddess worship may be coming together in groups for more formalized rituals, or it may be just women getting together and doing what women do. Women doing any of their tasks together can feel like Goddess worship. Probably many of them who do so would be horrified to hear it, but it's true nevertheless.

Goddess worship also can be individual meditation. If I meditate by myself, or work in my garden to make something grow, or bring some good thing to a friend or a family member, that's Goddess worship, too.

🐞 🐞 🐞

Relating to the Goddess has to be individually felt in order to be meaningful. I wouldn't presume to tell another woman how to think about it. I can't choose for others, because I don't like being chosen for, especially by those people who push a male god.

Women only need to understand that in the center of life, all things are connected. That understanding would be my idea of Goddess, that and anything else that would be completely contrary to the god concept. She would be without dominance, loving all things that are alive, and nurturing them. We need to care for other living things, making sure that they survive. That may mean controlling the humans.

Goddess worship includes feeding the birds and wild creatures, trying to cut down on our garbage, caring for the earth. My best interpretation of the Goddess is the shape of the earth. Inanna, Isis, Gaia, all the other ancient Goddesses are personifications of the earth we live on. She is the mother Goddess.

Goddess worship is a giving kind of thing, keeping the forest, keeping the wetlands, keeping the buffalo and other animals that are in danger of extinction. The Goddess can't become prominent as long as greed takes precedence over everything.

I'm probably known throughout the company I work for as a witch, but the one thing everybody knows about me is that I have integrity. As long as my beliefs are in accordance with my value structure, my way of living life, people know me as a good witch. If anything of you remains in the memories of others, it's not what you believe but how you live your life. I have integrity. I say what I think. I'm honest. I don't lie to anyone. Someone like me, who believes in the Earth Mother, can say what she thinks as long as she lives her life in the beautiful way. That remains in the memory. It's the memory you leave in the hearts of others that will change them.

🐾 🐾 🐾

I'm reminded of the line, "All acts of love and pleasure are My rituals." For each woman or each man, Goddess worship can mean whatever you recognize as divine presence or holiness or spirit. Any act that honors is worship, including acts where you honor yourself. Something as simple as drawing a very luxurious bath for yourself, or combing your hair longer than you usually do, or speaking to another woman in a way that honors her. These can be acts of Goddess worship.

It feels holy to me when things are moving easily, flowing. When things are beautiful and radiant, that feels divine. It can be a flash of sunlight through woods, scattering on the fallen leaves. That's divine. My idea of the Goddess is something like a mixture of all pleasures, beautiful sights, beautiful sounds. But discordant sounds can be a part of it also. It's not always perfect. I recognize the Goddess's ugly aspects too. My sense of beauty is not all light. There's a dark side. In kindergarten I was told to choose my favorite color for a picture, and I turned in a completely black picture. My teacher was horrified, but I thought it was beautiful.

🐾 🐾 🐾

The church implanted the idea that I could never be good enough to lead someone in worship. Each time I step into a women's circle, or speak out, or suggest something, the fear comes up that I can't do it because I'm a woman. I've done it enough, but still there's a little voice left over from all my negative training, every Sunday for an hour or an hour and a half—that's really hard to forget.

I try to remember not to judge people who are still on that path, because most of us were given no choice. I can understand that if they're getting fed on some spiritual level, with the music or the ritual or the lights or the stained glass or whatever it is, people can think they've received something good and want to keep returning. That's the sort of thing I'd like to have continuing in Goddess worship. Music is divine, no matter what the lyrics say. The idea of doing something ritually is appealing. Much of the ritual and symbolism in the Catholic mass felt rich to me. I liked getting dressed up for special occasions. As I heal the wounds left by the church, I may be able to reclaim other things that I liked about church services.

One of the most moving experiences of my life was standing in for the Goddess in a ritual of drawing down the moon. There was something like a veil that came down over me, and I saw through different eyes. My body felt very different. I started to feel a tingling in my toes. By the end of the ritual, I couldn't feel my feet at all. My hands seemed very charged. Afterward I felt dizzy, though I usually don't have dizziness or headaches. I hadn't expected anything to happen, but it was overwhelming. On the physical level alone, it was an amazing experience. Also, I had just started bleeding a few hours before, and it seemed a powerful time to work magic.

I feel that I shouldn't be the only one to have experienced this. As part of our ritual, it should be available to every woman when she feels like she's coming into her power. It's something I hope for.

         ઠ   ઠ   ઠ

Ritual is Goddess worship, and so is anything else that brings out the femaleness of a woman. Honoring her is worship. A Goddess religion should be out in the open, not underground as it is right now. A Goddess religion would cause men to look at women differently. They would have more respect. Respect for women should correspond with respect for the earth. We have to quit hurting the earth.

         ઠ   ઠ   ઠ

Stages of Goddess religion include grassroots gatherings, speaking out, women talking freely and openly, having environments where they can do that, and having the opportunities to do it. This doesn't happen everywhere. I know people who have moved to a new environment and spent literally years trying to find like-minded people. The stages require open environments where women can come together to talk and share.

I think we will slowly increase in numbers, and organize, and find ourselves in positions where we have to evolve ecumenically. Where women can talk comfortably together, and feel that they have power and strength, the religion may become generally established in an open society.

🐜 🐜 🐜

We can't deny that there is evil in the world. To say there isn't is foolish. People have to be held accountable for their behavior. Many women's spirituality people take ethics from the Wiccan idea: as you sow, so do you reap. It comes back to you. That's a good guideline, but I think it should be more sophisticated. What's right in one situation may not be right in another. Maybe the Goddess religion can deal more fully with that.

We're creatures that have the capacity to do some really horrible things. We're not going to deny that, but we should look at it more closely, not in a way that's damning or with a lot of artificial guilt. If people could come to some agreement on the subject of ethics, it would be a whole new world. Older women should help younger people to get to a higher level of psychological maturity, to learn how to take responsibility. Then we could have trust.

Women can help the Goddess movement by being role models. That speaks for the movement more than anything else. Those who choose to organize can do it, but I really do think it has to come from the grassroots level. It can't be monolithic. That would defeat everything that the Goddess is about. We should have many different kinds of structures for worship and coming together.

Goddess worship is one woman at a private altar, creating magic at that altar, or it is in the circles of women who come together, seeing the Goddess in other women and in nature, in the enjoyment and appreciation of what's beautiful in nature. We can worship what She has created or allowed to be created. What's ugly in nature is harder to accept, but it has become easier for me to accept those things when I understand about the Goddess having a light side and a dark side, creating and destroying. I can understand death, and the necessity for death, as part of the Goddess's plan.

When good people suffer, that's harder to take. It's rough to see people you love going through unnecessary suffering. I'd like to believe, but don't really believe, in the concept of reincarnation and karma and all that. That would conveniently explain it: suffering to hone the soul, so in the next life it would be different. But I don't accept that. I think a person should be able to make rational decisions about everything in life, including cutting off intolerable suffering by euthanasia, provided no one is pressured into it.

Religion is social. People go to church because their friends are there. They know everybody. Because the social church is part of their lives, it's hard for them to give it up. Goddess religion addresses all the issues of importance for women, and for the environment, so we need to develop the same habits in regard to Goddess religion. We might involve people who are friends of the environment. We really need an ecologically correct religion, one that would also address women's control over their own bodies, all the feminist issues, and teach the raising of children to be gentle people, boys as well as girls.

Parents should be equal, but the home is one area where women have power already, because children are usually closer to mothers than to fathers. That's a strength for women. However, the man in the relationship should be more involved with the children, to be a nurturing father, a student of child development, a decent father. People are becoming more aware of child abuse and wife abuse by men. These things are becoming less hidden and less acceptable. Goddess religion can see them as evils.

      🐌 🐌 🐌

Ritual is a good thing because it allows us to experience something nonphysical in a physical way. It allows us to put our inner visions into our experience.

      🐌 🐌 🐌

Women I know are gathering other women to them, making their homes available or finding other places where women can meet. Meeting in groups is one of the most powerful things we can do to foster Goddess worship. Just the act of coming together is magical. It only takes intention, because the magic happens spontaneously once the group is together.

The other thing is that it needs to be really democratic, not hierarchical. If it starts to feel like there's control coming from any individual in the group, then it changes. It's important that every woman feels as essential as every other woman.

Because Goddess religion is so connected with the earth, seasons, and cycles, its most important issue would be protecting our resources, living in a way that doesn't destroy. We must live with conscious awareness of our impact on other life forms. Loving yourself, and finding beauty and divinity in what's around you, are not incompatible with living in a way that doesn't scar the earth.

      🐌 🐌 🐌

Goddess worship is any thought that comes from inside of you, from a place of love or compassion or understanding, instead of guilt, obsession, shame, or cruelty. I can experience a form of Goddess worship just staring out the window. An active form of worship is reaching out to the women in your community, the women who are your friends and your family. I don't write off the women who don't support me. I just keep on loving them and trying to communicate. When love comes, it's very powerful and beautiful. It reaffirms me in every way.

🐜 🐜 🐜

I never believed in any of the "supernatural" in the way theology meant it—i.e, above the nature of man, godlike. Spiritual? Everything is spiritual. One is always spiritual when open, potentially able to see beyond one's immediate concerns. The key is awareness. People tend to get caught up in the narrow focus, seeing only their own immediate problem, forgetting to look beyond.

I'm a great believer in beauty as a revelation of the self, the world around one, or other people. If we look to really see, everything is beautiful. Looking, experiencing, is spiritual. Even violence or cruelty in nature is all of a part. Deliberate cruelty, unnecessary cruelty is revolting. But there are predator-prey relationships—for one to eat, the other must die. With our Disney way of looking at animals we may find this regrettable, but it is the way it is.

The problem with ritual is that you have to enter into a myth by the performance of certain acts, which then are going to benefit you. Whether people achieve it or not, the desired end of all religious actions is a state of ecstasy, a state of union with the divine, by entering into the myth through ritual.

I have never been in great ecstasy, but from my very limited experience in a Christian setting, I've found that being totally involved with the religious action can be a very satisfying thing. It gives focus to your life, in the way of a core or center that everything else spins out of. The closest I see it in the Goddess is the changing of the seasons, the wheel of the year.

That we take part in that is obvious, especially to a woman. I've read attempts to mythologize it. I don't think they work. We're not literal-minded. The idea of the Goddess who weds the god and becomes pregnant and delivers the spring is all very nice but it's not a message you can orient around you. Late twentieth century isn't going to buy it as a vehicle. A majority of people, because of late-twentieth-century technology, haven't the vaguest idea whether it's spring, fall, winter, or summer most of the time. They don't even know whether it's night or day. It's bright all the time. When you've got temperature-controlled cars, temperature-controlled buildings, how do you find nature?

We like to think moral tone results from a nice list of ten commandments, a list of dos and don'ts; but I don't think it does at all. Real moral tone has to come from the core of one's being, how one is in relation to one's own life and other people. There certainly are people who have no core. They have nothing there, just a big empty hole inside. That goes for the young people who are really sociopaths, who have no feeling for anyone, and people who are running around saying, "I've got mine, I'll get mine and that's all it's going to be about." They may not get theirs by mugging or zapping someone over the head, but it's the same basic lack of regard.

If the Goddess is seen as life affirming, and if enhancing and affirming life is Her principal tenet and core of belief, than all actions have to be in some sense life affirming. If I do something that negatively affects your life, I'm doing something against the basic tenet of my Goddess religion. That might be where we can start getting a grip on it.

The problems that we face as a society today don't have to do with morals so much as they have to do with the damnable emptiness of our lives. We've promoted having things as the greatest good, and have become a consumer society. There's nothing wrong with having, but if your whole existence is based on having more, you never appreciate what you have in the first place. You're too busy yearning for more. If you're not appreciating the present moment, what's happening to you? If you're always looking to get more, be more, have more, you're not rooted. Life is at this minute. We need to be more here-and-now-oriented, life-oriented; not tomorrow-oriented or yesterday-oriented or get-more-oriented.

There are two shopping channels on that crazy box. We have made shopping a great virtue. And it's very alluring. The goods are beautiful. We have a fantastic culture—just see all the goods that are displayed everywhere. There are fantastically beautiful things, a great array of stuff at moderate prices, given the general level of economies of the world. No matter how much you say, "I'm not going to get anything that I don't absolutely need," if you don't watch it you're coming home with more and more stuff. It's all too easy to make that your focus in our culture, which says this is the thing to do.

❦ ❦ ❦

One of the major differences between Christian and matriarchal beliefs is that Christianity tries to control your urges, control your very nature, instead of working with it. Goddess religion and Wiccan belief say that everything has a place in this world, and the prime rule is that you do no harm to anyone.

Goddess worship also is being conscious that everything you do has impact. It has some effect on yourself, or on somebody else, or on some part of the world. Whatever I take in affects me. Whatever I give off affects others. It's not easy to keep in mind; sometimes you think it doesn't really matter.

Goddess religion can be an honoring of the sacred in everything and everyone. I think that idea can make major changes in the structure of society. The Goddess religion encourages us to take ownership of whatever is going on around us, to participate. It's all about us and what's going on with us, as opposed to what's going on with the gods, and with whatever might be in an afterlife beyond where we are now. The Goddess is really about the here and now, and not being afraid to get your hands dirty.

There's been nothing in the media about Goddess religion, but there have been some notices taken of pagan religion. Some people have come to believe that the pentacle is a sign of devil worship. They don't know the difference. They think they see devil worshippers way on the left, and somehow they've managed to wrap this whole package up with paganism. Or they see things like people balancing eggs at the equinoxes, and a whole lot of New Age stuff, which has become very popular. The fundamentalists don't take that seriously. They don't know enough yet to be scared.

If the powers that be should realize that there are so many women getting involved in this, and taking it seriously, then they would feel very threatened. At this point it can be viewed as a joke, but it's really revolutionary.

Isolation of sacred spaces from the world at large will lead to a downfall of patriarchal religion. Basically, you're considered a Christian when you set foot in a church, but it's a lot harder to be

Christian elsewhere. If your sacred space is where you live, on the other hand, you're cognizant that your whole life is worship. You don't separate it out.

A temple doesn't have to be a patriarchal structure. There were temples when the matriarchy was still in effect. There are critical periods of time when people would want to be in the temple. I believe there are times, critical passages, key points in one's life, when a temple is important. But it needs to mesh with the world.

🐝 🐝 🐝

I think everything I do expresses Goddess worship. Getting up in the morning, saying hello to the day, even making breakfast. I know the Goddess is nourishing everything around me. In school, they never told us that we were connected to everything else. I think everybody could and should relate to the Goddess idea. Goddess religion would make the world more fruitful, happy, whole, non-linear, and loving.

🐝 🐝 🐝

Anything you can do for the earth, or for people, or for each other, constitutes Goddess worship. You don't have to be formal. You do have to be nice to people. That is Goddess worship.

Goddess worship may involve women being in charge, but we don't try to push our ideas down anybody's throat. We let people have their own opinions and think their own thoughts, whereas traditional religion is men who like to rule everything and shove their opinions down your throat. The Goddess definitely has my vote.

We shouldn't be controlled by patriarchal words; a woman should have her own ideas. There are many different Bibles, and they all pretend to be the true Bible. Did God own a printing press? Did he print one Bible and say, "Here's the one and only Bible"? You bet he didn't. Men have invented, written, interpreted, and twisted it around the way they want it to be.

No one has the right to dictate to you how you should feel

about any particular Goddess image. It should be whatever you need. I'm very close to Hecate but I do invoke other Goddesses.

   🐚 🐚 🐚

Individual women need to do some reading and educate themselves about what the old Goddess religions involved. I know some, but I'm sure I know much less than I think I do. Modern technology, with air conditioning, stereo sound, cars, and so on, has cut us off from looking at the stars and moon, being aware of the changing seasons, being in touch with things the way the American Indians were. Many religions are very sensitive to the seasons because they were made by people who lived outdoors.

We can die or live by what we believe. People die when they believe they've had a curse put on them. What we believe empowers us.

Like traditional religion, thealogy does have a certain ritual structure. I think people want a structure, the way a child wants discipline. We feel more comfortable with a certain amount of structure because we're trying to sort the world out. I think this is what draws people to religion.

   🐚 🐚 🐚

I think I have an archetype of human greatness that I love and admire. On the other hand, I think that to celebrate humanness too much is to put every other living thing at such risk that I don't like human beings at all. I wouldn't be sad if we all disappeared. I mind very much the way we wrench every living thing to our own machinations. That's very wrong. I'd like us to stop before we destroy everything. It seems to me that our best end would be to go up in the incense of celebration.

   🐚 🐚 🐚

I have watched young women get very excited through reading about the Goddess in books. Women can discuss books, then they can go into rituals together. That's a very effective method. At the end of the "Cakes for the Queen of Heaven" workshops, women go in two directions. Either they start a reading group, to read about women's spirituality, or they start a ritual group. Sometimes they do both. The reading group seems to peter out, but the ritual group doesn't. Once they have that feeling for the power of ritual, they will continue. Each woman goes up to her own comfort point. It's lots of fun as long as they can get out and celebrate the full moon together, but not many go beyond that.

There's a big gap between theory and reality. Feminist theory supposes that we all come to consensus, we all get along, we listen to others. That happens once in a while but not so often. It happens in small groups, but the dynamics of small groups are always changing. Of course, my ideal is that women should act according to what I consider the best of their natures: thinking of others, revering nature, doing all the good things. Goddess worship is living, breathing. It's all of every day. To be aware of that is relating to the Goddess.

꙳ ꙳ ꙳

After my daughter was born I was first exposed to the idea of the Goddess, and it made instant sense to me. I was invited to a circle. I didn't even know what a circle was. But I knew as soon as I sat down that I'd done this a thousand times before; I'd found my way back around to something very powerful. There was the blessing and the chanting and time for each woman to speak.

I don't view the energy of the universe as male or female, but I choose to participate in women's circles because they feel better to me. There's more connection, more good feelings, more positive nurturing energy. It's more fun to be happy and self-affirming than to be full of guilt. I like to connect with other participants and feel that spark of life that's in me. Mixed circles don't feed me in the same way. We need to focus our energy as women, to be there for each other. There's a different spirituality when women are together without men. Afterward I feel better able to deal with my daily life.

※ ※ ※

What I like best about the Goddess groups is the closeness with other women. I haven't found that anywhere else. It's a wonderful feeling; there's a closeness intergenerationally, which I think is very important. We need that. There's also an acceptance of how important it is to be a Crone—a feeling that this is a wonderful and honorable place in your life. When I went to my first Croning ceremony, I knew that I was ready to be a Crone.

I'm much closer to women now than I used to be. When the women's movement started, it was too competitive. In the business world there were women cutting other women's throats to get ahead. But the Goddess movement isn't anything like that. It doesn't matter who you are, or what you do. If you're there, you're accepted as another woman. I think that's very important. Whenever I leave a Goddess ceremony, I feel stronger. It brings forth my strength.

※ ※ ※

I like Goddess groups because they're small, and there's no organized hierarchy. It is women together celebrating the idea of changing the world through our combined energy. It's very positive, very strong, a feeling of community. It's scary to think that one day it might become an organized religion. Right now it's grassroots and it should remain so. It's not good to get too big, even though there is the problem of preserving positive power without organization. Goddess religion could turn around the environmental devastation, the wars and so on, if everyone felt the way we do about sustaining the earth and the environment.

※ ※ ※

I found my way to the Goddess through the "Cakes for the Queen of Heaven" course. The Goddess image really taught me how wonderful women are. The divine image came to me through women.

I found my own strength; it was there all the time but I didn't have a name for it before. After the Cakes course I got together with a small group of women who met every two weeks to meditate together, or do rituals, or just sit and feel the group dynamic. It was just what I needed. Later I began to do the reading, and attend the festivals, and I realized just how fast the Goddess movement is growing.

I like everything about Goddess groups. What's not to like? I like the festivals, and I love ritual magic. I like gathering people around to take part. I had some excellent teachers. At first I joined Dianic circles that included men, and I got used to that; but then I found the all-female circles more open, more rewarding.

🐜 🐜 🐜

I only heard about the Goddess four years ago when I had turned forty. I tried Science of Mind, and the Hare Krishnas. I was leaning toward Eastern religions and body-mind connections. But it was never enough. I was struggling to replace a male image with a female image. I like the idea of teaching children about the link that they have with their ancestors.

The majority of humans have the need for a symbol. We were told that God created "man" in his own image, but a woman needs an image too. What I like about Goddess religion is the polytheistic approach, in which each Goddess has properties one can call on. It makes sense to me. It's like the way Native Americans would call on the strength of certain totem animals when they did rituals. Even though I liked much of what I heard about Hinduism and Native American beliefs, they are not products of my culture. I wanted to connect with my Celtic roots.

In women's groups I especially like the chanting, the smudging, the candles, music, and movement. I like being with people of like mind, coming together to do what feels right. I like the idea of protecting our environment. I like dancing naked in the moonlight in my backyard.

10

THE NEW AGE

*M*ANY DIVERSE PRACTICES, PHILOSOPHIES, MATERIALS, and superstitions are subsumed under the blanket term New Age. Some of them are profound, others silly. Some are recreational, others commercial. Some are exotic, others homegrown. Some are free to all, others blatantly venal. Some are sincere, others deliberately fraudulent. And some are not new but thousands of years old.

Examples of subjects that have been jumbled together under the rubric of New Age are: acupuncture, altered states, aromatherapy, astral projections, astrology, ayurvedic medicine, Bahai, biorhythms, bodywork, cartomancy, channeling, clairvoyance, cryonics, crystal healing, divination, dowsing, dreamwork, est, firewalking, flat-earth societies, flower remedies, gestalt therapy, Hare Krishna, herbology, holistic medicine, homeopathy, I Ching, iridology, kinesiology, Kirlian photography, macrobiotics, metaphysics, miracle courses, Native American spirituality, naturopathy, numerology, palmistry, parapsychology, past-life regression, psychic self-defense, psychic surgery, psychokinesis, pyramidology, pyromancy, radionics, rebirthing, reflexology, reincarnation, rolfing, scientology, sensory deprivation, shamanism, shiatsu, spiritism, Tantrism, telepathy, therapeutic touch, transcendental meditation,

UFOlogy, Vedanta, vegetarianism, Wicca, yoga, and zen. Insofar as they espouse medical theories that have never been scientifically verified, Christian Science and chiropractic may be added to the list. Feminist spirituality is frequently included also.

New Agers often bandy about words for things that have never had any objectively demonstrable existence, such as: Akashic records, apports, Ascended Masters, Atlantis, auras, body meridians, chakras, chi, devas, ectoplasm, energy imbalances, engrams, ethers, extraterrestrials, Higher Beings, inner planes, Lemuria, levitation, light-bodies, negativity, psychic forces, sensitives, third eye, and vibrations of the "etheric" variety.

Some people think all spiritual feminists embrace every kind of New Age pseudotherapy or metaphysical misapprehension. But many such women reject the New Age connection as regressive and generally detrimental to their cause. They feel that if thealogy is to be taken seriously, it must be distanced from the New Age constellation of frivolous, flaky, or faddish attitudes.

Critics often focus on the flimflam aspects of the New Age, as one journalist said: "The New Age movement is really just an advertising scam, from crystal healers to weekend become-a-shaman workshops." Another speaks of "a large pool of New Age barracudas, where the most cunning and predatory among us devour everyone else . . . the New Age community in New York is comprised of many . . . acts of fraud and theft that go on disguised as 'healing treatments,' 'enlightenment workshops,' and 'spiritual guidance sessions.'" Even the more positive aspects of the movement have been criticized for exceeding their proper boundaries and limitations: "Positive thinking and creative visualization may provide the inspiration and principles that serve as guides for our actions, but they are not a replacement for building an accurate picture of the natural world. . . . Faith without evidence is self-delusion."[1]

Of course, faith without evidence has always been intrinsic to mainstream religions just as much as to alternative ones. To believe something improbable, without demanding any incontrovertible proof, is what all religionists regard as the essence of faith. In effect, religions train the public in uncritical acceptance of the unlikely or the impossible. There is no essential difference between belief in a channeled "Atlantean" priest and belief in a biblical prophet, between a mainstream spiritual counselor and a "Psychic Friend"; between the Holy Ghost and the Kalki Avatar; between holy relics and "power Wands"; or between healing by an apostle's laying on of hands and a New Age faker's laying on of crystals. All are equally unproved, and nevertheless seem equally credible to the faithful. On the subject of faith healing, one doubter wrote more than two centuries ago: "Neither doth fancy only cause, but also as easily cures diseases; as I may justly refer all magical and juggling cures, thereunto, performed, as is thought, by saints, images, relics, holy-waters, shrines, avemarys, crucifixes, benedictions, charms, characters, sigils of the planets, and of the signs, inverted words, &., and therefore all such cures are rather to be ascribed to the force of the imagination, than any virtue in them, or their rings, amulets, amens."[2] Today we'd say "placebo effect."

The prime phony miracle cure of past centuries in Christian Europe was holy water, which was sold to believers for every conceivable purpose. It was drunk to cure sickness, it was sprinkled on houses to protect them from storm damage; it was given to ailing cattle and chickens; it was put on infants' cradles and used as a fertility charm. It was even used to project a curse on an enemy. The church allowed, and profited by, all such superstitious uses "provided they were performed out of genuine Christian faith," as of course they always were, because otherwise why would anyone believe in their efficacy? Even the chalice of the eucharist was used as a magical remedy. A curate of Rye declared in 1538 that any child with whooping cough could be cured by drinking three times from the chalice.[3]

Saints' relics and healing shrines proliferated all over Christendom, many of them still claiming miracle cures. In England, hundreds of miraculous healings were attributed to the shrine of Thomas à Becket, and thirty-nine people were said to have been raised from the dead at the Holy Rood of Bromholm in Norfolk, vastly outshining the performance of Jesus himself. Unhappy wives, hopefully awaiting their husbands' death to free them from marital slavery, went to the shrine of St. Wilgerfort in St. Paul's. It was generally believed that if a woman offered the saint a peck of oats, her husband would be magically eliminated. For this reason the saint was nicknamed St. Uncumber.[4]

Christians believe that their faith is somehow to be distinguished from "superstitious" faith in the New Age variety of healings and miracles that make no reference to God, Jesus, Mary, angels, saints, or any other such mainstream entities. However, it is clear that they all pour from the same pot. Clay Fulks wrote: "A firm faith in the supernatural is of the essence of Christianity, and belief in the supernatural constitutes superstition." Ernest Renan in *The Life of Jesus* pointed out that no miracle, Christian or otherwise, has ever occurred in circumstances where it might be scientifically verifiable: "Experience shows, without exception, that miracles occur only in times and in countries in which miracles are believed in, and in the presence of persons who are disposed to believe them." Mark Twain succinctly described faith as "believing what you know ain't so." And confirmed skeptic Ambrose Bierce described faith as "belief without evidence in what is told by one who speaks without knowledge, of things without parallel."[5]

Centuries of intensive training in credulity has created a civilization ripe for exploitation by almost any belief system that comes along, which may be one reason why even the most bizarre New Age fantasies are finding large numbers of adherents. "Our culture in general is embracing mysticism. We read everywhere that vitamins can cure cancer, that chants can put a fatal disease into remission, that eating right can give one eternal life. The feminist culture has not been removed from this foolishness . . . women are being lulled into believing, even by some branches of the women's movement, that nonsense, not sense, is the way to analyze problems."[6]

Of course our culture has always embraced mysticism, and its religious authorities in general have always been hostile to science because of the scientific propensity to put the horse before the cart: proof before belief. H. L. Mencken, who defined metaphysics as "an attempt to prove the incredible by an appeal to the unintelligible," summed up the conflict between science and religion by saying that "the essence of science is that it is always willing to abandon a given idea for a better one; the essence of theology is that it holds its truths to be eternal and immutable."[7] Humans, more keenly aware than any other animal of their own impermanence, seem prone to adopt any illusion of permanence no matter how fantastic its claims; but scientists must try to remain open-minded in their search for facts, avoiding illusions or finding ways to keep them from contaminating objective results. Oddly enough, it is the eminently nonobjective New Agers who often accuse scientists of close-mindedness, because the scientific community does not readily embrace their improbable hypotheses. New Agers tend to forget the primary rule that extraordinary claims require extraordinary proofs, and the burden of proof lies on the claimant.

Disbelief is often labeled "negativity," the leading New Age bugaboo, virtually equivalent to the medieval bugaboo of heresy. "It is not unusual to come across New Agers who would refuse to condemn the mass murders of Charles Manson because it would be 'judgmental' to do so, who would believe that a flying saucer had just landed on the White House lawn because it would be close-minded to doubt it."[8] And yet the same "open-minded" believers will reject the well-documented findings of geologists, physiologists, anthropologists, mineralogists, physicists, and historians whenever they contradict a favorite illusion. Believers tend to fear those who would subject beliefs to empirical experimentation, for they know deep down that irrationalities would be nullified by this approach. The same fear underlies the fundamentalists' dislike of science and the churches' four-century warfare against the advance of scientific knowledge ever since the time of Copernicus and Galileo.[9]

> The habits of mind encouraged by television are not only analogous to New Age ideas; they enable those ideas to take hold. One can even see the New Age movement as a philosophy formed for the television age, in which objective reality has been abolished in favor of the endless flow of images. The New Age offers an answer to the problem of how to live in the world television portrays—a world that is out of control and impossible to understand, and yet filled with magic promises and instant transformations.[10]

It is hardly surprising to find that women, rebelling against the sexism of mainstream religions, would reach out to various New Age philosophies, where they often find some measure of spiritual authority that patriarchal theology has denied them. In the television-trained, undereducated, politically frustrated population, magic promises and instant transformations exert a powerful appeal; and the New Age seems to offer nondiscrimination of gender, if nothing else. Mainstream religious thinkers may even encourage the identification of women's spirituality with the New Age, knowing that its kookiness can help to discredit the Goddess movement that is increasingly viewed as a real threat to the religious establishment.

"It sometimes seems as though feminist spirituality is merely the women's auxiliary of the New Age movement," Cynthia Eller writes. "Spiritual feminists aspire to healing themselves and their sisters through a variety of less than medically and psychotherapeutically orthodox techniques, including homeopathy, chakra balancing, massage, Bach flower remedies, acupressure, and so on. . . . Magic is regarded by spiritual feminists to be a form of technology."[11] Of course this is not true of all spiritual feminists, but there is certainly justification for the charge. If the feminist spirituality movement should ultimately fizzle out as just another far-fetched fad, it could well be a direct result of too close an identification with other imaginative frivolities that constitute New Age thought.

> From the time feminist spirituality first emerged on the American cultural scene, it has been charged with abandoning a feminist social conscience in favor of a mindless feel-good spirituality. . . . All the candle wax in the world cannot convince men that there is something wrong with rape, or the government that there is something right about economic parity between the sexes. Political feminists do not fault spiritual feminists for bad intentions, but for ineffective methods. [12]

Rightly imaged, however, feminist spirituality does seem to have its effect. Many women trained by patriarchal religion to think of themselves as congenitally secondary to the godlike male (he, not she, created in God's image) have found in the Goddess movement a necessary first step toward achieving a sense of their own spiritual worth and autonomy. Judeo-Christian traditions generally relegated all women to the service roles: dutiful wife; uncomplainingly fertile mother; self-effacing pillar of the church; choir singer but never priestess; servant of God but never his decision maker. For some, the depth of self-obscurity to which patriarchy forced the feminine spirit has been truly devastating. Unconscious resentment of that lifelong oppression can surface and become purged through an acquaintance with Goddess traditions and an active participation in Goddess rituals. It can be an essential preliminary to developing the capacity for political action. If feminist spirituality can keep aloof from New Age fads, it may well evolve into a useful tool for women's empowerment, and remain viable long after those fads have run their course and gone the way of phrenology, snake oil, the phlogiston theory, and the gold-making Philosopher's Stone.

Women need to understand that the majority of New Age theories are as demonstrably false as those earlier ones, and therefore doomed sooner or later to similar decay and decline. Take, for example, the currently popular subject of crystal healing. The scientific truth is that "there is absolutely no evidence whatever that crystals emit curative energies . . . to claim that crystals can heal organic diseases is to be dishonest, fraudulent, and potentially harmful."[13]

The books written by self-styled "experts" on crystal healing constantly state absurdities that reveal an abysmal ignorance of their subject. For instance, it has been stated in print that rubies emit enough heat to bring water to a boil; that sapphire cures Alzheimer's disease; that smoky quartz is "suntanned" by sunlight that somehow passes through rocks to reach it; that zircon removes all sins; that jade is not a product of the earth but a "mutation" from another planet not even in our solar system; that amethysts "throb" at the rate of forty-two trillion beats per second; that emerald "aids the chlorophyll in the blood" (there is no chlorophyll in blood); that coral cures hemorrhoids; that crushed beryl should be dropped into sore eyes; that the earth produces no black crystals (a majority of minerals do form black crystals); that all you need to disintegrate kidney stones or gallstones is daily meditation with an agate; and so on, throughout thousands of foolish remarks whose authors seem to have no notion of the real nature and properties of minerals.[14] When "explanations" are offered, they tend to sound like this:

> An image of wholeness uses the medium of supradimensional unfoldment on the higher levels of Light and the medium of dimensionalized time-space in the lower realms as the fundamental polarized infrastructure through which an image *in potentia* becomes an actualized image unfolding in creation. . . . Precisely fluctuated proportional balances between the linear and rotational vectors of the spiraling wave-form is [*sic*] one primary means for the encoding and transfering [*sic*] of information. . . . The primary energy gridwork of the Earth is composed of superimposed icosahedral and pentagonal dodecahedral geometries surrounded by a hexahedron . . . outside of these intermatrix lattices, energy interactions between matrixes have a high degree of threshold barrier potential, and therefore primary intermatrix interactions do not normally occur. . . . The nature of the Thought-scenario coding is that of multidimensional supraholographic matrix symmetry relationships. . . . When each matrix level of the Code reaches its specific positional orientation, it is activated into actualization and thereby apportioned within its corresponding dimensional layer according to its code-patterns. . . . As a multidimensional whole the Code is quantumly transposed into countless symmetrically interrelated matrix levels. Viewed as a single Code extended into multifold dimensions of unfoldment, each-dimension thereof is angularly-geometrically synchronized. . . . Within the dynamics of interdimensional harmonic resonance, angular affinity relationships govern the access parameters of universal energetic interconnection and intercommunication. . . .
>
> A domain is a holistically homeostatic integrity zone. That is to say, domainship is a state of synergic wholeness wherein semipermeable boundaries and abiding internal energetic flow pat-

terns maintain a unit's homeostatic balance. . . . In order to create a domain, the collective energy dynamics of a gridwork need to be accurately oriented in its internal energetic interaction patterns such that it reflects the divine order.[15]

Did you understand that? Of course not. Neither did its author. It is an example of pure New Age gobbledygook: meant to impress, but never to inform. To the unlearned it might sound scientific, but in fact it refers to no phenomenon known to science and cites no scientific mechanism whatsoever.

We have a continent, with a hundred million half-educated people, materially prosperous, but spiritually starving; so any man who possesses personality, who looks in any way strange and impressive, or has hunted up old books in a library, and can pronounce mysterious words in a thrilling voice—such a man can find followers. . . .

I would be willing to wager that if I cared to come out and announce that I had had a visit from God last night, and to devote such literary and emotional powers as I possess to communicating a new revelation, I could have a temple, a university, and a million dollars within five years at the outside. And if at the end of five years I were to announce that I had played a joke on the world, some one of my followers would convince the faithful that I had been an agent of God without knowing it, and that the leadership had now been turned over to him.[16]

The gravest danger posed by New Age "healing" is that it may be substituted for genuine medical attention, so that an otherwise correctible pathology is allowed to go too far. Those who put their faith in mystics, gurus, homeopathic noncures, crystals, flowers, and all the other odd New Age pharmacopeia, can become martyrs to their cause, dying needless deaths because of ineffective treatments. Other than that, there is little harm in drinking herb teas, contemplating beautiful crystals, meditating on the inner light, and developing positive attitudes by whatever means may seem to appeal. Spiritual feminists certainly may make use of such practices without being taken in by the frauds and the fools. In all such matters, caution is strongly indicated. As George Santayana said, "To be boosted by an illusion is not to live better than to live in harmony with the truth; it is not nearly so safe, not nearly so sweet, and not nearly so fruitful."[17]

On the plus side, some aspects of the New Age have been beneficial to many. They have helped people get in touch with themselves and others, increased awareness of nature and ecology, and brought women to greater understanding of their spiritual authority. The New Age has evolved interesting music, playful toys, and new ways to enjoy oneself. It has allowed many people to eliminate residues of guilt, shame, or fear that made them unhappy. Wicca, Tantrism, and feminist spirituality alike have lent strength to the resurgence of the Goddess image and given women a rebirth of self-respect. If women use magic in "setting a table for the mind," as one interviewee put it, surely that is as valid a spiritual pursuit as weaving a church's altar cloth or arranging flowers for an Easter service. As long as one can avoid the charlatans and refrain from confusing symbol with fact, there is much to be found in New Ageism that may point toward a better philosophy of life in the future.

The best way to protect oneself from the charlatans is to maintain an openly skeptical attitude and ignore those who try to banish skepticism by labeling it "negativity." Beware of any and all claims of extraordinary powers, especially when they are being used for profit. Beware of alleged remedies whose proofs of efficacy depend on faith, or hearsay testimonials, or the patient's state of mind. Real remedies are proved by documented lab tests and clinical trials, and they work for everyone. Beware of practitioners who try to blame the patient when a miracle cure fails to work its miracle.

Remember that New Age–type remedies were the mainstay of medicine for thousands of years before modern methods of research made medicine an empirical science. During those times, up to a century or two ago, millions of people suffered agonies that modern medicine can easily relieve, and millions died of conditions that modern medicine can easily cure. Although the placebo effect works sometimes for some people, a positive state of mind can't combat a serious infection that needs antibiotics; acupuncture can't begin to deaden the pain of a tooth extraction like a hefty shot of procaine; prayer can't prevent death from a ruptured appendix; and not one of the touted New Age cures for cancer or AIDS has yet been seen to work. Beware of all claims of "miraculous" cures. When they are tracked down and followed by serious investigators, they have always proved false.

In general it is well to remember that it is far more likely that human beings will lie or will be deluded than it is that the laws of nature will be suspended or reversed in some miraculous way. One does not find the truth by accepting the improbable before eliminating the probable. We already know that people will cheat, people will devise schemes to bilk their fellow humans, people will invent specious theories and promote them without ever subjecting them to controlled tests. These things are probable. The improbable requires much more convincing proofs—testable, reproducible proofs—before it can be considered reliable; and it is the claimant, not the doubter, who must produce those proofs. When no objective proofs are forthcoming, walk away and keep your money in your pocket. Don't become one more support for Barnum's old adage that there's a sucker born every minute.

MODERN WOMEN TALK ABOUT THE NEW AGE

Sometimes, feminist spirituality is equated with the so-called New Age movement, a resurgence of very old age ideas about magic, spirits, amulets, mysticism, parapsychology, metaphysics, and various forms of "holistic" healing. The connection seems to be generally detrimental to Goddess religion because it enables mainstream folks to lump everything together as lunatic fringeism. Yet, in the view of most women who are involved with the Goddess concept, New Age is a fun fad whereas the Goddess is serious and likely to outlast all the channelers, crystal healers, necromancers, fortune tellers, and other New Age types. Some have even suggested that patriarchal authorities have emphasized whatever connections could be made in order to denigrate the Goddess movement.

☙ ☙ ☙

I don't believe that "anything goes" represents knowledge of or worship of the Goddess. The channelers, the rebirthers, the astrologers, the crystal people, and the Fairies speak a language I do not understand and, while I wish them well, they don't speak to me of the Goddess at all. Perhaps it is because the New Age has no historical nor academically scholarly dimension that it takes on for me so much of the pleasantly silly quality of wishful thinking or let's pretend.

☙ ☙ ☙

Sometimes people get into the Goddess religion and then drift off into some New Agey stuff. That's worrisome. New Age has deep roots in the supernatural. You're looking without, to things you can't control. You're looking for guidance to "channels" or "higher beings," for example. If you're not in control of your own life, then it's not your own wisdom from within you. The basic New Age premise is that you're subject to control from your betters. So New Age falls right in line with the patriarchal structure.

A lot of people drawn to Goddess religion are also involved with the supernatural: angels, channels, Christ-energy. When you've been brought up with a religion that tells you you're supposed to look to this god-structure, this omniscient being, for your answers, you tend to look to someone else or something else for guidance. But I think there is enough to do in the here and now, in the real world as most of us understand it. We don't need to get caught up in some sort of trip out into the ozone. In many ways that's a selfish trip, devoid of real understanding. It's creating another mythology to explain what you don't understand, or to exploit other people. It doesn't really create any societal change or make the world a better place.

☙ ☙ ☙

Mixing feminist spirituality with the New Age is a way of discrediting it, a way of saying that it's frivolous and superficial, that it doesn't have any real substance or scholarship behind it. of course that's not true. I point this out to people, and they're reluctant to show contempt in front of me.

🐾 🐾 🐾

I'm very resistant to things that I would classify as supernatural, like channeling. I have no interest in things like UFOs, the whole range of Uri Geller things, and all that stuff. It may be true but I don't really care enough to find out.

🐾 🐾 🐾

I don't think much of the whole New Age movement. It's wacky. It's fun, and it's "in," and all the rage, and I get the catalogs with angels and crystals and all that, but I wouldn't buy anything that has a crystal on it. It's demeaning.

If the Goddess religion is attached to that, then it makes the Goddess religion less. Even though there are some New Age elements in it, the Goddess religion is not New Age at all. Take meditation, for example. Meditation has been around for a long time. Just because New Agers use it, that doesn't make it any less valid. We can use crystals as symbols, and know and understand that.

I use magic all the time. I use the "correct" herbs, oils, colors. I turn the altar to face north. I do all that, understanding that it's all theatrical. It's part of creating a drama. It's setting a table for the mind. The mind can take the music and the incense and the colors, and it makes whatever happens more meaningful. But it doesn't mean that anything becomes objectively more meaningful just because I use a pink candle instead of a blue candle. It's decoration.

🐾 🐾 🐾

M.A.s and Ph.D.s from places like the Institute for Integral Studies are beginning to blur the line. Someone going to the Omega Institute sees so-and-so Ph.D. and such-and-such M.A. It doesn't matter to them where the degree came from. Those people are given an authority. That may be good, but in another respect, there's a lot of really kooky stuff out there. Some of it, especially in the therapeutic or medicinal fields, is pretty scary. People are getting herbalists' degrees through the mail—people who have no idea what they're talking about. They can poison or kill clients. There are people getting acupuncture degrees by mail. It's one of my jokes that you can walk in with a severed arm and they'll say, "Well, take some garlic and some ginger tea, and you'll be fine." Garlic is prescribed for everything.

I for one do not believe in astrology. But there's a certain amount of peer pressure in women's spirituality groups to believe in it. If you say you don't hold with astrology, everyone looks at you like you're a fascist or something. If you don't believe, they'll say you're very closed, very conservative.

I think you can be spiritual and yet not believe in angels, devils, gods, or Goddess. What is spiritual for me is my awareness of, and interaction with, the life force. The spirit that I breathe in is literally the spirit of Nature. I wouldn't say that I believe in a Goddess per se, like Hera or Isis or any of the old figures, but there is a powerful feminine spirit that is very real, very important not only to women's lives but also to men's lives. I make a definite distinction between the spiritual and the supernatural.

           🐞 🐞 🐞

With the word "Goddess," many people think "New Age." They write it off. I experience that often. I find myself trying not to use the word "Goddess" just because people don't take it seriously. But if I talk of God, I use the pronoun "she."

Supernatural stuff, divinities and so on, are really a construct of the human consciousness. It's an attempt to explain things that reside within your soul.

           🐞 🐞 🐞

I don't believe at all in New Age or supernatural things. I don't believe in visitations from ghosts or anything like that. I have no need for a sense of spiritual beings outside myself. If there is something that's wonderful, it's everywhere. It's in everything I touch. It's in myself, in other people, in animals. I don't need to have something from outside. The older I get, the less I want anything from outside.

When "supernatural" things happen, there's a natural cause, even if we don't know what it is. There's an explanation. We need to be smart enough to figure it out. There are many unknowns. Usually it's not important for us to know them, in order to be decent human beings and live peacefully with others. I don't call that process spiritual; I call it self-actualization or self-awareness.

🐜 🐜 🐜

Could there be anything that exists that is not natural? I don't think there could be. What people call supernatural phenomena are probably psychological. The spiritual exists for me in the everyday. I'd like to be a scientist, so I can learn about things that actually exist. I would do science in the time-honored way, because that's the best way and the only way we've ever had to discover what's true.

🐜 🐜 🐜

I make a distinction between what I think is valid and what is phony bullshit. There are things that go under the guise of supernatural that I tend to be very suspicious of. "Super" means "above," which again places our existence in a patriarchal-type relationship of upper and lower, or good and bad. I think that's part of the terrible angst we carry.

🐜 🐜 🐜

I would separate those notions of aliens and UFOs from the spiritual. I don't think of spirits in a negative way. I like to feel that I have spirit guides, higher forms perhaps, more enlightened, whether they're really inside me or not. It may be easier to think of them as being exterior. I'm pretty much a skeptical pragmatist, but it feels comfortable to think that there might be spirits guiding me. I guess "guiding" is really the best word. I feel that my life has been directed to this point. Somehow the Goddess has brought me to this place, in this time, to meet the people that I've met, to focus my life. I don't feel that at any given time; it's more in retrospect that I feel I have been guided. I feel that I should be looking back into the past, at my roots, to guide me into the future. Nature is my root.

I believe deeply in the spiritual, which is noncorporeal but profoundly real and important for humans, because it is where we locate all our altruistic and moral impulses, and where we are able to "connect" to the world and to the universe. In a Platonic sense, it is the "realest" reality, and certainly the one which raises humanity to its most admirable level.

I think of the spiritual as entirely natural because I think it is real. Therefore, I haven't any use for the "supernatural," if by that is meant the miraculous or the scary. I think the universe is tenderly indifferent to us (to paraphrase—badly—Camus), but that we cannot afford to be indifferent to it. Perhaps what we call the spiritual is that in ourselves which responds, with love, to the universe.

To me, supernatural is something that has never really happened; it takes place in the imagination. What we might call supernatural is something that we don't yet understand. Ghosts, saints, angels, spirits all are mythological-imaginary. Something really "of the spirit" doesn't relate to the supernatural at all. It is within us.

I had a tenth-grade chemistry teacher who was very interested in the supernatural: altered states of consciousness, ESP, psychokinesis, dream traveling. I spent a lot of time talking to him about psychic phenomena. He introduced me and a few others to reading tarot cards. That was already a break with my upbringing, which taught that it was very bad to use divination methods, even though they used the Bible for divination. Seeing the thealogy that's in the cards opened up another kind of awareness for me.

I don't believe that anything external influences the shuffling of the cards, or anything like that. I'm not even certain about how the randomizing works. I don't really work at it; but I'm not sure that working at it would be the right approach anyway. I do a half-hearted shuffle and just lay out the cards, and I can usually piece together a story. We put out some random symbols, and the way we put the story together constitutes a guidance. You can come up with a situation, and it can be cast in an if-then format. Usually the cards lead around to a certain course, and then to an outcome. It's just a matter of giving general advice.

Even if I'm not assigning mystery to a tarot card reading, I still live in a lot of mystery. I'm a rationalist, but I'm also a mystic. People's definitions or rejections of divinity are based on their experience, of course. I have problems with people who believe only what they can see, who can't even imagine that there might be a flow around them. That's what my spirituality is: feeling the flow.

Why else would we be wired to take pleasure in pretty colors? Randomness is the best architect of all. I've heard a lot of talk about drug design, and lo and behold, the random approach is best, and sometimes the thoughtful approach is worst. Evolution is right.

🐾 🐾 🐾

I don't believe there can be anything other than what's here, occurring. Spirituality doesn't have to involve strange experiences or UFOs or anything like that. Life is a transcendent experience but I wouldn't call it supernatural. I like the idea that insight is instinct. It's within us. Spirituality comes from the inside out.

❧ ❧ ❧

The Goddess for me is spiritual. Spirituality is healing myself, so I can go out and help others. I have more respect for spirituality than for all that New Age stuff. I'm a scientist by training, and very skeptical about people who claim to be psychic. I prefer the word "intuitive" to "psychic."

❧ ❧ ❧

The "supernatural," without being tempered by spirituality, is trash. There's so much silliness, like articles telling you "How To Tell If Your Co-Worker is a Space Alien." It turns out that it's somebody who dresses badly, who wears stripes with plaids, because aliens don't know any better. They haven't gotten it right. That kind of thing is so stupid.

❧ ❧ ❧

Women who are New Age spiritual often say divinity can't have any gender, we have to get beyond gender. I refuse to adopt that position. I think that's very unhelpful, also male-dominated and oppressive. I try to be a model for someone who sees things that way, and who lives her life that way. I think I'm not a very good model, because I'm single and a lesbian; I don't have children; I continue to make choices about my life that lots of women can't identify with. For me it has been a question of how do I present the Goddess as a live option, as something that really is the wellspring of my life?

❧ ❧ ❧

To tie the Goddess to the New Age is like hitching a racehorse next to a jackass. Development of the Goddess cause will be held back. They can't possibly pull together. New Age is all commercialism and silly playtoys for people with only the most tenuous grasp of reality. The Goddess, on the other hand, can be the core concept for some really profound philosophy. Goddess spirituality is about taking mature responsibility; New Age is about being childish and credulous, and wandering about begging for one phony guru after another to rob you. It is not empowering for women; it only takes advantage of them in a new way.

   🐾 🐾 🐾

All that New Age stuff is just another way for men to make money off credulous women, just as patriarchal religion has been doing for centuries. Women's energy is being exploited all over again, in a new way, but really in the old ways. What's the difference between listening to a guru and listening to a priest? It's all the same male elitism pretending to tell women what to do. We don't need that.

   🐾 🐾 🐾

The New Age movement has some very good and positive things going on. It is certainly a nonthreatening door to the ideas of Goddess power and transcendent womanhood. The down side is the almost obsessional quality I find in the literature and the groups about keeping everything nice and positive and sweetness and light. Denying the dark side of reality doesn't make it go away, so then it becomes "blame the victim" (you called that mugger to you with your fear and negativity), or "karmic debts" (what you did in a past life means you chose a child molester for a grandfather to learn the lessons you need in this life). This is very hurtful and evil. Some of the channeling and outer-space contacts seem far out to me also.

   🐾 🐾 🐾

The New Age is a smorgasbord. There's something for everyone. Some of it I don't think too much of. I think there are many charlatans, many fads. Some of it is rooted in old concepts, and they're very appealing, but other things have evolved that are not believable. People can get lost in those things. It's almost like the hippie movement, which started out with some really great ideas and then went in some wrong directions.

I don't like the title "New Age." I don't think it's new at all; it's very, very old.

&   &   &

I have strong opinions about the New Age. I think a lot of it is nonsense. I don't approve of the so-called healers who try to convince sick people that they should feel guilty about causing their own sickness. I feel sometimes that hardships or disabilities are just bad luck, or just the way it is, not anything that we cause or do to ourselves. I think it's extremely cruel to blame the victim. Yet people still believe in that sort of thing. It's no better than priests telling people they suffer because they're sinful.

I'm not sold on the idea of karmic debt, either. I don't really believe in reincarnation, though I think we are some kind of energy, apart from the material body. Personality or spirit may be an energy form but I don't think it necessarily remains intact, or in the same form, after death. I don't see much sense in the notion of being reincarnated intact in other life forms. I don't think I'll come back in another body. Who can know any of this? Even those who insist that they're sure can't be really sure because there's no real proof.

&   &   &

The Goddess is not New Age but Ancient Mysteries. I like creating rituals, and I like the humanistic view that people's gut beliefs can be different but they can create rituals together. I think religion should be a matter of personal search, not established hierarchies. Under Goddess religion, people could be taught not to hate and fight each other; mothers could refuse to send their sons to war. The Goddess movement allows for a polytheistic view that you can select different aspects or names of the Great Mother for yourself.

11

PROBLEMS AND FEARS

W OMEN IN THE FEMINIST SPIRITUALITY movement seem to be
caught on the horns of a dilemma. Experience has
shown them that organized religions are incorrigibly venal, that
they soon come to a point where their whole raison d'être is profit
making, and that their purported functions of help, charity, and
spiritual sustenance then turn into their exact opposites. The
results are horrifying enough to convince women that they would
rather not be organized at all.

During their witch-hunting period, Christian churches invented
and perfected the protection racket. Reginald Scot wrote in the sixteenth century that accused witches might obtain mercy if they
would "gild the hands" of their tormentors with money, and numbers of women paid the churchmen yearly fees to avoid prosecu-
tion. The inquisitors, said Scot, "have the authoritie to exchange the
punishment of the bodie with the punishment of the pursse," and
it enabled them to reap much profit.[1]

England's King Henry II was encouraged by Pope Adrian IV in
the twelfth century to invade Ireland as a business enterprise that
would profit the church, which seemed to have been dissatisfied
with the sums so far realized from that country. The pope told

Henry, "If you wish to enter that Island . . . to cause law to be obeyed and St. Peter's Pence to be paid by every house, it will please Us to assign it to you." The church similarly supported many other invasions and usurpations by rulers with whom it formed economic agreements, particularly in South America, where rapine and theft of native lands was firmly endorsed by churchmen who took their own share of New World gold.[2]

Emanuel Swedenborg complained of the situation in Europe of his own time: "Everywhere the convents, churches, and monks are the wealthiest and possess most land. The monks are fat, puffed up, and prosperous. . . . The houses are miserable, the convents magnificent, the people poor and wretched."[3] The sale of "indulgences" and other church favors for money, regardless of any moral consideration, has been an ongoing offense throughout history, as have the instances of murder and crime within the church. At least forty popes are known to have bought their way into office.[4] Modern assessments of criminal behavior among Catholic clerics demonstrate a proportion certainly no better than, but roughly the same as, the proportion in the general public.[5]

In today's world it seems nearly impossible to get any large project accomplished without organization; but having perceived religious organization as unsatisfying at best and oppressive at worst, women in their small, intimate Goddess groups may be establishing a large project in quite a different way. Perhaps it will become a truly collective project, made up of many autonomous subgroups which, like the circle, retain their democratic nonhierarchy while participating in a united whole. Perhaps the typically human fact that some people take on more of the work than other people need not lead to a rigid pyramidal structure. In less civilized groups, people do what needs to be done, and some do it better or more assiduously than others, depending on their personal tastes; but this does not necessarily create hierarchy. When there is a big chore demanding the efforts of the whole community, everybody pitches in.

In any event, what women in thealogy do not want—and perceive as a problem—is the kind of organization that has made mainstream religions intolerant, greedy, and exploitive. Bible-based fundamentalist Christianity has long since shown itself opposed to women's physical or intellectual freedom, and could be almost as oppressive, in the long run, for men. "Having fundamentalists in a nation is like having congenital imbeciles in the family—it's a calamity," says Fulks. "Allow their mountebank, swindling leaders enough control over society and though religious faith would flourish fantastically, society would revert to the sheep-and-goat stage of culture."[6] The Bible is not an adequate guide for a world on the brink of the twenty-first century. It may be a definite handicap, as Tom Paine suggested more than two hundred years ago:

> Whenever we read the obscene stories, the voluptuous debaucheries, the cruel and torturous executions, the unrelenting vindictiveness, with which more than half of the Bible is filled, it would be more consistent that we called it the word of a demon, than the word of God. It is a history of wickedness, that has served to corrupt and brutalize mankind; and, for my part, I sincerely detest it, as I detest everything that is cruel.[7]

Those who promulgate any kind of new ripple within the ever-swirling mass of religious thought are almost inevitably misunderstood, misinterpreted, and turned into ideological supporters of greedy successors. Sinclair wrote: "I care not how sincere, how passionately proletarian a religious prophet may be, the fate which sooner or later befalls him in a competitive society is to be the founder of an organization of fools, conducted by knaves, for the benefit of wolves."[8]

The morality enforced by religious organizations has been a patriarchal morality, often profoundly immoral from the humanistic point of view. It has rigidly suppressed human behaviors that provide mutual pleasure between individuals or sensual enjoyment, however harmless, for anyone. At the same time it has encouraged behaviors that give pain and anger, that intrude on the natural rights of others, that foment wars, crusades, and bigotry. Patriarchal religion has wandered very far afield from its own pre-

cept, "Do unto others as you would have others do unto you." The
so-called witches' creed, "Do as you will, as long as you harm
none," is almost the same precept after all. Each patriarchal religion claims to have a corner on morality, when it really has nothing
of the kind. "Among the many myths associated with religion, none
is more widespread—or more disastrous in its effects—than the
myth that moral values cannot be divorced from the belief in a
god."[9] What is morality? Do you believe in "holy war" or persecuting in the name of God, or do you believe in being kind to
others—*all* others?

Social problems need to be dealt with, whether under the auspices of a religion or not; but the religion that prevails should, at
the very least, not hinder humane solutions to social problems. All
over the country, women are taking it upon themselves to address,
in creative ways, social problems such as wife battering, rape, child
abuse, pollution of the environment, sexual harassment, and various kinds of crime. One woman alone founded Mothers Against
Drunk Driving (MADD) after her own child was killed by a drunk
driver, and a nationwide revision of laws came out of it. Women
can do much when they become determined to act.

The problems that face the Goddess movement will be solved
sooner or later, and the perceived difficulties with the organization
process probably will be solved in an unprecedentedly creative
way. What will happen after that, only Goddess knows—and Goddess is the collective spirit of women.

It is necessary, therefore, for women collectively to recognize
the dangers of patriarchal religious ideas and patriarchal political
influences, fueled as they are by enormous amounts of money.
Amassing tax-free fortunes is the one endeavor that churches seem
best at, especially because their adherents are often afraid to refuse
them. Elizabeth Cady Stanton perceived that "The Church has done
more to degrade woman than all other adverse influences put
together. . . . Out of the doctrine of original sin grew the crimes and
miseries of asceticism, celibacy, and witchcraft, woman becoming
the helpless victim of all the delusions generated in the brain of
man. . . . It is folly to talk of a just government or a pure religion, in

a nation where the State and the Church alike sustain an aristocracy of wealth and ease. . . . If all the church property in this country were taxed, in the same ratio poor widows are today, we could soon roll off the national debt."[10]

In 1895, Ouida wrote: "The modern followers of Christ have neither fear nor shame when they pile up gold on gold in their bankers' cellars through the death which they have manufactured and sold . . . but to the masses of men and women professing the Christian faith death has been and is the King of Terrors, from whose approach they cower in an agony which Petronia Arbiter would have ridiculed, and Socrates and Seneca have scorned. The Greek and the Latin gave dignity to death, and awaited it with philosophy and peace; but the Christian beholds in it innumerable fears like a child's terror of ghosts."[11]

A society that worships cruel deities invariably brings up its children with harsh physical punishments, for hurts inflicted in childhood are directly related to the deep inner fears that perpetuate cruel behavior in adults. European civilization during the Burning Times was a remarkably cruel society that not only associated piety with pain but also inflicted pain on the young and vulnerable without pity, making a virtue of what often amounted to sadism. Early Christian *Apostolic Constitutions* enjoined fathers to chasten their children severely: "Teach your children the word of the Lord, straiten them even with stripes [i.e., whippings] and render them submissive, teaching them from infancy the Holy Scriptures."[12] Sixteenth-century clerics on *Household Management* advised whipping not only infants but their mother also, even when her behavior was entirely respectable: "A good wife should be taught by her husband, by using the whip to her from time to time, but nicely, in secret . . . avoiding blows of the fist which cause bruises." Then as now, battering husbands were secretly ashamed of themselves and didn't want the world to know about their cruelty. However, the treatise granted, "Disobedient wives should be severely whipped."[13] All such brutalities were part of the process of instilling the fear of God.

During the time of the Inquisition, of course, the fear of God was a universal and well-justified fear of God's minions on earth, whose system of legalized extortion Lea called "unspeakably atrocious. It was a system which might well seem the invention of demons."[14] Not even men, not even clerics, could feel safe from the horrors of that five-century holocaust. "Under the autocratic regime of persecuting Christianity during the Middle Ages of Europe, Christian dogma was indeed accepted nominally by great intellects, but it was accepted under duress and with a reservation. . . . The men of highest intellect were compelled to express the faith that was in them in the most guarded language."[15] The unusually outspoken Jeremy Bentham (1748–1832) declared that Christian belief in life after death promotes more fear than happiness, because "People who do not believe in life after death do not fear being dead, but believers fear punishment more than they hope for bliss." He also noted that the clergy "consecrate mendacity, make irrationality meritorious, use force and fraud to promote their interests, and enter into unholy alliances with the state" to subjugate their fellow human beings.[16]

During the Burning Times it was not unusual for the children of accused witches to be beaten in front of the stakes where their mothers were being burned alive, which certainly would have made a lasting impression on any young mind. Throughout the nineteenth century, ecclesiastical writings for children emphasized the horrors of hell and the torments that naughty little boys and girls would have to endure, if guilty of such "indecencies" as playing in the park on Sunday, or going to the theatre.[17] Deeply offended by such psychological cruelties, Ingersoll wrote: "In every orthodox Sunday school children are taught to believe in devils. Every little brain becomes a menagerie, filled with wild beasts from hell. . . . To fill the minds of children with leering fiends—with mocking devils—is one of the meanest and basest of crimes."[18] Recognizing the imaginary nature of all these frightening nightmares, he remarked that "Fear paints pictures of ghosts and hangs them in the gallery of ignorance."[19] Today the pictures are graphic indeed; they are painted on big and little screens, in film and video, and many are the children who think the monsters they are watching just might be somewhere encountered in reality.

Fundamentalism still promotes belief in devils with the same superstitious fervor that past ages lavished on their belief in vampires, ghosts, revenants, trolls, succubae, goblins, dragons, and other evil spirits. The magic of modern technology can make all such things appear very real to the naive mind. Even after mature rationality has purged the psyche of most superstitious credulities, a residue of vague timidity can often remain, to be activated whenever religious questions arise. To some degree, nearly every woman in a patriarchal society has been affected by these deep-seated fears.

> Women have to suspect that the entire symbolic universe that surrounds them, which has socialized them to their roles, is deeply tainted by hostility to their humanity. This touches on all their most intimate relations, to mother and father, ministers and teachers, husband, male and female children. An entire social and symbolic universe crumbles within and outside them. They recognize in the familiar the deeply alien. . . . Few women have the courage to advance more than a few steps on this journey of recognition of sexism as evil, so vast and convoluted are the layers of enchantment, delusion, and seduction.[20]

Timidity is the real reason for the agnostic contention that it is better to believe in God and his hell, and to find them nonexistent, than it is to disbelieve and find too late that they exist after all. "It is a fearful thing to fall into the hands of the living God," says the scripture, ominously (Heb. 10:31). But can one really like—let alone worship—a god so cruel as to have invented hell in the first place, or a god so petty as to worry his head one way or the other about the beliefs of some of us human insects on an insignificant planet circling a minor star on the outer edge of an unremarkable galaxy in a universe of infinite numbers (as far as we know) of such galaxies? Can one like a god whose ego seem to require endless abject praise from these poor, inferior creatures, and who will admit believing murderers and other criminals into heaven while condemning to eternal torture the decent, honest nonbelievers who never harmed anyone in life? Can one like a god who provides human beings with rational minds, and then requires them to insult their own rationality by believing a host of impossibilities and absurdities as the price of salvation? Would any thinking person really want to spend eternity in the presence of such a God, who "so loved the world that he made up his mind to damn a large majority of the human race"?[21]

It is curious that the believers' notions of their postmortem rewards tend to be extremely vague, compared to the vivid immediacy of their visions of damnation. Theologians have never been very clear about the allegedly blissful existence in heaven, except to declare that it will not involve marriage. The old pagan idea that the bliss of deities and blessed spirits was like a perpetual orgasm went by the board, long ago, along with all other pagan celebrations of sexuality. Now there is some ill-formed notion of joining in the chorus of eternal praise that this enormously egotistical (or insecure) God seems to demand; but is choral singing really all that much fun? And if not, just what is the nature of the bliss promised to the faithful? On this point, God and all his angels are silent.

The ultimate human fear is said to be the fear of death. Humans alone realize that their lives will end, whereas other animals live in cheerful ignorance of the fact that some day nature will, in some way, recycle them. Religious faith is said to alleviate the fear of death, and that is its primary raison d'être. But what if one should realize that religion starts with the creation of fears that need not have been inflicted in the first place? In a way it may be said that, like advertising, religion first invents and promotes a need, and then offers something to fill the need.

There is little fear of death in cultures where it has been generally accepted as a part of life, where suicide has never been criminalized because it is accepted as a valid remedy for intolerable physical or mental pain. In Europe, suicide was originally criminalized by the church in its anxiety to prevent accused heretics from cheating the Inquisition before they were arrested. In default of a conviction, which the torturers obtained almost always, the church might lose its right to confiscate the property of the accused, a right that brought in enormous riches during the persecutions. Church authorities therefore declared suicide a mortal sin, and eventually ruled that self-killed heretics could be convicted postmortem, and their property taken away from their heirs. Still, the ruling on suicide remained a part of canon law, and is still used by some life insurance companies to avoid payment on policies.

As a result of this inhumane ruling, many elderly or terminally ill persons in our society are haunted by a fear worse than the fear of death: the likelihood of intolerable pain. The mercy we extend to our beloved pets is not offered to human loved ones under patriarchal laws. Surely a civilization affecting to be truly humane should junk all "religious" ideas that increase human suffering.

It is said that self-preservation is an instinct, even though some animals are known to destroy themselves "instinctively" when very ill, by ceasing to eat or move. But what is an instinct really, in human terms?

Nearly every living creature has a genetically built-in certainty about what it must do to find food, to reproduce its kind, to care for its young, to avoid its enemies, and so on. Humans call this certainty instinct. But humans have no real gut understanding of it. We, alone among all the creatures of this earth, are almost entirely devoid of instincts.

It's true that we talk of human beings doing things "instinctively," but that's a misuse of the term. By definition, an instinctive behavior is *always* seen in *every* individual of the species. An animal lacking its instinctive behavior patterns would be a genetic freak, like a bird without feathers or a fish without fins.

Even among higher mammals, instinctive behavior patterns are plentiful. No bear reasons itself into preparing for hibernation when cold weather comes. It just does it. No groundhog sits down to plan the building of its home tunnels. No beaver individually figures out how to build a dam. No animal mother has to be taught to bite off the umbilical cord and lick her newborn to stimulate circulation. It's true that newborn human beings do share the sucking instinct with the young of other mammals; but the newborn human doesn't even know how to get itself to the nipple, whereas most other mammals do.

Among humans, even those activities that seem closest to animal instincts, such as mating or maternal care, may deviate markedly or may not be done at all. We don't really know how it feels, as adults, to respond to an absolutely incontrovertible instinctual stimulus. Instead, we bumble through life presented at every waking moment with an almost infinite number of choices, more or less consciously considering many different possible behaviors and choosing one which might be quite different from what another individual has chosen.

We are somewhat helped by artificial, culturally imposed pseudoinstincts like customs, habits, rules, and laws, providing frameworks for behavior. But such artificial structures are highly changeable, and may be ignored by some individuals even when accepted by a majority. Unlike other animals, humans are quite capable of denying even the "instinct" of self-preservation by destroying themselves, or the "instinct" of species preservation by destroying their fellows. At times, large segments of the human race can be all too easily convinced that a concerted effort to destroy other members of their species is "right," as in the case of war. At times, many people can become convinced that it's "right" to eschew mating and reproduction of the species, as in the case of ascetic religious movements. We are capable of inflicting upon ourselves, for no good biological reasons, pain, injury, unwholesome or addictive habits, even mortal danger.

Theoretically, human intelligence has replaced the genetically built-in certainty of instinct. Our complex brains *should* be able to sort out all our choices and lead us to the correct ones. But intelligence as a survival tool is far less perfect than instinct. After all, intelligence has evolved only very recently, whereas instincts have been helping creatures along for several billion years.

As cultural animals, we direct most of our intelligence toward assimilating, reacting to, and internalizing various aspects of our culture, responding to the basic needs of life artificially, at second hand, through others around us. We "make a living," not as other animals do, by finding or catching food, but by fitting our mental and physical efforts into a cultural context. Yet culture is arbitrary and chaotic, often opposed to what an individual may perceive as beneficial to self or species. We can't determine black or white; our world has become a million shades of gray.

Still, deep within each human being there is that residual animal longing for instinctive certainty, for the urge that brooks no denial, the behavior that can't deviate, the Truth that can't be questioned. Many of us want this so badly that we imagine it into being. Unable to decide for ourselves how to live, we create all-powerful gods to tell us. We make up social rules and attribute them to deities so they may acquire the aura of certainty. Most unfortunately, those who become convinced of these divine origins of their customs often indulge in a form of species insanity by trying to destroy all who don't share their convictions. Many people will blindly, slavishly, adoringly follow anything that has the ring of certainty about it, no matter how absurd it may look to the reasoning intelligence. Consequently we have cultural structures packed with miracles, magic, theology, superstition, spirits, mages, religious and philosophical charlatans of every stripe.

In our cerebral, noninstinctive approach to the problems of living we are one of nature's more daring experiments. The conscious (as opposed to unconscious) mode of behavior has been tried only in a limited sort of way by other species. Certainly there are many animals who learn and reason as we do, but not on so grand a scale; they have not thrown away the crutch of instinct altogether. The human reasoning mechanism is something new on the earth, and like any other experimental model is still has plenty of bugs in it. We sense its inadequacies, and are afraid to trust it completely.

Moreover, the mechanism is still cumbersome, difficult, and tiring to use. To discover and learn the facts about the world we live in is a long, tedious process occupying many of our best minds for many lifetimes. Most people refuse to exert the patient concentration required by the pursuit of objective truth. They prefer the "flash" of instant enlightenment which probably *feels* like the animal's response to instinct even though it lacks a practical objective. Our instincts have departed, but they have left gaping holes that intelligence and imagination frantically strive to fill. That's why a meaningless phrase like "The meaning of life" can seem to have meaning. What does life really mean?

In Christian terms, the meaning of life is to find out whether a given individual will spend an afterlife in heaven or in hell—unless one believes in the doctrine of predestination, upon which the Presbyterian church was founded, even though its theologians now de-emphasize the fact. For most Christian sects, only the alleged existence of God and his rules and regulations are credited with the function of giving a meaning to life. One of the greatest of fears, according to theologians, is the fear of finding life meaningless because these existences are questioned. But real humans seem less afraid of this eventuality than theologians fondly believe. Josh Billings said, "It's better to know nothing than to know what ain't so." Thomas Edison snapped, "What does God mean to me? Not a damned thing! Religion is all bunk." George Bernard Shaw remarked that "The happiness of credulity is a cheap and dangerous quality of happiness, and by no means a necessity of life." John Morley opined that "All religions die of one disease, that of being found out."[22] These intelligent men, and many other people like them, obviously had no fear of going along from day to day without a "meaning" in the religious sense.

"If god can be his own sufficient reason, there is no basis on which to argue that the universe cannot likewise be its own sufficient reason, in which case there is no need to posit god in the first place."[23] Similarly, it is certainly possible to perceive each life as its own sufficient reason. That is why, as a symbol of Nature, the Mother Goddess makes more sense; for a mother demands nothing from her infant. A baby is its own sufficient reason and its mother loves it just because it is there. With this symbol to aid understanding, perhaps humans may finally banish irrational fears in the comforting thought that, like all other forms of life, we require no rationale. To be is enough.

The concept of the Mother Goddess also makes more sense as a way to alleviate the fear of death. In studying the so-called near-death experience we find the same symbolism recurring again and again: the feeling of propulsion through a dark tunnel, and a light at the end of the tunnel where some infinitely kind, caring individual will accept and comfort us. People with conventional Judeo-Christian acculturization tend to identify this individual as an angel or Jesus or God. But the nature of the entity is never quite clear. Because so many people describe the near-death vision in similar terms, we may assume that we are dealing with an archetype universally encoded in all human minds. An archetype has nothing to do with Judeo-Christian theology; it is a primitive substrate common to all human minds, and perhaps those of some animals also, and open to various interpretations.

What really happens when a person approaches death is that the brain begins to shut down. Present awareness is shut off first, then recent memories, then the not-so-recent memories are erased. Last of all, just before the brain-dead state, consciousness is reduced to its earliest experiences, which life has long since buried in the unconscious. The memory of the dark tunnel with the light at the end certainly recapitulates the first experience of every human life: passage into birth, and the first impact of light on eyes that have never seen light before. If so, the kindly being who waits to take care of us is no angel or Jesus or God; it is Mother.

Mother is the first divinity on whom we depend absolutely in our infant helplessness. Mother is the one we trust. The buried infant brain has never ceased to know this. Patriarchal religion takes that inner knowing and artificially masculinizes it.

Therefore, even though the biblical god is overflowing with hate, aggression, jealousy, cruelty, and spitefulness, theologians incongruously insist on describing him as a god of love; and Jesus is made into a male mother figure with his maternal qualities of sympathy, self-sacrifice, and tenderness toward little children.

Jesus then becomes a mother with a man's name, and the Bible has no better metaphor for the idea of a loving god than to make a pseudomaternal freak of him. Bible writers speak of him as a "nursing father" carrying the "sucking child" in his bosom (Num. 11:12), and early church authorities talked such absurdities as "the nourishing breasts of Christ," or the Holy Ghost mingling milk from "the Father's two breasts." Of course, at the fountainhead of Judeo-

Christian myth we find the ultimate absurdity, man giving birth to woman. Fundamentalist theology assiduously conceals the fact that the whole fable of Adam's rib was lifted from earlier Sumerian scriptures referring to the belief that the Goddess Nin-Ti, "Lady of Life" and "Lady of the Rib" gave mothers the power to create their babies' bones from one of their own ribs.[24] Prepatriarchal sources show that it was invariably the Cosmic Mother who was thought responsible for our remote ancestors' lives, and to whom they expected to return after death.

Creation myths are also archetypal images of the birth experience, with their usual elements of primordial darkness, fluid, churning motion, and the first visual impact of light. The biblical god said "Let there be light" (*Fiat lux*), but the idea was not original with him. Long before there were father gods, the Goddess was celebrated as the light bringer who opened the eyes of newborn children and allowed them to see light. As Juno Lucina or Diana Lucifera, She was revered throughout the Roman empire well into the Christian era.

Even when the Goddess is converted into the fearsome Crone, who takes all life forms back into Her ever-churning cauldron to make them anew, She is hardly as terrifying as the god who will condemn the sinner to an eternity of unbearable pain. The ancients believed in reincarnation; their Crone promised another birth later on, another mother, another infancy, another lifetime on earth. That was the original meaning of "born again." Thus in most ancient mythologies, the Crone merged with images of the Goddess-as-midwife, just as the elder priestesses in Her temples became the *obstetrices* who preserved the lore of the birth chamber.

Perhaps to alleviate the fear of death we don't really need the elusive hope of immortality, still vainly called "sure and certain" by those who possess no sure or certain evidence whatsoever for its reality. Just as creation myths recapitulate the archetypal Goddess as birth giver, perhaps a better respect for life can be achieved by recognizing the same archetypal Goddess as death bringer, personifying all of basic human experience. For centuries Western civilization has been enmeshed in its own foolish denial of death, without really facing or comprehending the fear. The Goddess worshippers of old managed it better.

MODERN WOMEN TALK ABOUT PROBLEMS AND FEARS

Perhaps the worst aspect of patriarchal religion is its dependence on the instilling of fear. To "put the fear of God" into someone is seen as beneficial; "God-fearing" is a synonym for "righteous." Actually, the fear emanates not from any supernatural source but from men who have the power to threaten and hurt those who don't share their vision of a punitive deity, and who don't give credence to their pretentious epiphanies. Women know all too well that patriarchal society is full of men who are willing to intimidate, batter, rape, or murder women. Numbers of such men tend to be increased rather than reduced by god-morality. But the Goddess movement challenges the fears of both men and women by the very fact that it seeks an end to fear. Women in the movement seem somewhat less concerned about possible attacks from outside than about possible disruptions within. Having given up a mainstream faith, such women have already displayed spiritual courage. Now their major fear is that what they have found could be lost before it come to fruition.

      🐚   🐚   🐚

One problem with Goddess groups is that once they get above a certain number of persons, they lose the appeal that they first had. Women are attracted to Goddess spirituality because, instead of being a nameless, faceless body in a pew within a large organization, they can be in a circle with people they know and can bond with. The individual's voice is heard. She is not passively receiving the Word. She gets to speak and actively take part. When the group grows too large, it's impossible to have everyone speak.

Also, I think it's the nature of pagans in general to shy away from anything that bespeaks structure. When the subject of organization comes up, having to be compartmentalized for effective functioning, pagans seem to become really anti-Aristotelian in their thinking. They reject the creation of an overall organization, and that's a problem. People resonate with the rotating leadership and rotating power. It would be interesting if they could find a way to do this on a large scale.

    🐝 🐝 🐝

We need to develop intercommunications among groups. There are many small groups all over the place, but they don't communicate. We need to organize. That's an awful word, I hate saying it, but I think it's true.

    🐝 🐝 🐝

I don't know whether I like the idea of an established Goddess religion. I could imagine Goddess temples with specific teachings, but I would rather see it as more participatory, honoring the being of each person, and teaching people how to be mature and responsible. We should teach ecological balance, and revering the earth instead of just exploiting it for our own ends. Can that be organized? We do need that.

    🐝 🐝 🐝

I have a real problem with those who confuse psychology with spirituality. Instead of addressing spiritual issues, some people are getting into the victimization-confessional mode, which makes me want to blow my brains out after fifteen minutes of listening to them.

There's a danger in becoming an indoor pagan. If you're going to get into Goddess worship, you should go outside. Changing the concept of the temple is essential in modern America where we've lost that sense of the wild. Restoration of the wild should be part of the Goddess idea. I'm sure of that, even though I'm from Brooklyn and scared to death of a moth.

In the druid fellowship, nobody can agree on the question of how we might become one of the mainstream sects. There's a group of people who want to establish a church, and another group that wants to remain apart from mainstream religion because they're rebelling against hierarchy, the very thing we hate. I never wanted to get into political hassles. I don't want to sit in meetings and fight with people. It's a lot of work and probably would kill all the fun. I love the Green Man grove because it's mostly artisans and artists, who do wonderful creative ritual things.

I've noticed that the media have stayed away from the Goddess movement. I'd like to keep it that way. I would not want people to adopt a Goddess religion because it's fashionable. I do not want the unwarranted attention of the media, because when the American media get their hands on anything, they trivialize it. Goddess worship is a mystery religion. Anybody who's truly practicing it keeps her mouth shut, because the energy is drained if you brag about what you do. The religion is very personal; you don't make a big show of it. Once the media get hold of it, you can forget it.

I hope we stay apart. I don't want the media around. I would be very uncomfortable with that. What makes Christian fundamentalism particularly repugnant is its blatant publicity. There are all those books in print now about Goddess religion. What protects it from being broken wide open? I like it as a very private form of worship.

                               🌿 🌿 🌿

I would like to do whatever I can toward establishing a Goddess religion. It's hard to envision, because you want to keep it very special, you don't want the wrong people coming to be disruptive or to make fun of it. You'd like to have things written about it, but you'd want them written in a positive way. I guess at this point the best thing is the grassroots undercurrent that's going on.

How can an organization take shape? How do you avoid a hierarchy, once you get into money and buildings and property? I want to see the movement grow and flower and become known and respected as a part of everyone's life. But at the same time I don't want to deal with money issues or hierarchies of any sort. I don't like politics and power trips. Whenever there's an organization, politics become involved on some level. How to keep good feelings and prevent power struggles?

I don't think the groups can be kept small forever. I don't think an established religion could be that spread out, and cut off, in little groups with no interconnection. They'd have to connect some time. One group might have a particular version that they think has more validity than another's.

The women's movement is a little ahead of the Goddess movement in terms of recognition. It might help if we can ride the coattails of the women's movement. As women gain power, they can bring along a view of the Goddess that will become acceptable to the majority.

God religion is necessarily very different from Goddess religion. I even hesitate to use the word "religion" for the latter, because that word conjures up all the patriarchal models. To me the word "religion" means a dogma, a hierarchy, a set of rules and regulations. What can we call the Goddess movement? "Worship" refers to something greater than yourself, and I don't quite see that in the Goddess. What I worship is myself, and you, and all of living nature.

Established religions always frighten me. I even had problems with the Unitarians, because I had the impression that they wanted me to move into this unthinking everything-is-fine sort of theology, to say we must work toward justice and that's all there is to it. My own experiences, if too strongly expressed, were not acceptable.

The group seemed to be composed largely of people trying to reconcile their Christian-Jewish divisions in their families, the "so-you-married-a-shiksa" syndrome. Most of the time it was the woman of the couple wanting to compromise. I don't think much effort was given to the development of a different understanding. It seemed to have become very stale. It's quite galling to be asked to support a minister whose sole job is to tell you stories (which you can get off public TV anyway), especially if you're being told that there is only one acceptable interpretation.

We need people to facilitate, to schedule, to do the nitty-gritty kinds of things. Setting up a Goddess church would be difficult. You do need to have committees of people to facilitate. You need someone to collect the money, to rent the space, to get the information out, to sponsor educational programs. If we collect money, some should go toward feeding and housing the poor. Our society is moved by money. Goddess religion may never be established unless it has a sound financial base.

🐒 🐒 🐒

I don't know how to respond to the idea of Goddess worship as a formal religion. I think organized religion is so bad, and Goddess worship is so positive! To organize it and make it anything like an institution would be an evil. It would be like a brilliant young woman in a stupid little man suit.

I don't know how to save it from that evil. It has been hard to find a way to keep it going, mechanically—to have a space for us to meet, to pay for the space, to get people to do a ritual every month. The more we have to organize, to facilitate those things properly, the less I love it.

I have in my psyche a model of how women work together, but it's never a powerful model. I think we need the power to bring this vision into being, so that it would be the power of great numbers, but it would be in the context of a culture that's totally patriarchal. It always seems to work out that when we want to organize, we get a bunch of us together, and then a few people do the work and the rest bail out when the going gets tough. You have a union model, where everybody starts by saying, our power is in numbers, and then it ends by giving the power to the people who are willing to do the work. I'm not happy with that. It's not my vision.

The very possibility of organizing and institutionalizing Goddess worship raises old anger and hostility in me. Yet at the same time I do see that without some sort of organization women's circles are nearly impossible to maintain. And unless there is some sort of publicity (ugh), how are other women to find the Goddess? Furthermore, because we have no dogma, and because circles are, by definition—and by conscious and deliberate choice—inclusive and nonjudgmental, they also include women whose vision of the Goddess isn't mine. Feminist/women's spirituality is not synonymous with Goddess worship, and Goddess worship and/or knowledge is not indiscriminate.

So, if we don't want to become hierarchical or dogmatic or create inner and outer circles, how can we be clear about exactly what Goddess worship is? And how can we construct Goddess circles that are inclusive, but not New Age? And is that something we should be doing? Clearly, these are questions to which I have no answer, and I find them very troubling.

I don't think I'm a counterculturist or a rebel—perhaps mine is a failure of imagination or an excess of historical information. Whenever I picture an "established" Goddess religion, it takes on the form of all other "established" religions—it becomes public and dogmatic, rigid, bureaucratic, and—well, hierarchical. Even to the extent that my full moon group has become "established," and has had to organize itself, I feel alienated from it. I do not feel either comfortable or happy in the larger groups which have formed. I see that the same small circle of women turns up for the "Wise Woman Council" meetings, and the same small circle makes most of the rituals and takes most of the responsibility for the group's relationship with its location. It's as if organization has an awful life of its own, and that its life/pattern is hierarchical and crystallizes itself into the same old division of those who do and those who are done for. On a larger historical scale, I can't find any exceptions to this pattern either, and very shortly this pattern becomes one of boss-functionary-follower—i.e., a hierarchy.

What does it mean to be "mainstream"? Politically influential? Rich? Numerous? And isn't power the only benefit Goddess worship could seek in these places?

Both the achieving of power and its exercise corrupt. So I'm stuck. I cannot advocate either power or powerlessness, since weakness is another kind of corruption—one that irresponsibly allows power an unlimited field. The shape of this argument, as you see, leads one to stockpiling atomic bombs. Just in case.

& & &

The Re-Formed Congregation of the Goddess has established itself as a legal church, and I think there are others as well. It means they get tax-exempt status, they can have buildings, they can have ministerial credentials for people, and they can do all the things that give you the perks. On the other hand, when they tried to buy some land recently, they ran into all kinds of local opposition. They got a different piece of land.

I don't know to what extent I think Goddess religions ought to move in the directions that the established churches have, because those seem to be pretty usurious and exercise a lot of power over the people in them, and determine what they must do in order to conform. They also seem to be based largely on the concept that there's we, who are the good people, and then there's all the others who are not. If we continue to do that, it doesn't seem to move us forward as a culture.

On the other hand, we need those structural perks that would enable us to live, to get enough money to go forward. Most of the women I know who are doing Goddess work have no money. We're not in the mainstream at all, in those ways.

I don't know what to do about government. I would want us to change some laws, as a result of having Goddess spirituality. But the idea of dealing with Congress just sort of makes me nauseated.

I wonder what will happen with men. Men are bound to be attracted, to want to be a part of this. They'll want to be in leadership roles, and I can't see that we can let that happen. It just runs into problems. I think the role of men in Goddess religion has to be supportive. It's so difficult, because I like men; I just don't want them messing this up.

& & &

Sometimes the movement has to be noisy. Sometimes it might go overboard, because you are going to get a few nuts in any movement; you're going to get some angry people, and people who are not very stable. Unfortunately, when the movement is criticized, critics are very quick to focus on the fringe element that makes the whole movement look bad. Fringe people are those who are dissatisfied with their lives, and generally unsuccessful in their relationships; injured people, damaged people, sociopaths or psychopaths. By reducing our infant mortality rate in saving the preemies, the FAS babies, the crack babies, we are producing a whole generation of people physiologically unable to cope.

We are trying to find our center. We're all trying to find where we belong in the scheme of things, to bring order out of chaos. We all have our problems and shortcomings. Any movement can be taken to an extreme, where it can be twisted and gets a bad name.

Another problem is that in any group there are those who just attend, and there are those who become involved. This is natural within a group. In every group there is someone willing to write down the discussion, to make reports, to do the work. Such people rise to the top like cream. There's nothing wrong with being willing to take some extra responsibility and do some extra work. And there's nothing wrong with simply attending, contributing to the room rent, participating in the ceremonies, but not having time or inclination to become any further involved. This is true in every group. But a group has to be structured to a certain extent. There are practicalities to be taken care of.

🐜 🐜 🐜

For me there's the problem of what is the function of religion. I always fear that when something becomes institutionalized, the same problems will recur. I worry about dogma and expectations of conformity, all the things that can undermine the nurturing, empowering parts of religion. Women are a lot better at consensus than men.

Goddess religion, then, would need to address all the issues of justice and the way it plays out in society. Goddess knowledge honors the individual authority, whereas the traditional religions place all authority external to the believer. Theologians have a really hard time giving the ownership of that back to the congregant.

Individual women need to grow more spiritual, to attend women's circles, to go on their own path. We need people who are trained in mental health and spiritual growth. The problem is that typically a person will have one without the other.

🐜 🐜 🐜

The religious impulse always divides itself into two aspects: the personal, mystical, individual impulse that finds expression in the individual's life, and the public, theoretical, theological cult aspect. There have been times when those two strands have come close together, and there have been times when they were very divergent, when the mystics were not seeing what the public cult was seeing, and vice versa.

From what little I know of Sufism, I think this is true in Islam. Certainly it is found in Judaism. Back in biblical times there were the prophets who were really out of sync with the cult, and the mystical systems of the Hasidim, the Cabala, and so on. In Christianity there was the same thing in both the Catholic line and the Protestant line. There were people like the Shakers, who really didn't have much of a public cult. It was essentially a private acting-out of impulse. They joined together to do it, but the impulse was coming from within.

Where we are with the Goddess right now is predominantly in the private realm. Individual women— and, increasingly, men— express their religious impulses or feelings in terms of Goddess. I'm not sure we're ready to go into the public cult phase, for two reasons. One, I think that comes about organically, when enough people have discovered it, and hold enough in common that they can come together and proclaim that. I don't know that we're there yet. Two, I'm disturbed by the culture that we live in, that wants to get a buck at any expense, that would exploit the development of public cult, in the sense of a process, creed, and worship. I don't know that we're ready to get there without being exploited. I don't know how we'd avoid exploitation.

Do we need a new religion? Maybe we do. Certainly the rise of Christianity came from people who were feeling left out of the popular cult of their time, who didn't feel that they were getting anything out of the popular cult. In the first few centuries of the Christian era there was great diversity. Everybody had a foot in half a dozen camps at the same time, and there was a certain amount of decline. In the third century, when Christianity got itself established—which was the worst thing that could have happened to it—there was a lot of breakdown. Maybe some of the breakdown does contribute to people banding together to protect what they find, though I'm not sure that's where we are at this exact moment.

I would like to see Goddess people becoming a bit more mainstream. There have always been very good people who have been considered marginal by society at large. A lot of Wiccans are perfectly ordinary rational people. They aren't weird. And yet they're still underground. I think if Goddess is going to become widespread, it has to become respectable. That's a problem the early church had, too. They were certainly underground, and not respectable, and had to move out of that.

I would like to see us join forces with other respectable things that are going on, to see people who are professedly Goddess invited to discussions, to get on panels, to present as Goddess persons an ecological viewpoint. Our thealogy is an ecological thealogy. We would like to be present as Goddess spokesperson in ecumenical activities in the community. When people are gathering to celebrate an event, or to protest something that a local Goddess group also dislikes, then I'd like to see someone who says, I am a member of Goddess group, and I want to join your protest, seminar, or whatever it is.

I know that many women are still in the process of liberating themselves, and this is necessary for them. But I am disturbed if the Goddess gets stuck there, if all the activity is simply getting ourselves together and having a campout and shrieking and yelling and running around nude and painting our bodies and having a good time and self-affirming ourselves. That's necessary, but I'd like us to move beyond it. I'd like us to get into harder and less theatric areas of concern. I really am hung up on ecological issues.

There are retreat centers where people can take time out from this very exhausting world, and simply stop for a week and try to get back into being in touch with nature, and just having some quiet enter their lives. I'd like to see Goddess people involved in that. That's what Goddess is all about, too.

In this age, when money is not plentiful for nonprofit affairs, I wonder if cooperation can be achieved. If someone already has this kind of thing going, would they be so threatened that they couldn't allow someone avowedly Goddess to be there? There are also women's centers. Could we have an openly, avowedly Goddess person present in those centers? Might not women who are openly Goddess ask to go on a board of one of these organizations?

I think we have a unique opportunity to develop a committed core of women who are moving toward openness about their religious orientation, and could possibly move into some of these spots where Goddess persons are needed.

       🐜 🐜 🐜

We need women who have enough money, and enough of a commitment, to establish a Goddess temple. We have to have someone to manage the money. How do we do it without becoming a hierarchical, patriarchal structure? It's difficult. If there's no hierarchy, who is going to be responsible? The responsible person almost invariably becomes a leader. It gets very complicated.

I have good firsthand knowledge of the workings of churches. You have to have committees for this and that, tending the grounds, upkeep, and so on. We need places that can be sacred space for us, and we're going to have to come to grips with the fact that we're going to have to finance it. We don't want to charge women to come to sacred spaces, but then we're reliant on somebody else's charity, men's charity. Men should not have to finance a movement to overturn their society. Men did it to women, historically, but we should proceed with more integrity.

When I think about the Goddess movement becoming a mainstream sect, I suddenly see a church building and everybody filing in, and the whole thing becoming perverted from what it originally set out to be. If we build temples, and create a structure, we're going to need someone to take care of the structure. We need priestesses to mind and take care of sacred temples. We can't ever get away from that. It's a job to do. How do we make it a meaningful job, yet not elevate it to the positions of power that priests enjoy right now? How do we get rid of that class structure?

One method is to get involved in the organization you're trying to change, then slowly but surely start seeding it, to raise the group consciousness level. People have a hard time with separation. Take a group of like-minded people out of mainstream society, and how long do you have to wait before they grow big enough to take over, or at least coexist without a threat of annihilation from the majority? Probably taking over the existing structure and seeding it is the best method. But it takes time.

Right now the Goddess religion involves groups of women, spiritual separatists. But there will have to be space for the men eventually. There are already Wiccans and other men who are into the Goddess faith.

We don't have any political power. We're not organized. When Christian patriarchs took over in force, they went on a massive witch-hunt against women who believed that they had a right to be as sacred as the men. I don't see that the patriarchs are too far from doing that again. They may say it differently, because it wouldn't be allowed to happen in quite the same ways, but I think it could happen.

We don't want to be martyrs. Goddess religion did not encourage martyrdom. When you talk of martyrdom and giving up your life for a cause, it goes against the grain of respecting and empowering ourselves.

🐝 🐝 🐝

I think a majority of women find it really hard to relate to the Goddess. They get frightened; they think it's some kind of religious anarchy. It's the most amazing thing. We have been kept so ignorant of our own history.

Sometimes women feel that their place, their orientation, is being questioned. They may feel that they're going to be ridiculed. I also think they're afraid to confront a man's reaction to their new interest in the Goddess. The way they were raised, the church they were raised in, may teach that Goddess faith is anarchy and blasphemy. Women have all these various concerns.

I was at a wedding recently, where a woman was saying something or other would happen, "God willing." I remarked, "or Goddess, as the case may be." The woman flinched and said, "Oh, well, I can't be *that* avant-garde."

Very often the political arm of the women's movement prefers not to speak of any spiritual quest, or beliefs that smell and smack of the New Age. The moment you try to introduce the idea that there's a spiritual component to the women's movement, they instantly get very defensive. They'll say, "That's not what we're here about; that's not what we're interested in. We're interested in stopping abuse, changing the lives of women for the better." Somehow there's a fear that women's spirituality threatens outreach and credibility. There's fear on various levels, for various reasons. They may think involvement with the Goddess would jeopardize them in the efforts in the mainstream. I can understand that. We don't all have to be custodians of the same ideas. Some people want to take care of trees. Some want to take care of historical landmarks. It depends on the group and how much they have to interface with the mainstream. You can be in the women's movement and not need to have the Goddess as a foundation.

But I hope that within three or four generations we will see Goddess religion established. There is much opposition from the religions now established, Muslim and Christian especially. The Muslims are absolutely willing to kill over this issue. Still, eventually there will be changes. There's some effort now to deal with those mutilations of women in Islam. I think that's very important. Horrible as they are to read about, the more these things come out, the more they're discussed, the more we talk about those priests who have abused children, the more we realize that these religions are not infallible. Their leadership can be wrong.

🐝 🐝 🐝

The designation of "witch" still scares a lot of people, even though witches' rituals have now been integrated into many churches, especially Episcopal churches. I'm surprised at many things that now pass as "Christian" though they are pagan.

There are circles of friends and acquaintances where witches are completely accepted. Then when you get out of the circles to more conservative areas, you suddenly hit this huge wall, where the idea of witches is very demonized. In California there's a Republican congresswoman who gave a speech blaming the earthquakes, mudslides, and wildfires in California on all the witches and feminists. And she's in Congress!

🐝 🐝 🐝

Women are terrified of talking, of standing up in front of a group of people and saying, "This is what I am, this is what I think, and if you don't like it, that's your problem." Women need to learn how to talk and articulate, and not do it in the way men do it, talking over each other. Women need to get together for more talking, and for taking control of whatever we can. Women getting together and talking would help establish Goddess religion because women would start thinking about things like having their own religion.

🐝 🐝 🐝

I was trying to think what it would take to have an established Goddess religion, and what keeps coming to my mind is that women need to know that we can have it. We need to be exposed to the idea of divinity as female. We need to believe that we deserve to have a divinity that meets our needs, responds to who we are, in whose image we are; and that we can have it. Many women get very attracted to this idea, and then they slide away. They think, "Oh, no, I can't do that. I can't have that. I can't make that choice on behalf of my own life."

I find that kind of thinking, repeatedly, in all kinds of ways, when I work with women. There's some barrier that we have to get past somehow, in order to say, "I deserve to make this choice for myself. Not only that, but if I don't make this choice, things will be in a real pickle."

I keep thinking it's like the instructions in airplanes: "Parents, put your oxygen mask on first, even though your inclination might be to do it for your child first." Your child can't help you if your child has the oxygen mask first and you don't. It has to be the other way around. I feel like that with women. There's some powerfully inculcated inhibition that I encounter all the time in women against making choices for themselves.

Women will get so enthusiastic about the Goddess, and will sing the songs, and look at different parts of our lives, and look at what Christianity and Judaism have done to us, and then in the end they'll retreat. They'll say, "Boy, this is great, but I just can't do it, my husband wouldn't understand," or "What would I tell my son?" or "My children will stand out from all the other kids at school if I do this." I don't know what to do about that. The only thing I've come up with is to continue to present it as an option, to continue to put it out there, to refuse to retreat from talking about the Goddess as "She," and about divinity as female.

How to help women realize that we can understand the issues, that we can make choices and decisions about them, and the decisions and actions we take matter? So many people feel so incredibly disempowered. The scope of the problem looks enormous. The scope of what any of us are able to do looks so small. We believe that we can't even find the problem, much less know what to do about it. I think that's a game that we've been enrolled in playing, somehow, that we don't know. But I think we do know.

The rejection of the male god and the patriarchal religion has really big consequences, on an external, daily basis. That's why I think it's such a big step to take. Often, women don't think they know enough to make such a decision on their own. That's really not true at all. One of the things patriarchy does to us is tell us not to believe our experience of what we know to be true, but to believe what we're told. Therefore we get into the habit of believing what we're told instead of what we experience and know to be true. Then, it looks as though one has to be an expert to really know. I think we need to undercut that whole way of thinking about the world and start from our own experience.

I think of my sister, for example, who is five years younger than I am and has two children, and I love her very much. She cannot bring herself to believe that she really knows anything about anything. She hasn't read enough. She doesn't know. I think, here is this immense amount of power going to waste because she doesn't believe she has it.

🐾 🐾 🐾

The problem that we have with trying to introduce Goddess religion to this society is the strong presence of Catholicism, Judaism, and Protestantism which say that Goddess religion is pagan, evil, or "New Age," which is really old age, older than Judaism and Christianity. The minute we sit in traditional churches and try to empower women, a lot of people get uncomfortable. The Presbyterian church recently did a thing called "re-imaging," where they were trying to re-image God, and this made a major to-do in the church.

🐾 🐾 🐾

People are so locked into the God image and the control of women by religion, that the Goddess isn't allowed into awareness. Where I came from, Goddess religion was heresy. I don't think women can really relate to the Goddess until they can experience learning it from another. We feel it inside, but we need to learn that it's okay to worship the Goddess of our belief, that the Goddess is a good Goddess, a giving Goddess, so that we don't have this fear of the male god figure who can have some kind of punitive effect on those who deny him. I think the only way we can get women to relate to the Goddess is to pass Her on to our daughters and other females. It's scary to many people.

                            🦋 🦋 🦋

A Catholic priest in India talked about a message coming into his head when he suffered a stroke. He said he was told to "bend to the Mother." He talked about the patriarchy, and the fear that resides in patriarchy, and about the darkness, and the fear that resides in the darkness. He said he realized now that the darkness was the darkness of love. I never heard that before. The darkness has always been fraught with such turmoil. But the idea of chaos, of going toward chaos, has become exciting. I've stopped spending my energy trying to talk myself out of it, I can see that's what life is. I've learned order through discipline, but that takes no skill. It's the other, natural, disorderly world that's interesting.

                            🦋 🦋 🦋

One of the nice things about aging is that you have time to go inward. The silence is comforting. Though I love people, I really do enjoy my times alone. Going within yourself brings a lot of strength. I don't have fears anymore. I go everywhere by myself. Many women don't. They are kept frightened by the media and by patriarchal training in disempowerment and low self-esteem. I say, make your own choices and go where you want to go. Goddess power can abolish fear.

                            🦋 🦋 🦋

How can we possibly be afraid of anything the Goddess represents, when patriarchal society has already shown us the absolute worst objects of fear that can possibly be? Women in this culture have known torture, and slavery, and rape, and war, and the theft of their children, and physical and psychological mutilation. The media continue to love showing women being stalked, or abused, or murdered; and that's part of the culture we're exposed to every day. Even if the Goddess were a real demon, She couldn't show us anything worse than what the patriarchy threatens all the time.

I think women's fear of the Goddess or of themselves is nothing but a projection of the real fear that they don't want to acknowledge, the fear of men and men's society and men's god. Women need to see what they're really afraid of, and cut it out of their lives and get rid of it.

12

MARY

M*ARIOLATRY HAS ALWAYS BEEN A* major problem for patriarchal Christianity. Mary was finally banished from the Protestant pantheon at the time of the Reformation; however, the Catholic Church has her still. Although the people have always adored her, early church fathers were bitterly opposed to her. Epiphanius said, "Let the Father, the Son, and the Holy Spirit be worshiped, but let no one worship Mary."[1]

Anastasius forbade Christians to call Mary the Mother of God, "for Mary was but a woman and it is impossible that God should be born of a woman."[2] The Marianites, an early sect claiming that Mary was truly divine, were persecuted as heretics up to the fifth century.[3]

Many pagan traditions imply that the Christian fathers' hostility was based on their unwilling recognition that Mary really was just one more incarnation of the ancient many-named Goddess, virgin mother of innumerable pagan saviors. Like Aphrodite Marina, she was named for the primal sea-womb from which the "Sun of Righteousness" arose reborn at each winter solstice. Aphrodite Marina as mother-bride of Adonis ("the Lord"), was incarnate in the virgin Myrrha; and early Christians referred to Mary as "Myrrh of the

341

Sea."[4] Myrrh was closely associated with the annual birth and death of both Jesus and Adonis (or Tammuz), who also came forth from Bethlehem.[5] Among Mary's many titles—such as Ark, Gate of Heaven, Garden of Paradise, Moon of the Church, and so on—one of the most prominent was Star of the Sea, a direct copy from the cult of Aphrodite-Ishtar.[6]

In various guises this Goddess was revered everywhere in the Greco-Roman world. In Egypt, as Mother Isis, She gave birth to the savior Osiris. In Phrygia, as Mother Cybele, She gave birth to the savior Attis. In India and Greece alike, as Maya, She gave birth to the savior Buddha or his counterpart Hermes. She was the original Virgin-Mother-Crone trinity standing as "the three Marys" at the foot of Jesus's cross, as "the three Moerae" at the foot of Attis's sacrificial tree, or as "the three Norns (Fates)" at the foot of pagan Scandinavia's sacred tree where the god hung in sacrificing himself to himself. The original female trinity was eventually Christianized as an all-male Father, Son, and Holy Ghost, though an earlier version was a trinity of God, Mary, and Jesus, perhaps modeled on the father-mother-child trinities of Egypt and Babylon.[7] Even after its masculinization, the Holy Ghost retained the form of the dove sacred to Aphrodite and Her Gnostic counterpart, Sophia.

The patriarchs erased Mary's powerful, threatening death Goddess or Crone form as soon as they could, but her maiden and mother personae were combined as in the temple hierodules of old, the *kadeshas* or *virgines* ("unmarried ones") who gave birth to godlings in all the shrines of the Mediterranean world. Among many such god-begotten, virgin-born heroes were Minos, Asclepius, Perseus, Sargon, Zoroaster, Heracles, Jason, and even Plato, who was said to have been fathered by the god Apollo.[8]

Temple maidens used to be routinely impregnated by gods, who obligingly took the form of priests or kings for the purpose. The Bible hints at some such practice in Mary's case, for the angel Gabriel, whose name means "divine husband," in the biblical expression for sexual intercourse, "came in unto her" (Luke 1:28).

This scriptural bluntness was much reworked by the ascetic churchmen of later centuries, who kept insisting that Mary's impregnation involved no impairment of her physical virginity. Very peculiar mechanisms were proposed for the occasion. It was claimed that the conception was brought about solely by a secret magic word, or that God's semen was filtered through a sacred lily to enter Mary by way of her ear. Even birth giving was supposed to have left her hymen intact. Pope Siricius excommunicated a number of literalists who declared that such a delivery would have been impossible. Birth stories seem to have been copied from the legend of Buddha's god-impregnated virgin mother Maya, who gave birth painlessly from her side. Mary's delivery involved no pain, no blood, and no afterbirth—though how the divine fetus could have survived without the all-important placenta has yet to be explained.[9]

From the second century on, churchmen began to insist that "ever-virgin" Mary never bore any other children, despite the Gospels' direct mention of Jesus' brothers and sisters. They began to explain away those inconvenient siblings by saying that they were really stepbrothers and stepsisters begotten by Joseph in a previous marriage. But St. Jerome insisted that it was "godless, apocryphal daydreaming" to imagine that Joseph had ever been married to anyone else, so about 400 C.E. the alleged brothers and sisters were reinterpreted as Jesus's cousins.[10] Theologians have never hesitated to read the opposite of what their so-called Word of God really says, whenever it suits their purposes. St. Ambrose quite shamelessly contradicted Holy Writ by asserting that Mary would never have borne any more children because she wouldn't "defile the heavenly chamber with the seed of a man."[11]

The idea that sex and normal maternity constitute "defilement" has been intrinsic to patriarchal Christianity from its inception. Its doctrine of original sin, perpetrated by Augustine, convinced the Western world that all creatures born of woman are automatically sinful *because* they are born of woman. The Marcionites even insisted that Jesus was never born at all because he would never touch polluted female flesh; instead, he descended from heaven fully formed as an adult.[12] The church debated for nearly two thousand years about whether Mary should be considered as sinful as everybody else, and did not adopt the doctrine of her Immaculate Conception (i.e., her own conception free of original sin) as an article of faith until 1854.

Mary has not provided much help for women in desperate need of self-esteem, for they know only too well that virginity and motherhood are biologically incompatible, and the traditional Virgin Mother sets up in men's minds an absurd ideal of purity that no woman can ever achieve—nor should she even aspire to it. As conceived and practiced by Christian ascetics, "purity" was a perversion. In most human societies, healthy sexuality seems to have been necessary not only to the comfort of the individual but also to the peaceful interactions of groups. Conversely, the world's most cruel and violently aggressive cultures have been those that burdened their own sexuality with the greatest number of restrictions and taboos. It was male fear of female sexuality that underlay such historical horrors as the Inquisition and the witch-hunts, and still contributes to such modern horrors as female genital mutilation, physical abuse of wives, daughters, and prostitutes, and untold millions of sexual maladjustments caused by religiously induced ignorance.

The doctrine of original sin was essential to the whole Christian message. Without it, no universal redemption would have been necessary, and there would have been no reason for a savior. The patriarchs made it a terrible curse on women that, "as the Church's celibates saw it, weighed down on the normal motherhood of normal mothers. But this curse is merely a monstrous product of neurotic sexual fantasy," says theologian Uta Ranke-Heinemann. "Traditional Mariology does not deserve its name. It has become a sort of anti-Mariology, since although it purports to exalt the greatness and dignity of women and to paint them in scholarly theological fashion against a gold background, in reality its clumsy fingers crush what constitutes feminine dignity."[13]

By making Mary the exception, radically and inexplicably different from all other women, churchmen painted themselves into a corner from which they couldn't emerge by insisting that she was, after all, just an ordinary human female. Already in the fifth and sixth centuries she was beginning to take on the aura of the old

Goddesses, particularly because the church placed her shrines in the same spots where the people were accustomed to pray to the Mother. Many a temple to Venus, Aphrodite, Freya, Hel, Diana, Juno, or Isis was simply converted into another chapel of "Our Lady." Sometimes, even the same pagan statue of the Goddess was retained and renamed, so that old Europe had quite a few versions of Mary-Minerva, Mary-Artemis, Mary-Sophia, and so on. The famous Black Madonnas present well-known examples, perhaps the most famous being the one in the "Druid Grotto" underneath Chartres Cathedral, who was called Mary although the gypsies worshiped her as their own Queen Kali.[14]

Although early efforts to get rid of Mary were sincere and strenuous, they were in the long run fruitless. The people refused to be deprived of a Mother Goddess. Like the Ephesians shouting down Christian bishops with "Give us our Diana!" Europe's pagans seemed to accept Christianity only on condition that a Great Mother figure would be retained.[15]

Once the church gave in and accepted her, Mary's cult displayed an extravagance of devotion that virtually overwhelmed the popularity of God or Jesus. Ashe says that the vitality of the church really depended on Mary rather than on either of the male deities; without her, Christ "would probably have lost his kingdom."[16] Some of Mary's devotees claimed that her power over God was absolute. She was the ruler of both angels and demons, queen of heaven, empress of hell, "lady of all the world," and a creatress who brought all things into being. Like God himself, she existed before the beginning of time.[17]

Most of all, Mary represented love, kindness, and mercy that were not forthcoming from her male consort. People in trouble prayed to the Virgin rather than to God, who was generally considered more punitive than merciful. Many believed that heaven had become available to humans not because of any goodwill on God's part, but only because of Mary's influence. The cathedrals that arose throughout Europe during Renaissance times were called not God's houses but "Our Ladies" or "Palaces of the Queen of Heaven."[18] It is perhaps notable that in all the alleged sightings of divine beings over the centuries, from Lourdes to Guadalupe, visions of the Virgin far outnumber the combined appearances of Jesus, God, angels, or saints.

Mary is shown in religious art with many of the attributes of the ancient Goddess. She has the moon and stars under her feet, she wears the blue robe that represents the heavens, she is haloed like the sun and decked with gems like Mother Earth. A thousand legends speak of her charities and kindnesses, and the extreme sacredness of her every part. St. Bernard was said to have been directly canonized by three drops of milk pressed for him from her breast.[19] Goethe addressed her as "Supreme and Sovereign Mistress of the World . . . equal with the gods."[20] What gods did he mean? Churches still make money from the pious offerings of pilgrims who travel long distances to behold scraps of Mary's garments, locks of her hair, some of her jewelry, fingernail parings, milk, tears, or any other relics that the inventive imaginations of priestly fabricators could devise.

So Mary is, in effect, the only mainstream Goddess generally known in Western civilization. Nevertheless, her own church denies her the status of divinity. Her church, which even identifies with her and names her Ecclesia ("the Church"), has conveniently forgotten that Mary's earliest churches were staffed by priestesses.[21] Its pope declared in 1977 that the all-male Ecclesia "does not consider herself [sic] authorized to admit women to priestly ordination."[22] The excuse given is that the congregation is supposed to see the image of Christ in every priest—presumably, even the all-too-many who have caused scandals by sexual abuse of women and both genders of children—but the churchmen don't seem to want to contemplate the idea that someone might see the image of Mary in a priestess.

The problem with Mary is that, although millions of people adore her as divine, her church will not. She is still presented not as a deity but as a historical woman, improbable though this may be found, even by the church's own scholars. She is supposed to be revered for her humanness, humility, and abject obedience to God's will. She is the all-forgiving, all-nurturing, all-devoted mother. Yet even this persona fails to ring true. What truly devoted human mother could stand and watch her only son bleeding to death on a cross, and not curse the father who decreed such a horror?

The men who purported to explain Mary's character seem to have had little understanding or sense of the real meanings of motherhood. They only wanted to make Mary the mother their own inner child always wanted: sinless, selfless, and sexless. For women, Mary's evolved image is a model that patriarchy wants them to internalize, not a model that will lead them toward a new world of feminist comprehension.

Mary is a good start, but she is only a start. She can't serve women well until churchmen stop chipping away at the divinity that common folk obviously want to give her—until churchmen agree to call her simply and frankly Goddess. She must blossom forth as a deity fully equal to God; indeed, even as his superior in moral tone and ethical teaching, since she was never the Goddess Militant, guilty of senseless aggression. To serve women well, Mary must be clearly once more the Divine Mother, not only of God himself but of all creation.

There is plenty of precedent for this view. Even within the church that resisted her, Mary's praises frequently presented her as the true savior, rather than her son. St. Anselm of Canterbury wrote to Mary: "By you the elements are renewed, hell is redeemed, demons are trampled down and men are saved, even the fallen angels are restored to their place, O woman full and overflowing with grace; plenty flows from you to make all creatures green again." In the eighteenth century, Alphonsus of Liguori said that "the most blessed Virgin rules over the infernal regions . . . the sovereign mistress of the devils."[23] The *Apocryphon of John* addressed her as "the image of the invisible, virginal, perfect spirit. . . . She became the Mother of everything, for she existed before them all."[24]

Thus Mary was not only a savior of souls, but also an eternal being, coeval with God and perhaps even more powerful. The prayer *Te Deum Laudamus* contains the line, "All the earth doth worship thee, Spouse of the Eternal Father." The English theologian Wyclif wrote: "It seems to me impossible that we should obtain the reward without the help of Mary. There is no sex or age, no rank or position, of anyone in the whole human race, which has no need to call for the help of the Holy Virgin."[25] In early Irish literature, Jesus was designated not the son of God but MacMaire, the son of Mary.[26]

Officially, the church always objected to such lavish Mariolatry but eventually came to understand that Mary was a tremendously powerful drawing card. Her dollars-and-cents value was incalculable. So she was accepted, because churches almost always accept anything profitable. Between the fifth and seventh centuries, a biography of Mary was invented, and various festivals were placed in the calendar to celebrate events of her life. September 8 was "discovered" to have been her birthday; her Annunciation took place on March 25, the vernal equinox, nine months before the solstitial birthday of the pagan sun god on December 25. It was decided that her death occurred on August 15, and a new word was invented for it: Dormition, or Falling-Asleep. Her first presentation in the temple was originally placed on November 21, but it was moved later to February 2 to coincide with Imbolg, or the ancient pagan Feast of Lights, sacred to Juno Lucina in Rome and to the old Goddess Brigit, whose priestesses tended the sacred fires in Ireland. The festival is now called Candlemas. To honor Mary's unimpaired virginity throughout the process of giving birth, a festival was curiously named the Solemnity of the Mother of God. Perhaps one reason Mary was so solemn might have been that, according to Francisco Suarez, she never in her life experienced any "venereal pleasure," nor did her holy impregnation arouse in her "any unbecoming movement of passion."[27]

And how were all these details brought to light? By assiduous scholarship? By fortuitous discovery of a Marian diary? By official records centuries old? No, none of the above. According to Pope Paul VI, the information about Mary's life was "made explicit through a slow and conscientious process of drawing from revelation."[28] This is a typically papal euphemism for "we made it all up."

But not quite all. There were numerous pagan precedents for Mary that found their way into the Gospels, in one form or another. The three Moerae that represented the ancient Triple Goddess appeared in the Nag Hammadi texts as companions of Jesus: "three who always walked with the Lord. . . . His sister and his mother and his companion were each a Mary. . . . The companion of the Savior is Mary Magdalene. But Christ loved her more than all the disciples and used to kiss her often on her mouth."[29] It was Mary Magdalene who was called the first of the disciples in Gnostic texts, who announced Jesus' resurrection to the other disciples, and who had anointed or "Christ-ened" him in the first place. Many colorful legends accumulated around her name.[30] She was supposed to have ended her miraculous career in France. Interestingly, Joan of Arc was executed for paganism as a result of having worshiped the Blessed Mary of Domremy, by hanging garlands on the Fairy Tree called *Arbor Dominarum*, the Tree of Women.[31] Of course, some version of Mary replaced the pagan Goddess in a thousand "Lady Chapels" all over western Europe.

Having found Mary impossible to erase, the Catholic Church has made a virtue of necessity and put her to good use. As she has a way of appearing in visions to ordinary people far more often than any other divine entity, the church has deigned to accept as "genuine" more than 350 of her appearances in the thirty-five years between 1951 and 1986 alone.[32] Every time she appears, there is an upsurge of piety in the surrounding area and an increase in church revenue; therefore it is beneficial to the ecclesiastical establishment to welcome her in.

Still, Mother Church is no mother but a patriarchal institution ruled exclusively by men, who were very cautious about accepting Mary, with her dangerous tendencies to take on Goddesslike characteristics. Goethe thought her "worthy of all worship, our chosen Queen," and as the Vierge Ouvrante she contained God, Jesus, and all heaven.[33] Many times she was seen as even better than God— more merciful, more inclined to listen, and possessed of the power to talk God into anything. She was his mother, the people reasoned, and he would obey her.

If Mary is to serve as an empowering model for women, this aspect of her tradition would have to be emphasized, while her meek, self-effacing, nonsexual, impossibly complaisant character would have to change. The church can't have it both ways: either she can be seen as a mortal woman, with ordinary mortal feelings and failings, and a mortal body that gives birth in the usual way; or she can be seen as a Goddess, eternal, omniscient, all-powerful, a supreme ruler of the spiritual realm. She has existed for too long in a nameless limbo between the two, neither quite human nor quite divine. If modern women need her, then let her be made available as a fully realized deity in her own right, a syncretic amalgam of all the thousand-named Goddesses of the past. Then Mary could, perhaps, evolve into a real force for change.

As she is currently pictured, Mary is more an offense to real motherhood than a glorification of it. As a physically impossible figure of myth, she bleeds off some of the devotion that should accrue to the real mothers of humanity—the women who quietly, faithfully love and nurture their children every day, establishing with them life's first all-important social bond, that mysterious blend of tenderness, generosity, compassion, sensuality, and acceptance that the Tantric worshippers of the Great Mother called *karuna*, and the West usually calls mother love.[34] The West has no formal acknowledgement of that power, the actual living model of blessedness, because the West has no generally recognizable Mother Goddess.

Perhaps we should learn from the ancients who named Christmas Eve "The Night of the Mother," and celebrated it in honor of the real force of motherhood that produces not just a mythical savior but every human life in the world. Women feel that force in the depths of their bodies as they strain to give birth, and as they look into the faces of their newborns, knowing that a lifetime commitment has just been established. The Egyptians revered that force; they said, in maxims written about 1500 B.C.E.:

> Thou shalt never forget thy mother and what she has done for thee. . . . For she carried thee long beneath her heart as a heavy burden, and after thy months were accomplished she bore thee. Three long years she carried thee upon her shoulder and gave thee her breast to thy mouth, and as thy size increased her heart never once allowed her to say, 'Why should I do this?' . . .

When thou art grown . . . cast thine eyes upon her that gave thee birth and provided all good things for thee, thy mother. Let her never reproach thee.[35]

Throughout the pre-Christian world it was generally acknowledged that "the blood of the race" is transmitted in the female line, and that mothers are the true creators of civilization. Properly pious men should do everything in their power to help the mothers' great work of racial upkeep, instead of hindering them as patriarchal society now does. The devotion accorded to Mary, whose impossible motherhood stands as a reproach to the real thing, should be transferred back again to the true fountainhead of all human love. Instead of the oxymoron of virgin motherhood, that disbelievable anomaly foisted on a credulous world by a woman-hating church, let true motherhood be revered and honored as we see it around us every day.

Mary is motherhood dishonored by men's rejection of her physicality, and cheapened by the very images that pretend to glorify her. As the famous Virgin of Guadalupe, for instance, she is outlined in neon lights, woven into bullfighters' capes, tattooed on human skin, portrayed in flowerbeds, and printed on throwaway mouthwash advertisements—even though her original shrine was built on the genuine site of "an important temple dedicated to the Aztec Virgin Goddess Tonantzin, 'Little Mother' of the Earth and Corn." Mary's "Miraculous Medal," struck in the middle of the nineteenth century, was touted even more crudely, crassly, and cynically than the most primitive superstitious fetish: "Persons who wear it indulgenced will receive great graces, especially if they wear it around the neck."[36]

Mary has become a profitable commodity for the church, which derives enormous revenues from relentless promotion of tasteless artifacts like the cheap plastic portraits of her, and thousands of shrines where secret fakery causes her pictures to weep or bleed, where her idols are supposed to work just like a medicine-man's voodoo mask, where the trusting faithful are told that innumerable miraculous healings have occurred, though not a single one has ever been properly documented. Arrogant princes of the church don't believe for a minute in Mary's unbiological existence, but they give her to the naive masses as a sop, to stave off the rebellion of the Goddess-hungry. As much as the smirking blond bimbo standing by the shiny new car, Mary has become a sales gimmick. She brings ever-increasing profits into a rigidly patriarchal organization that is already obscenely rich.

Symbols are all very well, but they should stand for some aspect of reality that gives them a true meaning. Just as the Goddess was once absorbed into the figure of Mary, perhaps Mary should be reclaimed and expanded again into the Goddess who represents Everymother and the life force that creates and shapes us all. Instead of celebrating Christmas as a birthday, perhaps we should celebrate it as a birth-giving day—for is not every birth a miracle? Is not nature wonderful enough? Instead of picturing a ludicrously mature infant sitting up on his mother's lap and graciously receiving the gifts of kings, shouldn't we picture a genuine infant, utterly helpless, unable to control his body, wholly dependent on the selfless attendance of Everymother, who really deserves the gifts.

The real world, and real motherhood, should be seen as more sacred than anomalous myths, and more divine than any figments of men's imaginations. Just as every man is first created physically, socially, and emotionally by a mother, so also every god was first created by the Great Mother; and Mary, as Mother of God, deserves to be restored to the symbolic throne of the Creatress.

MODERN WOMEN TALK ABOUT MARY

Women raised in Catholicism may project their yearning for female divinity upon the Virgin Mary, the nearest approach to a Goddess that the church has ever allowed its congregations to have. An enormous pressure of public opinion forced the church to admit Mary to its pantheon, although early in its history the church tried to abolish her altogether. After several centuries it was found that Europe's new converts flatly refused to abandon their Mother Goddess and demanded some ongoing simulacrum of Her. Mary filled the need. But after centuries of official disparagement in opposition to the people's devotion, is Mary sufficiently Goddesslike for the modern woman? Opinions are divided.

🐜 🐜 🐜

I can't put myself back into the Catholic place, but I do remember that the Virgin meant more to me than all the rest. I remember praying to her. I think it's natural for girls to be drawn to Mary.

🐜 🐜 🐜

I would pray to Mary. I believed that she would hear my prayers. She was the Mother; she would take care of everything, like your mother takes care of you. I was always communicating with the woman. But it disturbed me that the statues of the saints in church were always higher than the Virgin Mary. I wondered, if she's the mother of God, why is she always down on her knees? If they're giving the Mother figure this importance, why is she not equal? Why is she always lower? The woman was always lower, kneeling. Those are the images that you receive. I didn't want to internalize that.

The idea of a virgin mother is utterly confusing. Those two words just don't go together, no matter what the church says about it.

🐜 🐜 🐜

Patriarchal theology is violent and has many unnatural stories, like Mary's impregnation through her ear or through the top of her head. The stories are unreal. Mary was the right-to-lifer's ideal: She was given no choice.

🐜 🐜 🐜

The only thing we were given as girls was the Virgin Mary, and she was always demure, and weak, and not allowed to have any power.

🐜 🐜 🐜

Thealogy doesn't emphasize submission. It goes the other way. Therefore, Mary is not the greatest model for women to be emulating.

🐜 🐜 🐜

I looked at statues of Mary, but they never filled my heart the way the stories and parables seemed to say they should.

🐜 🐜 🐜

I've been initiated into the Vedantic tradition, specifically because of the Mother. I didn't realize that I hadn't prayed since I was a child, until I prayed again to the Mother. I remembered a prayer that I used to say as a child, on my knees in front of my bed, and I realized that it was a prayer to the Mother. "Holy Mary, give me your help, and never let me stray far from you. Make me a good child, so that I can love learning. Bless my good parents and always give them good health." It's a beautiful prayer.

  That was the last time I prayed, and really believed, and felt connected. I was praying to the Mother then. My spiritual teacher refers to Kali as the Great Mother, or Durga, or the Virgin Mary, or the Black Madonna, or the Virgin of Guadalupe. She sees them all as parts of the Great Mother. It's so moving to talk with her about the Mother.

🐜 🐜 🐜

To the Lutherans, Mary was a sweet girl but rather stupid. Her attitude was, "Okay, God, whatever you say; I don't know about this, but okay, yes, sir." They claimed Jesus was this fully formed person well before the whole God and Mary thing came about, and she had nothing much to do with it. She was just a receptacle, a physical carrier. The incest interpretation only became clear to me when I started reading about all the usual Goddess-god interactions in other mythologies.

    🐜 🐜 🐜

The only female role model the Christian tradition provides is the Virgin Mary, the personification of submission. In accepting this prototype, women contribute to their own oppression and debasement.

Although Protestants do not deify and hold Mary up to be emulated in the way that Catholics do, they have not provided any other role models for females. The theme of female submissiveness pervades literature written for women.

For thousands of years, women have not created mythology or symbolized their values in any formal way. They have instead subjected themselves to and participated in man-created mythology, allowing men to interpret the universe for them and determine their place in the social order.

Far from being honored by God's choice of her as the vessel for his son as the mythmakers claim, Mary was degraded to a nonperson, one who had another's will imposed on her without choice. The attitude that women should feel honored to submit to men persists to this day. One must question why men have such a need to dominate women and why women so willingly submit to domination by men.

Instead of being venerated, Mary is to be pitied. She symbolizes woman mercilessly exploited; to worship her is to worship woman debased. Women cling, of course, to the old mythology that represents comfort and tradition to them. They try to deny its misogyny and even to make it "feminist" and "liberating" by rewriting it somewhat and making its language gender-inclusive. That is not enough. It is time for women to be iconoclastic, to shatter the myth of Mary and other male-created myths that negate the essence of their being. Women must get back in touch with their power and creativity and create myths and symbols of their own to celebrate their spirituality.

13

VISIONS
OF THE FUTURE

*I*MAGINE A WORLD IN WHICH no child is ever born unwanted or unloved. No child is born to a mother too young, too poor, too busy, or too ignorant to care for it properly. Consequently, no child is abused, neglected, or abandoned. Unwelcome births are prevented by general everyday use of birth control or abortion, which are considered the just choices of women, and not any man's business. Thus, every pregnancy carried to term is the result of conscious planning and preparation by responsible adults. Every baby is welcomed with joy and is tenderly nurtured. With women in control of their own reproductive functions, human populations do not outgrow the capacity of their environment to sustain them.

Imagine a world in which these loved and wanted children are raised gently, without harsh punishments or implanted fears. They are not exposed to acts of violence. They are not encouraged to play with imitation weapons in games of aggression. They do not sit for hours in front of television sets watching cartoon creatures smashing, shooting, or blowing each other up. They do not witness any murders, rapes, physical assaults, or battles presented in the guise of entertainment, for such things are not considered enjoyable.

On the other hand, sexuality is not only considered enjoyable but is honored as a sacred ritual that puts humans in touch with a higher, warmer kind of interpersonal communication. Sexuality and sin are not linked in the public consciousness. Sensuality in general is freely enjoyed as a positive interaction with others and with the environment. Young people are carefully trained, as they grow into adolescence, in the right use of their sexual capacities. The 10 percent of us who seem to be born with a homosexual orientation are freely permitted to take the route that seems natural to them, without censure or blame. Rape is unthinkable because no one, man or woman, is conditioned to associate sex with cruelty.

Imagine a world in which cooperative groups help each other raise the children, care for the sick and the aged, maintain and create the evolving culture, and do the work of the community, each person contributing according to her or his capacities. Imagine a world in which people are taught to help one another as readily as, in our world, they are taught to compete. Imagine a world in which no group, race, nation, color, or ethnic background is considered inferior to any other, but all are appreciated as authentic manifestations of human diversity. Though people may differ, they can recognize each other as siblings, all children of one Mother Earth. Imagine a world in which intolerance is unknown, and war unthinkable.

Imagine a world in which the unique, sentient lives of animals are as well respected as the unique, sentient lives of people; where no wild creature is ever killed for "sport," and no domestic animal is abused. People do not use natural fur, ivory, horn, or other animal products that involve gratuitous slaughter or species endangerment. If animals are slain for meat, it is done humanely, without causing suffering, and no part of the carcass is wasted. Pets are cared for with competence and kindness, so that their lives and deaths are made as comfortable as possible.

Humans, too, can be assured of comfortable deaths. In cases of painful terminal illness, euthanasia is both legal and customary. Each person is granted unchallenged control of her or his own life, including the decision to end it. Like birth giving, voluntary death is viewed as the rightful choice of a mature individual, to be supported and helped by others.

Imagine a world in which no one is very rich or very poor, but everyone has enough to live comfortably. Acquisitiveness and conspicuous consumption are not admired, but rather viewed as bad manners. Therefore, envy and greed are not common motivations. People work hard to win their neighbors' respect, to express their own creativity, to enjoy the privilege of education, and to take pride in using their strengths and their inventiveness to help others. Those who can't work—the very young, the very old, and invalids—are lovingly cared for. The moral code presents helpfulness as a primary virtue, and causing unhappiness as a primary sin. People trust one another. "Do what you will," say the teachers of ethics, "as long as you harm no one." And they say all acts of love and pleasure are righteous.

In short, imagine a world in which every person may enjoy what every good mother wishes for her child: a useful, happy life that develops her or his capacities to their full extent, and fosters positive, rewarding relations with others. If there be a religion in this world, it would be one that projects that maternal guardian spirit onto Mother Nature, Mother Earth, symbol of the feminine forces of our uniquely life-giving, life-sustaining planet. No punitive, demanding god would have a place there, but rather a recognizably metaphoric embodiment of the milk of human kindness, idealized and writ large as a supreme Mother Goddess, not transcendent but immanent in the human spirit.

Such is the world toward which the new women's spirituality points as its Utopian goal. Who can say it is not achievable? What we can imagine clearly enough, we may well be able to do.

As an author I have the privilege of meeting many women in the still-amorphous Goddess movement. These intelligent women tend to be skeptical of the claims of patriarchal religions and other supernaturalistic beliefs. They know that every god in history is made in the image of man, with many of man's faults, such as jealousy, greed, self-conceit, and cruelty. Their Goddess is emphatically *not* God-with-a-feminine-suffix. She is a deity with whom women can feel comfortable, created according to women's morality and priorities, which are different from those of men. Though men have always lied about the source of their god-vision, women's Goddess is a conscious and deliberate act of their creation, springing from the only true source of any deity, the archetypal human mind.

Thus is seems that, for the first time in history, a truly honest religion is taking form. It is to be hoped that the Goddess movement will continue in this direction. Religion has been a con game for much too long. It's time for the world to receive a better idea from its women, who can supply a sensible spirituality for sensible people.

MODERN WOMEN'S VISIONS OF THE FUTURE

Women foresee increasing acceptance of the Goddess, and postulate several improvements in cultural and social relations as a result. Most people who imagine a society overtly dedicated to the Goddess image perceive it as a kinder, gentler way of life, focused on nature, ecology, and reduction of interpersonal or intergroup violence. These are laudable aims, perhaps less achievable in the context of patriarchy than they would be under the visions of female authority.

🐾 🐾 🐾

I think it's going to take a lot of exposure to get more people interested in the Goddess. We should be open about it, talk about it, share it with others. The idea has to spread from person to person. However, I wouldn't want it to be pushed down people's throats, like Christianity. It should be more of a grassroots movement.

🐾 🐾 🐾

I can imagine a Goddess-based religion, but I can't say when it will occur. The women's spirituality movement is pointing in that direction. I don't believe it will ever be as structured as traditional religions, because women don't establish hierarchies. Women in a group try to work together and not against each other.

🐝 🐝 🐝

An established Goddess religion would infuse the world with trust and compassion. It would be caring, which is one thing sadly missing from our society. We should listen to people with compassion, not with judgment, mean-spiritedness, or odious comparisons. I can see some pretty intense beauty in most people.

If a woman can listen to her heart, it doesn't matter what she deifies. A Goddess religion is what we want in our souls. When the Goddess religion comes about, it will be very natural. It will just happen, like when you start or end your period. The main thing is for each individual woman to get comfortable with herself and listen to her heart.

Goddess religion may help this country change its priorities. I'd like to see education, welfare, and eldercare getting all the money they need, and the military would have to hold bake sales.

🐝 🐝 🐝

The world is corrupt, and an established Goddess religion would absolutely turn that upside down: it would be the opposite of what we have now. Women, because of their role as mothers, have a caring and a respect for others that men somehow don't have. I don't think women would ever create wars, in the way that men do. When you've given birth to children, you aren't going to send them out to kill each other. I don't understand that in men. Women would be more cooperative, would find other ways to solve things, rather than having to pick up arms and go to war. Women have more spirit of cooperation, and the Goddess religion reinforces that.

More publicity for the Goddess religion will help bring it into public view. The more the public can see it, the more it gets mentioned and becomes a household word, the more accepted it will be. That's the best start we could have for it. It is going very quickly, and I think there will be some backlash. We're already seeing a lot of backlash against feminism. At this point in time, the Goddess religion is not yet prominent in the public mind. If it were, the churches would be scared shitless.

I see the Goddess religion coming into power more as an evolutionary process than as a revolution. Individual women will be changed, and then their impact on society will change society. The fact that there has been a merging of spiritual feminism with political feminism probably represents a step in that direction. I know many women who are involved in women's spirituality are not particularly political. They don't see a need to be political. Still, you have to be somewhat involved with politics if you want to help change laws. You have to have people who are going to be in decision-making positions who have the same sense of values that you have.

I like the fact that each woman can create her own sacred space and invite other women to share it. Everywhere we gather, we make that sacred space. I envision something like a plot of land, with areas for open-air and enclosed events. In this place, a clearing can be a sacred space for any ritual. Caves were wonderful sacred spaces. Women feel that the Goddess-oriented sacred space is a place where every woman is welcome.

The raising of offspring should be one of our most sacred priorities. Teaching and taking care of children is going to mark the success of the Goddess religion. If we can nurture the children and bring them up properly, then they're going to do their own work as they come of age. This can break patriarchal control. Maybe we need Goddess day-care centers. The grassroots movement at that point would be tremendous.

🐾 🐾 🐾

I think the Goddess movement is healing for the earth, and it is infiltrating many spheres of activity. It's a white middle-class phenomenon at present, but no people can dismiss it. It's going to be with your daughter, or your granddaughter. It potentially includes all women, Native American, African American, European, Asian, and every other cultural background. Many of them have always had Goddesses of some sort.

🐝 🐝 🐝

A combination of pagan and Goddess beliefs in the Unitarian Universalist context will be very useful. What is needed is for women in other religions to reach out and take the power of female images for themselves. I was thinking of Hinduism, or some of the African religions, or other oriental religions whose details I don't know. Women want to exert more influence, without being hierarchical. We want our ways of thinking and being to have more respect and more elbow room. That is beginning to happen now. I don't really know how to nurture and foster it any more than by doing just what we are doing. We need safe places where thealogy can be explored.

It would be helpful to provide Goddess concepts in acceptable bite-size bits, as in details of stories. The more there is of that kind of palatable snippet of a different way of looking at the world, the more the Goddess will be brought into mainstream culture.

It's clear to me that religion is an expression of what people want. There may be nothing actually out there. We'll never know. Whether it's really true or not is irrelevant. We construct the world we live in, based on our beliefs. Spirituality emanates not from reality but from the belief system.

Sometimes, to find out what we really mean, we must take three or four different statements and see where they overlap. It's an imprecise way of communicating, but I think it's the way our brains operate, both male and female. That's how I think of thealogy. We'll say things that are overlapping, one almost like another but different. No one is an exact overlap of anyone else. That's our richness. But in male theology, the rules are like something drawn up by lawyers. Rather than becoming richer, they only get more and more precise.

🐝 🐝 🐝

Even though the Goddess religion will change the way girls are raised, it's even more essential to change the way they're treated by men. The world needs enlightened men brought up by feminist mothers. Men have to learn that their worth is not based on whom they can control.

An established Goddess religion would change everything. More people would be happy in themselves and their relationships. The struggles I see around me are based on people's issues with their self-worth. A Goddess religion instills a really good, honest sense of self-worth. I don't know anything else that does that. Once a child loves her/himself, you don't have to teach morals. If people love themselves, they're going to act in a way that's loving to others That's so much easier and more harmonious, a typical Goddess teaching.

         🐜   🐜   🐜

There are lots of things women can do to help establish Goddess religion, many resources for us now to get our own orientation. We have a lot available to us. We can share that with other women. We can lead in small groups. I try to bring the Goddess into everything I do.

I teach people how to take the law school admissions test. I make a circle in the room before people come in. I bring it in because it changes the energy. We can talk about it overtly in lots of different ways. That's why "Cakes for the Queen of Heaven" is so important to me. My cofacilitator was frustrated with it because it's so elementary, but it attracts women for whom these are new ideas, and who need to step in. The second course is a follow-up on how to have a Goddess practice, for people who are interested in that. There has to be a choice, where we can keep presenting the option all the time.

We can get training. We can be as public as we feel safe being. We can extend those boundaries to where there's more safety. I feel a responsibility that way, since I'm less vulnerable than a lot of women, because I don't have a family. I don't have children that can be taken away, and my job can't be taken away from me—on that ground, anyway. That's not true for a lot of women. If a husband came and said that he thought his wife was practicing Goddess religion, and was a witch, she could very easily lose her children in a custody battle. It isn't a simple thing at this point. But those of us who can, can push those boundaries back, and make it safer.

I think another important step, for someone like me who was brought up in a city, is to have an experiential understanding of the connectedness of all life forms, rather than simply a theoretical understanding. It makes it much easier, for me, to make those kinds of choices that promote life rather than destroy life. I often think that's what has really happened in our culture, that we're so separated from the results of our decisions that we pay no attention. We make these crazy decisions, when we can't see what actually happens.

I'm beginning to think that money is a really crucial issue, that we need to have money. Women who are doing this work need to be financially supported.

Another thing Goddess religion would do, or I hope it would do, is to really let women know that we have to be in charge, that men have got to listen to us. It isn't just that we had a swing to matriarchy on the one hand, and a swing to patriarchy on the other hand, and now we're going to be in the middle and everybody's going to be in charge. It isn't going to be like that. We can't be like that for a lot of generations.

🐜   🐜   🐜

I think a Goddess religion would change the moral tone of society by equalizing women with men. I don't see a Goddess religion as having women control men. I think of the Goddess being there for both women and men. Anybody in a church might say, well, God is there for women; but what I see in the current religions is a lot of domination over women. I don't believe that in the Goddess religion there would be a similar domination over men.

That would be one of the main changes that we'd see if we had a Goddess religion in the mainstream: equal sharing, equal responsibilities in everything. There wouldn't be boy toys and girl toys. Responsibilities around the house wouldn't be male versus female. All the executives in a company wouldn't be male, with a token female. There would be more cooperation between people than controlling.

&   &   &

When enough individual women come forth and say, Goddess is my orientation, my belief, then we'll begin to get some recognition. Individual women need to come forth and say, Here I am, and band together for support and expression. We need to slow down, to recognize natural times and natural cycles. Don't buy into everything that comes along.

It's almost as if the mind—anybody's mind—doesn't have the material to give answers at this point. We're still programmed with the old program. All we can do is be aware that there is a need. This is what happens when you get caught in the transition period, which is what we're living in.

We've moved out of the theological age into the psychological age. We did that back in the '50s and '60s. After the Second World War we started moving into the psychological age. We have looked to psychology for answers, where previous generations looked to theology. I don't think it's giving us any more answers than theology gave us, but psychology and the other social sciences are building blocks.

Psychology itself has changed greatly. Certainly the Jungians are out there in force, more than they were twenty years ago. Freud has completely disappeared into the background. He's no more than a historical footnote. Day-to-day therapy is pragmatic in the extreme, and being pushed even more in that direction by our health-care system. Economic realities are governing psychology right now. I think Freud and Jung and company were looking for more universal answers, but then psychology left universal answers behind and got caught up in its need to cope with hard-core problems. The Goddess may take us the rest of the way toward our answers.

The Goddess is about being life-affirming. What is going to happen with the Goddess religion is that it will be all new. Even the old Goddess religion—what we know of Crete and the old matri-archies—seems to be still concerned with death and an afterlife. Certainly that's what Christianity is concerned about. Christianity is entirely aimed at an afterlife. While in the past couple of centuries it has come more into being life affirming (giant strides from the medieval period), there is still this concentration on the afterlife. But what the Goddess religion is going to be about is life itself, life affirmation, life enhancement, We need to let go of the afterlife aspect because a lot has changed.

When the religions were forming, life expectancy was very short. It was natural to want more. Now we have a long life expectancy, and it's getting longer by leaps and bounds. Emphasis has got to move away from a hope for more, later, to making the best of what's here now. When you have a long period of time to do something with, you've got to do the best you can. So I think the Goddess religion is going to be all new; it's going to be all discovery. Things are changing and we can never go back.

We are just at the very beginning of the new Goddess. I am amazed at how much has happened in the past ten or twenty years, the steps we have taken toward forming that new culture. It has gone much faster than I would have thought possible. It's coming, even though it's not going to be arriving overnight.

We have a long way to go, to get rid of what we have now and come to a life-affirming age. If you take a really long view—and for those influenced by the Goddess, a long view is automatic—you can see that there's still a long stretch ahead of us. I don't think we're going to blow ourselves up, but we might make life very difficult for ourselves on this earth.

A religion needs two things. It needs myth and rite. Goddess is developing some rite, with elements that are pretty common everywhere now. But myth is missing. I haven't the vaguest idea how you go about getting yourself a myth. I suppose it will come of its own accord. That's how most things develop. You can't force it. It's like having a baby. You can say, I want to deliver on such-and-such a date, but if the baby and the hormones aren't ready, it's not going to happen. Giving birth to a Goddess myth is a process.

I don't think we've really developed a thealogy yet. Theology is systematic, logical. It has a philosophic base. Given the original premise, one thing follows another. I don't think we've begun to systematize a set of thoughts about the Goddess. We are still, possibly, in the myth-making stage. The myth of a religion tries to answer basic questions. How did we get here, why are we here, why are things like they are? Maybe that's what we're doing right now, trying to think of another way of coping with why things are what they are. Through our interest in ecology, our interest in natural cycles, we are trying to find out.

Original sin was a metaphor for human limitations. Why is there death? Why do we get sick? Why is work so hard? Why don't things turn out the way we want? Why are people evil? Why are things nasty? The answer to all of it was original sin. If we didn't have original sin, those things wouldn't be. Today we have a different set of whys. Why is there death? Well, because that's the natural cycle. Even though that's hard for us to accept, that is the reason. We know why there is illness. We may not know what to do about it, but we know the why. We don't need "why" answers so much any more. Maybe what we need are "what" answers or "how" answers.

What we need to ask ourselves in the late twentieth century is: How come our technology is outpacing our knowledge of how to live? How come I'm running so fast and getting nowhere? How come I'm so tired all the time? There are so many demands on us. Maybe these questions need a myth to help us find the answers. One way or another, universal questions are going to get asked. As life gets more stressful, they probably will be asked more urgently. Maybe the Goddess is the best way of coping with such questions.

🐝 🐝 🐝

I like the distinction between authority and power. It shifts the ground of discussion in a most interesting way. That's a really neat idea, the vision of our winning not by struggling for power but struggling for authority, or finding authority, or becoming authority. It seems to me that a cogent distinction between authority and power is that authority people want to make it a tradition, to hand on the authority, in order to teach others how to "author" their own lives; whereas power people are devoted to keeping the power. In terms of future vision, this makes a really precise distinction between the male, patriarchal, status-quo political vision and that difference I would have women make. I would like there to be less power and more authority.

I picture power here and authority there, but empowering is in the middle space. What I would want, and what the women I know would want, and actually what the men in my world would want, is for people to be empowered and authoritative. I see that is how I've spent my life as an educator, making people more authoritative. I have never been interested in having anybody I cared about exercise power. It sucks—and I don't mean that vulgarly, I mean it's like a vacuum cleaner. It's only a remover; it can only take.

The truest part of myself and all the women I know is that we weave, and connect, and tell stories, and make patterns, endlessly, endlessly. That is the true essence of woman in society, as instinctual and blind as spiders' weaving. I think the spider is wonderful; I think Arachne is a splendid symbol.

One of the things that Goddess worship does is bring to the fore all of the essential questions. It's a forum that we've lost. I see this as the most powerful immediate political effect of Goddess worship: bringing women together again to talk. I can't believe it's an accident that the centerpiece of Goddess rituals is the passing of the talking-stick, and the re-voicing of women—not just in a political way or an organized way or a collective voice, but in making space for each individual woman who holds the stick to speak, and to be voiced as an individual who is simultaneously part of the group.

Ultimately, better-served women will better serve the world.

I think we should educate all the senators, and have a Goddess person as advisor to the president. Actually, the only way is grassroots. The Goddess philosophy should be there so people can know about it without having anything forced on them. All teachers should take classes in Goddess lore.

First and foremost, a woman should honor herself and her cycles. She can teach her kids, her husband, her family. She can bring people to her. She can form clubs, women taking care of women. It will grow.

🐜 🐜 🐜

Goddess worship is infiltrating the mainstream religions. It's the coming form of mainstream. In the womanchurch mode of Catholicism there's an enormous move toward this. They're making enough noise to make the men worry. As there are more women ministers in Protestant denominations and women rabbis, you can see them sneaking things in, even though they're not making all the changes at once. Little by little, people get more used to it. When I visit Protestant churches, I'm amazed to see that they've been able to sneak in enough so that, in the older times, people would have been shocked to think they were even considering it.

🐜 🐜 🐜

If we had a Goddess religion it would have to be legally approved to function, to perform handfastings and all that sort of thing. There you are, back to needing the legal certificate. I might be taking too short a view, because I want everything to happen *now*.

People who believe in Goddess and believe that the existing world has value are speaking out, trying to avoid pollution of the mind, heart, and spirit, The more we do, the more it's going to ripple outward. I don't like to use the word network; it's too linear and square. I like the word connection.

Goddess religion would address the issues of basic respect for other people, other things, other countries, the earth. If that could be fostered, the world would be a great place. In a way, the ideological is the social; the personal is political. Think globally, act locally. These are Utopian ideas: we have to change the way people think about things.

I hope that if Goddess thealogy becomes the basis for churches, they don't become the Church Militant, but rather the Church Triumphant.

Certainly I don't believe in the flip-flop: give women the same kind of power that men have now. That's unrealistic. You have to work through the system that's here, and try to change it. You can go outside the system and create your own lovely little system, and that's fun, but we have to operate in a male context and yet make points and change things. In order to change anything, however, you have to maintain the outsider point of view, looking in; otherwise you just join the Old Boys' Club. It seems to me that women are smart enough to be able to change the patriarchal system at the same time that they're envisioning something else. We haven't much choice.

Things are coming in from many different cultures and many different spiritual positions. The ripples spread. I want to do as much as I can do in the time that I have to do it. That's what I'm working for.

It's so encouraging now just to hear the bits of things that college students are doing. Several groups of undergraduates are doing rituals. There's a place in nearly every town where you can go to look for ritual tools. Seven years ago there was nothing.

In the last fifteen years. I gently tried to radicalize as many as I could. As Emerson says, a mind once stretched never goes back to its original size. Any little bit can stretch it that much more. I want the women of the future to find the Goddess and to bring the men along with them.

         🐾   🐾   🐾

Once established, Goddess worship will completely change society as we know it. It will give young girls and young women a better feeling about themselves. It will give things like education and the nurture of young children as much value or more value than war making. It will also invite men to balance their aggressive energies, giving them permission to get in touch with their nurturing side.

To be female is not to give anyone else the license to dominate you or beat you or denigrate you in any way. I like the model of a society where people are not greedy for material possessions, but freely give among themselves whatever is needed. Experience is better than possessions—the experience of songs, poetry, art. It's a very attractive model. My idea of what a Goddess religion would bring to society is that it would give everybody permission to be what they are by nature. Men wouldn't have to put on hard shells of aggression. They could let their tender side show.

We need the people who are writing the books, putting together the workshops, writing the curricula, and teaching. I'm interested in Native American figures like Changing Woman and Spider Woman. One could almost make a ten-week curriculum on those alone, and also the Mayan and Inca Goddesses. I haven't yet acquired a warm personal image of the Asian or African Goddesses, but I have read about them and want to learn more.

Goddess religion should address social justice, equality for all. It should stress that what women do is as important as—or more important than—making money or making war. It might be similar to what Gnostic Christianity was intended to be, except that it went off in other directions. Goddess religion should let everyone develop his or her potential, in an atmosphere where people can thrive because they don't have to waste time and energy defending themselves from others of their own kind.

🐿 🐿 🐿

Goddess religion should remain decentralized. That's difficult. As Goddess women, we feel funny about taking control of a group. But there has to be a balance. Nonhierarchical organization can work. All it takes is to meet in small groups where we can reenergize ourselves, then go out into the world and behave as Goddess people should. If enough of us do that, we'll have it.

The question is, what to do with men? Even if they didn't have more than their share of power, which they do, we'd still have to involve them. Men's Wiccan practice is different from Goddess practice. I've never particularly understood male Wiccan practitioners. Once we did try to have a mixed men's/women's group, but it petered out, mainly because only one or two of us did the work to keep it going.

The Goddess has to do with linking our bodies with the body of Mother Earth. It has to do with how we treat each other, too. Goddess-oriented women are supportive and compassionate and open-hearted. If we could get those ways of treating each other to spread out to the whole world, it would be a revolution indeed. I don't have a whole lot of hope that it will happen in my lifetime. But it's coming along very fast in the United States and Europe. The developing countries, which used to be closer to the earth-based religions, are now becoming consumerist. They're trying to imitate us. That's going to be a problem for the earth.

The social, larger-world aspect of the Goddess religion is important to me. It breaks my heart to see the abuses in the world: the hungry Third World children, the violence against women and children in our own society. I'm not convinced that political action helps. It seems the men are going to do what they want anyway. I'm skeptical about all their motives; there are too many moneyed interests.

The issue of violence against women is ideal for the Goddess movement. We should support women who are trying to get out of relationships like that. We need to give them healing, then start working on the men. Social justice is very important to me, even though I haven't yet found my place in it. I feel that there is guidance in Goddess.

        🐾 🐾 🐾

Goddess religion may be established only with the downfall of patriarchy. It may never become mainstream, as long as we have politicians and governments that we subsidize without complaining, that are run by patriarchal thought processes. If not mainstream, Goddess religion will remain underground, known, hoped

for, wished for, but still an underground bible. It won't win as long
as our real god is greed. A church doesn't exist today unless it is
constantly saying to its people, "God needs money."

Martyrdom serves no useful purpose. Why should a woman be
like Jesus, willing to be hung on a cross? Through the centuries
women have been sacrificed even more horribly, against their will.

My feeling is that if everybody stopped thinking about himself
so much, and at least once a day thought about somebody else, no
one would ever need help again. I would hope that Goddess religion, knowledge, thealogy would always be more other-directed
than patriarchal theology.

🐌   🐌   🐌

Goddess religion needs to be established in a peaceful way, quiet,
settled; but there must be a strong statement made. Men must
finally listen to women.

The Full Moon circles and the rituals that we do will help establish Goddess religion. We must teach the men. I'm learning, myself,
and I share it with my male friends. Some men accept it and like it.
They too feel something wrong with the patriarchal society. They
know a balance is needed. It's definitely happening.

🐌   🐌   🐌

The Wiccan movement and the Goddess movement are occasionally mentioned on TV and may slowly become incorporated into
mainstream culture, but many people still think they're something
brand new. They're still unaware of the long, long background, the
great old traditions. With increasing openness to discuss the belief
system and its history, more women will be drawn to it, and there
will be more about it in the media.

Two recent TV shows incorporated the theme into a plot, but it
was not at all informative. Still, dissemination may start in the
entertainment industry because of its lifestyle. When it is broad-
cast, it contacts the whole culture. This is good. There has to be

exposure. People should know what we really are. There are still some who think we're a bunch of lesbian women out to castrate all men; they have no idea of what the movement is really like.

🐜 🐜 🐜

Goddess religion is a mythopoesis, a slow development of a standard message. If it has anything like a dogma, it's kind of leftist, kind of pantheist, definitely immanent. Our society has a whole supermarket of religions to choose from. Is Goddess religion going to exclude men? Shouldn't there be a god somewhere, too?

I think Goddess religion is actually becoming established with astounding speed. Among alternative religions it is already one of the most popular. There are more feminist spirituals than anybody else. Our goal should be to get as close as possible to expressing the true spiritual.

🐜 🐜 🐜

I don't quite know how men fit in, and that's a problem. I would imagine that women would want to be involved in spiritual functions with men, to go to church together. You have a family of boys and girls, you go to church together.

I know there are spirituality groups that have both men and women, but I don't feel really good about them. I like the private groups for women. There's something wonderful about women being with women, and not having men present. I wouldn't want to give that up, not yet; we have such a long way to go.

If women governed the churches and men were just part of the congregation, the way it is now but in reverse, it would be unfair to the men, just as it's unfair now to the women. I'd rather see men going off and being spiritual together, and women going off elsewhere and being spiritual together. Most worship could be separate, with joint events occasionally. The more I think and read about it, the more it seems we—men and women—are almost like two separate species. We have different cultural needs.

In an ideal world, both men and women would be different. Men wouldn't be threatening in any way. They'd be more nurturing, less warlike, more like women and therefore more acceptable human beings. Goddess worship could contribute to that.

We need to make more women aware of the Goddess, to let them know that it is a legitimate spiritual path, not something wacky. If they think it's something wacky, we're not going to get them at all. It would be really wonderful to get more women involved, to have this become a religion with as much validity in the world's eyes as Catholicism, for example. That's a dream, but a lot of hard work can make it come true.

An established Goddess religion could change the moral tone of society when a large number of people become involved in it. It's possible. Certainly there would be a great deal more respect and equality for women. The society encourages or discourages certain types of character development. If women were equally represented in elective positions, all over the world, I think you'd have a tremendous influence for peace. If there were still wars, they'd be very limited. Testosterone causes a great deal of trouble.

🐝   🐝   🐝

I think the idea of an established Goddess religion is far in the future, but it certainly would not give much support to wars. Nor would there be support for the violence to women and children, nor for the violence to the planet and the creatures on it. There would be tolerance of other life forms, because we are all Her children. She cares for all of us.

Women have to go slowly in their small groups, but the groups are coming together more and more. That is happening. There are meetings throughout the country now, with larger groups. I think, also, that people are finding the Goddess in ordinary life, and in art: graphics, plays, books. There is the Great Mother breaking through.

🐝   🐝   🐝

A Goddess idea is good because women should be in charge of their own thoughts. In traditional or standard religions, people aren't in charge. They have no power. They must conform to the prevailing theology. The majority of women need to understand that they are permitted to achieve spiritual awareness through their own ideas. Lesbian women in the seminary are developing Goddess imagery, inserting it into the canon. I think we have started a revolution. This isn't by chance. We're working on it every day. Many people have been working on it for a long time. Changes are coming even to the mainstream religions. I don't know that the Catholic Church is going to change much, though, which is really sad, because they have a lot of goodies. They have Mary. They have many updated pagan images that have been converted into saints. They have a long history of defining concepts.

I can relate to the extreme importance of having a Goddess image. It's difficult to explain to traditional Christians how I feel about this. The masculine image of the divine is not something that we should unquestioningly accept.

One of the important things for a Goddess religion to become generally established is that there has to be a service component. It's good to disperse your experience, to tell the world. People may not be convinced, but at least they should be exposed to it. People can choose what they want. It should be available. Goddess religion should address freedom of thought, human rights, the rights of children, the rights of families. We should expose women of other cultures to the idea that they can take charge of their thealogy. Even if they don't necessarily break with the views that they were raised with, they can take them and transform them.

   🐏 🐏 🐏

To help institute a modern religion of the Goddess, one should do the following things:

Be a living part of one (or more) small circles of Goddess worship—sisterhood is powerful.

Recognize the Goddess in the everyday things that women do.

We create life and maintain it. We weave connections. We are the communicators, the diplomats, the sharers, the healers. We can make our lives a celebration of these values, each one of us on an individual level. In this, I think we can teach by example.

Contribute time and money to political candidates who stand for Goddess's values. To stores and businesses that embrace environmentally safe procedures and products. To battered women's shelters and to early childhood education. To literacy programs.

Study. Read books about the Goddess and about ritual. If you can, write them. Travel to sacred places—by thought and by reading. Create sacred spaces in your life, and at least one sacred place where you can go. I think we need a touchable "sacred," one that can be studied physically, sensually, materially, as well as conceptually.

Be kind to others and to yourself. The heart of that kindness is, at its best, a recognition—bone deep and absolute—of the value of what you offer.

Be courageous. Our blessing "Thou Art Goddess"—is cause for courage, as well as for joy and kindness.

🐞 🐞 🐞

The Goddess movement is essential for our survival. We can't correct the damage we've done to the environment until we drop all that has come about from the Christian perspective. There's no way that will ever heal. As long as we go around thinking it's all right to dominate, we will be wrong. I want the world to be a better place for my children.

🐞 🐞 🐞

Now that I know how old the Goddess religion is, and how long it prevailed among human beings, I think there must be a way that we can get back to that. But it wouldn't be like a takeover, the way men take things over. We need to get back to the extended family structure that the ancient women had. Women's groups feel more and more like mutually supportive family members.

The Goddess movement is immensely important for the future of the planet, because it embodies ecological concerns that patriarchy has always ignored. Patriarchy also has fragmented the family and separated people; there's always a we-and-they dichotomy. I think the Goddess movement can work, first through women, then by extension through all humanity, to bring a new sense of family. We have to learn to live together. Women can do that, and that's their strength. Every time I spend a weekend or a festival with a group of women, I just know that it's the real source of caring.

14

THE UNKNOWN
A Conversation

*E*CHOING THE CLICHÉ THAT HAS been heard through the centuries, my friend said, "People need to believe in God because it's a comfort." Is this truism really true?

Personally, I could see nothing comfortable about an arbitrary belief imposed on the unknown, and I said so. "People don't want to face the unknown," she answered.

"Well, you don't face it anyway, if you don't know it," I remarked. "The universe is full of unknowns. Even most of what is now known to scientists is still unknown to a majority of laypersons. Not knowing is our usual state of existence. If people are upset by not knowing, how come they don't make more of an effort to learn about what *is* known?"

"That would mean study and concentration," she said. "People don't want to concentrate. They want to be given simple, understandable answers and reassurances, like God is there, God loves you, everything's okay. That's comforting."

"That's infantile," I snorted. "Babies need that, but grownups shouldn't. How can it be comforting to believe what you know, deep down, is improbable? That kind of comfort is a thin crust over an abyss."

381

"Maybe so," she answered, "but most people seem to be infantile in that way. The idea of the unknown is too much for them, even though the word is somehow attractive. They'd rather call it God and assume it to be known in some sense."

"There lies one of the paradoxes," I said. "Theologians say God is unknowable, then go on to explain in great detail that they know all about him. If you equate God with the unknown, then by definition you are worshiping what you know nothing about. How could you know whether 'the Unknown' even wants to be worshiped? The whole concept is without sense."

"Does it make any more sense to call it Goddess?"

"It does if you understand Goddess not as a transcendent reality, like God is supposed to be, but as a metaphor: the embodiment in a word of Earth, Nature, the life force in general, the biological creative and nurturant power that is predominantly female. I don't envision Goddess as a substitute for my own ignorance. I'm content to let the unknown be unknown."

"Well, that's you," she said. "Most people want some kind of explanation for the unknown."

"I have no problem with that," I said. "Curiosity is a fine thing when it impels us to find out more about our world, or ourselves, or whatever. Curiosity is important. But curiosity should seek real answers, not be slaked by improbable stories made up by people devoid of genuine knowledge. Fairy tales are entertainment, not enlightenment. There's nothing wrong with imaginative entertainment; but it shouldn't be mistaken for enlightenment. For instance, we can enjoy science fiction without supposing it to be real science. Explaining the unknown becomes unintelligent and unintelligible when it crosses the line and becomes fiction claiming to be fact."

"Don't you think fiction can present facts—about human nature, for example?"

"Of course it can, and often does. But that's not the same as, say, presenting biblical myths as literal history. Literature can be metaphorical enlightenment, but there's a basic dishonesty about giving people the traditional impossibles (like a virgin birth) and demanding an implicit belief in their reality. That's insulting to the human intellect. One should be free to criticize and reject explanations that contradict the laws of probability."

"Shouldn't one also be free to choose the impossible explanations as well?"

"Yes, if that's really what is wanted. Unfortunately, in matters of religion it's not a truly free choice. Religious belief is so pervasive a part of our culture that most people grow up taking it for granted, then in adulthood they can't think it through anymore. They have accepted the improbable, and it takes on the same aura of 'comfort' connected with childhood notions generally. Belief in God is the adult version of belief in Santa Claus, only without the eventual letting-go. For my part, as a child I was troubled by the nagging suspicion that Santa Claus didn't make sense, and I was greatly comforted by the revelation that he wasn't an alien spiritual being after all, but only a metaphorical expression of my own parents' real love, which I could trust. The transition from God to Goddess is also something like that."

"Most people want more meaning to life than seeing it just as a biological or sociological condition, especially if their human relationships are less than satisfactory."

"But belief and meaning are not the same thing. There are lots of rational ways to give meaning to one's life: raising children successfully, doing good work, helping others, learning, teaching, creating art, meeting personal goals, even the acquisition of money or power. These are meanings. Mere existence, all by itself, can't mean anything. It just *is*."

"That's the point," my friend said. "People want their *is*-ness to mean something."

"What kind of something?" I asked.

"I don't know. That's the unknown that needs faith."

"I hardly think the human species can be justified in thinking that its mere existence has a transcendent meaning, other than the obvious fact that it is causing mass extinctions of other species by overproliferating itself. What meaning will we have, after the almost-inevitable has happened, and we have joined the other 99 percent of all species that have ever lived on earth and are now extinct? Some species will survive us and go on to reproduce their kind in a different, humanless world. Until the sun stops radiating heat and light—which it will, eventually—life forms probably will continue to evolve on this planet; but our existence here is temporary and provisional. We've been here for a very short time compared to most other species, and we seem to be eating ourselves out of house and home at a very fast rate. Can that be construed as a meaning?"

"No, but that's an awfully pessimistic view of humanity."

"It's a realistic view. We have no reason to believe ourselves intrinsically different from any other species just because we have developed language and technology. We have disabled or destroyed most of our natural enemies and so have become our own natural enemies. Unlike the majority of other species, we kill our own kind with great enthusiasm. We may dominate the earth today, but that's no guarantee that we will be here tomorrow, when the earth no longer produces what we need for survival. Species come and go, and may change the environment for better or worse, from their own point of view. The earth doesn't care. The universe doesn't care. The life force—or Goddess—will go on evolving, until conditions no longer support the process. Where is any transcendent meaning in all that?"

"You don't see anything good in human existence, then."

"I didn't say that. From the human point of view, there is much good in human existence, even when it's bad for other creatures. Much of what we create is enjoyable and useful, and may even be harmless, though that's a moot point. Cutting down trees to build a house, we destroy the homes or livelihood of innumerable insects, birds, or small mammals like mice and squirrels. In building a town, we destroy thousands of acres of natural habitat and all its creatures. If a man enjoys going out in the woods and shooting deer, are the deer having a good time? Every day we kill millions of animals for food, for clothing, or for nothing just because they get in the way of our cars. To eat is good, from our viewpoint. To go somewhere is good, even if it means polluting the environment and piling up road-kills. Our is-ness hurts the rest of the living world mainly because there are too many of us. When the human population of this planet was very much smaller, our predatory ways didn't make a vast difference. Now they do. If there were such a God as some people presume, do you think he would have deliberately arranged such an imbalanced world?"

"Theologians are always pointing out the folly of trying to comprehend God by the rules of human logic."

"Well, of course they are, because logic won't support their premises. That method has been tried and tried again, without much success. So they advise faith as a substitute for logic. I think that's a profound mistake. The only thing we've ever really had going for us, as a species, is our ability to reason. Now we need that ability more than ever, if we are to get past the present 'Sixth Extinction' without doing ourselves in along with everything else. It's faith that told us we were so superior that we have a right to exploit and destroy other creatures. It's faith that told us women were born to be men's slaves. It's faith that tells us we're virtuous when we go to war and kill multitudes of other humans, besides all the other life that our wars blow up, trample, shoot, crush, or poison without even noticing. It's faith that teaches us to be irrational and to convince ourselves of the improbable. It's faith that loads us with guilt for being sexual creatures, denies the inevitability of our death, forces too many young females to bear unwanted throwaway children, fosters interracial hatreds, and demands too many of our resources that could be more sensibly and humanely utilized.

"It's faith that has encouraged us toward literal belief in angels, devils, ghosts, vampires, familiar spirits, chimeras, witchcraft, sorcery, divination, miracles, necromancy, spiritualism, resurrection of the dead, past lives, snake oil, space beings, vibrational healings, channeling, psychic levitation, or psychic friends, as well as gods. Considering that these concepts have been created by human minds and by nothing else in nature, it seems begging the question to say they shouldn't be subject to human reason. Mental constructs are subject to mental rules above all. Therefore we have every right—maybe even a duty—to think about these things before committing to a belief in them. Every theologian knows that faith has to be instilled before a child matures enough to be able to think. That way, rationality can be forever closed out of that area of the mind that clings to faith."

"Rationality is also closed out of those areas that we call love, sympathy, sorrow, anger, and most other emotions. Yet they certainly exist."

"Of course, but they exist *in us*, not elsewhere. Sane people direct their emotions toward the actual individuals or circumstances that have stimulated them, rather than supposing that these emotions apply to the unknown. We have no reason to believe that the natural universe of phenomena, known or unknown, is subject to human-type emotions. Despite millennia of straining to discover God in objective reality, no such discovery has been made. God is still not demonstrable, except as metaphor, so I would as soon call it Goddess as anything else."

"Would you call your Goddess concept a faith, then?" my friend asked.

"No. I'd call it, perhaps, a poem, or a work of art, or an idea, remembering always that ideas are human products. I'm not so crude as to propose literal belief in a Big Mama sitting up in the clouds or under the mountains. I'd prefer the idea of Goddess to be known, not unknown. We must stop pretending that fiction is fact, or that we know the unknown. Goddess may be our psychological experience of Mother, or a personification of earth, or a longing for womanlike tenderness, or a fitting reverence for the female creative principle, or any other reasonable description. It should never imply a blind faith that ignores reality. I prefer the word Goddess because it's fresh, without those ever-so-numerous traditional connotations of intolerance and oppression that hang about the word God."

"So you're comfortable with the thought of leaving the unknown to remain unknown?"

"Perfectly. I don't insist on any undefined transcendent meanings. As far as I can tell, the cosmos just is, and we are too insignificant a part of it to assume any reason or purpose for it. Anyway, the whole idea of purpose is a human invention in itself. The real pur-

pose of any living thing is to stay alive as long as possible and produce more of its kind. Beyond that, we are in the realm of fable."

She laughed. "And humans are so much better at making up
fables than they are at finding out truths, right?"

"Right. Fables are fun, and truth is hard to discover. Every American child, growing up with storybooks and TV cartoons and fantasies of every kind, is fed a hundred fables for every one truth. For
most, it's infinitely easier to remember that Cinderella wore a glass
slipper than to remember the distance from earth to the sun. We
condition our children to be believers rather than truth-seekers."

"I know that Christian churches made a terrible mess of their
own credibility during the nineteenth century, when they were
busy denying just about every scientific breakthrough that came
along, because it didn't agree with Scripture; and I know that some
of them still do that. But most mainstream sects today are perfectly
willing to accept scientific truth. They say that faith is concerned
with a 'higher' truth, meaning more elegant thoughts, I guess, or
something closer to an ultimate truth."

"Yes, but each sect's 'higher' truth differs from the next one's,
and truth is hardly the word to describe any subject about which
there is endless disagreement. Truth is a matter of proof, not a
matter of opinion. All of Judeo-Christian history has been filled with
mutually contradictory 'truths,' their believers all trying to diabolize,
discredit, or even slaughter one another, and to make more converts
than their rivals. Still, a lie remains a lie no matter how many people
believe it. It has often been said that if there were a God wishing to
get a particular message across to human beings, he has certainly
gone about it in the most muddleheaded way imaginable."

She gazed into the middle distance for a while, cogitating. Then
she said: "You're right about that, but surely religion in modern
America has outgrown all those murderous rivalries and diaboliza-
tions. There are many churches, and they have different theologies,
but they tolerate one another. You don't see Presbyterians attacking
Lutherans, or Catholics bombing synagogues."

"Don't you? How about recent events in Ireland? The fact is that
religious battles are going on all the time. What is the bombing of

an abortion clinic but an act of religious terrorism? What about all the religious strife in the Muslim world?"

"Well, they're at a lower level of intellectual sophistication, I guess. There will always be ignorant people; and bigotry and intolerance are the products of ignorance. The ordinary, decent (I almost said God-fearing) American is willing to accept neighbors who have differing beliefs."

"Yes," I said, "and that diversity may be one of our best saving graces. Religion in modern America is a scrap-heap of loose boulders trying to pretend that it's a monolith—that is, each boulder tries to pretend that all the others, basically, agree. Such diversity of opinion is surely better than Europe's condition when the medieval church really was a political monolith, self-empowered to dominate, confiscate, excommunicate, and use torture and the stake to eliminate heterodoxies. America's founding fathers were absolutely right to insist on total separation of church and state. They were still, historically, close to the horrors of truly monolithic religion. We have forgotten how evil the combination of church and state can be, how threatening to the basic principles of democracy and intellectual freedom. And there are fundamentalist forces today trying to bring that situation back."

"I know," she said, "and I find that scary. Fanatics are always dangerous, and ignorant fanatics are worst of all. There's a really puzzling unknown for you—why is it that people who profess the strongest faith in a loving God are most prone to be filled with hate and violence?"

"I think it's probably due to some remnant of rationality that suspects their faith might be questionable after all; so they perceive anyone with different opinions as a threat. Those who want to kill heretics are really trying to kill the heresy within themselves. After all, they are adult human beings with some sort of a brain, and some part of that brain whispers that the god they think is so real is actually the Unknown. This is an intolerable thought and they project it outward, onto others, to get rid of it."

"Still, you can't deny that every religion has many people who are truly kind, loving, and tolerant, and who feel that their faith has made them so, and who practice what is generally described as Christian charity."

"Certainly I don't deny that," I answered. "I'm not sure, though, just how much of their goodness can be attributed to their faith, and how much really belongs to their basic character and the way they were raised. It's possible that people are made essentially kind or cruel by factors having nothing to do with religion, and then any religion they adopt will prove to be an expression of those factors. That's why it's so important to train children in every religious tradition, no matter what, to be honest, responsible, and helpful to others. That's the only way we can ever have a comfortable society."

"Another Unknown," she laughed. "How to raise children? Of course all those male psychologists have been blathering about it for decades without making much of a difference, and of course you'll say that mothers know best, and that's another manifestation of the Goddess."

"Sure," I said. "Mothers do know best, and left to themselves, most of them would raise children lovingly and tolerantly, teaching them to get along with others, allowing them to enjoy themselves, and also insisting that they respect knowledge and apply themselves to learn. Mothers would do that because they would want their children well prepared to have happy and useful adult lives. In a patriarchal society these things are not always so easy. There are many other distracting elements and forces involved in our children's socialization."

"Television being a big one, of course," she said. "And just look at the heavy sell that television gives 'the Unknown'! All those programs about the paranormal, *Encounters, Sightings, The Extraordinary, Unsolved Mysteries, The Other Side*, which seem to say that the Unknown is encountered almost every day in such forms as telepathy, ghosts, angels, prophecy, aliens, UFOs, and all kinds of magic. And lots of pure fantasy as well, sci-fi, *Outer Limits*, ghoulies and ghosties in horror flicks, lots of make-believe scares, as well as religious programs. Skepticism is never even mentioned as a possibility, but 'willing suspension of disbelief' is certainly encouraged."

"Yes, if there's any disbelief there in the first place to be suspended. Most children simply take it in without making any distinction between probable and improbable, and so do most childlike adults. In modern America there is no really distinct line between religion and show business. Hollywood has been creating religion for many years; millions of people are more familiar with the gospel according to Cecil B. de Mille than with the gospel according to Matthew. The convincing immediacy of film media always tends to blur the line between fantasy and reality for a large segment of the audience. There are even people who completely identify actors with the roles they play.

"Early training in credulity can leave people vulnerable to any number of fringe beliefs that present fantasy as reality; and credulity as a character trait is encouraged in every child who grows up hearing that blind faith is a virtue, whereas doubt and questioning are sins. Religion's war against fringe beliefs is not a war of the rational against the irrational; it's a contest between different fantasy systems, the mainstream ones having more political and financial clout, and therefore able to advertise themselves into respectability. Miracles, magic, drama, and charlatanism all have a common root. So it's no wonder that a believing society is plagued by spellbinders, gurus, psychics, channelers, fortune tellers, and miracle mongers of every stripe. No matter how often it's shown that psychics' predictions don't come true, transcendental meditators don't levitate, crystals don't cure cancer, telepathy doesn't work, dead people don't talk, and 'speaking in tongues' is just meaningless babble, all the negative instances are ignored because all the trained believers are more comfortable with belief than with disbelief. Superstition therefore reigns everywhere, and the most shameless frauds are more popular than debunkers. This is the shared insanity of modern culture."

"So how is the concept of the Goddess any less insane than the rest?"

"Ah. Here we have a unique opportunity, a way to create a really new thing in cultural attitudes. Throughout the matrifocal period of human history, the Goddess was taken literally, just as the god is now by most believers. Then She began to be discredited, and over several thousand years Her literal existence came to be denied. Now She can return in a new, more realistic form: not literal. She can be clearly recognized as a human construct—a valuable, even essential metaphor of feminine forces in nature, a cherished symbol, a means of understanding, something like a national flag or a totem. Her literal existence can still be denied, you see, which places Her in a stronger position than the god whose followers don't dare deny him. We can say, no, the Goddess is not any Big Mama sitting up in the clouds, so don't bother to insult your intelligence about Her. She exists as an archetype, as a universal human concept, and She doesn't need your credulity. Paraphrasing Pogo, women can say, We have met the Goddess, and She is us."

My friend looked thoughtful. "That's rather deep," she said slowly. "You seem to be saying that to deny the reality of the Goddess is to enhance belief in Her."

"Not belief, exactly. It would be better to call it usefulness. As a concept, She works—especially for women, who need such a concept and have needed it for centuries now. This involves admitting that all deities are nothing more and nothing less than human concepts; and that admission alone would represent a step forward in human thought, bringing us a little closer to the kind of mental sophistication that would engender real tolerance and clearer vision. Belief is not proof, and it's high time we recognized that. We need not confuse our symbols with reality in order to make use of symbols. We know that a national emblem is not literally the physical country, but the emblem is useful nevertheless. So it is with the Goddess. She does not require us to believe anything against our common sense."

My friend smiled. "I begin to see. It really is a rather new way of looking at the idea of deity."

"It's also a new way of dealing with the unknown: We don't have to pretend to know it. Thealogians don't have to fill us full of guff about what the Goddess thinks, and wants, and commands, the way theologians have been pretending to know such things about their god all these centuries. Furthermore, thealogians don't have to make any silly assumptions that a future science will disprove and shatter the faith of believers who have been taught to view them as eternal truths. Thealogy can leave the unknown alone, to be gradually discovered by the scientific method, the only way that really works. We can perceive the Goddess as collectively human, and immanent, and pragmatic. It seems to be that, given all this, She may have a longer life expectancy in human culture than any of the father gods who have foolishly tried to do without the principle of motherhood."

"I don't know why, but that does kind of soften any fear of the unknown," she said. "What we don't know isn't so frightening. It's what we do know about the evils of patriarchal society that I find most frightening. If the Goddess idea can mitigate some of those evils, I'm all for it. But what about that final unknown—the life-after-death unknown? I think that's what lies at the core of most religious belief. We want to be told that we aren't going to stop existing."

"You're right, of course; but the problem with patriarchal religion is that it has introduced the ultimate sadism into its afterlife idea: for our trivial sins, a hell of agony that never, ever ends. Surely nonexistence would be better than an existence like that."

"Yes, but hardly anybody ever believes that he's going to hell. Why, the church gives ritual assurances of blessed afterlife even to Mafia murderers and thieves and other criminals, no matter what they've done; they can always buy their way into heaven, it seems. They would have us believe that even the angels rejoice at the arrival of a 'prodigal,' or a sinner who managed to get enough deathbed-time to repent."

"Well, even with the assurance of heaven, what is that? The patriarchal theologians never came up with anything better than an eternity of singing praises to God. Who but egotistical man could have invented a God whose heavenly bliss consists of hearing his own praises sung by blessed spirits, day and night for all eternity? The worst old-fashioned Oriental potentate was never *that* puffed up with himself. And why would a creator of an unthinkably vast universe require so much flattery from mere human beings, dead or alive?"

She laughed. "I've read that the ancient pagans described heavenly bliss as an eternal orgasm. Now *that* I wouldn't mind believing. But matters of love get terribly confused. Christianity teaches (according to the Gospel) that there is no marriage in heaven. But most people want to envision a reunion with loved ones. And what about multiple marriages? Are you supposed to meet all the husbands you may have had, or they meet all their ex-wives, and so on? It could get really complicated."

"One of the first things that turned me against Christianity," I said, "was the discovery that animals were not allowed in heaven. Some of the individuals I have loved most in my life have been animals. When I heard that there would be no afterlife for them, when I was a child, I decided then and there that I wanted no part of God's heaven. We're also told that heaven belongs to the poor in spirit. What fun would it be to spend eternity with the poor in spirit?"

"So, what do you think you will be after you die?"

"Either ashes or rotting meat. In either case, all my atoms will return to the environment in some form, and be dispersed into other substances and/or entities. The pagans had a much more sophisticated idea in their eternally churning cauldron, the Crone's image of cyclic life-and-death."

"But what about your soul?"

"What is soul, other than the consciousness and feelings that I have while my brain is alive and functioning? Soul is to the body what music is to the violin. When you smash the violin to atoms, it doesn't play music any more. When all my gray matter is dispersed into the atmosphere or the soil or whatever, I have no more consciousness. I'm back where I was before I was born, that is, nowhere."

"Then what do you think it is that we call soul or spirit?"

"I think soul is not a *thing* but a *function*, an attitude; say it's what Freud described as the oceanic feeling, or our own sense of what we perceive as being best about ourselves. Physically it's just one more astronomically complicated series of electrical patterns in the brain, perhaps a little more complicated than those in the brains of other mammals, because it's all mixed up with verbiage and imaginary concepts; but not much more complicated. We think and feel, apes think and feel, dogs and cats and horses and elephants and whales all think and feel in the same way, essentially. The Christian idea that humans are fundamentally different from all other creatures, and superior, and empowered by God to exploit all the rest of them with total callousness, is one of the maddest and most dangerous ideas ever evolved by that supreme egotist, man. "

"Well, it all makes sense, in a dismal sort of way. But the majority of people really don't want to give up whatever personal vision they may have of some kind of immortality."

"What's dismalest is the way our sense of God-given soul has led us to mistreat Mother Earth and Her creatures, whereas our pagan ancestors were wiser about walking in balance on the land, not hoarding what you don't need, using the gifts of nature without wasting them. These are things we need to relearn. I think the Goddess movement will prove to be of significant use in relearning them. As women were the first religious teachers of the human race, so they need to be again. We don't need immortality if we can create a paradise on earth, where people can be happy as well as productive, creative, responsible, and kind. Utopia!"

"Of course a real Utopia is impossible."

"Yes, but *that* journey will be the important thing, not the impossible destination. The women are setting their feet on the path. The old paths have led into ugly thickets and dead ends. It's time for a new way to be tried, don't you think?"

"I do."

"Then let's try."

NOTES

INTRODUCTION

    1. Barbara G. Walker, *The Woman's Encyclopedia of Myths and Secrets* (San Francisco: Harper & Row, 1983), p. 769.

    2. Roger E. Greeley, *The Best of Robert Ingersoll* (Amherst, N.Y.: Prometheus Books, 1977), p. 36.

    3. Homer Smith, *Man and His Gods* (Boston: Little, Brown, 1952), p. 286.

    4. Walker, *Woman's Encyclopedia*, pp. 599–602.

    5. Charles Bufe, ed., *The Heretic's Handbook of Quotations* (Tucson: Sharp Press, 1988), p. 217.

    6. Walker, *Woman's Encyclopedia*, p. 387.

    7. Bufe, *Heretic's Handbook*, p. 215.

    8. Annie Laurie Gaylor, ed., *Women without Superstition: No Gods—No Masters* (Madison, Wis.: Freedom From Religion Foundation, 1997), p. 283.

    9. Anthony Flew, *God: A Critical Inquiry* (LaSalle, Ill.: Open Court Publishing, 1984), p. 101.

CHAPTER 2: WHAT IS THEALOGY?

1. Barbara G. Walker, *The Woman's Encyclopedia of Myths and Secrets* (San Francisco: Harper & Row, 1983), p. 592; Charles Bufe, ed., *The Heretic's Handbook of Quotations* (Tucson: Sharp Press, 1988), p. 215.

2. Walker, *Woman's Encyclopedia*, p. 387.

3. Homer Smith, *Man and His Gods* (Boston: Little, Brown, 1952), p. 227.

4. Naomi Wolf, *The Beauty Myth: How Images of Beauty are Used against Women* (New York: William Morrow, 1991), p. 289.

5. Aubrey Menen, *The Mystics* (New York: Dial, 1974), p. 149.

6. Uta Ranke-Heinemann, *Eunuchs for the Kingdom of Heaven*, trans. Peter Heinegg (New York: Doubleday, 1990), pp. 334, 347.

7. Bufe, *Heretic's Handbook*, p. 169.

8. George H. Smith, *Atheism: The Case against God* (Amherst, N.Y.: Prometheus Books, 1979), pp. 247, 240.

9. Bufe, *Heretic's Handbook*, p. 173.

10. Walker, *Woman's Encyclopedia*, pp. 495–97.

CHAPTER 3: BREAKING AWAY FROM THE PATRIARCHY

1. Naomi Wolf, *The Beauty Myth: How Images of Beauty are Used against Women* (New York: William Morrow, 1991), p. 283.

2. Charles Bufe, ed., *The Heretic's Handbook of Quotations*, (Tucson: Sharp Press, 1988), pp. 124–25.

3. Geoffrey Ashe, *The Virgin* (London: Routledge & Kegan Paul, 1976), pp. 178–79.

4. Vern L. Bullough, *The Subordinate Sex* (Chicago: University of Illinois Press, 1973), p. 114.

5. Barbara G. Walker, *The Woman's Encyclopedia of Myths and Secrets* (San Francisco: Harper & Row, 1983), pp. 921–27.

6. Bufe, *Heretic's Handbook*, pp. 121, 123, 210.

7. Mary Daly, *Beyond God the Father* (Boston: Beacon Press, 1973), p. 69.

8. Carole Gray, "Nineteenth-Century Women of Freethought," *Free Inquiry* 15, no. 2 (1995): 33.

9. Uta Ranke-Heinemann, *Eunuchs for the Kingdom of Heaven*, trans. Peter Heinegg (New York: Doubleday, 1990), p. 189.

10. Tama Starr, *The "Natural Inferiority" of Women: Outrageous Pronouncements by Misguided Males* (New York: Poseidon, 1991), pp. 122, 205.

11. Ranke-Heinemann, *Eunuchs*, pp. 97, 107, 127, 135.

12. Riane Eisler, *Sacred Pleasure: Sex, Myth, and the Politics of the Body* (San Francisco: HarperSanFrancisco, 1995), p. 193.

13. *New Age Journal* (August 1995): 139.

14. Jerry Mander, *In the Absence of the Sacred* (San Francisco: Sierra Club, 1991), p. 391.

15. Tim Leedom, ed., *The Book Your Church Doesn't Want You to Read* (Dubuque: Kendall/Hunt, 1993), p. 357.

16. Bufe, *Heretic's Handbook*, pp. 122, 197.

17. Leedom, *Your Church*, p. 386.

18. Bufe, *Heretic's Handbook*, p. 209.

19. Genevieve Vaughan, *For-Giving: A Feminist Criticism of Exchange* (Austin: Plain View Press, 1997), pp. 322,353,384.

20. Annie Laurie Gaylor, *Women without Superstition: No Gods—No Masters* (Madison, Wis.: Freedom From Religion Foundation, 1997), p. 124.

21. Ibid., pp. xxii, 469, 528.

CHAPTER 4: WHAT'S WRONG WITH PATRIARCHY?

1. Sir Thomas Malory, *Le Morte d'Arthur*, vol. 2 (London: J. M. Dent & Sons, 1961), p. 179.

2. Barbara G. Walker, *The Woman's Encyclopedia of Myths and Secrets* (San Francisco: Harper & Row, 1983), pp. 635–44.

3. Ibid., pp. 436–48.

4. See Henry Charles Lea, *The Inquisition of the Middle Ages* (New York: Macmillan, 1961).

5. Terry Davidson, *Conjugal Crime* (New York: Hawthorn Books, 1978), pp. 98–99.

6. Uta Ranke-Heinemann, *Eunuchs for the Kingdom of Heaven*, trans. Peter Heinegg (New York: Doubleday, 1990), p. 336.

7. June Stephenson, *Men Are Not Cost-Effective: Male Crime in America* (New York: HarperCollins, 1995), p. 355.

8. Charles Bufe, ed., *The Heretic's Handbook of Quotations* (Tucson: Sharp Press, 1988), p. 201.

9. Stephenson, *Men Are Not Cost-Effective*, p. 236.

10. Helen Ellerbe, *The Dark Side of Christian History* (San Rafael, Calif.: Morningstar Books, 1995), p. 186.

11. Bufe, *Heretic's Handbook*, p. 180.

12. Ibid., p. 161.

13. Ranke-Heinemann, *Eunuchs for the Kingdom of Heaven*, pp. 132, 133.

14. See Joan Morris, *The Lady was a Bishop* (New York: Macmillan, 1973).

15. Ranke-Heinemann, *Eunuchs for the Kingdom of Heaven*, pp. 127, 133–34.

16. Robert Briffault, *The Mothers*, vol. 2 (New York: Macmillan, 1927), pp. 493–94.

17. Ibid., vol. 3, p. 373.

18. Bertrand Russell, *A History of Western Philosophy* (New York: Simon & Schuster, 1945), p. 366.

19. Homer Smith, *Man and His Gods* (Boston: Little, Brown, 1952), p. 263.

20. Tim Leedom, ed., *The Book Your Church Doesn't Want You to Read* (Dubuque: Kendall/Hunt, 1993), p. 413.

21. Davidson, *Conjugal Crime*, pp. 99, 211.

22. Amaury de Riencourt, *Sex and Power in History* (New York: Dell, 1974), pp. 263, 364.

23. Mary Daly, *Beyond God the Father* (Boston: Beacon Press, 1973), p. 4.

24. Nelle Morton, *The Journey Is Home* (Boston: Beacon Press, 1985), p. 105.

25. Ann Oakley, *Taking It Like a Woman: A Personal History* (New York: Random House, 1984), pp. 116, 118.

26. Adrienne Rich, *Of Woman Born: Motherhood As Experience and Institution* (New York: W. W. Norton, 1976), pp. 67, 270.

27. Percy Bysshe Shelley, *The Necessity of Atheism* (Amherst, N.Y.: Prometheus Books, 1993), pp. 43, 64.

28. Monica Sjöö and Barbara Mor, *The Great Cosmic Mother: Rediscovering the Religion of the Earth* (San Francisco: Harper & Row, 1987), pp. 193–94.

29. Annie Laurie Gaylor, ed., *Women without Superstition: No Gods— No Masters* (Madison, Wis.: Freedom From Religion Foundation, 1997), pp. 27, 216.

30. Genevieve Vaughan, *For-Giving: A Feminist Criticism of Exchange* (Austin: Plain View Press, 1997), pp. 264, 318.

CHAPTER 5: PHYSICALITY

1. Barbara G. Walker, *The Woman's Encyclopedia of Myths and Secrets* (San Francisco: Harper & Row, 1983), pp. 910, 921.

2. Ibid., p. 823.

3. Heinrich Kramer and James Sprenger, *Malleus Maleficarum* (New York: Dover, 1971), p. 44.

4. Helen Ellerbe, *The Dark Side of Christian History* (San Rafael, Calif.: Morningstar Books, 1995), p. 33.

5. Uta Ranke-Heinemann, *Eunuchs for the Kingdom of Heaven*, trans. Peter Heinegg (New York: Doubleday, 1990), pp. 194, 325, 328.

6. Ellerbe, *Dark Side of Christian History*, pp. 104, 106, 102.

7. Ranke-Heinemann, *Eunuchs for the Kingdom of Heaven*, pp. 55, 228.

8. Tama Starr, *The "Natural Inferiority" of Women. Outrageous Pronouncements by Misguided Males* (New York: Poseidon, 1991), p. 102.

9. David F. Noble, *A World without Women: The Christian Clerical Culture of Western Science* (New York: Knopf, 1992), p. 132.

10. Mary Condren, *The Serpent and the Goddess: Women, Religion and Power in Celtic Ireland* (San Francisco: Harper & Row, 1989), pp. 153, 148.

11. Noble, *World without Women*, p. 133.

12. Elise Boulding, *The Underside of History* (Boulder, Colo.: Westview, 1976), p. 365.

13. Herbert J. Muller, *The Uses of the Past* (New York: New American Library, 1954), p. 160.

14. Boulding, *Underside of History*, p. 370.

15. Noble, *World without Women*, pp. 105, 230.

16. Condren, *Serpent and the Goddess*, p. 168.

17. Noble, *World without Women*, p. 284; Condren, *Serpent and the Goddess*, p. 179.

18. Noble, *World without Women*, p. 139.

19. Phyllis Chesler, *About Men* (New York: Simon & Schuster, 1978), p. 198.

20. Charlene Spretnak, ed., *The Politics of Women's Spirituality* (Garden City, N.Y.: Anchor/Doubleday, 1982), p. 270.

21. Jack Lindsay, *Origins of Astrology* (New York: Barnes and Noble, 1971), p. 106; Walker, *Woman's Encyclopedia*, p. 635.

22. Ernest Crawley, *The Mystic Rose*, vol. 1 (New York: Meridian Books, 1960), p. 319; Walker, *Woman's Encyclopedia*, p. 145.

23. Crawley, *Mystic Rose*, vol. 1, pp. 79, 241.

24. Spretnak, *Politics of Women's Spirituality*, pp. 272–73.

25. Walker, *Woman's Encyclopedia*, p. 637.

26. Spretnak, *Politics of Women's Spirituality*, p. 269.

27. Starr, *"Natural Inferiority" of Women*, pp. 52–53.

28. Joan Morris, *The Lady was a Bishop* (New York: Macmillan, 1973), pp. 106–11.

29. Ranke-Heinemann, *Eunuchs for the Kingdom of Heaven*, pp. 23–25.

30. Morris, *Lady was a Bishop*, p. 111.

31. Monica Sjöö and Barbara Mor, *The Great Cosmic Mother: Rediscovering the Religion of the Earth* (San Francisco: Harper & Row, 1987), pp. 185, 197.

32. Ibid., pp. 193, 195.

33. Chesler, *About Men*, p. 220.

34. Ranke-Heinemann, *Eunuchs for the Kingdom of Heaven*, p. 316.

35. Walker, *Woman's Encyclopedia*, p. 171.

36. Chesler, *About Men*, p. 222.

37. Ranke-Heinemann, *Eunuchs for the Kingdom of Heaven*, p. 318.

38. Walker, *Woman's Encyclopedia*, pp. 170–71.

39. Andrea Dworkin, *Right-Wing Women* (New York: G. P. Putnam's Sons, 1978), pp. 80–82.

40. Rosemary Radford Ruether, *Sexism and God-Talk: Toward a Feminist Theology* (Boston: Beacon Press, 1983), pp. 143–44.

41. Roger E. Greeley, *The Best of Robert Ingersoll* (Amherst, N.Y.:

Prometheus Books, 1977), p. 47.

    42. Ruether, *Sexism and God-Talk*, p. 235.

    43. Greeley, *Best of Robert Ingersoll*, pp. 35, 76.

CHAPTER 6: REPRODUCTION

    1. Barbara G. Walker, *The Woman's Encyclopedia of Myths and Secrets* (San Francisco: Harper & Row, 1983), pp. 312–13.

    2. Charles Bufe, ed., *The Heretic's Handbook of Quotations* (Tucson: Sharp Press, 1988), pp. 150, 125.

    3. Tama Starr, *The "Natural Inferiority" of Women: Outrageous Pronouncements by Misguided Males* (New York: Poseidon, 1991), p. 109.

    4. Uta Ranke-Heinemann, *Eunuchs for the Kingdom of Heaven*, trans. Peter Heinegg (New York: Doubleday, 1990), pp. 96–97.

    5. Starr, *"Natural Inferiority" of Women*, p. 124.

    6. Ranke-Heinemann, *Eunuchs for the Kingdom of Heaven*, p. 275.

    7. Bufe, *Heretic's Handbook*, p. 125.

    8. Starr, *"Natural Inferiority" of Women*, pp. 130, 138.

    9. Ranke-Heinemann, *Eunuchs for the Kingdom of Heaven*, pp. 267, 210, 270.

    10. Riane Eisler, *Sacred Pleasure: Sex, Myth, and the Politics of the Body* (San Francisco: HarperSanFrancisco, 1995), p. 309.

    11. Ranke-Heinemann, *Eunuchs for the Kingdom of Heaven*, pp. 25, 74–75, 195.

    12. Starr, *"Natural Inferiority" of Women*, p. 198.

    13. Ranke-Heinemann, *Eunuchs for the Kingdom of Heaven*, p. 261.

    14. Eisler, *Sacred Pleasure*, p. 314.

    15. Ranke-Heinemann, *Eunuchs for the Kingdom of Heaven*, p. 249.

    16. Walker, *Woman's Encyclopedia*, p. 4.

    17. Starr, *"Natural Inferiority" of Women*, p. 88.

    18. Ranke-Heinemann, *Eunuchs for the Kingdom of Heaven*, pp. 83, 159.

    19. Ibid., pp. 62, 286, 83, 85, 149.

    20. Ibid., pp. 197, 288.

    21. Eisler, *Sacred Pleasure*, p. 206.

    22. Ranke-Heinemann, *Eunuchs for the Kingdom of Heaven*, p. 163.

23. Ibid, pp. 139, 141, 155.

24. Eisler, *Sacred Pleasure*, p. 316.

25. Ranke-Heinemann, *Eunuchs for the Kingdom of Heaven*, p. 186.

26. Walker, *Woman's Encyclopedia*, p. 708.

27. Eisler, *Sacred Pleasure*, p. 102.

28. Walker, *Woman's Encyclopedia*, p. 709.

29. Robin Lane Fox, *The Unauthorized Version: Truth and Fiction in the Bible* (New York: Knopf, 1992), pp. 117–18.

30. Andrea Dworkin, *Right-Wing Women* (New York: G. P. Putnam's Sons, 1978), pp. 143–44.

31. Robin Lane Fox, *Pagans and Christians* (New York: Harper & Row, 1986), p. 439.

32. Walker, *Woman's Encyclopedia*, pp. 599–602, 879–83.

33. Fox, *Pagans and Christians*, p. 460.

34. Marilyn French, *Beyond Power: On Men, Women, and Morals* (New York: Summit Books, 1985), p. 542.

35. Erich Fromm, *The Anatomy of Destructiveness* (New York: Holt, Rinehart & Winston, 1973), p. 151.

36. Ibid., p. 168.

37. Starr, *"Natural Inferiority" of Women*, p. 81.

38. Dworkin, *Right-Wing Women*, p. 191.

39. Fromm, *Anatomy of Destructiveness*, p. 288.

40. Carol Gilligan, *In a Different Voice* (Cambridge: Harvard University Press, 1982), p. 183.

41. Fred Hapgood, *Why Males Exist* (New York: William Morrow, 1979), pp. 11, 16, 19.

42. Genevieve Vaughan, *For-Giving: A Feminist Criticism of Exchange* (Austin: Plain View Press, 1997), p. 248.

43. Marina Warner, *Alone of All Her Sex: The Myth and Cult of the Virgin Mary* (San Francisco: Harper & Row, 1989), p. 57.

44. Annie Laurie Gaylor, ed., *Women without Superstition: No Gods—No Masters* (Madison, Wis.: Freedom From Religion Foundation, 1997), p. 547.

Chapter 7: Doctrines

1. Uta Ranke-Heinemann, *Eunuchs for the Kingdom of Heaven*, trans. Peter Heinegg (New York: Doubleday, 1990), p. 319.
2. Vern L. Bullough, *The Subordinate Sex* (Chicago: University of Illinois Press, 1973), p. 114.
3. Tama Starr, *The "Natural Inferiority" of Women: Outrageous Pronouncements by Misguided Males* (New York: Poseidon, 1991), p. 185.
4. Charles Bufe, ed., *The Heretic's Handbook of Quotations* (Tucson: Sharp Press, 1988), p. 125.
5. Starr, *"Natural Inferiority" of Women*, pp. 72, 33, 88.
6. Helen Ellerbe, *The Dark Side of Christian History* (San Rafael, Calif.: Morningstar Books, 1995), p. 99.
7. Bufe, *Heretic's Handbook*, p. 165.
8. Ranke-Heinemann, *Eunuchs for the Kingdom of Heaven*, pp. 178–79.
9. Amaury de Riencourt, *Sex and Power in History* (New York: Dell, 1974), p. 227.
10. Robert Graves, *The Greek Myths*, vol. 2 (New York: Penguin Books, 1955), p. 277.
11. E. O. G. Turville-Petre, *Myth and Religion of the North* (New York: Hold, Rinehart & Winston, 1964), p. 187.
12. Barbara G. Walker, *The Woman's Encyclopedia of Myths and Secrets* (San Francisco: Harper & Row, 1983), p. 656; Andrew D. White, *A History of the Warfare of Science with Theology in Christendom* (New York: George Braziller, 1955), p. 319.
13. Joseph Campbell, *The Masks of God: Occidental Mythology* (New York: Viking, 1964), pp. 196, 199.
14. Walker, *Woman's Encyclopedia*, pp. 436–48.
15. Bullough, *Subordinate Sex*, p. 176.
16. Geoffrey Ashe, *The Virgin* (London: Routledge & Kegan Paul, 1976), p. 208.
17. Homer Smith, *Man and His Gods* (Boston: Little, Brown, 1952), p. 206; Walker, *Woman's Encyclopedia*, p. 387.
18. George H. Smith, *Atheism: The Case against God* (Amherst, N.Y.: Prometheus Books, 1979), p. 300.
19. Robin Morgan, *The Anatomy of Freedom: Feminism, Physics, and Global Politics* (New York: Anchor/Doubleday, 1982), p. 244.

20. Smith, *Atheism*, p. 84.

21. Ruth Hurmence Green, *The Born-Again Skeptic's Guide to the Bible* (Madison, Wis.: Freedom From Religion Foundation, 1979), p. 100.

22. Smith, *Atheism*, pp. 100, 322.

23. Philip Rawson, *The Art of Tantra* (Greenwich, Conn.: New York Graphic Society, 1973), p. 112.

24. Walker, *Woman's Encyclopedia*, p. 489.

25. Walter Kafton-Minkel, *Subterranean Worlds: 100,000 Years of Dragons, Dwarfs, the Dead, Lost Races, and UFOs from inside the Earth* (Port Townsend, Wash.: Loompanics Unlimited, 1989), p. 280.

26. Ellerbe, *Dark Side of Christian History*, p. 161.

27. Bufe, *Heretic's Handbook*, p. 215.

28. Ibid., p. 217.

29. Ellerbe, *Dark Side of Christian History*, pp. 38, 77.

30. Bufe, *Heretic's Handbook*, pp. 174, 183, 217.

31. Ibid., pp. 200, 175.

32. Ellerbe, *Dark Side of Christian History*, p. 183.

33. Ibid., p. 184.

34. Upton Sinclair, *The Profits of Religion* (New York: Vanguard, 1927), pp. 116–17.

35. Bufe, *Heretic's Handbook*, pp. 171, 174.

36. Miles R. Abelard, *Physicians of No Value: The Repressed Story of Ecclesiastical Flummery* (Winter Park, Fla.: Reality Publications, 1979), pp. 44–45, 79.

37. Elise Boulding, *The Underside of History* (Boulder, Colo.: Westview, 1976), pp. 356, 372.

38. Joseph Campbell, *The Hero with a Thousand Faces* (Princeton: Bollingen, 1949), p. 249.

39. Joseph Campbell, *Myths to Live By* (New York: Viking, 1972), p. 89.

40. W. Arens, *The Man-Eating Myth* (New York: Oxford University Press, 1979), p. 161.

41. Walker, *Woman's Encyclopedia*, pp. 748–54.

42. Arens, *Man-Eating Myth*, pp. 160, 67.

43. H. R. Ellis Davidson, *Gods and Myths of the Viking Age* (New York: Bell, 1981), p. 110.

44. Walker, *Woman's Encyclopedia*, p. 267.

45. Arthur Avalon, trans., *Mahanirvanatantra* (New York: Dover, 1972), p. 273.

46. Graves, *Greek Myths*, vol. 1, pp. 94.

47. William Woods, *A Casebook of Witchcraft* (New York: G. P. Putnam's Sons, 1974), p. 183.

48. Bufe, *Heretic's Handbook*, pp. 160, 162, 164, 167.

49. Ranke-Heinemann, *Eunuchs for the Kingdom of Heaven*, pp. 240, 241.

50. Ellerbe, *Dark Side of Christian History*, p. 100.

51. Leonard W. Levy, *Treason against God: A History of the Offense of Blasphemy* (New York: Schocken Books, 1981), pp. 217, 219, 286, 290.

52. Herbert J. Muller, *The Uses of the Past* (New York: New American Library, 1954), p. 250.

53. Smith, *Atheism*, p. 195.

54. Annie Laurie Gaylor, ed., *Women without Superstition: No Gods—No Masters* (Madison, Wis.: Freedom From Religion Foundation, 1997), p. 13.

55. Richard Leakey and Roger Lewin, *Origins Reconsidered* (New York: Doubleday, 1992), pp. 347, 357.

56. Gaylor, *Women without Superstition*, pp. 324, 195, 225, 446.

CHAPTER 8: THE GODDESS IMAGE

1. Gordon Stein, ed., *The Encyclopedia of Unbelief* (Amherst, N.Y.: Prometheus Books, 1985), p. 186.

2. Joseph Campbell, *The Masks of God: Occidental Mythology* (New York: Viking, 1964), p. 70.

3. Ibid., p. 153.

4. Arthur Avalon, trans., *Mahanirvanatantra* (New York: Dover, 1972), pp. 47–50.

5. John Weir Perry, *Lord of the Four Quarters* (New York: Collier Books, 1966), pp. 10, 180, 217.

6. James B. Pritchard, *The Ancient Near East*, vol. 2 (Princeton: Princeton University Press, 1958), pp. 135, 202.

7. Ibid., vol. 1, pp. 65, 97, 232–33.

8. Maarten J. Vermaseren, *Cybele and Attis* (London: Thames & Hudson, 1977), pp. 83–87.

9. Ibid., pp. 109, 115.

10. Campbell, *Occidental Mythology*, p. 728.

11. Jack Lindsay, *Origins of Astrology* (New York: Barnes & Noble, 1971), p. 289.

12. Walter Woodburn Hyde, *Greek Religion and Its Survivals* (New York: Cooper Square, 1963), pp. 61, 76, 77, 84.

13. Elaine Pagels, *The Gnostic Gospels* (New York: Random House, 1979), pp. 30–31.

14. Ibid., p. 30.

15. Ibid., pp. 57–58.

16. Ibid., p. 29.

17. C. K. Barrett, *The New Testament Background* (New York: Harper & Row, 1961), pp. 218–19.

18. Raphael Patai, *The Hebrew Goddess* (n.p.: Ktav Publishing House, 1967), pp. 147, 161.

19. Ibid., p. 240.

20. Pagels, *Gnostic Gospels*, p. 57.

21. Brian Branston, *The Lost Gods of England* (London: Thames & Hudson, 1957), p. 65.

22. Walter Kafton-Minkel, *Subterranean Worlds: 100,000 Years of Dragons, Dwarfs, the Dead, Lost Races, and UFOs from inside the Earth* (Port Townsend, Wash.: Loompanics Unlimited, 1989), p. 281.

23. Jerry Mander, *In the Absence of the Sacred* (San Francisco: Sierra Club, 1991), p. 333.

24. Branston, *Lost Gods of England*, p. 130.

25. Nelle Morton, *The Journey is Home* (Boston: Beacon Press, 1985), p. 142.

26. Ibid., pp. 107–108.

27. Naomi Goldenberg, *Changing of the Gods* (Boston: Beacon Press, 1979), pp. 107–108.

28. Charles Bufe, ed., *The Heretic's Handbook of Quotations* (Tucson: Sharp Press, 1988), p. 174.

29. Ibid., p. 207.

30. Barbara G. Walker, *The Woman's Encyclopedia of Myths and Secrets* (San Francisco: Harper & Row, 1983), p. 291.

CHAPTER 9: RITUALS AND PURPOSES

1. Clement A. Miles, *Christian Customs and Traditions* (New York: Dover, 1976), pp. 22–23.

2. Ibid., p. 269.

3. Ruth Hurmence Green, *The Born-Again Skeptic's Guide to the Bible* (Madison, Wis.: Freedom From Religion Foundation, 1979), p. 228.

4. Helen Ellerbe, *The Dark Side of Christian History* (San Rafael, Calif.: Morningstar Books, 1995), p. 153.

5. Francis Hitching, *Earth Magic* (New York: Pocket Books, 1978), pp. 207–10.

6. M. L. W. Laistner, *Christianity and Pagan Culture in the Later Roman Empire* (Ithaca: Cornell University Press, 1951), pp. 6–7.

7. Roger E. Greeley, *The Best of Robert Ingersoll* (Amherst, N.Y.: Prometheus Books, 1977), p. 17.

8. Paul Johnson, *A History of Christianity* (New York: Atheneum, 1976), pp. 222–23.

9. Miles, *Christian Customs and Traditions*, pp. 221–22.

10. Hitching, *Earth Magic*, p. 213.

11. Barbara G. Walker, *The Woman's Encyclopedia of Myths and Secrets* (San Francisco: Harper & Row, 1983), pp. 116–18.

12. Ibid., p. 1058.

13. W. Carew Hazlitt, *Faiths and Folklore of the British Isles* (New York: Benjamin Blom, 1965), p. 399–402.

14. Walker, *Woman's Encyclopedia*, pp. 624–28.

15. Hazlitt, *Faiths and Folklore*, p. 27

16. Miles, *Christian Customs and Traditions*, pp. 190–92.

17. Walker, *Woman's Encyclopedia*, p. 754.

18. Ibid., pp. 267–68.

19. Robert Briffault, *The Mothers*, vol. 3, p. 248.

20. Hazlitt, *Faiths and Folklore*, p. 447.

21. Tama Starr, *The "Natural Inferiority" of Women: Outrageous Pronouncements by Misguided Males* (New York: Poseidon, 1991), p. 131.

22. Hazlitt, *Faiths and Folkore*, p. 453.

23. Greeley, *Best of Robert Ingersoll*, p. 67.

CHAPTER 10: THE NEW AGE

1. Robert Basil, ed., *Not Necessarily the New Age: Critical Essays* (Amherst, N.Y.: Prometheus, 1988), pp. 321, 322, 326, 344, 350.

2. W. Carew Hazlitt, *Faiths and Folklore of the British Isles* (New York: Benjamin Blom, 1965), p. 103.

3. Keith Thomas, *Religion and the Decline of Magic* (New York: Scribner, 1971), pp. 30, 50.

4. Ibid., 26–27.

5. Charles Bufe, ed., *The Heretic's Handbook of Quotations* (Tucson: Sharp Press, 1988), pp. 194, 181, 182, 169.

6. Robert Seidenberg and Karen DeCrow, *Women Who Marry Houses: Panic and Protest in Agoraphobia* (New York: McGraw-Hill, 1983), pp. 141–43.

7. Bufe, *Heretic's Handbook*, p. 163.

8. Basil, *Not Necessarily the New Age*, p. 327.

9. See Andrew D. White, *A History of the Warfare of Science with Theology in Christendom* (New York: George Braziller, 1995).

10. Basil, *Not Necessarily the New Age*, p. 283.

11. Cynthia Eller, *Living in the Lap of the Goddess: The Feminist Spirituality Movement in America* (New York: Crossroad, 1993), pp. 64, 109, 116.

12. Ibid., pp. 186, 197.

13. Henry Gordon, *Channeling into the New Age* (Amherst, N.Y.: Prometheus Books, 1988), pp. 41–42.

14. See Barbara G. Walker, *The Book of Sacred Stones: Fact and Fallacy in the Crystal World* (San Francisco: Harper & Row, 1989).

15. Randall N. Baer and Vicki V. Baer, *The Crystal Connection: A Guidebook for Personal and Planetary Ascension* (San Francisco: Harper & Row, 1987), pp. 8, 19–25, 61, 252.

16. Upton Sinclair, *The Profits of Religion* (New York: Vanguard, 1927), p. 254.

17. George H. Smith, *Atheism: The Case against God* (Amherst, N. Y.: Prometheus, 1979), p. 188.

CHAPTER 11: PROBLEMS AND FEARS

1. Reginald Scot, *Discoverie of Witchcraft* (Yorkshire, England: Rowman & Littlefield, 1973), p. 27.

2. Helen Ellerbe, *The Dark Side of Christian History* (San Rafael, Calif.: Morningstar Books, 1995), pp. 63, 90.

3. Ralph Shirley, *Occultists and Mystics of All Ages* (New York: University Books, 1972), p. 93.

4. Ellerbe, *Dark Side of Christian History*, p. 51.

5. See Emmet McLoughlin, *Crime and Immorality in the Catholic Church* (New York: Lyle Stuart, 1962).

6. Charles Bufe, ed., *The Heretic's Handbook of Quotations* (Tucson: Sharp Press, 1988), p. 194.

7. Ibid., p. 208.

8. Upton Sinclair, *The Profits of Religion* (New York: Vanguard, 1927), p. 275.

9. George H. Smith, *Atheism: The Case against God* (Amherst, N.Y.: Prometheus Books, 1979), p. 275.

10. Annie Laurie Gaylor, *Women without Superstition: No Gods—No Masters* (Madison, Wis.: Freedom From Religion Foundation, 1997), pp. 113, 141, 158.

11. Ibid., p. 261.

12. M. L. W. Laistner, *Christianity and Pagan Culture in the Later Roman Empire* (Ithaca: Cornell University Press, 1951), p. 31.

13. Tama Starr, *The "Natural Inferiority" of Women: Outrageous Pronouncements by Misguided Males* (New York: Poseidon, 1991), p. 134.

14. Henry Charles Lea, *The Inquisition of the Middle Ages* (New York: Macmillan, 1961), pp. 60, 97, 257.

15. Shirley, *Occultists and Mystics*, pp. 31–32.

16. Gordon Stein, ed., *The Encyclopedia of Unbelief* (Amherst, N.Y.: Prometheus Books, 1985), p. 56.

17. Barbara G. Walker, *The Woman's Encyclopedia of Myths and Secrets* (San Francisco: Harper & Row, 1983), p. 388.

18. Bufe, *Heretic's Handbook*, p. 196.

19. Roger E. Greeley, *The Best of Robert Ingersoll* (Amherst, N.Y.: Prometheus Books, 1977), p. 100.

20. Rosemary Radford Ruether, *Sexism and God-Talk: Toward a Feminist Theology* (Boston: Beacon Press, 1983), pp. 173–74.

21. Greeley, *Best of Robert Ingersoll*, p. 36.

22. Bufe, *Heretic's Handbook*, pp. 169, 186, 182, 177.

23. Smith, *Atheism*, p. 252.

24. Walker, *Woman's Encyclopedia*, pp. 728–29.

CHAPTER 12: MARY

1. Geoffrey Ashe, *The Virgin* (London: Routledge & Kegan Paul, 1976), p. 151.

2. Amaury de Riencourt, *Sex and Power in History* (New York: Dell, 1974), p. 150.

3. Robert Briffault, *The Mothers*, vol. 3 (New York: Macmillan, 1927), p. 183.

4. Ashe, *Virgin*, p. 48.

5. Briffault, *Mothers*, vol. 3, p. 97.

6. Barbara G. Walker, *The Woman's Encyclopedia of Myths and Secrets* (San Francisco: Harper & Row, 1983), p. 604; Briffault, *Mothers*, vol. 3, p. 184.

7. Ashe, *Virgin*, p. 206.

8. Homer Smith, *Man and His Gods* (Boston: Little, Brown, 1952), p. 183.

9. Uta Ranke-Heinemann, *Eunuchs for the Kingdom of Heaven*, trans. Peter Heinegg (New York: Doubleday, 1990), pp. 6, 342.

10. Ibid., p. 31.

11. Ashe, *Virgin*, p. 182.

12. Vern L. Bullough, *The Subordinate Sex* (Chicago: University of Illinois Press, 1973), p. 112.

13. Ranke-Heinemann, *Eunuchs for the Kingdom of Heaven*, pp. 342, 345.

14. Walker, *Woman's Encyclopedia*, pp. 890–92.

15. Ibid., p. 233.

16. Ashe, *Virgin*, p. 236.

17. Walker, *Woman's Encyclopedia*, p. 603.

18. Ashe, *Virgin*, pp. 203, 217.

19. Bullough, *Subordinate Sex*, p. 170.

20. de Riencourt, *Sex and Power in History*, pp. 250–51.

21. Ashe, *Virgin*, p. 231.

22. *Time*, Feb. 7, 1977, p. 65.

23. Marina Warner, *Alone of All Her Sex: The Myth and Cult of the Virgin Mary* (San Francisco: Harper & Row, 1984), pp. 241, 329.

24. Elaine Pagels, *The Gnostic Gospels* (New York: Random House, 1979), p. 52.

25. Carol Ochs, *Behind the Sex of God* (Boston: Beacon Press, 1977), pp. 72, 74–75.

26. Mary Condren, *The Serpent and the Goddess: Women, Religion and Power in Celtic Ireland* (San Francisco: Harper & Row, 1989), p. 161.

27. Warner, *Alone of All Her Sex*, pp. 66–67, 39.

28. Ibid., p. 334.

29. James M. Robinson, ed., *The Nag Hammadi Library in English* (San Francisco: Harper & Row, 1977), pp. 135–36, 138.

30. Walker, *Woman's Encyclopedia*, pp. 613–16.

31. William Woods, *A Casebook of Witchcraft* (New York: G. P. Putnam's Sons, 1974), p. 38.

32. Robin Lane Fox, *Pagans and Christians* (New York: Harper & Row, 1986), p. 375.

33. Walker, *Woman's Encyclopedia*, p. 610.

34. Ibid., pp. 495–97.

35. Ibid., p. 682.

36. Joe Nickell, *Looking for a Miracle: Weeping Icons, Relics, Stigmata, Visions and Healing Cures* (Amherst, N.Y.: Prometheus, 1993), pp. 29, 32, 170.

BIBLIOGRAPHY

Abelard, Miles R. *Physicians of No Value: The Repressed Story of Ecclesiastical Flummery*. Winter Park, Fla.: Reality Publications, 1979.

Arens, W. *The Man-Eating Myth*. New York: Oxford University Press, 1979.

Ashe, Geoffrey. *The Virgin*. London: Routledge & Kegan Paul, 1976.

Avalon, Arthur, trans. *Mahanirvanatantra*. New York: Dover, 1972.

Baer, Randall N., and Nicki V. Baer. *The Crystal Connection: A Guidebook for Personal and Planetary Ascension*. San Francisco: Harper & Row, 1987.

Barrett, C. K. *The New Testament Background*. New York: Harper & Row, 1961.

Basil, Robert, ed. *Not Necessarily the New Age: Critical Essays*. Amherst, N.Y.: Prometheus Books, 1988.

Boulding, Elise. *The Underside of History*. Boulder: Westview, 1976.

Branston, Brian. *The Lost Gods of England*. London: Thames & Hudson, 1957.

Briffault, Robert. *The Mothers*. 3 vols. New York: Macmillan, 1927.

Bufe, Charles, ed. *The Heretic's Handbook of Quotations*. Tucson: Sharp Press, 1988.

Bullough, Vern L. *The Subordinate Sex*. Chicago: University of Illinois Press, 1973.

Campbell, Joseph. *The Hero with a Thousand Faces*. Princeton: Bollingen, 1949.

———. *The Masks of God: Occidental Mythology*. New York: Viking, 1964.

———. *Myths to Live By*. New York: Viking, 1972.

Chesler, Phyllis. *About Men*. New York: Simon & Schuster, 1978.

Condren, Mary. *The Serpent and the Goddess: Women, Religion and Power in Celtic Ireland*. San Francisco: Harper & Row, 1989.

Crawley, Ernest. *The Mystic Rose*. 2 vols. New York: Meridian Books, 1960.

Daly, Mary. *Beyond God the Father*. Boston: Beacon Press, 1973.

Davidson, H. R. Ellis. *Gods and Myths of the Viking Age*. New York: Bell, 1981.

Davidson, Terry. *Conjugal Crime*. New York: Hawthorn Books, 1978.

de Riencourt, Amaury. *Sex and Power in History*. New York: Dell, 1974.

Dworkin, Andrea. *Right-Wing Women*. New York: G. P. Putnam's Sons, 1978.

Eisler, Riane. *Sacred Pleasure: Sex, Myth, and the Politics of the Body*. San Francisco: HarperSanFrancisco, 1995.

Eller, Cynthia. *Living in the Lap of the Goddess: The Feminist Spirituality Movement in America*. New York: Crossroad, 1993.

Ellerbe, Helen. *The Dark Side of Christian History*. San Rafael, Calif.: Morningstar Books, 1995.

Flew, Anthony. *God: A Critical Inquiry*. La Salle, Ill.: Open Court Publishing, 1984.

Fox, Robin Lane. *Pagans and Christians*. New York: Harper & Row, 1986.

———. *The Unauthorized Version: Truth and Fiction in the Bible*. New York: Knopf, 1992.

French, Marilyn. *Beyond Power: On Men, Women, and Morals*. New York: Summit Books, 1985.

Fromm, Erich. *The Anatomy of Destructiveness*. New York: Holt, Rinehart & Winston, 1973.

Gaylor, Annie Laurie, ed. *Women without Superstition: No Gods—No Masters*. Madison, Wis.: Freedom From Religion Foundation, 1997.

Gilligan, Carol. *In a Different Voice*. Cambridge: Harvard University Press, 1982.

Goldenberg, Naomi. *Changing of the Gods*. Boston: Beacon Press, 1979.

Gordon, Henry. *Channeling into the New Age*. Amherst, N.Y.: Prometheus Books, 1988.

Graves, Robert. *The Greek Myths*. 2 vols. New York: Penguin Books, 1955.

Gray, Carole. "Nineteenth-Century Women of Freethought," *Free Inquiry* 15, no. 2 (1995).

Greeley, Roger E. *The Best of Robert Ingersoll*. Amherst, N.Y.: Prometheus Books, 1977.

Green, Ruth Hurmence. *The Born-Again Skeptic's Guide to the Bible.* Madison, Wis.: Freedom From Religion Foundation, 1979.

Hapgood, Fred. *Why Males Exist.* New York: William Morrow, 1979.

Hazlitt, W. Carew. *Faiths and Folklore of the British Isles.* New York: Benjamin Blom, 1965.

Hitching, Francis. *Earth Magic.* New York: Pocket Books, 1978.

Hyde, Walter Woodburn. *Greek Religion and Its Survivals.* New York: Cooper Square, 1963.

Johnson, Paul. *A History of Christianity.* New York: Atheneum, 1976.

Kafton-Minkel, Walter. *Subterranean Worlds: 100,000 Years of Dragons, Dwarfs, the Dead, Lost Races, and UFOs from inside the Earth.* Port Townsend, Wash.: Loompanics Unlimited, 1989.

Kramer, Heinrich, and James Sprenger. *Malleus Maleficarum.* New York: Dover, 1971.

Laistner, M. L. W. *Christianity and Pagan Culture in the Later Roman Empire.* Ithaca: Cornell University Press, 1951.

Lea, Henry Charles. *The Inquisition of the Middle Ages.* New York: Macmillan, 1961.

Leakey, Richard, and Roger Lewin. *Origins Reconsidered.* New York: Doubleday, 1992.

Leedom, Tim, ed. *The Book Your Church Doesn't Want You to Read.* Dubuque: Kendall/Hunt, 1993.

Levy, Leonard W. *Treason against God: A History of the Offense of Blasphemy.* New York: Schocken Books, 1981.

Lindsay, Jack. *Origins of Astrology.* New York: Barnes & Noble, 1971.

Malory, Sir Thomas. *Le Morte d'Arthur.* 2 vols. London: J. M. Dent & Sons, 1961.

Mander, Jerry. *In the Absence of the Sacred.* San Francisco: Sierra Club, 1991.

McLoughlin, Emmet. *Crime and Immorality in the Catholic Church.* New York: Lyle Stuart, 1962.

Menen, Aubrey. *The Mystics.* New York: Dial, 1974.

Miles, Clement A. *Christmas Customs and Traditions.* New York: Dover, 1976.

Morgan, Robin. *The Anatomy of Freedom: Feminism, Physics, and Global Politics.* New York: Anchor/Doubleday, 1982.

Morris, Joan. *The Lady Was a Bishop.* New York: Macmillan, 1973.

Morton, Nelle. *The Journey Is Home*. Boston: Beacon Press, 1985.

Muller, Herbert J. *The Uses of the Past*. New York: New American Library, 1954.

Nickell, Joe. *Looking for a Miracle: Weeping Icons, Relics, Stigmata, Visions and Healing Cures*. Amherst, N.Y.: Prometheus Books, 1993.

Noble, David F. *A World without Women: The Christian Clerical Culture of Western Science*. New York: Knopf, 1992.

Oakley, Ann. *Taking It Like a Woman: A Personal History*. New York: Random House, 1984.

Ochs, Carol. *Behind the Sex of God*. Boston: Beacon Press, 1977.

Pagels, Elaine. *The Gnostic Gospels*. New York: Random House, 1979.

Patai, Raphael. *The Hebrew Goddess*. N.p.: Ktav Publishing House, 1967.

Perry, John Weir. *Lord of the Four Quarters*. New York: Collier Books, 1966.

Pritchard, James B. *The Ancient Near East*. 2 vols. Princeton: Princeton University Press, 1958.

Ranke-Heinemann, Uta. *Eunuchs for the Kingdom of Heaven*. Translated by Peter Heinegg. New York: Doubleday, 1990.

Rawson, Philip. *The Art of Tantra*. Greenwich, Conn.: New York Graphic Society, 1973.

Rich, Adrienne. *Of Woman Born: Motherhood as Experience and Intuition*. New York: W. W. Norton, 1976.

Robinson, James M., ed. *The Nag Hammadi Library in English*. San Francisco: Harper & Row, 1977.

Ruether, Rosemary Radford. *Sexism and God-Talk: Toward a Feminist Theology*. Boston: Beacon Press, 1983.

Russell, Bertrand. *A History of Western Philosophy*. New York: Simon & Schuster, 1945.

Scot, Reginald. *Discoverie of Witchcraft*. Yorkshire, England: Rowman & Littlefield, 1973.

Seidenberg, Robert, and Karen DeCrow. *Women Who Marry Houses: Panic and Protest in Agoraphobia*. New York: McGraw-Hill, 1983.

Shelley, Percy Bysshe. *The Necessity of Atheism*. Amherst, N.Y.: Prometheus Books, 1993.

Shirley, Ralph. *Occultists and Mystics of All Ages*. New York: University Books, 1972.

Sinclair, Upton. *The Profits of Religion*. New York: Vanguard, 1927.

Sjöö, Monica, and Barbara Mor. *The Great Cosmic Mother: Rediscovering the Religion of the Earth*. San Francisco: Harper & Row, 1987.

Smith, George H. *Atheism: The Case against God*. Amherst, N.Y.: Prometheus Books, 1979.

Smith, Homer. *Man and His Gods*. Boston: Little, Brown, 1952.

Spretnak, Charlene, ed. *The Politics of Women's Spirituality*. Garden City, N.Y.: Anchor/Doubleday, 1982.

Starr, Tama. *The "Natural Inferiority" of Women: Outrageous Pronouncements by Misguided Males*. New York: Poseidon, 1991.

Stein, Gordon, ed. *The Encyclopedia of Unbelief*. Amherst, N.Y.: Prometheus Books, 1985.

Stephenson, June. *Men Are Not Cost-Effective: Male Crime in America*. New York: HarperCollins, 1995.

Thomas, Keith. *Religion and the Decline of Magic*. New York: Scribner, 1971.

Turville-Petre, E. O. G. *Myth and Religion of the North*. New York: Holt, Rinehart & Winston, 1964.

Vaughan, Genevieve. *For-Giving: A Feminist Criticism of Exchange*. Austin: Plain View Press, 1997.

Vermaseren, Maarten J. *Cybele and Attis*. London: Thames & Hudson, 1977.

Walker, Barbara G. *The Woman's Encyclopedia of Myths and Secrets*. San Francisco: Harper & Row, 1983.

———. *The Book of Sacred Stones: Fact and Fallacy in the Crystal World*. San Francisco: Harper & Row, 1989.

Warner, Marina. *Alone of All Her Sex: The Myth and Cult of the Virgin Mary*. San Francisco: Harper & Row, 1984.

White, Andrew D. *A History of the Warfare of Science with Theology in Christendom*. New York: George Braziller, 1955.

Wolf, Naomi. *The Beauty Myth: How Images of Beauty Are Used against Women*. New York: William Morrow, 1991.

Woods, William. *A Casebook of Witchcraft*. New York: G. P. Putnam's Sons, 1974.

INDEX